NEO TERRORISM
An Indian Experience

NEO TERRORISM
An Indian Experience

A.K. LAL

GYAN PUBLISHING HOUSE
NEW DELHI—110 002

Neo Terrorism: An Indian Experience
(Terrorism)

Rs. 690

ISBN: 81-212-0828-9

The views expressed in this book are those of the author alone and not of the Indian Army, the Ministry of Defence or the United Service Institution of India or the Publisher.

Published in 2005 in India by
Gyan Publishing House
5-Ansari Road, Daryaganj
New Delhi-110 002
Phones: 23282060, 23261060 Fax: (011) 23285914
E-mail: gyanbook@vsnl.com
Visit our website at: http//www.gyanbooks.com

Lasertypesetting by: Varsha Graphics, Delhi
Printed at: Delux Offset Press, Delhi

Contents

Foreword

I consider it an honour and privilege to be writing the Foreword of a book written by a close associate and a highly spirited Infantry officer belonging to the Punjab Regiment, of which I am the Colonel of the Regiment. In this well researched book the author, Brigadier A K Lal, has done yeoman service by covering the entire gamut of terrorism and its linkage to military strategy. The book is designed to bring an exhaustive analysis of all facets of terrorism in the aftermath of recent terrorist attacks in America.

There is no denying the fact that terrorism is at the very heart of this new paradigm of international conflict. It is, moreover, an increasingly popular ideology of conflict within nations, as discontented factions, disappointed with the attainments of aspirations and impatient with the processes of democracy, obtain freer access to large arsenals of sophisticated small arms and explosives, as well as to the skills to use them. Indeed, the power, the weaponry and proficiency of terrorist groups appears to be accelerating at a rate much faster than the countermeasures available to civilized society.

The use of terror in one form or the other has been there since the dawn of history. Terrorism in modern times appeared with its bloody manifestations during the French Revolution. In the late 19th Century, radical nationalist groups like Irish, Macedonians, Serbs and Armenians used terrorist methods in their struggle for autonomy or national independence. Internal terrorism is relatively a new phenomenon in world politics, state terrorism and revolutionary terrorism being the major categories. Whatever may be the ingredients of terrorism, these acts ought to be condemned internationally since terrorist activities are brutal in nature and have little regard for humans or humanity in general.

The combined impact of various international and internal factors have led to the proliferation of various terrorist movements and separatist insurgencies that have swept across South Asia in the recent past, the most prominent ones being the sponsored Kashmiri terrorism in India, the persistent insurgencies in its North Eastern States, and the Tamil problem of Sri Lanka. The Maoist revolutionary anties in Nepal and the Chakma movement in Bangladesh are among the more obvious of the numerous other areas of potential strife within the subcontinent that could spawn terrorist movements in the foreseeable future.

Since Kashmir is a first hand Indian experience, it has been appropriately taken by the author as a backdrop, time and again, to explain various live situations in this book. In India's case, the need of the hour is to identify India's growing stature and thus the responsibility for reorganizing its military doctrines, (including terrorism), and strategies for the security of its areas of influence and subsequently areas of interest. Pakistan's proxy war through networking of terrorists, and a counter to them, has to be developed in a much more cost effective manner (other than loss of human life) than hither-to-fore, by synergizing technology with organizations and doctrines. Insurgencies and terrorist movements in other parts or India, namely the North East and other neighbourly states, need to be addressed holistically too.

Having realized this need of the hour, the author has chosen a very relevant topic for his book. Unfortunately, the long-standing dispute between India and Pakistan over Kashmir has tended to distort the understanding of this issue. The world community tends to equate the state with Kashmir Valley and the Valley with Kashmiri Muslims. The 'Kashmir issue' is thus presented as an intractable 'territorial dispute' between two belligerent neighbours, or, at best, as Kashmiris' struggle for an independent state of Jammu and Kashmir. Little is known about the plurality of the state with diverse communities such as Gujjars, Bakkarwals, Kashmiri Pandits, Dogras and Ladakhi Buddhists for whom the right of self-determination has little appeal, and even less is known about their political aspirations and political choices. Each is engaged in a little battle for nurturing its socio-cultural identity, seeking avenues of social and economic development and creating its own political space.

India in South Asia is now perhaps the most heavily militarized region in the world, and nuclear India remains boxed between the region's two other nuclear powers – China and Pakistan – and while both are in land continuity with India, diplomatic relations with them are far from perfect. But despite this, India sadly lacks national security awareness and its people remain inadequately informed about the military issues that concern every citizen.

Thus, in writing this book, the author has made an attempt to fill various voids pertaining to terrorism in our contemporary military literature. To achieve this, he has covered the whole spectrum of terrorism to include its global manifestations, concepts, thoughts and doctrines of terrorism. He has also, in a most professional manner, analysed the various facets of NBC terrorism threat perceptions, spelt out a viable counter terrorism and weapons of mass destruction (WMD) terrorism strategy to include legal aspects as well.

There is now a genuine need for a nationwide debate on the security policies of India, and the intellectual pluralism that stems from it could in turn provide its politico-bureaucratic elite the national mood towards military issues and enable them to direct the country's policies in the right direction. Fortunately, across India today the media, a number of academics and intellectuals have started to debate issues of national security.

Looking ahead, we must be clear of the threats we are likely to face. We must also be clear as to which directions could such threats come from and the types of conflict we will be involved in : conventional, insurgency or terrorism based, or even nuclear, biological and chemical. A lucid grasp of these issues will enable us to be clear in the end about how to defend our future.

The author has done a marvelous job in putting together a complex subject which is mostly read, talked about and understood by only a few professionals. He has written the book in a way that the general reader, to include the student and professor, civil and defence personnel, the media and political leaders alike, will find a valuable reference book to help them form their own opinions and come to their own respective judgments in this crucial field of national security. I therefore take pleasure in recommending this absorbing and authoritative book to all those who take interest on matters military and in national security per se.

(Shankar Parasad)
Lieutenant General
Inspector General Army,
Director General Infantry,
Colonel of the Punjab Regiment

Preface

I have been involved in counter-terrorist operations for more than 30 years of my army life. My impressions, which reflect in this book, are a life long effort and experience, both at the strategic and the tactical, ground, levels. I had the opportunity of *Questioning* or *Interrogating* hundreds of these revolutionaries or mostly unlawful elements or terrorists.

My father, then Captain Brij Mohan Lal, had been a commissioned officer in the British Indian Army and has the unique distinction of participating in the Second World War in the Burma campaign. With him was yet another distinguished soldier, Captain SK Sinha, who later retired as Lieutenant General and is presently the Governor of Jammu and Kashmir. My impressions as given by both of them have been unique in comprehending the human psyche in war, which blurs the distinction between a *brave act* and a *terrorist act*. The Japanese terrorist acts against the enemy soldiers had drawn parallels to the worst examples in history.

I have also gathered many impressions while discussing with Pakistan's previous Chief of Army Staff, General Jehangir Karamat (who resigned in opposition to Nawaz Sharif's policies including the establishment of a National Security Council in Pakistan), whilst he attended an *Asian Security Seminar* at the India International Centre, New Delhi, in January 2001. Many linkages on Pakistan's military strategy and terrorism have thus been drawn and speculated.

I am also grateful to the former US Ambassador to India (earlier American Ambassador to Islamabad), Dennis Kux, who during his visit to India in March-April 2001, interacted with me on many issues during various presentations, which I had conducted. I have had some very interesting discourses from experts on terrorist issues, based in the UK including Robert, J. Bunker, during the Asian Security Seminar in January 2001, in New Delhi. In this regard, very clear articulation by Arundhati

Ghosh on the emerging WMD terrorist threat has been beneficial to the extent of sharing perceptions with another outstanding personality in the Indian strategic scene.

The Army has given me the ground experience and a laboratory for strategic thinking. In the coming decades, the contours of wars that are likely to emerge in the 21st century and the relevance, of asymmetric warfare in this context have been analysed, to bring out the symbiotic linkages between terrorism and military strategy.

Global terrorism of the past cannot be discussed without the anatomy of terrorist movements in the South-Asian region including the *Deadly-Triangle of Terrorism* formed within the geographic confines of Afghanistan – Pakistan – Kashmir. Being close to the former Soviet Union (FSU), proliferation of Weapons of Mass Destruction (WMD) has occurred in this region, adding a new dimension to the threat. Thus, the necessity of formalising civil defence mechanisms on this account. The recent articulations by President George Bush, earlier CIA reports and the anthrax attacks post 11 September 2001, have only testified these facts.

Another very disturbing trend is the 'Pan-Islamic' agenda or the new kind of Jehad[1] (Distorting the very meaning of Islam and Jehad). This kind of a fissurous tendency, if not managed, may even accentuate a kind of Samuel Huntington's thesis of a *Civilizational Clash* in which case it becomes Islam versus Christianity or Judaism, or even Islam versus Hinduism. Some came out with a theory of a *Varna-Clash* in which the divide is along race and colour. The need is to comprehend the cancer of terrorism and tackle it at the the root, if possible through the United Nations. The counter-strategy obviously could have the thrust of *Eradication of Poverty Zones* and *Eradication of Illiterate Zones*. But, to be more frank, the issue is much more complex. Yet another factor which would have to be controlled is the *Evilness of Mind*. . . and this may not be possible always.

1. Here, in this book, *Islamic Jehad* or Islamic Terrorist should not be misconstrued commonly, for it is only referring to those small percentage comprising extremist terrorists. The word *Islamist* broadly signifies the preponderance of the political aspect in which it categories the majority of Muslims who are virtuous and practice Islam.

Therefore, the best solution is to evolve *counter-methods (positivity)*, which balances the *negativity* of human nature.

In this context, talking of *negativity* as a defence concept for a modern nation state Pakistan fits the role. I would also like to mention having read the book *The Quranic Concept of War* as formulated by Pakistan's Brigadier S.K. Malik in 1979. The theme of this book has basically articulated terrorism in these words *Terrorism, is the quintessence of the Islamic strategy for war. Terror struck into the hearts of the enemy is not only a means, it is the end in itself.* I have been thus analysing Pakistan's stratagy, since then. Having myself operated for almost quarter of a century both in Kashmir and the North Eastern parts of India, I could distinctly see the different texture of terrorist and guerrilla activities in these two different geographical areas. In the North-East, terrorist actions are more loosely controlled without in fact any military strategy. However, in the Kashmir state, the complete modus operandi of terrorism is strictly executed as per military precision. The tactics of infiltration and regrouping across the LOC are all controlled by the ISI, who it appears has perfected the art of a new *Net War* concept, which will be discussed in the book.

Further, Kashmir is an Indian experience, which has been taken as a backdrop, time and again, to explain various live situations. In India's case, the need of the hour is to identify India's growing stature and thus the responsibility for reorganizing its military doctrines, (including terrorism) and strategies for the security of its areas of influence and subsequently areas of interest. Pakistan's proxy war through networking of terrorists and a counter to them has to be developed in a much more cost-effective manner (other than loss of human life) than hither-to-fore, by synergising technology with organisations and doctrines. Insurgencies and terrorist movements in other parts of India and neighbouring states need to be addressed holistically too.

An in-depth analysis has been done on issues of WMDs, their usage by terrorists, and consequence management. Having experience as the Director of Nuclear Strategy in Army Headquarters, helped me to do some constructive work on emergency responders to such incidents. This resulted in creating an infrastructure in the way of organising response teams to such incidents.

A study has been carried out here on the requirement of a counter-intelligence structure. Israeli model towards this end has been compared and aspects of the *Balance of Terror* philosophy discussed. In the fast changing scenario of post '9-11' lot of legal conventions are coming to the fore and the same have been summarised.

I must confess that, initially, research with the IDSA was focused on the subject *Nuclear Biological and Chemical Terrorism: A South Asian Perspective*. Later, my work at the United Service Institution of India got broadened to link various facets of military strategy with terrorism, as obtained in the Indian subcontinent and especially so in the post '9-11' scenario.

An *NBC Technical Manual* has also been added, which actually can become the *First Aid Kit* during such incidents. If one carries the manual, one can become and enroll as a first responder in such a crisis.

New Delhi **A K Lal**
January 2004

Acknowledgements

My initial work on this project began at the Institute of Defence Studies and Analyses (IDSA) which was furthered at the United Service Insititution of India (USI) where it finally took shape while interacting with many visiting specialists on this subject. While writing this book, many interviews and inter-active sessions were organised at the Ministry of Defence, Ministry of External Affairs, Defence Research and Development Organisation, Institute of Defence Studies and Analyses (IDSA) and the United Service Institution (USI) of India, New Delhi. The author is thankful to Shri IK Gujral, Shri Jaswant Singh, and Dr APJ Abdul Kalam.

I owe inspiration and motivation to Lieutenant General Satish Nambiar (Retd), presently Director, United Service Institution of India. My many discussions with Lieutenant General Nambiar helped me in formulating this book. I also would like to convey my deep gratitude to Major General YK Gera (Retd) for all his help.

I also owe many impressions due to the platform provided at the Institute of Defence Studies and Analyses (IDSA) and the United Service Institution of India (USI), especially our earlier Directors of IDSA, Air Commodore, Jasjit Singh (Retd) and Dr K Santhanam, and the Deputy Director, Commodore, Uday Bhaskar (Retd). The consultations and discussions with Major General VK Shrivastava (Retd) while at the IDSA have also been of worth.

I have been studying terrorism and military strategy for more than quarter of a century. Over this long period, I had the opportunity of not only reading about such matters but physically experiencing the phenomenon of terrorism and the loss of human life.

In the 1970s, the insurgencies, which one experienced in the North-East of India, had very little terrorist content except for some unplanned aberrations. However, the same type of guerrillas, in recent period have become terrorists of sorts, armed with the latest technology. I had the opportunity of interrogating or interviewing them in hundreds of numbers, which gave me an insight on such individuals. In the early 1990s, one came across many of these pseudo fighters, some of whom were trained with the ISI (Pakistan) sponsored links in Afghanistan.

During my various stints in the field including Jammu and Kashmir, I had the opportunity of speaking to hundreds of locals, both Hindus and Muslims. In fact both live in amity and have narrated, time and again, their choice of a secular India rather than an unstable 'Islamic' state. The indigenous Muslim even now follow many Hindu rituals.

I am extremely grateful to those who have given me advice and guidance like Shri I K Gujral (ex-Prime Minister of India) over many long sessions and Arundhati Ghosh, who gave me an international level appraisal of real politic on various issues, time and again. I also had the unique access to the present President of India, Dr Abdul Kalam, who was very kind in enunciating his vision for peace and global security.

The guidance of and interactions with the Director IDSA, K Santhanam and with Major General VK Shrivastava have been very helpful.

My interactions with Sujit Dutta and Shitij Prabha of IDSA gave me new insights into their experience. I am indeed also grateful to Sridhar, a specialist on the issues of Taliban and Osama Bin Laden.

I also learnt and documented many ground facts due to being a part of the defence community, with whom I argued and debated on future counter-terrorism strategies including WMD.

I would like to acknowledge the support of my wife Akanksha and my two daughters, Shilpi and Shikha, for painstakingly correcting volumes of my writings and giving it the shape it is in now.

In this complete research process, I came to acquire primary original source material and many other open source materials, which I have quoted, where applicable. Reference to more than a hundred periodicals and news papers may have been done over and above my personal impressions, all of which cannot be quoted.

In spite of the diversity of my primary, secondary and open sources of reference, it may not be conducive to reveal all the names of so many persons, whom I have met and discussed this subject, more due to security reasons and their life being endangered thereafter. Exposing a *Human Source* is not my endeavour, more as an ethical code of conduct and their own personal security. Therefore my omission at places of precise sources should be understood in the correct perspective.

I would like to dedicate this book to my great master Pujya Rajagopalachari, who imbibed in me the need to search for the inner self and seek inner vision and strength.

One

Global Narrative

The Power Shift

The 11 September 2001 attacks on America was a culminating act of the process of a challenge to global security. It was a logical conclusion to an emerging scenario. A terrorist act with a mass killing impact was expected. It was not a question of . . . *will* it happen? But obviously.....*when* will it happen?

This event should not be looked as a single aberration. It has to be diagnosed and treated. Therefore, there is an urgent requirement for an analysis to include aspects endangering global peace on a wide spectrum of issues ranging from politics, economics, education and ideological beliefs, which in turn are causing the *Wheel of Power* to turn. In other words it is causing a *Power Shift* as well as an *Ideological Rift*. In the emerging world order, the power shift curve appears to be leaning more towards Asia and even India in the South Asian region. Similarly the *Ideological Rift* between cultures and religions are widening. The case of Islam versus Christianity or Islam versus Judaism is tilting towards negativity. Both these issues will be debated further so as to correctly perceive the problem and identify terrorism as the prime threat to global security.

As of now, the threats are only multiplying; due to the proliferation of weapons of mass destruction (WMD); evolution of new technologies and military capacities; as well as the shrinking of global resources and environmental degradation which may challenge the very survival of human race. The determinants to global security are many, encompassing a wide spectrum of complex issues[1]. However, the focus here will remain on the cancerous growth of redefined terrorism or the so-called 'Neo-Terrorism', which may encompass a new dimension of the WMD, from an Indian perspective. The linkage to military strategy and the various counter-strategies would also be discussed, to include civil defence mechanisms (more against WMD threats) and the various legal aspects.

Terrorism is proliferating and challenging the coherence of nation-states. It is taking a heavy toll on human life. Abetment by big powers is a reality. Terrorism can see the demise of a nation in the Twenty First Century. Global security doctrine needs to be analysed with the terrorist factor as it dangerously portends towards world peace. The Asian countries especially South Asia should come under an 'Anti-Terrorist Umbrella' (ATU).

The transition to the new millennium has given birth to a more complex world ridden with unequal distribution of power and resources, where American dominance would reach its peak. The dynamism of which would impact and affect the common man. The proliferation of WMD would only intensify with biological weapons becoming more potent and where cyber and anonymity would make wars without geographical boundaries and that too when they become tools in the hands of terrorists. Terrorism would transcend frontiers creating an invisible front. The prognosis about a future world can be inter-related to the following propositions:

- World population is growing at 1.5 per cent per annum. It would imply a continued addition of 100 million people every year. Food growth will continue declining causing a dangerous imbalance.[2]
- Great power relations will be in a flux, as differences over economic and strategic issues would encompass a kaleidoscope of self-interested factors. The emergence of European Union and the fast developing economies of South Asia would unbalance core issues.
- Regional boundaries will be increasingly blurred due to the exploding Information Technology and applications of space, which will unite the globe.
- Economic wars would become more relevant rather than war for barren territories. Nevertheless certain nation states would remain in bellicosity over neighbouring territories due to historical and ethnic complexities.
- The hierarchy of superdom is uncertain due to the emerging economies and unification of Europe. Impact of Euro dollar would impinge on security of other states.
- Technology, including military technology will spread rapidly, as there is an ongoing renaissance and a Revolution in Military Affairs (RMA) impacting national strategies. Faster absorption of RMA by any state would be militarily rewarding.
- Spread of NBC weapons would affect military equations. Their proliferation would continue in conflicting situations or terrorist attacks.[3] Refinements of fourth generation nuclear technology would localise effects as compared to large area destruction and may become more popular as per already created world opinion towards total ban of nuclear weapons.
- Global distribution of power will change, as the centre of gravity would shift to Asia and the energy resources of Central Asia would become a core issue in world politics and the paradigm of power.

• Bigger powers will be more vulnerable to attack as WMDs proliferate and terrorism expands into various shades and potencies. In fact it may cause a *Revolution in Terrorist Affairs (RTA).*

RMA effect would also be utilised by the "High Tech Terrorists". Low intensity conflicts and insurgency would persist till there is an economic revival of the afflicted area and till the seeds of political conflict are extinguished. South Asian region would be more vulnerable in this context. As a corollary, an intensive effort to check and prepare for this menace would have to be evolved globally.

There will be many other extra security related issues, the interplay and interpolation of which would fabricate the destiny of future generations. The impact of information technology and the fast inter-related space capabilities would transcend the very concept of existence of human civilisation. Therefore, an analysis and assessment for future global power play would be fabricated on the following :-

• Balance of power could change dramatically over short periods - as was the case with US and Germany between1870 and 1910. China is already a global player and the revival of Russia cannot be overruled.

• Direct satellite will facilitate transmission of high-speed wireless data, which will be highly robust and mobile. Application of satellite technology is already revolutionising information and battlefield capabilities. This obviously is also having an impact on terrorist and *Counter Terrorist Operations (CTO).*

• Space based communication systems and the synergisation with internet capability will usher an era of real time information and command management. This would enable forming a global CTO network, may be under the aegis of UN or regional forums.

• NBC threat will proliferate beyond 2025 in the security structure in which non-state groups will also be players.

• NBC shadow for overseas and expeditionary military operations would persist, to serve 'US' interests including complementary operations to support allies. A pre-emptive strike to set back a potential enemy's nuclear or chemical programmes would remain a possibility.[4] The recent announcement of Bush against the *Axis of Evil* has to be seen in this context.

• Counter-proliferation via air strikes, special operations forces, or insertion of software agents that would softly kill weapons could prompt targeted countries to be neutralised and destroyed even before actual operations. In other words, it would usher in a period of new methods of warfare including those through non-state players, or the so-called *Asymmetric Warfare*, below a particular threshold level of total war.

The Asian region can be broadly divided into two segments on the basis of ground realities.[5] One, the western region—Pakistan, Afghanistan and parts of West Asia, where strife and realpolitik are the predominant forms of politics. In the eastern segment of the continent of which India is first, followed by South East Asian countries and Japan, the progress is much more in all aspects, especially economic and military co-operative arrangements. China is the most dominant country. It would continue to emerge as the peer competitor to US as per the current trends of growth of an approximate level of 10 per cent. However, these projections have the potential of getting upset due to wild card shifts in a nation's capability; either due to maligned social fibre or unequal distribution of power and wealth. The re-emergence of Russia and the consolidation of the European Union (EU) will yet be a factor to be watched. Here, we would also focus on the "Rise of Asia" situation with special reference to South Asia. The focus is already shifting towards Asia as its old tradition of isolation fades to merge with the global economy and other higher issues of inter-dependence between the world states. The following are the emerging trends in Asia:

- Asia is burgeoning with conventional militarisation. Thus instability is likely to persist. This is getting accentuated by a rising population of 1.8 per cent, which may create demographic and population security hazards.[6]
- Terrorism may continue flourishing in Asia due to the dynamics of the great power game.[7] Terrorist groups may consider the Asia-Pacific region as an attractive theatre of activity.[8] Even possession of WMDs by them cannot be overruled, due to existence of a black market on this account as well as not quite a strong security check.
- Pivotal states in Asia would remain to be Russia, China, Japan, India, Pakistan and Indonesia. India is gearing up to become the fourth largest economy of the world. It already has the fourth largest army in the world. India again is the fourth country in the world, which can launch satellites.
- The first war of Twenty First Century launched by America against terrorism would continue for many years. This obviously would cause new alliance in Asian security requiring remoulding and re-structuring.[9]

As a consequence of the above, the fundamental structural fabric of the Asian continent is undergoing a metamorphosis, the attributes of which are:

- Asia-Pacific region has the potential of becoming the economic giant, which will shift the focus away from the present alignments. Today, Asia consumes roughly 30 per cent of all US merchandise export supplies and U.S. imports 40 per cent of Asian merchandise. The trend will continue in favour of Asia.
- External threat dynamics is likely to increase due to changing environment towards multi-polarity. This trend is contrary to the forces of unipolarity and emergence of newer military-technologies, as were on display in Kosovo and Afghanistan and now Iraq. However, the strategic balance is not likely to change at least for a decade, in favour of the Asiatic landmass.
- Internal conflicts, turbulence, political transitions will keep this region unstable, disallowing smooth growth and free prosperity. Issues like Taiwan or Sino-Japan tensions could become future flash points. The Kashmir imbroglio would persist. This trend will repel trends of unification and also affect trade and commerce in South Asia. They may thus dictate and define new parameters of terrorism.

Coming closer home, the South Asian nuclearisation coupled with the changing nature of terrorism, including WMD potential would pose a challenge to this region and in turn to the world. The post 11 September events have shown Pakistan to be the epicentre of terrorism. America's objective is to cause systemic change in this turbulent terrorist/Jehadi ridden region by a combination of cooperation and coercion to control any breeding ground of terrorism. This approach implies that the requisites for local hegemony will be treated as a *lesser included capability* which automatically derives from India's capacity to stand shoulder-to-shoulder with the great powers in Asia and beyond. This perspective has precipitated because weakening India would only allow China to expand in the Asia-Pacific as its tentacles have already reached Myanmar and the Coco-Islands, with Pakistan also converting into a natural ally of China; with the turmoil in the trans Caucasus Central Asia and Persian Gulf and when Indian energy dependence only increases. Thus, India cannot remain underdeveloped and isolated; it would have to face bigger challenges in times to come be they terrorist, missile or nuclear threats from belligerent neighbours.[10]

The Indian Ocean is already bristling with nuclear submarines, aircraft carriers and flotillas. Diego-Garcia is an American base. In the Indian Ocean Rim (IOR) there are many ongoing insurgencies and terrorist activities. Thus, the whole Asian and particularly the South-Asian region is bridled with weapons and tensions, a factor to be guarded for peace. South Asia will emerge as a new economic bulwark and "Growth Pole" in which India will emerge a very important player. RAND report by Charles Wolf et al 1995 suggests that keeping by the conservative growth rate of 5.5 per cent, the Indian economy will grow from 1.2 trillion in 1994 to 3.7 by 2015 - an increase from 46 per cent of Japan's 1994 GNP to 82 per cent of its GNP in 2015. India's GNP is likely to increase from 24 per cent of China's total to 27 per cent by 2015. This enhanced economic growth should increase military capability. India's military stock would constitute 79 per cent of China's military stock by 2015.

Against this backdrop, the potential of India has to be understood. May be, India's potential will fructify into greater stature. India sits strategically in the South-Central Asian region. It hugs the Islamic bloc on the West and the Southeast Asian bloc on its East. It is estimated that India's average growth of GDP is likely to increase. And if this trend continues to remain around 5.5 to 6 per cent up to 2010 AD, it would allow India to become an economic fulcrum in Asia and may be even beyond. Yet, there could be many imponderables to this achievement. The point to understand is that India's growth would automatically stymie the growth of various terrorist movements by 2025 or so.

Further, it is worth highlighting additional growth patterns in this region to understand the economic dynamics of this region and the concurrent understanding of their mitigating effort on seeds of terrorism, in a longer perspective:

- Highest sustained economic growth (averaging 6 to 8 per cent). The downward trend in SE Asia has yet to affect substantially China and India, both countries having strong fundamentals.
- Some of the countries (about eleven) identified as emerging markets are China, India, Indonesia, Poland and South Africa.
- Wealth and prosperity of US will continue to have linkages with Asia. US imports 42 per cent of its goods from Asia-Pacific region in contrast to 20 per cent from Europe, 19 per cent from Canada, about 12 per cent from rest of North America and 5 per cent from rest of the world. Similarly, American merchandise export is in the following zones: Asia-Pacific 30 per cent; Europe America 16 per cent; rest of the world 5.6 per cent.[11]
- US Commerce Department estimates that rise of import in above mentioned emerging markets would be $ 1000 billion by 2010 AD than it was in 1990.[12]
- Both, China and Japan emerge as peers to US (Japan's biggest weakness is that its economic vitality is dependent on good political relations with its trading partners).
- Japan has structural economic problems, however China

enjoys the same and its Achilles heel is the 'Fossil Fuels'. Thus, long-term Chinese strategy would be to secure areas of oil resources and corridors to obtain them. This justifies their naval growth and the ascending nexus with Pakistan. Although Japan has the 3rd largest military budget, yet it may not be able to match China.

- RMA diffusion in national strength is occurring fast in the Asia-West Pacific region. Asia is riddled with boundary disputes, some of which date back to the colonial era. These may become flashpoints in future on the smallest of pretexts and may, thus, be an overriding factor for peace. In this context, terrorism may get indirectly linked to newer dimensions being a product of tensions and rivalries. The disputed areas are:

  (a) Sino-Japanese dispute over Senkaku Islands.
  (b) Russia-Japanese dispute over northern territories and the Kurtles.
  (c) Sino-Indian border dispute over Aksai Chin and the North East boundaries.
  (d) Sino-Indian border dispute over Spratly Islands.
  (e) India–Pakistan dispute over Kashmir.
  (f) Chinese-SE Asian dispute over Spratly islands.
  (g) Sovereignty dispute over SE Asian straits.
  (h) Enhanced militarisation to the extent of rise of 10 per cent in defence expenditure by China and change in force structuring and strategic orientation. Other Asian states are following the same route. Threat of open ocean contingencies is shaping military structures.

Having scanned the environment and the global trends, one would like to draw linkage of terrorism to India's ancient history. Terrorism can easily be compared to a demon of Indian folklore or mythology called Raktha Beeja Asura. Every drop of blood shed by this demon would produce another demon of equal capability, which used to frustrate Gods. The Lord in a famous hymn in *Bhagavad Gita* had promised that whenever there is decline of righteousness (Dharma) and rise of unrighteousness (Adharma), he would manifest himself as an embodied being (*Bhagavad Gita,* Hymn IV. 7, 8). The threat to India, therfore, remains real.

It will not be unnatural if the chemical attack by a religious sect in a Tokyo sub-way can also happen anywhere in Delhi. Similarly, nuclear leakage and pilferage has to be considered a serious threat. In attempting to gauge its likelihood, we must first acknowledge that we do not know how much, if any, may already have been stolen. There is too much of it unaccounted for. In the US and the non-communist world, more than 9000 nuclear power plants are operating. Each has the capacity to produce bomb-capable plutonium, some up to 300 kilograms a year - all together a total of about 45 metric tons a year, the equivalent of at least 6,000 nuclear weapons. Approximately twenty plants, in seventeen countries, can now process plutonium from reactor fuel cycle and breeders that make it difficult to estimate accurately how much plutonium will be in circulation by the year 2005. Transport of so much dangerous material in open commerce may well turn out to be the Achilles heel of the nuclear industry, a prime target for terrorist theft. The Americans were worried about 'Bio-attacks' by Iraq. The Anthrax attacks in the post '11 September' period is a warning signal. There is a need for a 'Global Security and Counter-Terrorist' doctrine to be evolved by nations and universally by the United Nations, to include 'Medical Aid and Survival Measures' at global level. Piecemeal attendance to issues like ban of land mines and such, is not good enough.

There is a need for evolving a universal counter-terrorism doctrine sanctified by a UN resolution akin to the NPT, the CWC or the CTBT. In fact, the threat of WMDs through terrorist acts is much larger than a missile misfire. There is scope for instituting such like counter strategies, after identifying the CBW threat spectrum in the coming new age. A new type of warfare through Weapons of Mass Disruption (WMDR) also seems to be emerging and can be also categorised as a WMD. (Discussed in the chapter on 'Redefining Terrorism')

In combination with these global trends and the power shift, which is occurring, one has to also analyse the trends of ideological beliefs viz Islam versus Christianity or Islam versus Judaism, and the ideological shift, which, it appears, is overtaking the 'power shift'. Here, it would be very appropriate to peep into the historical perspective of the idea of Islam's conflict with Westernisation and modernity. Iranian scholar and diplomat Fereydoun Horeyda believes that Christendom has subjugated Islam since the Twelfth Century. Christian states were established evicting Islam in countries such as Spain or Portugal, but was followed soon by riposte led by the Kurds who defeated the crusaders during the period from 1187 to 1192. Very soon Spain was recaptured. These earlier Islamist rule, unfortunately, consolidated their power further by fermenting religious beliefs of the so-called "Islamness". This was the beginning of the 'Ideological Rift' in the Twelfth Century, which initiated the concept of Islamic militancy akin to brutality and ruthlessness. Chengiz Khan's invasion into India only testifies the same.

There have been cases of burning of Indian epics; the Nalanda library was burnt. The attack by the Taliban on the Bamiyan Buddha statues is a repetition, in the Twentieth Century, of their psyches). During the period of the First and Second World War, Christianity again dominated the scene. In fact, the British carved the Middle East, which again was a psychological and ideological blow as felt by the 'Ulema of Islam'. In fact the Iranian revolution in the 1970s was basically a counter-reaction to Americanism or Western domination. They introduced a complete 'Neo Islamic Education' system, with the aim of breaking away from the shackles of Western education.

In today's modern world, where information and media are the key players, it has only accentuated the cumulative effects over the centuries to increase the ideological divide. Unfortunately, the erstwhile USSR's occupation of Afghanistan and the American help to organise militants against Russian occupation, created a Frankenstein and a popular cause like Jehad, for mobilising Islam against the Western world itself.

Jehad has now become the rallying point for Muslims. Jehad, when amplified signifies holy war to evict non-Muslims from their lands[13], which were Muslim lands earlier. India also becomes the objective of this war in spite of Kashmir's accession to India and the legal position being very clear. Pakistan has not recognised this accession, but has been seized by a hate - India obsession.

Partition: The Indian Experience

As regards the Indian experience, it will be worth recapitulating the salient aspects and the truism on Kashmir to get the right perspective of an area which appears to be connected with the epicentre of terrorism. Walter Lawrence, ICS, CIE, the Settlement Commissioner for Jammu & Kashmir State 1897 stated, which testifies India's historical claim:

"Let the World know that Kashmir till 14th Century was a Hindu state till the Muslim ruler Sikander came from across the Khyber pass and terrorized the people by rape and murder to cause conversions".[14]

The ramifications were that he divided brothers and sisters into different religions. In actual fact, it just remains a case of removing the veil of ignorance from the face of this most beautiful and lush valley of the world.[15] In fact, Kashmir is a case of a "Great Power-struggle and a Great-Game" being played by various powers, some at the global level, some at the regional level and some at the sub-continental level. Unfortunately, akin to Afghanistan it happens to be a powerful battle ground having geo-strategic leverages and significance. May be the Asian landmass, will supersede Mackinders concept[16] of the European landmass, in the evolving Twenty First Century.

It will re-structure and re-mould global politics and economics, where the concept of terrorism would be an unacceptable aberration. As is already known, the geographical confines of South of Central Asia and West of South Asia may qualify to be called the region of 'Breeding Terrorism', unfortunately with a religious hue. It will be unnecessary to argue as to who created this 'Frankenstein', the beast which has at last come out of the bottle of the genie, in one of the biggest terrorist strikes in the history of humanity. Undoubtedly, the creation of this organised 'Evil Empire' was a product of cold war rivalries. But unfortunately, even in the post cold war period, the great Jehadi machinery became a 'Strategic Weapon' to fulfill the so called 'Pan-Islamic Aspirations' as enunciated by Osama Bin Laden. It also helped Pakistan fulfill and consolidate its frontiers across Afghanistan and of course towards Kashmir, which was the unfinished agenda. Realistically speaking, one can say that it has been the Kashmir imbroglio, which has been the 'oxygen' of this great and nefarious movement. Therefore, at this juncture it becomes necessary to understand the problem of Kashmir a little more in the global context, to clear the perspective of the Indian experience.

The accession of J&K to Pakistan was a critical need from the geo-economic strategic point of view. This was perceived to be necessary because four out of the five rivers in West Pakistan, that is, the Indus, Jhelum, Chenab and Ravi, originate from across, and in, the mountain reaches of J&K, and the fifth (the Satluj and Beas combined) flow through the state of Himachal Pradesh bordering J&K on its southern flank. Being agro dependent, water becomes a primary source of concern for Pakistan. Obviously, geo-economic compulsions make it important for Pakistan to possess Kashmir. 23 years after the event (and ten years after the Indus Water Treaty) General Akbar Khan wrote:From the economic point of view, the position was equally clear. Our agricultural economy was dependent particularly upon rivers coming out of Kashmir. The Mangla head-works were actually in Kashmir and the Marala head-works were within a mile or so of the border. What then would be our position if Kashmir was to be in Indian hands?"[17]

Mohammed Ali Jinnah as the Governor General of Pakistan gave orders on 26 October, 1947 with a view to seize "Muslim areas around Poonch which controlled the headwaters into West Punjab of Pakistan". This fact has been testified by a British Army officer who was Military Attaché to General Douglas Gracey, the Commander of the Pakistan Army in the period in 1948-49 to an

Indian Army officer[18]

This is not to suggest that the issue of 'Theocracy' was not important in deciding Pakistan's attitude toward Kashmir. After all, Pakistan itself was sought on the basis of the two-nation theory that Muslims constitute a separate nation and should have a separate state, and, hence, all Muslim areas should be part of Pakistan. Islam had been used as the raison d'etre of Pakistan itself. The effort to enlarge the territory of the new state before independence by trying to usurp certain states had not succeeded and by themselves had given the lie to the rationale confined to 'Muslimity' constituting the basis of Kashmir's inclusion in Pakistani territory. But Pakistan's leadership, over the years, has been distorting the realities. It is true that the sub-continent was partitioned along communal lines in 1947, but this analogy was applicable only to the areas and provinces directly ruled by the British. In the North-West Frontier Province, a referendum had to be held in spite of its population being overwhelmingly Muslim, since this area was not directly administered by the British.

The British ruled only some parts of India directly and these areas were designated as "provinces". About 54 per cent of the territory of erstwhile British India came within this framework in 1947. It is this area that was to be partitioned in accordance with the dispensation of transfer of power when India attained independence and Pakistan was created. Factors like geography, demography, etc, were to be kept in mind and a Boundary Commission was set up to draw the boundaries of the proposed state of Pakistan carved out of India.

However, the balance of 46 per cent of the total territory of the pre-independence India, was controlled remotely by the British through treaties made with rulers and kings of nearly 564 states. A separate Chamber of Princes was instituted for deliberation on decisions pertaining to these princely states such as and was thus called the 'Paramountcy of the British'. On 25 July 1947, Lord Louis Mountbatten, the Viceroy addressed the Chamber of Princes and stated, "The States will have complete freedom.... Technically and legally when they become independent." He invited the rulers to make up their minds, preferably before 15 August 1947, when India would become independent and paramountcy would lapse, leaving these rulers, sovereigns of independent countries.

The Muslim League headed by Mohammed Ali Jinnah, the creator of Pakistan, had insisted that since sovereignty would be restored to the princely rulers, their decision also should be the criterion for accession. They had taken the position before independence that the rulers would have the right to accede to either of the new state or even remain independent. Liaquat Ali Khan, who was to be Pakistan's first Prime Minister, had stated that after transfer of power, "the Indian States will be free to negotiate agreements with Pakistan or Hindustan as considerations of contiguity or their own self-interest may dictate, or they may choose to assume complete and separate sovereign status themselves". The case of Junagadh's accession got sanctified further when Mohammad Ali Jinnah again reiterated to them that the "Ruler of a state had an absolute right", to accede to either country. But they did not allow the same logic for J&K, and invaded it instead. Nevertheless, the 'two nation theory' undercut this principle when he lured the Hindu ruler, Maharaja of Jodhpur, to almost accede to Pakistan in return for use of Karachi as a free port. Similarly, Hindu states like Bikaner and Jaisalmer were also approached, which was in complete contrast to Jinnah's theological school of thought for partition. Therefore, the logic of demanding Kashmir is immoral.

India on its part, took the idealistic position that the will of the people was important if not the over-riding factor for a decision on accession of a state to India or Pakistan. The Congress was also vehemently opposed to any state staying independent after transfer of power. The Maharaja sought a 'stand still' agreement with India and Pakistan to maintain the status quo. India did not agree to the proposal. The Indian leadership had been insisting that such an agreement could be signed only after accession. Pakistan, however, agreed, but imposed an economic blockade to force the decision in Srinagar. Then followed the invasion by Pakistan and the subsequent many wars for Kashmir.[19]

The key issue, therefore, is that there was never a question of partition of these states on communal grounds, or their accession being governed by this factor. The Radcliff Boundary Commission award partitioning the subcontinent into two countries, thus, applied only to the British ruled provinces and not to the princely states.

In totality, Kashmir's strategic significance becomes vital as the pivot of greatness. Again, examining in the context of the religion of Kashmir: "The Indifference shown in the matter of Mosques and Mullahs may be accounted for by the fact, that the Kashmiri Sunnis are only Musalman in name. In their heart they are Hindus, and the religion of Islam is too abstract to satisfy their superstitious cravings."[20]

Further, it can be quoted: "It was only natural that the Musalmans, when they were converted to Islam, should cling with tenderness to the old religious places, and should adopt sacred spots already familiar to the country-side. But I attribute much of the delightful tolerance which exists between the followers of the two religions chiefly to the fact that the Kashmiri Musalmans never really gave up the old Hindu religion of the country".[21]

Another interesting historical fact, which requires understanding, is that Kashmir's 'Sanskritistion' occurred way back through the *Rajatarangini* of the Kashmiri poet Kalhana. It narrates:

> "It comprises in eight cantos of Sanskrit verse the history of the various dynasties which ruled Kashmir from the earliest period down to the time of the author, who began to write this work in A.D. 1148, in the reign of king Jayasimha. Although Kalhana himself mentions several historians as his predecessors, none of their works have come down to us. The Rajatarangini has thus become the most direct source of information on the ancient history of Kashmir. Allowing for the legendary character of much that is related in the first three cantos regarding the earliest dynasties and discarding the artificial chronology of these portions, we retain in Kalhana's work a connected account of Kashmirian history, which has well stood the test of historical criticism."[22]

The above can be accepted as the history till the time of Walter R. Laurence. One can even trace that Kashmir is the birthplace of the fair-faced Pandu race and furnished sovereigns to the plains of Hindustan[23].

Now coming directly to the middle of the 21st century, the period of the unfortunate partition of the Indian Subcontinent and Pakistan's option of a 'Two Nation Theory'. This theory was theocratic in nature, whereas India believed in secularism. Narrating the analogy of the Instrument of Succession it is said:

"The accession of J&K state to India was unconditional, as was the accession of all other states to India or, for that matter. Pakistan. The Governor General, Lord Louis Mountbatten, while accepting the accession of J&K, wrote back to the Maharaja: 'My government feels, that as soon as the (Pakistani) raiders are beaten back and peace is restored in Kashmir, the question of accession should be decided *according to the will of the people*'." (Emphasis added). This clearly indicated the intentions, subject to the aggression by Pakistan being vacated first, something that has still not happened. It also needs to be noted that the accession had the full and unconditional support of the National Conference, the primary political party enjoying overwhelming popularity in the state.

It is a historical record that Lord Mountbatten had visited

Srinagar in June and advised the Maharaja to accede to one of the two countries. He had given him Sardar Patel's message that were he to accede to Pakistan, "it would not be considered an unfriendly act" by India. Patel, it may be recalled was the second seniormost leader in Jawaharlal Nehru's Cabinet and minister for states affairs at that time. Meher Chand Mahajan, the J&K Prime Minister, who brought the Maharaja's letter of accession, appears to have held out a threat to Nehru. According to Abdullah, who was present at the meeting, Mahajan told Nehru: "The army must leave for Srinagar today otherwise I shall proceed straight to Mr. Jinnah and sign an agreement with him." Nehru walked out of the meeting in anger saying, "If you favour an agreement with Pakistan (you can) leave at once." Abdullah persuaded Nehru to accept the accession, and pleaded with Mahatma Gandhi to send the Indian Army to defend the state.[24]

Further, India's case of Kashmir's integration is natural, as India has only got integrated with the lost kin (converted by purging and coercion). Therefore, Maharaja Hari Singh's accession to India was a moral obligation. He allowed integration of the lost tribe with mainland India. These sentiments persisted till about. It was around 1984 after which an 'Ideological Rift' on communal lines started showing. It will be worth identifying the reasons, which precipitated this.

The Jehad against the Russian occupation of Afghanistan, created Pan-Islamist sentiments in the Muslim world, even to the extent of diffusing minor differences between various sects like that of the Shia-Sunni. In furtherance to this, Zia-ul-Haq's approval of the Jamaat-i-Islami approach to Islamisation of Pakistan was wholeheartedly appreciated by the Shiite Iran and the consequent flow of massive funds. This concept of Muslim brotherhood also transcended into Kashmir causing an 'Ideological Rift' with their earlier nationalistic sentiments. Simultaneously, the ISI was already training many Muslims from other countries (presumably for operations in Afghanistan), which further created an euphoria and camaraderie within certain Islamic groups. The cries of massive rigging during the late 1980's state elections in Kashmir, changed the heart of the many leaders, who were popular and had political aspirations. They now were exploited by the ISI to create a psychological shift in favour of Pakistan.

By 1988-1990 the ISI was able to create a wedge between the indigenous Kashmiris and the Central Government. Meanwhile, with the slowing down of the Afghan conflict, Pakistan was able to convert the direction of the proxy war from its North to its East, declaring Kashmir within the confines of a Jehad. Since then till date, terrorists from other countries are fighting in Kashmir.

There is yet another phenomenon, which has gone unnoticed over the last decade. That is, gauging the aspirations and sentiments. The inputs from Siddhartha Varadharajan[25] are important :

> "From the frozen, glacial wastes of Siachen down through the rocky valleys of Skardu and Gilgit and up to the heaven like abode of the Hunzakuts, there is a palpable undercurrent of dissatisfaction with Pakistan. And though the longing for self rule and even Azaadi does not match with what exists in Indian Kashmir in either scale or intensity, it is clear that Islamabad, which has been ruling, the region since 1947 can no longer take the sentiments of people here for granted."

For possibly the first time since partition, a correspondent from an Indian newspaper has managed to travel to this remote, sensitive corner of undivided Jammu and Kashmir. The picture that emerges from several days of interaction with people here is one of frustration at the lack of self-government and constitutional rights: "Nobody has loved Pakistan more than the people of Gilgit-Baltistan", says Hussain Shah, a retired army officer who now heads the Nationalist Muttahida Quami Party. "But our rulers are tyrants. The East Pakistanis were the most patriotic Pakistanis but they were driven away. That is what is being done to us".

"The situation here and in Indian Kashmir is very different", says Ali Mardan, editor of the Gilgit-based weekly, *Naqqara*. "There, the struggle has been going on for some time whereas here it has not even started properly. But if the government continues to ignore the grievances of the Northern Areas, it could even end up facing an armed struggle". Says Major Shah, "In Indian-occupied Kashmir, the government tried to incorporate people against their will. So they revolted. Here, people told the government, 'Give us the rights of Pakistani', but Pakistan says no. The end result is no one respects self determination".

The problem in the Northern Areas (NAs) stems from the region's peculiar constitutional status within Pakistan. Unlike Azad Jammu Kashmir (AJK), which has its own 'Prime Minister', Supreme Court and budget, the NAs are in limbo. "We are neither a province of Pakistan nor a self-ruling region like AJK", says Shah. The 'legislative council' set up for the region in 1973 is a toothless body subordinate to the Pakistani bureaucracy. The Chief Secretary is all-powerful and the NAs' over-all head, or 'chief executive', is the Federal Government's Minister for Kashmir Affairs. "In Pakistan Baltistan", says Mardan, "to date, we have never had a local Chief Secretary or Police Chief. They are either Punjabis or Pathans".

Though there are six organisations in the NAs seeking self-determination, none favour integration with India. However, overall attitudes towards New Delhi are surprisingly unconventional. "I salute India", says Shah. "Even though a Kashmiri can become prime minister, no non-Kashmiri can become chief minister of J&K. But in the Northern Areas, an outsider is our chief executive". In Pakistan, they like to say "Farooq Abdullah is a puppet chief minister", he says wryly. "But Pakistan is not even prepared to let us be puppets".

This could become the main plank of India's counter-terrorist strategy by allowing POK's nationalistic integration with Kashmir, which by itself could become an autonomous state within the constitution of India. It is here that the paradox lies. On one side, is Kashmir's cultural linkage with the Hindu rituals and on the other is the call of the 'Pan-Islamic' cause. (Having talked to several Kashmiris, one is able to ascertion that their leanings are more towards India even now) But the tide may turn if India loses its secular face. Therefore, India's main counter proxy war strategy would be its very pluralistic composition, and very military posturing in which the costs of maintaining the proxy war becomes so high that the perpetuating state abandons the Islamic and Quranic policy towards becoming a modern state.

Terrorism : Redefining the Contours

The words 'Terror' and 'Terrorism' have become semantic tools of the powerful in the western world. In their dictionary, it means "Intimidation" by the 'systematic use of violence' as a means of both governing and opposing existing governments. The current western usage has restructured the scene, on purely ideological grounds, to the retail violence of those who oppose the established order[26]. Historically speaking one can trace certain aspects of the traits of terrorism to the ancient civilisations of Greece and Rome. Even the Vedas and *Mahabharata* have glimpses of terrorist acts. Our epics narrate acts of terror. Samsaptakas were ones who had taken a vow to conquer or die, and never to retreat. The Samsaptakas were suicide squads, vowed to some desperate deed. This is akin to present day suicide squads called Fidayeen.[27] Terrorism thrives on fear. By manipulating fear in a special way, terrorists have always been able to affect human behaviour in a fashion disproportionate to their effort. All violence, as Hannah Arendt has reminded us, is unpredictable. Unlike power, force or strength, violence is always applied with unforeseeable effects. The turn of the century has distinctly seen a resurgence of religious (Islamic) oriented terrorist groups (like Taliban, etc) giving essence of a Pan Islamic agenda.[28] The recent attacks on America was clearly aimed at teaching America a lesson to lay off Muslim world in general and Saudi Arabia in particular. But what shook the world is the ability of terrorists to hit at will. Since the close of the Eighteenth Century, we have had a great many instances and fighting for the liberation of countries, ranging over a wide landscape of operational groups, like the anarchists, separatists, Marxist-Leninists, Naxalites reactionaries, Islamic fundamentalist and every conceivable brand of debauch, anti-imperialist and so called national liberationists. Their intellectual and spiritual role model have been a gallery of heroes ranging from Marx, Lenin, Trotsky, Sorel, Marighella, Mao, Giap, Fanon, Marcuse, Malcolm X, Guevara, Debray, and Guillen to Osama-Bin-Laden. What could this tangled skein of programmes and participants possibly have in common? Probably it ranges from nationalism to vandalism. Therefore, it is very difficult to divide righteousness or treachery being executed by such groups. They serve a cause which could be for the good of a nation or be the very foundation of deceit and criminality. There is a very thin line dividing the difference between terrorism and insurgency or secessionism. The core difference lies in its essence having a political motive or otherwise. The other main issue is the type of tool used; the mechanism and tactics of terrorism. And their linkage with military strategy as in the present context.

With the backdrop of this global and regional narrative bringing out the mosaic of global security, let us address the principles re-defined or the so-called 'Neo-Terrorism' phenomenon. It could not have been expressed better than by India's then Foreign Minister Jaswant Singh:

> It dramatically redefines 'conflict' through a rejection of all restraints or means. India has lived with clandestine war, proxy war, state-sponsored terrorism, cross-border terrorism and what not, but terrorism accepts none of this, it redefines political geography, for it accepts no boundary, it is an ideology in itself, it conquers and colonises the mind through terror. It has thus redrawn the contours of geo-politics. Why? Principally, because terrorism converts the strengths of freedom and democracy into its principal weaknesses. First, terrorism is also predicated on exploitation of technology, then of communications, and again of employing the resultant exposure, or the "oxygen of publicity". Secondly, terrorism exploits the confidentiality of our modern

> financial and banking systems. Thirdly, spread of terrorism is facilitated by today's free movement within and between countries. Our past perceptions no longer hold good because terrorism questions both the instruments and the established hierarchies of power. Terrorism is redefining 'power'. It rejects all traditional norms of international order like, 'balance of power', 'spheres of influence', even of 'coalition of forces'.[29]

Therefore, one can analyse the shades and meaning of this adjective encompassing a wide range of issues impacting on individual psyche and creating fear; it impinges on the 'Theory of Nation-States' as well. It exploits the globalisation of freedom and modern technology. It is an evil, which can only be tackled by a global consensus.

Further, as explained by Jaswant Singh is the aspect of using this new definition 'Neo-Terrorism' as part of a state strategy sponsoring the same. He comments thus:

> "It works for establishing the hegemony of terror. Terrorism rejects all established boundaries, treaties, limitations and norms—whether geographic or moral. Despite these anarchic attributes, terrorism is employed as an instrument of state policy. The ultimate peril of adopting this path is, in the early stages, discounted by them on the anvil of convenience, because the tool of terrorism is a low cost option in the short term, but always desirable in the immediate term. When I say this I am not making a normative or a moral judgment. This is the objective reality, for terrorist organizations are like cellular structures. They are not like beehives, dependent only on a 'Queen Bee'. Terrorism is not unlike tissue, a 'system', each cell of which, in a sense, is self-contained and can reproduce itself in identical forms."[30]

In the South Asian region, one can flag the historical text along three distinct lines. Firstly, during the colonial period in the Twentieth Century, anti-establishment or terrorists movements were more related to independence. Secondly, during the post-colonial period upto 1972, which saw the emergence of sub-nationalistic type movements; and thirdly the period thereafter (including the Afghanistan imbroglio) in which, both the varieties of terrorist movements, one based on religion (Islamic jihad type) and the other type with roots in ethnic sub-nationalism (Sri Lanka/ North-East India, etc.) had surfaced and have even sustained, to now grow into serious threats.

Further, trying to define state military terrorism, it would mean: "Formulating an organisation in the other state with the view to carry out controlled violence so as to target the civil and the military assets or personnel and cause a Psycho-Traumatic Terrorists Impact (PTTI) on individual citizens/soldiers behaviour culminating in affecting the collective behaviour and psyche of the state polity being terrorised with the ultimate aim of setting military objectives and a political goal" (Explained subsequently).

In totality, terrorism has various shades and levels of operation; starting from armed robbery, which has a singular impact to state sponsored terrorism which has a strategic impact on a nation's security. As a corollary, there has yet been another dimension of 'Religious Terrorism' based on fundamentalism or a religious ideology. This obviously is fissiparous in nature as the global civilisation is divided in multifarious religions. However, for students of 'Military Strategy' who want to understand 'The Art of War',-the definition and impact of terrorism takes an entirely different connotation of 'Using terrorism as a tool of Military Strategy'. It further gets more complex, when applied in a historical and geographical context in an area of dispute between two nation states, and especially so, where there are strands of insurgency, or where the seeds of a classical form of guerrilla warfare[31] exists. The guerillas, who traditionally fight the government machinery, of late have been trying to use terrorism as a tool, to keep the population on their side by force and fear. A close study of terrorism in the Asian region, reveals a new trend of religious terrorists fighting out of their land for a larger religious aim. Yet another phenomenon, which has emerged is the concept of asymmetric warfare by the weaker side in the form of sponsoring terrorism. Further, the state sponsoring terrorism creates a nucleus of a heterogeneous kind, having religious affinity but nationalistic and ethnic diversity. Further, they are armed with the most sophisticated weapons and communication system. The individuals of such a group, all have different ideals. One is fighting for nationalistic cause, whilst the other may be fighting for a religious cause. The guerrilla or the indigenous element becomes the eyes and ears, whereas the outside elements become the muscles supported by skeleton structures of an interested nation. The chemistry thus created makes a 'Devastating Impact' in the state being terrorised into submission. Unfortunately, at times the state sponsoring such groups looses control of these Frankensteins, who may in the momentum of things touch the extreme end of the violent spectrum by a 'WMD' usage as they already have 'Anarchist or Apocalyptic' tendencies.[32]

Contemporary terrorism is replete with examples of the threat and use of chemical and biological (CB) agents. Of late even use of radiation weapons has been reported and so also nuclear hoaxes.

On the other hand, there are pure religious based groups, which have no nationalistic vision or guerilla ingredients but seek 'Ideological' or 'Pan-Religious' goals. The 11 September 2001 attacks on the US may fall within this purview. They would be referred to as Islamic Terrorists[33] coming from various nationalities.

Therefore, one can identify yet another landmark contour in terrorist characteristic of having the ingredients of a guerilla or an insurgent, who are Jehadis but are trained and possess the best and most sophisticated weapons and communication systems including satellite telephones. In a way it is causing "Revolution in Terrorist Affairs" (RTA). Thus they can be called "Neo-Terrorist" or "Jehadi-Techno Terrorists'[34]. Here, in this work, the focus would be on this guerrilla type "Jehadi-Techno-Terrorist" (JTT) and their impact on classical military strategies and national security.

At this juncture, it is worth analysing the historical perspective of various mixed guerrilla and terrorist movements across the globe. Since guerrillas use terrorism as part of their strategy, both definitions have a purpose and tendency of becoming synonymous. Therefore, while understanding the new contours of the evolving definition as discussed above, the base of 'guerilla theology' remains constant, at least in as far as its impact on military strategy is concerned. It is, therefore, an oxymoron to de-link both the activities. What, therefore, really becomes important is to establish a linkage between 'Guerilla -Terrorist' and 'Military Strategy' so as to be able to redefine the new emerging phenomenon. Maybe, the answer is to recapitulate and flag historical events, pertinent to the subject,[35] in which the classical/conventional armies operating in foreign land lost to opposing indigenous forces, created with a mix of the conventional model and supported by local guerrilla type forces, which acted as force multipliers. The result was the eviction of the purely classical army. Further, evolution of this form of warfare and its impact also needs to be recounted.

1807-1813. France under Napoleon occupied Spain, whose guerrilla movement combined with Wellington's British Army, threw off the yoke of Napoleon's army. (This is the first formalised combination of guerrillas and conventional army to throw the classical army of Napoleon out of Spain).

1812-1813. France under Napoleon reached the gates of Moscow, Cossacks the guerrillas, waged a successful guerrilla war and made them retreat, and struck at the retreating army at will.

1814. Early guerrilla campaigns in South America bore success. In fact, the American civil war followed the pattern of a guerrilla war. (But somehow or the other, nobody at this instance could really draw or grasp the strategic impact of such a form of Warfare).

1900-1902. The guerrilla campaigns in South-Africa during the Boer War contributed to the evolution, both of the guerrilla and counter guerrilla type of warfare.

1916-1918. During Arab revolt against the Turks, T E Lawrence was the first man to breach Turkish defences [first time very important].

1918-1940s. In the interim period, between the two World Wars, the communist form of guerrilla warfare took roots in Russia as well in China (Mao-Tse-Tung's War was called a people's war or a guerrilla war). The communist were fast enough to pick up the dictums of this war from the experiences of TE Lawrence by adding the aspects of economic and political goals.

Karl Marx, and Lenin in October 1906 in their writings had already paved their way for Guerrilla Warfare Techniques (GWT). The word 'Partisan' was used first time in meaning acts of terrorism and robberies. Similarly Bolsheviks seized political power in Russia in 1917-18, without much military activity and more through guerrilla type operations. However, after seeing Lawrence's success in 1916-1918, Lenin further developed the theme and fully adopted guerrilla warfare to the 'Art of Revolution'. The basic tenets laid down by Lenin were[36]:

- Intelligence of enemy movements, while keeping your own plans hidden, is the prime tactical secret.
- Avoid the enemy's strength. (It is worth noting that within this formula Lenin adopted one half of the motto of the Jeune Ecole, the initiators of the 'guerre de course'—'Shamelessly attack the weak; shamelessly fly from the strong').
- By employing rigidly controlled units, the Communist leaders could out-manoeuvre larger, less mobile forces.
- Deliberate use of terror is a means of breaking down resistance while keeping your own people under control.
- A flexible attitude must be maintained. The weapon chosen e.g., the strike, insurrection, robbery or military action, must suit the circumstances.

Similar work subsequently was done in 1937 by Mao-Tse-Tung during the Chinese struggle and war within. The dogma so created has influenced the complete region including South-Asia and India where movements like the Nepali based Maoist guerrillas or the

Indian Naxalites have their principled routes. Let us recollect Mao's dissertation on the subject[37]:

- Guerrilla operations are a necessary part in a war of revolutionary character. They must not be considered as an independent form but as one step in the total war, one aspect of the revolutionary struggle.
- Without a political goal, guerrilla warfare will fail, if its political objectives do not coincide with the aspirations of the people.
- Because guerrilla warfare basically derives from the masses, it is supported by them and can neither exist nor flourish if it separates itself from their sympathies and co-operation.
- All guerrilla units must have political and military leadership.
- Guerrilla strategy must primarily be based on alertness, mobility and attack.
- During the progress of hostilities, guerrillas gradually develop into orthodox forces that operate in conjunction with units of a regular army.
- An opinion that admits the existence of guerrilla war but isolates it is one that does not properly estimate the potentialities of such a form of making war.

He also developed a concept that guerrilla force in due time should be upgraded and developed into regular army to defeat the opponent. (The weakness of Chiang Kei Shek has to be recapitulated in this context). Similarly, one can draw many other historical examples during the middle portion of the last century. To recount a few:

- Russian Partisan Directive of 1933[38] laid down guerilla doctrine in case some body attacked Russia.
- In the period 1940-45, German invasion spurred guerrilla movement in Russia but a similar movement could not succeed in Norway, Holland, Belgium, France, Denmark, Italy, Poland, or the Balkans and therefore the Germans continued with their occupation of these areas.

Yet another historical model needs examination, where, although guerrilla movements took roots, but were defeated by government forces due to more successful handling of counter guerrilla operations. These examples are being drawn with a view to develop pros and cons and thus bring out the correct lessons and be able to develop counter-strategies for controlling such movements.

1952-1960. British government machinery defeated the communist guerrilla in Malaya.

1955-1959. The guerrilla organization named Ethniki Organosis Kyprion Agoistan (EDKA) took roots against Arch Bishop of Cyprus. The combined Algerian and French National Army defeated the insurrection. The guerrillas lost due to application of new counter-revolutionary doctrines.

Having seen the historical linkages of a guerrilla movement and counter-movements as well as its use as a military strategy, one needs to interpolate the same on the current strategies, with the uniqueness where guerrillas use terrorism as a tool of military warfare. One can differentiate the various kinds of warfare under the general head of *'Shades of Warfare'* as a function of terrorism. (Fig. 1.1).

Fig. 1.1: Shades of Warfare.

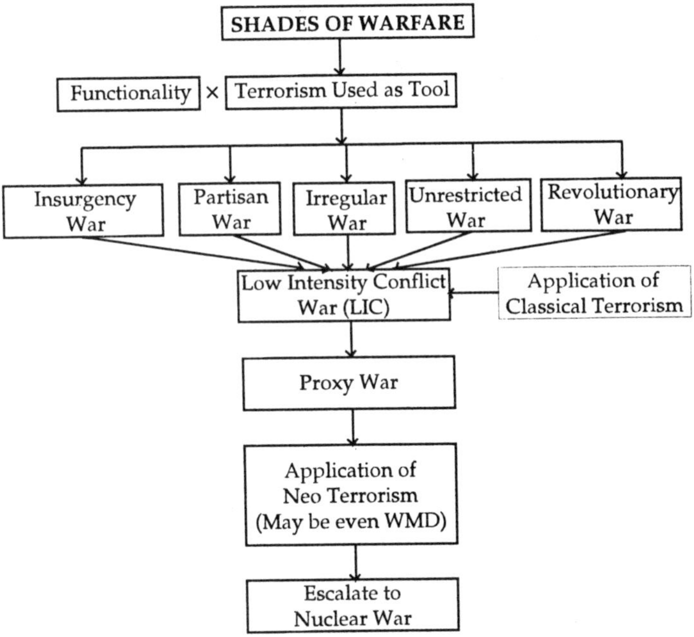

Therefore, one can see the various connotations, having subtle differences where the product of 'Terrorism' changes the content of warfare. Here the focus would be on a *'Neo-War'* created by the Jehadi type Guerrilla Terrorist (JGT) whose strengthened nucleus acts as a force multiplier to bleed the nation being terrorised and engage it in a kind of low intensity conflict or 'LIC', when the equation is judged between two asymmetric nation states. 'Proxy war' is a higher definition of 'High Intensity' rather than 'Low

Intensity', in which the external forces may be playing the 'Great Game'. However, what one has to worry about is the application of the 'Neo Terrorist' in such conflicts. The conflagration really becomes a 'Nuclear Flash Point', if the asymmetric state, which is sponsoring such terrorism is also nuclear and where proliferation of WMD can occur due to lack of controls.[39]

Further, if the dimension of WMD terrorism is added as a strategic leverage it can be classified as a *'Neo-War'*.[40] One can see the cycle of escalation, viz if conventional or classical guerilla terrorism is applied, it escalates the situation to LIC-Proxy war. However if 'JGT' nucleus is applied with WMD Potential, 'Neo-War' escalation occurs.

Now let us see the perception of WMD terrorism and how does it affect the human bondage to fear at the individual and the state level:

(a) Any destructive device as defined in section 921 of 18 USC, section 2332a, (which reads) any explosive, incendiary, or poison gas, bomb, grenade, rocket having a propellant charge of more than four ounces, missile having an explosive or incendiary charge of more than ¼ ounce, mine or device similar to the above; (b) poison gas; (c) any weapon involving a disease organism; or (d) any weapon that is designed to release radiation or radioactivity at a level dangerous to human life.[41]

The above is also listed in the Federal Response Plan (FEMA 229, Change 11 February 7, 1997). The definition under section (A) proves too inclusive with references to conventional military but somehow or the other appears vague, as it does not talk of a nuclear chain reaction. However, the military provides a far more practical explanation. Joint Publication 1-02, DOD Dictionary of Military and Associated Terms, published in March 1994 describes Weapons of Mass Destruction as follows:

In arms control usage, weapons that are capable of a high order of destruction and/or of being used in such a manner as to destroy large numbers of people. Can be nuclear, chemical, biological, and radiological weapons, but excludes the means of transporting or propelling the weapon where such means is a separable and divisible part of the weapon. Also called WMD.[42]

It should be noted that the DOD term CBRN, which describes 'chemical, biological, radiological, or nuclear' capabilities is synonymous with WMD and, in fact, is currently preferred because of WMD definition problems. This definition incorporates the (B)-(D) sections currently utilised by federal law enforcement and expand the older Nuclear, Biological, and

Chemical (NBC) term to incorporate non-nuclear 'radiological' WMD incidents.[43]

New contours and perception of technology have developed in some counter-terrorism strategy, based on the concept of Weapons of Mass Disruption which target human bonds and perception, rather than tangible assets, at the systemic level. These capabilities are derived, in many instances, from advanced (cyber or Bio cocktails) forms of weapons, which could eventually be employed by terrorists globally.

—Robert J Bunker

The perception of an immediate WMD threat currently dominates American Federal counter-terrorism planning and the implementation of response efforts articulated in Presidential Decision Directive 39 (PDD-39).[44] Of late, another danger based on a different and less recognized form of emergent mass effects weaponry has also been disturbing. This type of weaponry, known as Weapons of Mass Disruption, has the effect to disrupt large segments of infrastructure without causing the high levels of physical destruction associated with traditional forms of WMD.

There is yet another school of thought vis a vis the decades-old linear trends in traditional WMD employment who argue that the traditional record does not support the dominant view of its likelihood of use due to it being counter-productive. A substantial body of empirical data backs up these arguments, which draw upon weapon performance, cost-benefit considerations, and known behavioural patterns[45]. Beyond the traditional WMD discussions, however, a new debate may be forming. It is based upon concern over potentials of WMD. The '9-11' WTC disaster can definitely be categorized in this class, as not only it disrupted the social fabric but also hit the financial markets. In this context, one has to examine even 'lasers' as causing a disruption effect. Lasers make ideal terrorist weapons and, in fact, possess a number of advantages over Surface-to-Air Missiles (SAMs) in the areas of availability, functioning, and operational deployment[46]. To further complicate matters, lasers, like computers, are drastically falling in price and their performance levels are greatly increasing. With a basic form of Directed Energy Weapons (DEW) now being employed for both criminal (police helicopter directed) and unknown (commercial aviation directed) purpose, speculation concerning the future employment of more advanced forms of DEW with mass effects potentials can no longer be discounted. One has, therefore, to redefine, WMD; many of which are cyber-based will be discussed in relationship to WMD and with regard to weapons morphology and effects. The catastrophic potential of this new form of weaponry is implicitly recognized in Executive Order 13010, Critical Infrastructure Protection[47]. While the intent of the theory and redefinition is not to specifically explore this weaponry in any great depth, but only provide a useful conceptual framework in which to better understand new perceptions of mass effects weaponry developed in some counter-terrorism strategies.

The origins of the term WMD can be traced back to Barnard Baruch's usage in a '...1964 speech before the United Nations advocating creation of an international agency to be given exclusive jurisdiction over all nuclear weapons'.[48] Global perceptions remain focused on nuclear weaponry as the de facto form of WMD with the dominant thinking drawing upon strategic bombing concepts, which developed over the previous decades and more recent seminal works such as Bernard Brodie's *The Absolute Weapon*. The term WMD based on Nuclear, Biological, and Chemical (NBC) perceptions developed as a useful concept and spread in the WARSAW pact thinking, talking of contaminated environments, and disarmament (propaganda) literature. It then diffused into Western and UN disarmament and arms control nomenclature. This shift in terminology appears to be cultural with nuclear weapons no longer being viewed for their deterrent and strategic utility but rather as people killers.[49]

Military perceptions regarding WMD/CBRN are not clear for the new types of weaponry, which are coming to the forefront during the era of RMA. Many weapons are challenging our perceptions of traditional WMD. They are products of RMA like, information warfare (IW), cyber warfare (CW), directed energy weapons (DEW) and advanced non-lethal weapons (Advanced NLW) with much overlap and confusion. More details of the same will be discussed in the chapter on threat perceptions, bringing out morphology and many other aspects. The inclusion of Disruption in WMD is to conceptualise a new capability, which advanced weaponry could provide, rather than a mass destruction incident. The term 'Weapons of Mass Disruption', (WMDR) while in existence for a few years, has never been adequately conceptualised, and the concept has never differentiated between mass disruptions incidents, which can be created by virtually any form of weaponry and those designed to be actual WMDR.[50]

WMDR Weapons : Morphology and Impact

In order to overcome these deficiencies in the current WMDR concept, three forms of weaponry characteristics must be considered.

The first is the simplicity in construction, designing and delivery (SCDD). The second pertains to level of effect and the third to the target set being influenced. The SCDD is a very important factor in usage. For example, a small chemical or bio-agent can be carried secretly hidden in torch cells, umbrellas or even clothing. Similarly, level of effect is based on a continuum from the individual to the group to the systemic. (In this connection, the original relationship has been identified by Robert J Bunker in his article on WMDR). Determining the specific firebreaks between these thresholds of effect has been and always will be problematic. Generally, the individual threshold = 1 and group threshold is equal to 1+. The firebreak between the group threshold (1+ to n) and the systemic (n+) represents a vast grey area. Primarily the type of weapon being employed usually determines it. Conventional weapons, both lethal and non-lethal (NLW)), do not possess inherent systemic effects potential and, therefore, are excluded from this designation unlike CBRN. However, the WMD/WMDR category produces the psycho-traumatic threshold impact (PTTI) due to the magnitude of physical or economic danger, traumatising human mind. The same are shown in the diagram for three levels and types of impact. (Fig 1.2)

Fig. 1.2

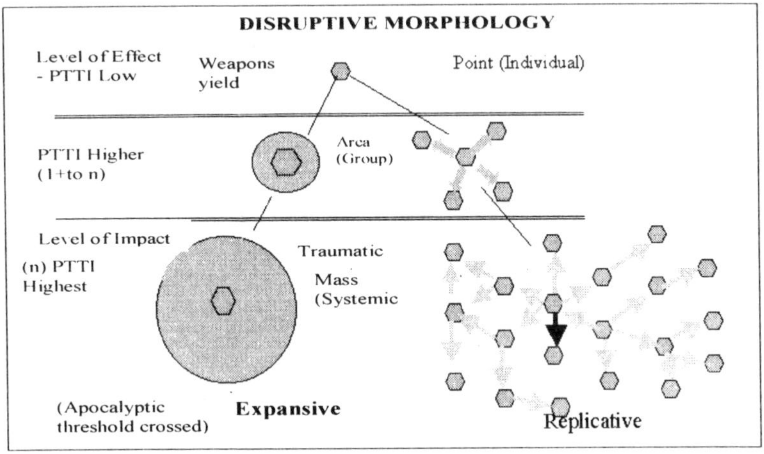

(Courtesy Robert J Bunker)[51]

Basic conventional weaponry is divided into two types, point impact and area impact type. Point weapons, such as small arms, influence one target at a time, causing singular effect whereas 'Area weapons', such as bursting devices (grenades and bombs) and automatic weapons, are able to influence a greater region of operational space because of their reflective and explicative properties, respectively. Bursting devices expand from a point to a larger area of effect via blast or lethal (non-lethal) fragmentation and are thus able to inflict damage or disruption upon a group of individuals. Automatic weapons possess such high rates of fire that they too can replicate, in a primitive mechanical sense, enough points of impact (individual bullets) to influence a larger area of effect. The utilisation of Kalashnikov series of automatic weapons have brought a Revolution in Terrorist Affairs (RTA) and has given a new dimension to the definition of emerging terrorists.

CBRN and newer forms of weaponry are in a class by themselves because of their mass effects potential. This greater threshold of effect extends beyond a group of individuals into the systemic. Once again, expansive and replicative weaponry properties come into play. A chemical weapon, when released, expands into a given volume of space, such as a subway in the case of the 1995 Tokyo Sarin attack. The same principle holds true for a nuclear device, which multiplies from the point of fission into an expanding mass derived from an atomic chain reaction. The replicative characteristic of mass effect weapons, on the other hand, is based on more of a biological/systems approach. Biological and digital viruses expand from the point of effect and replicate themselves from the group to the systemic level within a given population such as humans and computers, respectively[52]. (Fig 1.3)

Fig. 1.3. Bonds/Relationships.

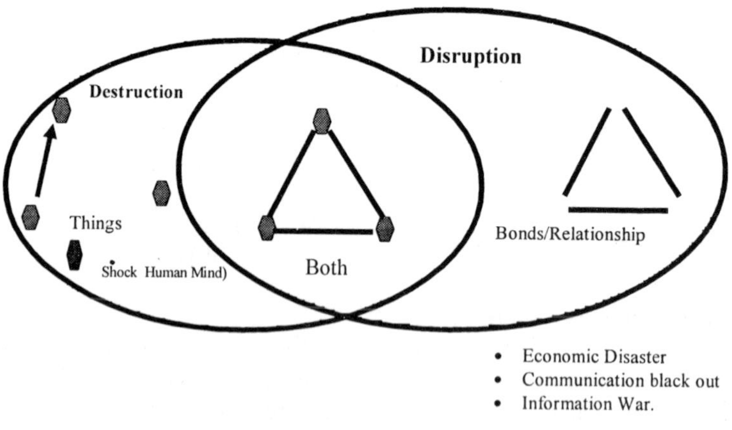

With regard to weapon target set of effects, two tangible objects can be influenced. The material damage and the shock effect on the mind (Fig.1.3). The first object is 'things' represented by people or, material. Things are the primary target of conventional weaponry and WMD (CBRN). The physical difference between them is simply based on individual, area, and mass effect, as discussed earlier. In sum, thing-influencing weapons are generally meant to kill and damage and are generally considered lethal when employed against human beings. The second object is the shock effect pulverizing the mind due to enormity of the damage, which crosses the threshold of human imagination, breaking the bond between perceptions of fear and destruction.

The third target set, which can be influenced by weapons, is composed of 'bonds-relationships'. Rather than targeting a thing, the relationships within a thing, between it and other things, or between a thing and its environment are the focus of attack.[53] These relationships can be degraded, severed or altered.[54] At a group level, land mines can stop a squad of soldiers attempting to move through a defile. It does not matter if the barrier is physical, using lasers, sticky-foam and heat-tabs, or non-physical, using optical or acoustic devices. The final outcome is still that the relationship of the squad (thing) to its avenue of approach (environment) has been degraded or possibly even severed. The crashing of a computer network, by means of Radio Frequency Weaponry (RFW), such as a Transient Electronic Device (TED) or High-Energy Radio Frequency (HERF) device, on the other hand, represents a systemic level incident. In this case, the synergy represented by the networked users has been disrupted even though the users themselves have not been injured.

The area of overlap between these target sets allows for both thing and bond-relationship targeting taking place simultaneously. This dual target set convergence represents a concern because of what might be termed a 'Domino-Effect' taking place due to its significant high-order Psycho-Traumatisation Terrorism Impact (PTTI) and information operations potentials in addition to systemic physical effects. Nuclear devices with their heat/blast, electromagnetic pulse generation, and terror effects can influence both these target set. Arguably, bio-terrorism or chem-bio cocktails based upon both lethal and non-lethal pathogens also falls within this category. Besides the effects of mass incapacitation and/or death generated by such weapons, their employment would also degrade and alter the bonds-relationships within a society, as would nuclear weapons. Examples of such degradation include the loss of confidence in governmental institutions.

A biopsy of the impact of WMD/WMDR terrorism and human mind would reveal the various levels and thresholds of a psychotraumatic effect culminating in a collective impact. This is based on the principle and theory of the area [πr^2] depicting a higher PTTI or lower, which itself depends on the type of weaponry used, as shown in the figure 4 below. In the case of WMDR/WMD, the circle theory gets applied manifold depending on the colossal devastation. Thus it has not been depicted by a circle and would have to be perceived as extremely PTTI. (Fig. 1.4)

From the preceding analysis, we can conclude that for a weapon to fit the criteria of that of a WMDR it is required to possess three organic characteristics. First, it must have easy SCDD for application; second it must have the inherent potential, via expansive or replicative properties, to have a threshold of effect of which allows it to influence a mass (systemic) level area of operational space. Third, it is required to influence the bonds and relationships within a thing, between a thing and another thing, or between a thing and its environment or disruption purposes. Despite this focus upon weapons which organically possess mass (systemic) effects potential, it must be constantly remembered that all weapons possess the ability to generate mass destruction, mass disruption, and mass destruction and disruption incidents if creatively employed by terrorists, against targets such as dams, nuclear or chemical plants and petroleum/natural gas pipelines and storage facilities[55]. Further, weapons can be combined in what has been termed a hybrid attack or hybrid threats which combine modes of attack as a force multiplier/disruption enhancer, as in the case of a conventional power plant bombing taking place in tandem with an information attack on electric transmission, distribution, and/or control systems. With the above caveats, however, the following forms of weaponry appear to meet the WMDR criteria. This is explained by Robert Bunker, an expert on the subject based in UK.

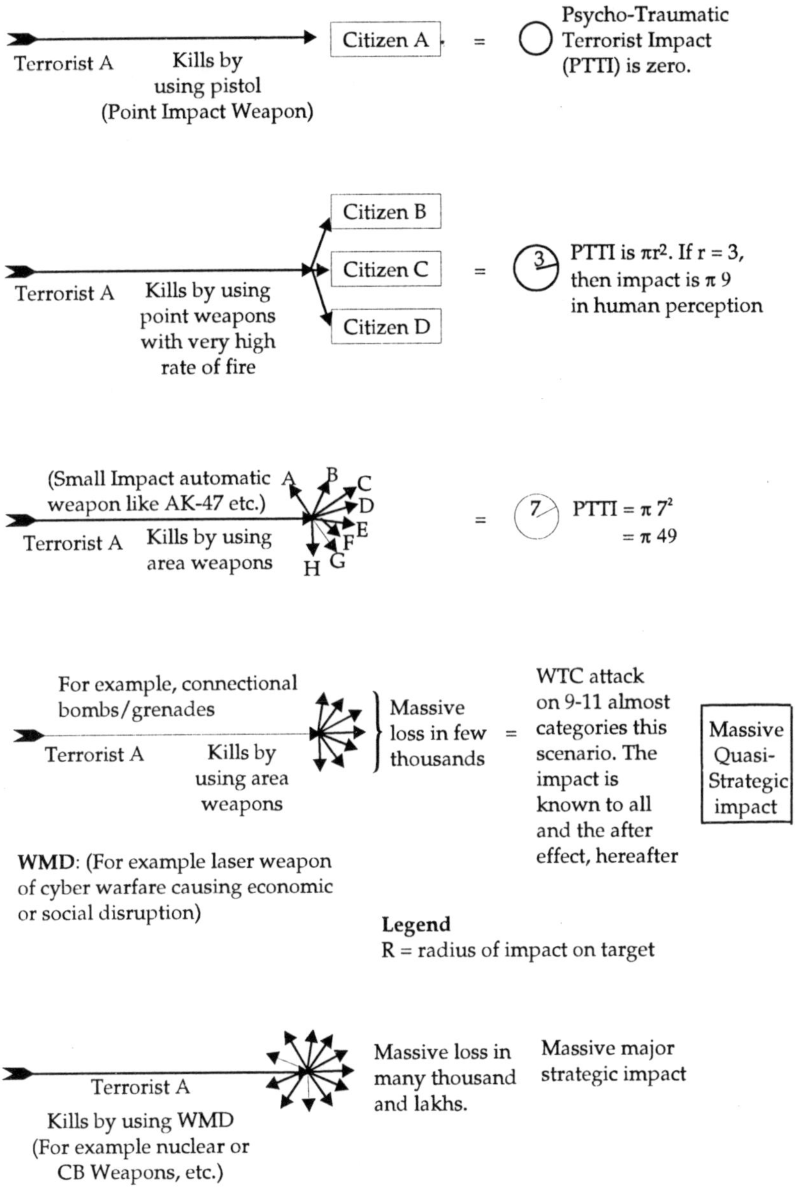

Fig. 1.4. Threshold of Psycho-Traumatic Effect.

Cyber Warfare, RFW, isotropic radiators, and computer viruses represent newer forms of weaponry while advanced non-lethal chemical agents, non-lethal biological viruses, liquid metal embitterment compounds, and genetic altering radiological devices overlap with the older CBR components of CBRN.[56] As a result, depending on the intent of use (lethal or non-lethal) and sophistication of the CBR weaponry involved, these devices have the potential to be considered as either Weapons of Mass Destruction or Weapons of Mass Disruption. Nuclear devices, because they exhibit heat/blast, electromagnetic pulse generation (EMP), and terror effect, should be cumulatively reconsidered as WMDR rather than simply WMD as should possibly some forms of bio-weapons, which also now blur our perceptions of WMD and WMDR. Cyber Warfare can distort information in computers and even make them dysfunctional in operations causing disruption in activity or WMDR. (Table 1.1)

Table 1.1

Expansive Properties	*Replicative Propertises*	*SCCD*
Radio Frequency Weaponry (RFW, HERF) Isortopic Radiators Non-Lethal Chemical Agents Direct energy weapons (DEW) Radiological Devices (Genetic Alteration) Liquid Metal Embrittlement (LME) Cyber warfare (CYW)	Computer Viruses, Non-Lethal Biological viruses, Atomic chain reaction, radio-active effect	CB cocktails, Suitcase nuclear bombs (Whenever available), Bioagents carried in living organism or powdered form like Anthrax etc. DEW platform can be easily carried in aircrafts and automobiles

To elaborate further the theory of mass effect has attempted to explore an emerging class of weaponry and its relationship to traditional perceptions of WMD in order to increase awareness and, in fact, better understand the emerging type of threat it will probably represent to law enforcement professionals, first responders, and military personnel engaged in counter-terrorism activities and consequence management in the years to come. While this mass effect weaponry is far less destructive than WMD as it may not multiply collaterals or proliferate like nuclear variation, its wide scale disruptive effects make it in some ways a more sophisticated and insidious option for terrorists. It provides them with the capability of disrupting our infrastructure in order to shut down large segments of our society without inflicting wide scale environmental and human destruction in the process. It is against such mass bond-relationship that our domestic efforts must also now focus upon in addition to the more traditional ones already recognised with regard to WMD, as potentially a terrorist weapon.

Therefore, one can redefine the classical sense of terrorism to a modern sense: 'Neo-Terrorism', is cellular in nature having heterogeneous components of religious fanatics (for example, the so called Jehadis) and indigenous insurgents or guerillas (but akin to the common denominator of religion) who are state sponsored with state-of-the-art weapons and communication systems - and who operate on a type of doctrine (like Netwar) to fulfill a greater strategy. If one analyses them, the common factor is religion but the aims of the same cell or group could be different ranging from, for example, 'Pan-Islamisation' having traces and attitude of a civilisational differential or nationalistic cause. These 'Neo-Terrorists' are causing a 'RTA' and could also use WMD or even WMDR for achieving their aims.

In this book, the focus would remain on these type of 'Neo-Terrorists' who do not aimlessly carry out action but are linked to a stratagem of a military nature to fulfill many aims-may be national or even religious. At least this is what the Indian experience is.

In the Indian environment, one can redefine terrorism to be based on cellular structures like the nucleus of an atom having electrons circuiting around. The composition of the nucleus is tactically heterogeneous with its elements of the Pan-Islamic Jehadies, the indigenous terrorist from Kashmir, foreign terrorists and the sub-control element like the intelligence component who may be belonging to the perpetrating state (Fig.1.6). The electron element or the so-called 'Over Ground Workers' (OGW) provide the live information and guidance for tactical operations to the nucleus or a terrorist group. These OGWs again may be of various types and operate at various levels. The group of three to four terrorists with composition of religious, money, organisational or guerrilla type moves in the inner periphery. The outer periphery or the electron path consists of over ground workers, mostly working for money. In totality, it appears to be a kind of a money channel sustaining the terrorist industry. In fact a deep analysis and interaction with many such captured groups reveals money as the prime mover. Further, the epicentre collectivity of the mass of such cells are orchestrated in synergy with military strategy causing cumulative strategic and tactical impact.

Therefore, the Indian experience is unique and may be a laboratory for nations wanting to pursue the strategy of asymmetric warfare or proxy warfare. This model should be countered by a uniform global counter-terrorism strategy without a second thought as this could accentuate to a dangerous world especially with the proliferation of WMDs and fissiparous tendencies, which are being articulated paving way to 'civilisational clashes'.

The mass of such cells (Z, X....Y) is created by organisational and communication interconnectivity due to which inherent flexibility and operational sustainability is created. If Z is destroyed, then Z1 and others remain to carry out the tasks. Meanwhile Z is recreated over a period of time. Therefore they operate like an amoeba and appear amorphous beyond destruction as shown in Fig. 1.5 below. These cells are further geographically and tactically disposed to remain relevant, district or area wise.

Fig. 1.5. Cellular Structures : Terrorism Groups.

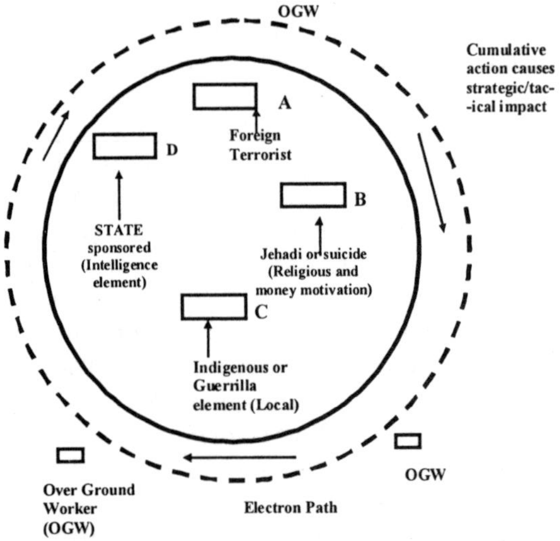

In the modern era, where revolution in terrorist technology and communication is occurring, one can therefore reword to specifics and reality as it exists today and re-define terrorism as "A systemic societal failure and a social observation in which a group of networked people, motivated by money, religion, political or an ideological divide, cause monitored, but random violence, on the other post of the society to achieve disproportionate leverage in fulfilling their apocalyptic aims".... This definition can be further expanded to encompass the emerging threats of WMD and WMDR also.

In the Indian sub-continent, statistics show prevalence of maximum and wide network of terrorist groups, as it is an ideal breading ground.[57] It will be 'unrealistic and un-strategic' to think that they are autonomous and caused only by poverty. The seeds of insurgency and revolutionary movements are obviously present, akin to any country in the Asian or African landmass, but what one has to identify is the ulterior motives of nations who may be regional contestants and who may want to curtail our national prowess. Therefore, their linkages, with the neighbouring region cannot be eye washed. The China-Pakistan strategic and complementary net and the emergence of the ISI in the 1980s-1990s as a control force cannot be overlooked (The CIA-ISI-China linkages during the Taliban-Soviet confrontation is an overt factor) as the mother/an

Fig. 1.6. Networked Groups of Terrorism.

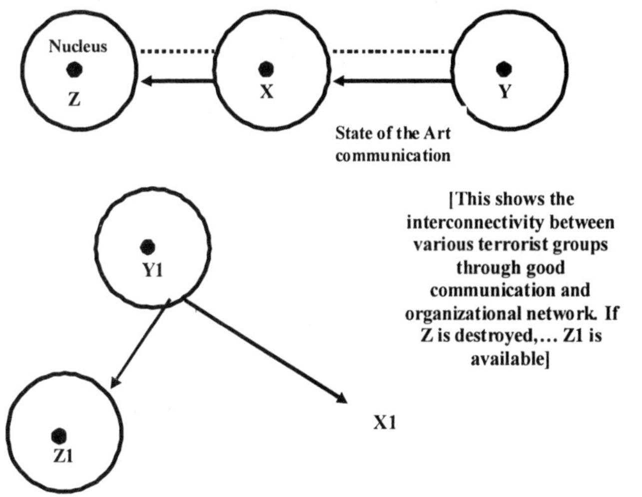

umbrella organization which was sustained and financed (including the narcotics-arms-terrorism-self financing vicious cycle) as a part of the global cold war momentum and having extended its branches to these potentially fermenting social aberrations in India. Their operations in fact had widened in a large arc to the nations in the neighboured of the Indian subcontinent, which were cultivated as bases for covert secessionist operations. In this, in logical conclusion, all such internally organized movements got harnessed and nurtured. (for example the NSCN or the ULFA connection is very well known. Even the Nepalese Maoist movements are beyond doubt being catalysed by these external forces). The technology of networking, which was till now conceived tactically or operationally functioning in a particular limited geographic region got expanded into a strategic networking in which an effort was made by some hidden hand to integrate all such insurgent and terrorist movements in South Asia, ranging from the LTTE near the Indian Ocean to the movements in Kashmir and Afghanistan. Obviously, such an intricate and wide networking would strengthen them many fold. Further, also due to the proliferation of WMD (More after the demise of FSU when many NBC related items were available for sale) this kind of dangerous technology could therefore be accessed. Therefore any strategy to counter terrorism would also have to be dealt with a 'Grand Strategy' approach under the aegis of United Nations for a global fight against terrorism.

During the cold war era of international politics, it has been seen that 'Big Powers' have used pure terrorism or abetment of guerrilla or insurgency movements in areas outside their sphere of influence to enable creating leverages and bargaining ground.[58] The other 'Big Power' obviously counters it and applies a 'counter-weight' of a similar nature, having secessionist and terrorist elements. But the September 2001 attacks on America has changed all these paradigms with the only 'Super Power' declaring all out war against terrorism in any form anywhere in the world. So, will it change India's case? The Naxalite movements, the North East insurgencies and in areas of South East Asia. Will they all go and wane in the coming decade.[59]

In summation, one can redefine and classify various shades and grades of terrorism in the following spectrum as per the ingredients and characteristics so contained. In the classical sense, the main ingredients of terrorism could be the 'causal' or 'motivational' factors, i.e., nationalism or a religious case, type of technology i.e. weapons and communication systems used, and the impact at target end, i.e., WMDR or WMD or conventional.

Fig. 1.7. Classification : Terrorism.

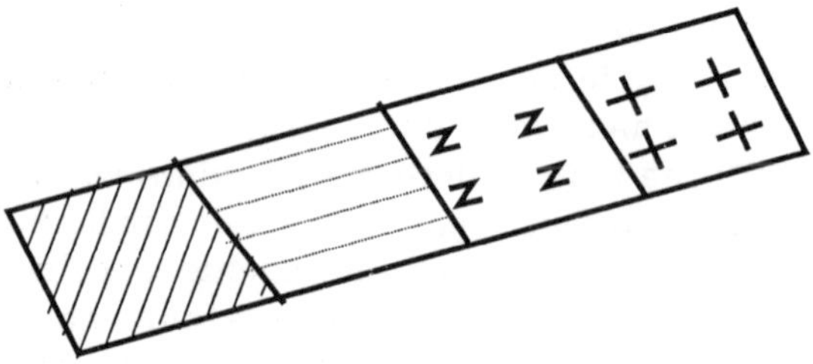

Type of Aid	*Cause/ Ideology*	*Type of Technology*	*Impact on Target end*	*Classification of Terrorism*
No aid	Individualistic	Conventional	Conventional kill ratio	Terrorism/ Classical Terrorism.
State Sponsored	Religion (Pan Islam /Secessionist)	Weapons of the ***'RMA'*** type	Neo-Violence (Higher kill ratio)	Neo-Terrorism
-do-	-do-	-do-	Hyper-violence (very high kill ratio including economic/cyber disruption)	WMDR Terrorism
?	-do-	NBC	Extremely High	WMD Terrorism

Therefore the type of terrorism, which was applied on ***'9-11'*** could be categorized as being **'Neo-Terrorism'** causing a WMDR PTTI. Similarly, the type, which India is experiencing again could be classified as ***'Neo-Terrorism'*** causing the **'Third Manoeuvre'**. What India has to be care full is to contain the present level, lest it becomes WMDR or WMD.

References

1. As enunciated by Shri Jaswant Singh, (former Foreign Minister of India) at the Annual "Cariappa Memorial Lecture-1998" New Delhi. Also a complete elaboration on these aspects has been done in his book *'Defending India'*.
2. Nicholas Polurin, *Population and Global Security* (UK: Oxford University Press, 1966), p. 10.
3. John Norris and Will Fowler, *Brassey's Modern Military Equipment (UK)*, p. 110.
4. Strike on Iraq in 1999 could fall in this category. North Korea, Iran, Iraq, and some other countries may be neutralised under the new counter-proliferation initiative (CPI) role of NATO.

5. Sujit Dutta, *From Realpolitik to Co-operation: The Evolving Transition in the Asian Security Scenario* at the Asian Security Seminar at the Institute of Defence Studies and Analysis, New Delhi, January, 2001, p. 3.
6. Nicholas Polurin. A poor country with a population growth of 2.5 per cent requires economic growth of 5 per cent to achieve 2.5 per cent capita economic growth.
7. Unfortunately, Taliban was created to checkmate enlargement of former Soviet Union (FSU) but instead it became the breeding ground of religion motivated terrorists who themselves have challenged American way of life.
8. "The United States security strategy for the East Asia-Pacific Region 1998" *Strategic Digest,* Vol. XXIX.,(January 1999P, p. 36.
9. India now being an important partner with America in the war against terrorism would change the flux of inter-state relations in the region.
10. In addition, the big power game between America and China is likely to shift to Kashmir from Afghanistan causing terrorism and instability.
11. "Sustaining US Engagement: US Strategic Vision for a New Century", *Strategic Digest.* Vol. XXIX, (January, 1999), p. 39.
12. Vishnu Prajapati,(ed). *South Asia Power and Politics,* p. 71.
13. Yossaf Bodansky, *'Bin Laden' The man who dared America,* Rose Villa CA: (Prima Publishing, 1999), p. xii.
14. Walter R. Lawrence, *Valley of Kashmir* (Kesar Publishers:, New Delhi,(1967), p. 302. Another interesting aspect is the interviews carried out by author with the Sarpanch (Head of the village) of Nariala village of Dalogra block, Rajauri District (J&K). The great great grandfather of the Sarpanch was called Mohd Baksh, great grandfather Ch Hoshmal, grandfather Ch Wafaruddin, father Ch Gulamuddin. They claim to have lineages to Krishna Dynasty of Kashmir, which ruled Kashmir till 1423 when they were dethroned by Muslim invaders.
15. In fact, the author has interacted with more than hundreds of Kashmiris, in private and in civil dress. They do not consider themselves different from Hinduism, which till today is reflected in most of their customs, especially during marriage.
16. Halford J. Mackinder said any one who occupied Europe ruled the world. This was more applicable to the 19th and 20th century.
17. General Akbar Khan, *Raiders in Kashmir,* (Delhi: Army Publishers, 1970, p. 10).
18. That time Capt BM Lal recounts the story very vividly. He has many written proofs of similar accounts.
19. Jasjit Singh, Pakistan occupied Kashmir under the Jack Boot, p. 8.
20. *Ibid.,* p. 286.
21. *Ibid.,* p. 286.
22. *Ibid.,* p. 180.
23. Copy note 1 in p. 183.
24. Jasjit Singh Pakistan occupied Kashmir under the Jack Boot, p. 9.
25. Siddhartha Varadharajan, *Times of India* (New Delhi), March 2002.
26. Peter C.Sederbergn, *Terrorist Myths, Illusion, Rhetoric and Reality,* UK, Prentice Hall Englewood Cliffs, p. 23.
27. *Mahabharata* by C. Rajgopalachari published by Bharatiya Vidya Bhawan p. 472.
28. Sreedhar,'Taliban's Afghanistan': Looking into Future', *Perceptions Journal of International Affairs,* Vol. V No. 4 December 2000, February 2001, p. 34.
29. Reflection, "September 11, 2001 and after", Strategic Analysis, December 2001, Vol. XXV, No. 9

30. Reflection : September 11, 2001 and after.
31. Guerilla Warfare is that form of warfare adopted by strategically weaker side to give it the capability of taking the tactical offensive at chosen place and chosen time.
32. The case of Chechnya, terrorist movements in Central Asian Region (CAR) and the Indian Subcontinent (Kashmir) fall within this concept.
33. Although Islam decries terrorism and Jehad has a much wider and positive definition, but unfortunately in the post 11 Sep. crisis scenario, Jehadi has been misunderstood as an Islamic Terrorist. To avoid ambiguity and cause distinction between a conventional terrorist and religious oriented the word being now coined is – "Jehadi Techno-Terrorist" (JTT) or a Neo-Techno-Terrorist (NTT) signifying the class as prevalent of the Osama Bin Laden (OBL) group or the ones operating in Kashmir.
34. As per the 'Concise Oxford Dictionary' terror means 'extreme fear' or 'affected with terror' and terrorist is defined as 'One who favours or uses terror-inspiring methods of governing or of coercing government or community'.
35. Obviously, to bring out strategies and counter-strategies against terrorist, the sub-continental setting and narrative would be used as a backdrop for better comprehension.
36. *Guerrillas a History and Analysis* Arthur Campbell, p. 65.
37. *Ibid.*, p. 66.
38. *Ibid.*, p. 66.
39. Again the case of Chechen rebels reminds us of the 'radiation weapons' used by them against the Russians.
40. WMD state sponsored terrorism would put the security template and chances conflict resolution in the lowest part of the ladder of success. Due to the catastrophic impact of such a situation a 'Neo-War' terrorization phase will occur, challenging not only regional security but also global security. A modern Terrorist who has harnessed, 'RMA' and would obviously escalate the situation into a new phenomenon of a 'New war' or 'Neo-War.
41. Term definition accessed from the Los Angeles County Emergency Operations Bureau (EOB) website.
42. Term definition accessed from the Defense Technical Information Center (DTIC) website at http:www.dtic.mil/doctrine/jel/doddict/data/w/06538.html.
43. Robert J Bunker, "Weapons of Mass Disruption and Terrorism" in Journal offprint *Terrorism and Political Violence*, (A Frank Cass Journal), p. 39. Further, many ideas have been taken from the authors presentation at the India International Centre during the Asian security seminar Jan 2001 New Delhi.
44. PPD-39 is a classified government document. An unclassified version of this document generated as a result of a Freedom of Information Act request by the Federation of American Scientists (FAS).
45. See Ehud Sprinzak, 'The Great Super Terrorism Scare', *Foreign Policy*, No. 112 (Fall 1998), pp. 110-124 and David C. Rapoport, "Terrorism and Weapons of the Apocalypse", *National Security Studies Quarterly,* 5/3 (Summer 1999), pp. 49-67. Rapoport cites the best empirical studies to date, W. Seth Carus, "Bioterrorism and Biocrimes", Working Manuscript (Washington, DC: National Defense University, December 1998) and a CNS Monterey Institute study, "Terrorism in the USA Involving Weapons of Mass Destruction (Monterey, CA, 1998).
46. For a discussion of this topic see Robert J. Bunker, "Terrorist Laser Employment Against Civil Aviation : Issues, Concerns, and Potential Incidents", *Transit Policing 8* (Spring 1998) pp.7-8, 21-28.

47. Executive Order 13010, signed 15 July 1996, addresses the disruptive impact of RFWs and cyber attack potentials against the nation's critical infrastructure. This document can be accessed at the White House website.
48. Barnard Baruch was a close associate of President Truman, William C. Green, 'Semantics of "Weapons of Mass Destruction", paper presented at the Western Political Science Association Conference, Seattle, Washington (25 March 1999), p. 5.
49. *Ibid.*, pp. 5-7.
50. The same problem exists for mass destruction incidents. Any weapon creatively employed has the potential to generate systemic level destruction. For example, a crude improvised explosive device (IED) attached to a chlorine tank will result in a mass HAZMAT incident. If the attack were timed so that the prevailing winds took the resulting cloud into a residential neighbourhood in the middle of the night or into a school yard during the day, mass casualties would be expected.
51. The diagrams (figures) have been re-conceptualised based on the work of Robert J. Bunker and presented during the Asian Security seminar New Delhi in January 2001. The author had many interactions with Bunker and has now given his perceptions.
52. For the replicative potentials of a computer virus see the recent example of the 'Melissa macro' or W97M-Melissa virus. Geoff Becker, 'Rare Warning of Computer Virus Issued', Associated Press (27 March 1999).
53. At a higher dimension of bond-relationship targeting, targeting the internal relations of information within an object would become a hyper attack.
54. With regard to the bond-relationship targeting concept, see Robert J. Bunker, 'Higher Dimensional War fighting: Bond-Relationship Targeting and Cyber shielding', Paper presented at The Future of War, The Ivan Bloch Commemorative Conference, St. Petersburg, Russia (24-27 February 1999).
55. With regard to these recognised vulnerabilities, see The Report of the President's Commission on Critical Infrastructure Protection.
56. Potentially lethal second order effects from RFW and computer virus employment are recognised. In those instances, as in the case of a passenger jetliner falling from the sky because of RFW use, that weapon could be said to possess WMD characteristics even though it is generally viewed as a Weapon of Mass Disruption. As such, a cyber attack against an aircraft could be termed a 'virtual' attack.
57. China is almost has the same level of societal growth and maybe poverty but does not have such terrorist movements. May be the basic reason being the factor of communism as a political factor.
58. The battles in Vietnam, Afghanistan and Sri Lanka (LTTE) and many such likes can be categorised towards it. In this context abetment in Kashmir has to be seen from a much wider angle.
59. America's warning to LTTE on this account appears to be an indicator of revised American policy. One has to, therefore, watch very carefully.

Two

Classical Military Strategy, Doctrine and Terrorism

(Thired Manoeuvre Linkages and Prospects of Weapons of Mass Destruction)

It will be unfair to the reader to deal with a terrorist strategy without understanding the nuances of classical strategy and doctrines of military warfare. Terrorism involves violence. Violence can be countered by military counter-violence. If this violence gets linked to insurgency and state policy or an ideology, it takes the shape of political overtones. If this violence further gets sponsored by a neighbouring state, it amounts to breaking the code of conduct of International norms as laid down vide United Nations General Assembly (UNGA) Resolution 380 (V), 1950 which declares "Fomenting of Internal Strife" as aggression. Again in 1974, the UNGA, vide resolution 3314 which was further amplified vide (Article III) that "the sending by or on behalf of a state of armed bands, groups, in regulars or mercenaries which carry out acts of armed forced against another state of such gravity or its substantial involvement therein" also amounts to aggression. In short, state sponsored terrorism in another state is illegal as per international norms.

The moment terrorism is state sponsored, there has to be an underlying linkage with military strategy. Let us first examine the classical definition of strategy and doctrine and thereafter identify the basic tenets of terrorist strategy and doctrine, ranging from conventionality to the extreme weapons of mass destruction (WMD) spectrum. Let us identify the interplay between each level when 'Terrorism' is employed as an 'Art of War' or as part of military strategy which satisfies and fulfils the emanating war philosophies of direct or frontal attacks and the manoeuvre attacks, in the form of terrorism. They can in fact be coined as the 'Third Manoeuvre' for ease of understanding.[1]

Strategy can be defined as the art of applying force so that it makes the most effective contribution towards achieving the ends set by political policy and 'The art of the dialectic of two opposing wills using force to resolve their dispute.[2] Yet another definition by

Von Clausewitz is thus: "The employment of the battle as the means towards the attainment of the object of the War"[3]. In other words, strategy forms the plan of war, fitting into the scheme of a grand strategy or national policy. Undoubtedly, there is always a partial overlap between policy and strategy. Let us now see the specifics and understanding of a classical sense of doctrine and what could be the contours of a *'Terrorist Doctrine'*.

Doctrine is the interface or the bridge between conceptualisation and an action plan. It interprets the grand strategy into higher directions embodied in 'strategic thought' into a working guideline. In other words, doctrine operationalises war. In fact, there are various interpretations of such doctrines. JFC Fuller defines doctrine as 'The focal idea of an army'. Nevertheless the above, that doctrine consists of a set of beliefs about the nature of war and the keys to success on the battlefield.[4]

Let us examine yet another opposite view of doctrine (as given by Fuller) as a dogma causing rigidity and ensuring failure. In his book, *The Reformation of War,* Fuller writes:

> "In itself the danger of a doctrine is that it is apt to ossify into a dogma, and 'if seized upon by mental emasculates who lack virility of judgment, and who are only too grateful to rest assured that their actions, however inept, find justification in a book, which, if they think at all, is, in their opinion, written in order to exonerate them from doing so. In the past many armies have been destroyed by internal discord, and some have been destroyed by the weapons of their antagonists, but the majority have perished through adhering to dogmas springing from their past successes, self destruction or suicide through inertia of mind."

Therefore, one can see transformation of doctrine with time and modernity, which is equally important. Here, the whole exercise, obviously, is to identity newer doctrines pertinent to existing scenarios of unconventional and proxy wars. To quote Fuller againg from his book *The Foundation of the Science of War*, on the need of doctrinal changes with circumstances:

> "which to be effective must be elastic enough to admit mutation in accordance with change in circumstance. In its ultimate relationship to the human understanding this central idea or doctrine is nothing else than common sense – that is, action adapted to circumstance".

The same analogy when applied to terrorist doctrine or counter-terrorist doctrine, some important essentials emerge. Firstly, if terrorism is applied in its purest form it does not stand even a partial moral test. It becomes more a situation of 'tit for tat', leaving very little space for any strategic leverage. It becomes an 'eye for an eye' argument and any advantage is squared off. However, if it is used and mixed with guerrilla or insurgent movement, in the country being attacked, it gets elevated to a politico-military strategic level. Therefore, here in this work, we will talk more of such a nature where a combination of this kind exists. The doctrine of terrorism-cum-guerrilla warfare tends to exploit the adversary's population base as a force multiplier to enable successful terrorist or guerrilla operations against the security forces, so as to make a psycho- traumatic impact in the environment. The idea is to paralyse administration and governance, forcing the aggrieved state to a compromise. The basic theme of such a terrorist doctrine would rest on mobility, decentralisation and initiative rather than being traditionally disciplined and controlled centrally.[5]

Looking back at the strategic level, employment of a guerrilla or an insurgent in terrorist mode over a wide front would entail a kind of 'indirect strategic manoeuvre' or the so called "third manoeuvre" with maximum leverage in making the attacked country's defence untenable. "Battles", stated Churchill, "are won by slaughter and manoeuvre. The greater the general, the more he contributes in manoeuvre, the less he demands in slaughter".

While bloodless war is not a real prospect we must not dismiss the comparison between the two elements of attrition and manoeuvre and it is the manoeuvrist approach which we seek to follow. Terrorism and abetment of terrorism in neighbouring states is a manoeuvre of a protracted nature. In this approach, the organiser of terrorism aims at disorganising the enemy's overall cohesion and will to fight. It calls for an attitude of mind in which doing the unexpected, using initiative and seeking originality is combined with a ruthless determination to succeed. For any terrorist act undertaken to achie political leverage, this aspect is of paramount importance.

Yet another principle, which cannot be overlooked in laying the treatise for a terrorist campaign is the aspect of the classical understanding of the tempo of operations and thereafter its application to the unconventional warfare template.

We have defined "Tempo, as the rhythm or rate of activity of operations, relative to the enemy". Tempo has three elements; speed of decision, speed of execution and the speed with which a force transits from one activity to another. Liddell Hart graphically illustrates this while talking about the German invasion of France in 1940[6], in which the Germans outclassed the French. Similarly, terrorist operations require a controlled tempo over the whole front, so as to outdo the defender in predictability and time and space.

Therefore, the dogma of terrorism when used in the pattern of guerrilla warfare and applied as a military strategy can be listed along following lines: (The modern terrorist warfare as unleashed in Kashmir by Pakistan can be traced back to the historical roots of guerrilla warfare):

(a) It must be dynamic and maintain momentum (otherwise it allows security forces to rest and recoup).
(b) It should maintain rhythm and tempo (otherwise it dampens impulse of the population).[7]
(c) Static or fixed defences have no role (otherwise they are overcome easily by a conventional attack).[8]
(d) It reverses warfare by seeking to avoid battle.
(e) Evades tactical battle, where success is not ensured.
(f) Hit and run tactics.
(g) Synchronisation of operations to produce strategic leverages.
(h) Effect is cumulative as the number of strikes (N) on security forces (SF) are square of impact (I) by a ratio of direct proportion, i.e., $N= I^2$ or $N^2 = I^4$ or $N^3 = I^9$. Therefore, the number of incidents have a cumulative effect in tipping the scales.
(j) Ambiguity and intangibility also act as force multipliers.
(k) Inverts on the main principle of orthodox war. 'Concentration' is taboo. Dispersion is the key word.
(l) Ratio of 'space to forces' is the key (as vividly explained in Lawrence's mathematical calculations about the Arab revolt, which the Turks had to hold a post every four square miles. A similar case exists India's counter to terrorist pattern of attacks in Kashmir). Therefore, terrorist operations should be orchestrated to force the security forces towards this grid intensive deployment. (A counter to this would be discussed in the last chapter).
   (i) Rugged terrain gives them hiding place and concealment.
   (ii) Geo-political imperatives influences population attitudes. More successful in a situation of nuclear stand off and asymmetry.
   (iii) Exploiting situation of 'asymmetry' thus starts from a lower capability.

At the highest national policy level one can see the interplay between various levels of policy, strategy and tactics. Looking back again at the apex level, where the national security objective, political will and morale would be identified from which should emanate a military strategy of indirect approach or using terrorism as a manoeuvre and thereafter the doctrine which builds the military capability and creates the necessary force structures (combination of guerrilla-cum-terrorist forces) the tactics, (of evaporation) weapons and light equipment fall in place as shown in Fig. 2.1.

Fig. 2.1.

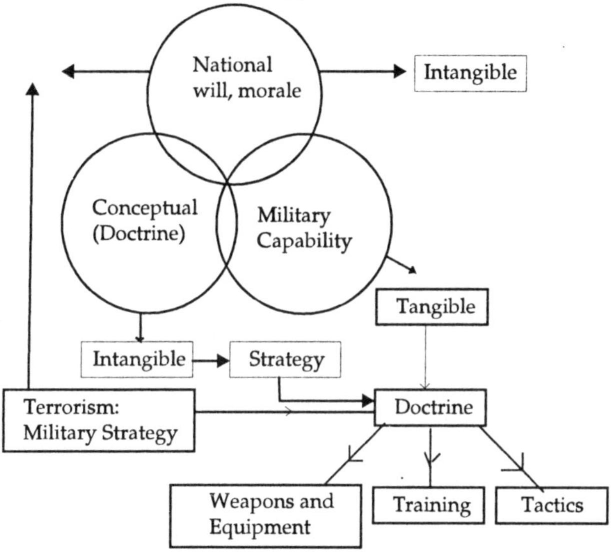

In any war against terrorism, real time input is the key. Invariably where it does not happen success is not achieved. A state wanting to use terrorism in another state should have the components of fighting power based on the factors enumerated in the figure above. As can be seen conceptually, the terrorist doctrine should exploit 'intangibility' of operations. However, any military activity traditionally becomes tangible. Therefore, terrorist strategy and doctrine should be dependent on not holding ground and giving a conventional battle. Terrorists should be intangible and should evaporate like ether. However, their weapons should be pulverizing but light and they should have sufficient training in minor tactics. The terrorist be trained and grounded to exploit the four pillars of successful fighters, namely, moral, physical, conceptual and organisational.

The Morale and Motivational Component

Field Marshal Earl Wavell gave a pertinent advice, albeit not for terrorist purposes, "The real way to get value out of the study of military history is to take a particular situation, and as far as possible get inside the skin of the man who made the decision, realize the conditions in which the decision was made, and then see what way you could have improved upon it." This is achieved by a high level of motivation like the Jehadi and the Madrasas concept or policies akin to it. The LTTE was able to create suicide squads. Similarly Islam grounded terrorist groups have created the Fidayeen.

The Physical Component –Equipment Issues

I will turn next to the physical component as it manifests in our equipment or the physical means to fight. It is not surprising that history is littered with lessons, both good and bad, relating to equipment, the transition from one equipment to another and the influence that results. The introduction of the stirrup, the transition from 'pike to shot' and from 'cavalry to tanks' are just some of the examples. The present day modern weapons are more terrorist friendly being lighter and having faster rate of fire. (Imagine a terrorist using ancient weapons. Kill effect or the terror effect will proportionately reduce). Therefore, one can say that the more lethal (Lethality = L) the weapon, the more the terminal terror (Σ) effect. One can draw an analogy: $L^2 = \Sigma^4$ or $L^4 = \Sigma^{16}$. [9] (In this connection also refer to circle theory in).

The path of history is replete with costly examples of the failure of equipment programmes. But there are also some lessons that illustrate the ability to take battlefield equipment and technologies and utilise them so that their effect is far greater than their individual contributions.

The Conceptual Component

If equipment can be a battle winner, it is the understanding of how best to use that equipment that will win campaigns.

The tank, the wireless and the dive-bomber each had an individual contribution to make to the changing nature of war fighting. However, it was the 'concept', the doctrine if you like, which put these three ingredients together in what we now call Blitzkrieg, to revolutionize warfare. This example from history will tell us a lesson all too easily forgotten. While individual equipments may achieve evolutionary improvement in battlefield capability, it is the intellectual approach, which will frequently bring together a variety of equipments to exploit their full potential. A modern terrorist who enjoys organisational strength like Netwar (explained later) and who has the correct concept of employment would achieve a much higher terminal or terrorist effect [It can be considered as summation of cumulative and total terrorist effect]. One of the concepts is to formulate a 'Netwar' concept, which has been articulated in various 'RAND' reports. The historical analysis and the aspect of transformation of warfare should be factored in making any doctrine. It is worth quoting the impact of 'Concept' by an example in history.[10] The concept should logically flow to creation of a tailor made organisation.

The Organisational Component

A doctrine has to be executed by an organisation. History is replete with examples of force structuring based on the concept and weapons of employment. The American air land doctrine dictates creation of smaller forces but with better strategic and tactical mobility. Any terrorist networked organisation will be operating in very small groups of sections and half sections, who may be deployed in a grid system conjoint with population basis. It is in this context that the doctrine of netwar has evolved.

Therefore, one can say doctrine is the product and mix of various factors and assets ranging from the higher directions, grand strategy, operationally and organisationally-networked forces intertwining the following:

(a) National security goals.
(b) Technology type and number of weapons.
(c) Organisational goals.
(d) Philosophy and ideology.
(e) Motivation and morale.
(f) Enemy or adversary's capabilities.
(g) Historical analysis and inputs.

Of all the factors mentioned above, most of them are self-explanatory. However, the last aspect needs some deliberation. The value of history in developing military doctrines of counter-terrorism is an important facet, normally overlooked in the Indian subcontinent. If one remembers the famous quote by General A A Svectin, "Military doctrine refers to the point of view from which military history is understood and is experienced and lessons learnt. Doctrine is the daughter of history . . . Doctrine is needed so that in the realm of military thought on army does not represent human dust, but a cohesive whole . . . should be predatory and stern, ruthless towards defeat and the defeated.'

Applying the historical analogy to the Indian sub-continental scenario, it can be said that India's military doctrine till now has shown traces of only a 'defensive' doctrine or 'a reactive stance' to the influx of the *Jehadi* terrorists. It is only recently that a wholesome doctrine with all the ingredients including the historical input is under formulation. (However, a tentative doctrine against terrorism/netwar has been discussed subsequently in the last chapter). On the other hand, the Pakistanis have exploited their historical success against the Soviet invasion of Afghanistan from 1979 onwards. They established a similar model against India, more so after the erstwhile Soviet withdrawal from Afghanistan in 1990. For example, to offset Pakistan's military asymmetry against India it tried to establish a military strategy and doctrine to unleash a terrorist oriented 'netwar' against India, so as to keep the Kashmir issue burning at the international level and to stem the Indian conventional superiority by keeping the operations below tolerance thresholds.

New Concepts and Thoughts: Unconventional Warfare

Unconventional warfare or so called unrestricted warfare is a technique by using terrorism as a tool which can be employed by a state at various levels having the following interpretations.

National/Strategic Level. This implies planning at the highest level so as to achieve national objectives. The military strategy serves these objectives. The military strategy takes on an indirect approach.

Fig. 2.2.

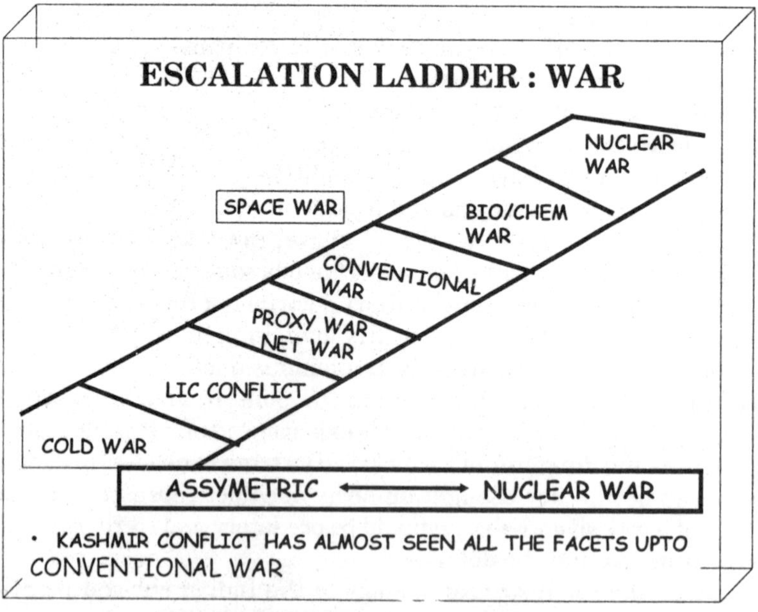

Operational Level. The strategy of indirect approach in its application form is executed by a field directive of using a combination of insurgents and terrorists, all operating at the tactical level through the means of terrorist tactics.

Tactical Level. At the tactical level it implies infiltration and move of small tactical groups who operate under the doctrine of 'netwar' as explained subsequently. They carry out attacks on soft or hard targets causing panic amongst the civil population, and lowering the morale of the security forces.

If one examines the escalation ladder of war, (Fig. 8), one can identify, such kind of terrorist or netwar at step 2 (LIC) or step 3 (Proxy war) of the ladder. As can be seen, war is fought below the threshold, short of a conventional war, which becomes the military strategy of the attacker. In other words it is also known as 'Asymmetric Warfare'. (The Kashmir conflict has almost seen all the facets conventional war with threats of a nuclear war). In case the terrorists (more state sponsored) come out with a wild card of threatening to use WMD, then the total scenario changes causing an extremely volatile instability. At this juncture it will be worthwhile to speculate a 'Terrorist Nuclear Strategy' and what could be its parameters. It would amount to working as deterrence, against any major counter-terrorist action. The terrorists would conceal their weaponry, but would require state support for using a means of delivery. They may also declare 'No first Use' and 'Partial Mutual Destruction' philosophy, in other words saying, you may not be able to destroy me pin-pointedly but I will at least partially destroy you. A nuclear strategy by terrorists has to be thought along the lines of 'Axis of Evil' as already articulated by Bush.

Pakistan in fact has asimilated a mililtary, and yet not so military, strategy by which sub conventional war in the form of 'terrorism' has been put forth as a tool of military operations. It must be noted that "Alliance and Network" would be yet another organisational principle linking terrorists networks or states supporting them. India's Op Parakram was a laboratory for strategic studies in which Pakistan's 'Protracted Proxy War' (PPW) against India underwent the following stages:

(a) The first stage was of Pakistan's Strategic offensive since 1990s and India's strategic defensive. (The initiative was in Pakistani hand).

(b) The second stage was of Pakistan's strategic defensive. Since the 11 September and 13 December 2001 attacks on the US and Indian Parliament and India's preparation for the counter-offensive created an Indo-Pak military stand off passing the initiative back in Indian hand.

(c) The third stage was one of India's strategic counter-offensive and Pakistan's strategic retreat (This then becomes an imbroglio due to the complementary Pak-China strategy and consequent abetment).

(d) Since then, the terminal terror (Σ) effecthas remained below the specified thresholds as seen in the various terrorist incidents.Incidents with mass kill effects were absent.

Historically, governments can be usurped by following methods:

Guerrilla War — In this, Mao Tse Tung is one of the leaders who could achieve success by this method. On the contrary, historically since 1945, forces that have been defeated were in Greece, Yugoslavia, Malaya, Kenya and Philippines.

State sponsored — In the prevailing international environment, especially in Asia, one of the main countries which has been sponsoring terrorism is Pakistan.

Revolution — One can recollect the great French Revolution and the revolutionary forces of Mao Tse Tung.[11] But in the contemporary world, this is a remote possibility, where full scale societal changes occur through a moral civil disobedience movement.

Demographic shift — Hannisation of the area like China has changed the demography of Tibet. One can relocate population and try to usurp the state. Take the case of Pakistan vis-a-vis Kashmir.

The strategy is in making the occupation of the country so expensive so that the governing power quits like Britain withdrew from Palestine and Cyprus. There is yet another method of governance by coercion and terrorism like the totalitarian systems where invariably the press is gagged. It has a tendency to externalise internal tensions and to use war as a raison d'etre of the continuation of the system. Also, totalitarian states have a tendency to regard themselves as 'menaced' by a combination of hostile powers, or at least pretend that they are encircled with problems, requiring totalitarian handling. One can recollect the May 1939 slogan of Einkrei Sung (on encirclement) which dominated the headlines of German propaganda. Similarly, in 1963, Indonesia declared itself threatened by the existence of federation of Malaysia. Stalin's attitude after the conclusion of the Nazi-Soviet Pact of August 1939 also testifies the totalitarian mentality. Terror is a basic tool and instrument in the hands of totalitarian rulers. Its largely deliberate and well-calculated use is one of the criteria, which distinguish most totalitarian systems from the earlier types of benevolent despotism and autocracy. According to Karl W. Deutsch, three important facets of totalitarian regimes are: extreme mobilisation of effort, unity of command and power of enforcement.[12] All the three facilitate use terror as a weapon.

Pakistan has harnessed the complete *Jehadi* machinery and interestingly also satisfies the interpretations of the Maoist 'People's War Concept'. Needless to say, innocent children are being brain washed in the Madarsas on a single track of Islamic education with no other subjects of pure science and arts. These young minds are nurtured to achieve military ends if need be. By this dispensation and operational art of using terrorism as an adjunct to military strategy, Pakistan has been able to pin down the large Indian Forces as well as bleed them economically offsetting India's high defence budget of 2.5 per cent of gross domestic product (GDP). This has had a further cascading effect , cutting down Indian teeth in regional affairs and may even be serving to China's advantage. However, the post 11 September 2001 events have turned this apple cart of asymmetric warfare in India's favour with the changed international opinion and America's declared policy of fighting terrorism till the end.

It is said that the best 'Art of War' is 'No War' and yet achieve tangible politico-military objectives. The recent India-Pakistan stand off has to be seen in this perspective. Yet another state, which has been following such a policy, has been 'Palestine'. Even the age old Indian epics have mentioned 'terrorism' as a tool of political and military strategy. However, one has to pin down the tolerance levels and identify the contours of terrorist structures of violence. Three such distinct contours are :

(a) The corps or the central structure, which integrates the various Tanzeems giving them motivation and directions.

(b) The operational or the theatre level. By giving ISI related support of intelligence, communication and launch bases, on own side short of the 'LOC'.

(c) The tactical or the sector level support across the 'LOC'.

Shades and Levels of Military Support

Fig. 2.3.

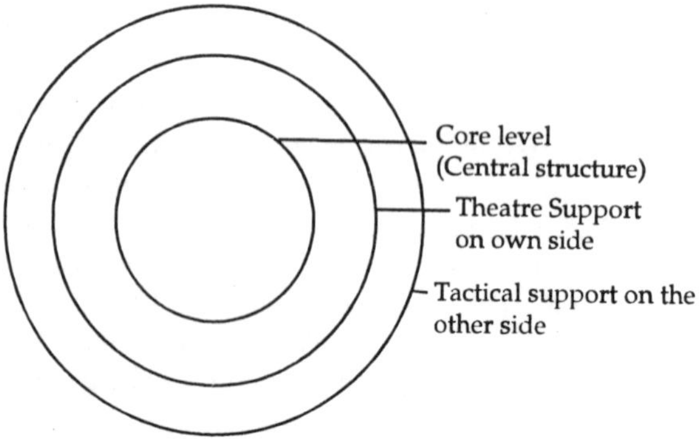

Now coming back to the roots of classical strategy, the aim is to carry out operations which are complementary to the conventional military deployed along the 'LOC', so as to deploy and absorb at least one third force of the opposing side, thus blunt the strategic conventional edge of the opposing side. As regards form of manoeuvre, it is replicating the model of an indirect attack by a classical 'Turning Movement' (like the famous Inchon landings in the Korean War in the 50s or Field Marshal Slims' turning movement by 4 Corps across the Irrawady in the Burma campaign). The daily infiltration by terrorists is equivalent of this kind of turning movement, or the so-called 'Third Manoeuvre' (First manoeuvre may be on the left flank, the second manoeuvre may be on the right flank and the third manoeuvre being in depth areas).

To elaborate further, frontal attack should be simultaneously done with an intermediate attack and if possible also in the open flank of depth in the hinterland. Elucidating a case study is warranted. Let us assume that a 'Terrorist Group' has infiltrated into another country. It will involve infiltrating through the gaps in the international border and would amount to employing tactical principles of infiltration. This group when it moves inside some distance (about 5-10 kms), it would require logistical support and other field support elements in the form of guides and intelligence. Subsequently, this column would have to be concentrated at a hide out or enclave, where they shift frequently and do planning of operations. These operations may range from hard targets to soft targets. The type of target chosen depends upon the orders given as part of higher directions, to drive fear and helplessness in the minds of the people, the military or the political leadership. As a cover up or as a smoke screen, employing some percentage of terrorists with the locals (recruited more by fear) shows indigenous nature and hardcore trained group. In fact a nation can intelligently provide military leadership to these small groups of terrorists. (Pakistani model of terrorist operations is akin to these parameters).

Yet another aspect of military strategy, which is being, employed, is the harnessing of Revolution in Military Affairs (RMA) which in turn is causing a 'Revolution in Terrorist Affairs' (RTA) as outlined below. Due to the influx of lighter and newer weapons with a high rate of fire (like AK-56) as well as availability of hi-tech equipment including radio sets and satellite telephones, which gives added flexibility to tactical operations, the terrorists are enabled to carry out more successful operations as well as cause more casualties. Here, at this stage one shudders to think of a contingency in which these ruthless perpetrators manage to take possession of weapons of mass destruction.

In the present scenario, since after America's offensive in the Afghan war, enough evidence towards possession of WMDs as before has been confirmed. What therefore is worrisome is the capability of terrorists to strike at will. The existing levels of WMD proliferation may accelerate such a proposition. America is thereby trying to put the logic of building a 'Ballistic Missile Defence (BMD) against such rouge elements'. It appears justifiable after the terrorsit attacks on America. Possession of WMD weapons by such non-state actors would obviously require the support of nation-states. This will see the emergence of a coherent military strategy as a deterrent to these small groups of terrorists.

One can define the broad contours of the terrorist nuclear doctrine along the following lines:

(a) **No First Use** or a **Blackmail Posture** as the terrorist groups would want to terrorise rather than use nuclear weapons first. In the subsequent chapters I have covered the emanating threats not only due to proliferation and smuggling from the regions of former Soviet Union, but also due to existence of a black market. The use of radiation weapons also remains a possibility. However, they will still be vulnerable to strikes by state forces, and destruction. But their strategy would be punitive strike in case the country being blackmailed takes initiative in neutralising the same, by conventional methods or makes any first move in this direction without abiding by the blackmailer's demand. (There is another school of thought saying that the terrorist will purely strike with WMDs rather than use WMD for purposes of blackmail).

(b) **Survivability** of weapons would of paramount importance. Thus, they would have to be hidden deep underground and located in wide dispersion. May be, state support alone can make survivability and disposition possible.

(c) **Deterrence** would be the main purpose of a terrorist's possession nuclear capability; implying that the opposite side should operate within threshold.

(d) **Command and Control** would obviously be delegated to the main head of terrorist group. However, a line of succession is also likely to be laid. The orders for execution are likely to be given by word of mouth or a designated code word by electronic communication.

Terror strikes at odd hours, frequently causing psycho-traumatic problems and capitulation of the population's will and welfare. It is ubiquitous and clandestine and hangs like the sword of Damocles. The actions are more prophylactic and preventive. This makes the population vulnerable and remains in a state of perplexity and ambivalence whether to help the terrorists or not. Normally, the fear of the terrorists outweighs the danger of state forces who operate with in democratic norms. (An illustration of this is Pakistan's creation of terrorism in Kashmir and the restrained and democratic handling by Indian security forces).

Having identified various governance tools, one can say that in the modern era, where all out war is not possible, terrorism is a likely philosophy to be used for political ends. Let us analyse this further by articulating the method of this 'invisible' warfare. Let us amplify and elaborate the concept of 'Netwar', which is the art of terrorist warfare.

Doctrine of Net War

In actuality, the phenomenon of *"Netwar"* denotes an emerging mode of conflict at societal levels, involving measures short of

---

Netwar

Conflict and crime at societal levels that involves:-

- *Measures short of war.*
- *Protagonists who rely on.*

Network forms of organisation, doctrine, strategy, communications and technology attuned to information age.

- *Protagonists likely to consist of dispersed small groups, but with state of the art communications.*

---

war, in which the protagonists use — indeed, depend on using network forms of organisation, doctrine, strategy, and communication. These protagonists generally consist of dispersed, often small groups who agree to communicate, coordinate, and act in an inter-netted manner, often without a precise central leadership or headquarters. Decision making in this context may be deliberately decentralised and dispersed. Thus, Netwar differs from traditional modes of conflict and crime in which the protagonists prefer to use hierarchical organisation, doctrines, and strategies, as in past efforts to foster large, centralised mass movements along Leninist lines.

Despite the modernity of the concept, history is replete with instances of Netwar. The irregular warfare in North America during the French and Indian Wars, and the American Revolution in the eighteenth century; the warfare waged by indigenous Spanish guerrillas against the Napoleonic occupation in the early nineteenth century, are some of the examples. In contrast to the currently emerging examples of Netwar, the early cases were forced, largely by the circumstances, into Netwar-like designs; these were not designs that were determined by explicit doctrine, or that could be sustained for long, or over great distances.

Thus, we can see that the phenomenon of Netwar is not entirely new. There are numerous examples from the past. In the present day scenario the Netwar is growing and spreading both quantitatively and qualitatively much different from what has been witnessed in the past. It is becoming both plentiful and powerful enough to compel a rethinking of the overall nature of potential threats, and of the roles and missions for responding to them. The Taliban in Afghanistan possessed a Netwar (capability).

Net War Design Elements

- *Web or Dispersed, Interconnected "Nodes"*
  - *— Nodes may be large or small in size.*
  - *— Tightly or loosely coupled to each other.*
  - *— Inclusive or Exclusive in Membership.*
  - *— Specialised in Segmentary.*
- *Flat structure: No central command, little hierarchy, much consultation, local initiative—A "Panarchy".*
- *Central Doctrine and Decentralised Tactics.*
- *Dense Communication of Functional Information.*
- *A distinctive design with unique strengths.*

The Revolution in Military Affairs (RMA) is providing modern armies with a qualitatively better Observation, Orientation, Decision and Action (OODA) capability. Obviously, the modern army with satellite surveillance and guidance is in a position to strike huge conventional armies. Imagine Rommel's Panzer divisions like in the

North African campaign, all concentrated and lined up for a blitzkrieg. The modern army would reduce them to ashes within hours. May be the answer for the weaker side is to reorganise on the patterns of smaller groups or in other words, evolve a Netwarfare doctrine, which neutralises modernity to a certain extent. Let us amplify the thought process further.

With the advent of better technology and the 'RMA', the Netwar concept is becoming a portentous threat by integrating global terrorist networks. The resurgence and impact of the same is still emerging; its organisational, doctrinal and other dimensions are yet to be fully defined and developed. The modern Netwar concept comprises of a web of dispersed, interconnected "nodes". The nodes may be individuals, groups, formal or informal organisations, or parts of groups or organisations. The nodes may be large or small in size, tightly or loosely coupled, and inclusive or exclusive in membership. They may be segmented or specialised. They may look quite alike and engage in similar activities. The boundaries of the Network may be sharply defined or blurred in relation to the outside environment.

The organisational structure is quite flat. There is no single central leader or commander. The network as a whole (but not necessarily each node) has little or no hierarchy. There may be multiple leaders. Decision-making and operations are decentralised. The design is both headless and hydra-headed.

Types of Networks. The networks come in basically three major types, as shown in Fig. 2.4.

Basic Types of Networks

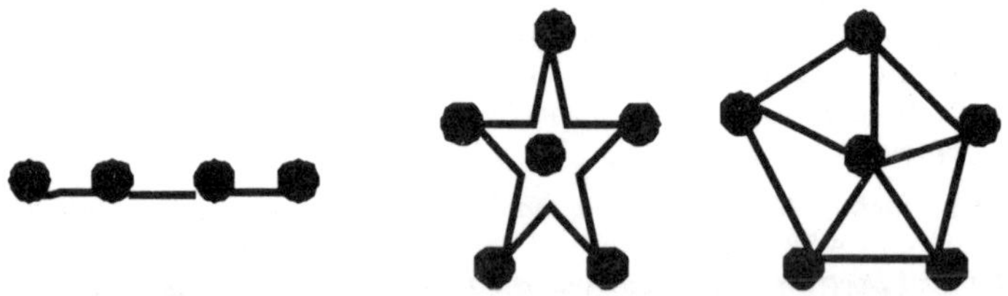

Chain Network **Star Network** **Multi Channel Network**

- **Each type suits different purposes and situations.**
- **Multi channel Network gives high potential.**
- **Mixture of all three may be more advisable.**

(*Source:* RAND Report).

Chain or Line Network. This is the one in which people, material or information moves in linearity and they move along a line of separated controls, and where terminal-to-terminal communication travels through the intermediate nodes or centres.

Star, Hub or Wheel Network. In this, a set of sub units/ groups are connected to a central but non-hierarchical unit/group/ organisation and must go through that unit/group/organisation to communicate and coordinate with each other.

All Channel Network. In this there is multi-channel connectivity with everyone connected to everyone. This is most difficult to organise and sustain. This form is gaining new strength from the information revolution and wide area satellite connectivity. If all stations have a 'Satcom' then each can be connected to the other.

The capacity and capability of this non-hierarchical design for effective performance over time may depend on a powerful doctrine or ideology, or at least a strong set of common interest and objectives, that spans all nodes, and to which the members subscribe. Such a structure can enable them to be "all of one mind like one entity" even if they are dispersed and dedicated to different tasks. The Netwar thus can provide a strategic and operational centrality that allows for tactical decentralisation. It can set boundaries and provide guidelines for decisions and actions so that they do not have to resort to a hierarchy—"they know what they have to do."

Strengths of Netwar Design

- *Offensive potential adaptable, flexible, versatile vis a vis opportunities.*
- *Functional Differentiation with Interoperability.*
    - *Interoperability.*
    - *Impressive Mobilisation and Penetration.*
    - *Capabilities.*
    - *Capacities for Stealth and for Swarming.*
- *Defensive potential: redundant, robust resilient in the face of adversity.*
    - *Difficult to crack and defeat as a whole.*
    - *Great deniability.*
- *Offense and defence often get blurred and blended.*

The Netwar design has unique strengths for both offensive and defensive operations. In case of an offense, Netwar has better OODA and thus is more adaptable, flexible, and versatile vis-à-vis opponents. This may be particularly the case where there is functional differentiation and specialisation among the network's nodes. These nodes-level characteristics, rather than implying a need for rigid command and control of group actions, combine with interoperability to allow for unusual operational flexibility, as well as a rapidity of manoeuvre and an economy of force. Further, during the course of a Netwar offensive, networked forces will be able to manoeuvre well within the decision making cycle of more hierarchical opponents. This suggests that other networked formations can reinforce the original assault or they can launch wide based swarm attacks upon other targets. This will present the defender with a dilemma as to how best to deploy their own reserves and available forces. The defender will not be able to identify the centre of gravity of the attacking force.

In terms of their defensive potential, networks tend to be redundant and diverse, making them robust and quite resilient in the face of adversity. Because of their capacity for interoperability, and their absence of central command and control structures, such network designs can be difficult to crack and defeat as a whole. In particular, they defy counter-leadership targeting (i.e. *"decapitation"*) as well as provide enough dispersion to dissipate the enemy's conventional strength.

The blending of offensive and defensive operations will entail mixing the strategic and tactical levels of operations. An apt example of this is the Netwar-like guerrilla campaign in Spain during the Napoleonic wars. In this campaign much of the time, the guerrillas and the small British expeditionary force pursued a strategic offensive aimed at throwing the French out. However, more often than not, pitched battles were fought on the defensive, tactically. Similarly, where the guerrillas were on the defensive strategically, they generally took the tactical offensive. The war of the Mujahideen in Afghanistan provides an excellent contemporary example.

The latest satellite communications tele systems, including satellite communications, advanced telephone, fax, electronic mail (e-mail), and computerised billboard and conferencing systems—all contribute to Netwar, and their roles in recent conflicts are often remarked about. Such technologies enhance the capabilities of networked members not only to coordinate with each other, but also to collect intelligence related to the external environment and also of the adversaries. The availability of the state of the art communication means and inter/intra connectivity also popularly referred to as global connectivity enable broadcast or otherwise transmission of messages to target audiences. Intelligent and well thought out plans to master the plethora of communication means and space connectivity will enable countering of the netwar in our context.

The concept of "Network-Centric Warfare" rests on an

important doctrinal notion; victory in future battles will depend more on who has best "Networks" than on who has the strongest "platforms". But so far writings about this concept have focused mainly on technological level, i.e., on the information and communication "grids" that could enable the concept. The applicability of this concept at strategic level will be primarily to keep the opponent unbalanced. The capture of objectives and their subsequent consolidation will perforce have to be through conventional battles. The relevance, efficacy and validity of this newly emerging concept of war have been amply demonstrated in the recent conflict in Afghanistan. Had the Taliban dispersed in the mountains rather than giving consolidated battle at Kabul or Kandahar, the situation would have been different. The actual application of a netwar concept would have then taken place, in which the Taliban alliance would have struck at will in the form of terrorist attacks.

Netwar can be countered by improving ground troops satellite connectivity. The emphasis should be to shift ground-based intelligence to space-based system towards the mission specific satellite. Nevertheless, the above, again it is space alone, the domination of which can again counter a Netwar concept due to the real time information management followed by precision response which can even destroy smaller groups hiding alone even in caves. Therefore, in totality, there is a need to understand the metamorphosis, which is taking place in warfare, mainly due to space being militarised, which in fact is also affecting the traditional principles of war.

Pakistan's proxy war in Kashmir is basically a 'Netwar' where terrorists of various nations have been integrated into a web. These groups operate with the modus operandi as already explained. Therefore Pakistan's strategy has been to unleash proxy war on India through multi-national trained terrorists, who have been mixed with local Muslim population (more by coercion) so as to cause the classical 'turning movement' as a 'Third Manoeuvre' and achieve, yet another politico-strategic goal of a wedge and leveraging Kashmir out of Indian hands.

Another factor, which needs debating, is the concept of 'Balance of Terror' more relevant in the Palestine versus Israel situation. Palestinians call 'Mustafa' as a suicide squad. The main motivation behind this being what the Koran says, as per perceptions of *'Mustafa'* squads: "Israelis have occupied your land and they have to be evicted" (Islamic Jehadi).

The ongoing conflict therefore appears to be endless where each side is maintaining a stance of 'Balancing Terrorism' so that it remains below threshold of war, but at the same time continues to draw international attention and Arab support. The Israelis in retaliation have been conducting military strikes purportedly to kill these terrorists. Therefore a helpless and vicious circle of violence continues in West Asia. What one has to worry is that this *'Tit for Tat'* or the *'Balance of Terror'* syndrome should not escalate to WMD terrorism, as discussed in the next chapter.

References

1. The first manoeuvre could be classical military manoeuvre by the army, the second type of manoeuvre could be through air.
2. General d' Armee Andre Beaufre, *Strategy of Action;* (Armand Colin, France, 1966), p. 19. English Translation by Faber and Faber, London, 1967.
3. General Von Clauswitz, *On War* (Translated by Colonel J.J. Graham, London, 1944-49) p. 165.
4. Jack Snyder, *The Ideology of the Offensive: Military Decision Making and the Disasters of 1914,* Ithaca & London: Cornwell University Press, 1984, p. 27.
5. As if to illustrate this very point, referring to the situation in 1940, Robert Allan Doughty says: "French and German doctrine thus differed sharply on several key points. While one emphasized methodical battle, firepower, centralization and obedience, the other emphasized continuous battles, mobility, decentralization and initiative. Thus during the fighting around Sedan, the doctrine of the Germans provided them with a distinct advantage over the French".
6. The pace of panzer warfare paralysed the French staff. The orders they issued might have been effective but for being, repeatedly, twenty-four hours late for the situation they were intended to meet and execute.
7. The tempo of operations by the US led coalition on the 2001 Afghan War was so accelerated that the Talibans couldn't regroup.
8. The rout of the Taliban occurred in Afghanistan (2001) as they tried to hold fixed defences, which is an anti-guerilla warfare stratagem.
9. This has been deduced after detailed survey and analysis, as the author has taken part in various counter terrorist operations. If a 3.3 bolt-action rifle is used then the terminal effect will be much lesser than the effect of using a AK-56 weapon.
10. Some recent works by David Rowland, a historical analyst on *Breakthrough and Manoeuvre.* As a concept this excellent work (DOAC R9412) identifies the three major factors: Surprise, Air Superiority and Aggressive manned Reconnaissance as key to the breakout. In 158 campaigns examined, when all of these were absent no breakthroughs were achieved and the chance of campaign success was negligible. Where all three were present there was a 98% probability of breakthrough and 89 per cent probability of campaign success. The study also highlights shock, attack intelligence, mobility and attack logistic superiority as important elements. The doctrinal influence of such work is important and we can ignore such well-researched and pertinent work only at our peril. Similarly, the concept of 'Blitzkrieg', although advocated by Liddell Hart but was applied by the Germans with great success in Second World War.

11. Analogy drawn from the works 'Strategic Problems of China's Revolutionary, Mao Tse-Tung's War' (1936), selected works of Mao Tse- Tung, Lawrence and Wishart, London, 4 Vols., 1954, Vol. 1, pp. 193-196.
12. Karl, W. Deutsch, 'Cracks in the Monolith' in Carl J. Friedrich (ed.), Totalitarianism, *(Harvard University Press, Cambridge, Massachusetts, 1954)*, p. 309.

Three

Terrorism and Weapons of Mass Destruction: Threat Perceptions (And Beyond)

"The future may see a time when such a (nuclear) weapon may be constructed in secret and used suddenly and effectively with devastating power by a useful nation or group against an unsuspecting nation or group of much greater size of material power."

Henry Stimson to Harry Truman
25 April 1945

"Terrorism is no longer something that is read about happening in foreign lands. It is our real threat and our vulnerabilities are real here, particularly against chemical and biological weapons."[1]

Senator Carl Levin (D. Michigan)

"With advanced technology and smaller world of porous borders, the ability to unleash mass sickness, death and destruction, today has reached a far greater order of magnitude. A lone madman or a nest of fanatics with a bottle of chemicals, a batch of plague-inducing bacteria, or a crude nuclear bomb can threaten or kill tens of thousands of people in a single act of malevolence. These are not far-off or far-fetched scenarios. They are real—here and now.

Secretary of Defence, USA, William S. Cohen[2]

The concept and nature of classical terrorism is being re-shaped in the modern era. An analysis on the historical perspective and the emerging trends indicate the fructification of the changing nature of such a threat. The answer therefore lies in a critical appreciation of the threats and thereafter establishing response mechanism at national and global levels.

Terrorism

- Concepts and Nature Being Re-shaped in the Modern Era.
- There is ongoing 'Revolution in Terrorist Affairs' (RTA).
- The Ongoing Evolution of Operational Philosophy of Terrorist Groups, may result into a WMD Related Threat in a future scenario.
- Turn of the century distinctly seen resurgence of Religious (Islamic) Oriented Terrorist Groups.

In fact, there is an ongoing *"Revolution in Terrorist Affairs" (RTA)* due to the impact of modern technology, globalisation and the proliferation of Weapons of Mass Destruction (WMD). However, the classical definition of terrorism and its causal factors continue to have the same historical roots as hither-to-fore. As we transcend the new millennium, we can marginally see the transformation in the changing nature and shades of terrorism. The ongoing evolution of operational philosophy of terrorist groups, now appears to be even encompassing the upper limit of the spectrum of violence ranging from the lower level of sub-nationalism, ideological fundamentalism and to the extreme end of transnational state sponsored terrorism precipitating, may be, into a WMD related threat in a future scenario. In this book, the focus would remain more on the South-West and South-Asian scenario, the dynamics of which presently, comparatively pose more threat to this zone than ever before. In the post-'9-11' scenario, many Anthrax attacks in USA and confiscation of a vast amount of literature on the subject of designing NBC weapons by Taliban and other groups have only testified earlier speculations.

Carrying out a holistic appraisal from historical times and thereafter joining the strands with the modern trends of technology and globalisation can only support this deduction. An analysis of the WTC strike and its impact on USA, may classify the '9-11' strike within the category of a WMDR (Discussed in Part II), as it has beyond doubt disrupted the American economy and its systems.

WTC ATTACK: CHRONOLOGY OF EVENTS

8:50 AM :	American Airlines flight 11, a **Boeing –767** with 81 passengers takes off at Boston to LA, crashes into northernmost twin tower of WTC.
9 AM :	A Second American Airlines flight 175, again a **Boeing – 767** with 56 passengers taking off from Boston crashes into southernmost of the twin towers.
9 : 25 AM:	In New York Stock Exchange tradings supended. Evacuation of people begins.
9:50 AM :	The Federal Aviation Administration grounds all the flights as a precautionary measure.
10:09 AM:	Southernmost tower collapses.
10:26 AM :	International flights re-routed.
10:30 AM:	Northernmost tower collapses.
10:30 AM :	Emergency declared in New York.
10:35 AM:	Washington and New York airports closed.

IMPACT OF TERRORISM ON THE USA

- Aviation, tourism and other related i3ndustries affected.
- US Congress passed 5 billion dollars as compensation to airlines.
- Six top US airlines announce 85,000 jobs lay off.
- Unemployment rises to all time high of 6%.
- Afghanistan campaign further drains US economy.
- IMF cuts its forecast for world growth from 3.1% to 2.6%.

  (All these contribute to 'Disruption' and thus one can call this '9-11' attack as a WMDR attack)

Further, if one traces the sequence of terrorist attacks on US citizens since 1979, the '9-11' attacks appear to have raised the higher spectrum of violence and this strike therefore can be classified as WMDR. What one has to speculate is the emerging threat of a WMD attack from the sequence in the graph given below:

TERRORIST ATTACK ON US CITIZENS SINCE 1979-2000

09 Nov. 1979	US embassy in Tehran stormed. 52 US citizens taken hostage and kept for 449 days.
16 May 1981	Explosion in New York airport. One killed. Explosion claimed by Puerto Rican Resistance Army.
18 April 1983	Suicide car bomber blows up US embassy in Beirut killing 17 Americans.
23 Oct. 1983	Shiite suicide bomber blows up US marine barracks in Beirut killing 241 marines.
14 June 1985	A Gunmen seize an aircraft. Compels the pilot to land at Beirut. They demand release of Arab terrorists.
05 Sep. 1986	Hijackers seize a Jumbo jet at Karachi. 22 people killed when commandos storm the plane.
21 Dec. 1988	Pan Am Boeing 747 explodes over Lockerbie, Scotland, killing 270 people.
26 Feb. 1993	Bomb explodes below the car parking area of WTC at New York killing six people.
19 April 1995	Former US soldier Timothy Mcveigh carries out a bomb attack on Federal Building in Oklahoma killing 168 people.
25 June 1996	Truck laden with bomb explodes outside mall frequented by US soldiers in Riyadh killing 19 of them.
07 Aug. 1998	Car bombs rip through US embassies in Nairobi and Dar-e-Salam killing 224 people; Osama-bin-Laden is the main suspect.
12 Oct. 2000	USS Cole bombed by a suicide boat. 17 US soldiers killed; main suspect Osama-bin-Laden.
11 Sep. 2001	WTC and Pentagon rammed by aircraft killing thousands.

The terrorism onslaught has wrecked the US. The country has lost more than 100 billion dollars, 100,000 jobs lost, hurtling the economy to recession. It is estimated that New York alone needs approximately 90 billion dollars for rebuilding.

Fig. 3.1.

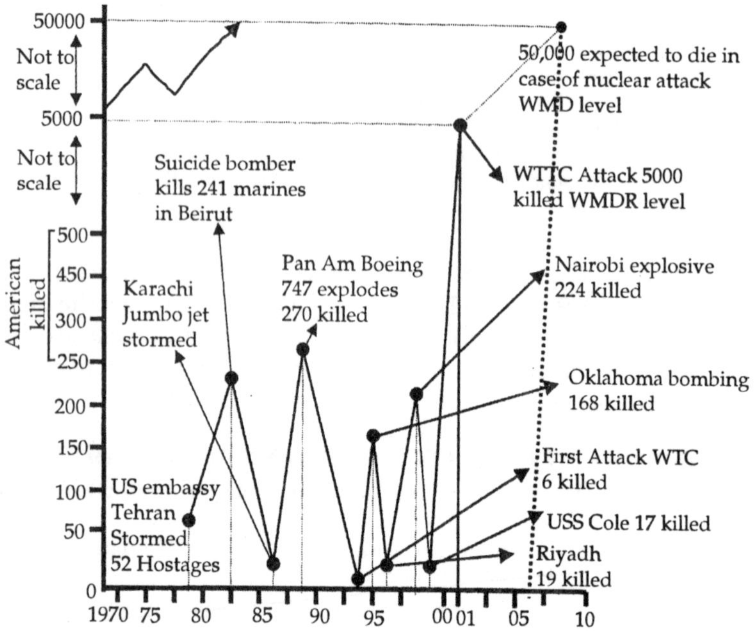

As can be seen graphically that the quantum of casualties, which occurred on American citizens by such terrorist attacks in the period from 1980s to 1990s has been having a pattern in which killings have been in hundreds (below five hundreds or so). However, the '9-11' terrorist attack has shown a complete escalation in the casualty rate to almost 5000. This classically therefore falls in the category of a WMDR attack, (As there was complete disruption in social and economic life), where there has been a quantum jump in casualties. What one dreads in the future is the anticipated WMD attack as shown in dotted lines, which may result in mass destruction and casualty up to about 50,000 or so. (Fig. 3.1)

DIALECTICS OF WMD TERRORISM

Global View: Changing Nature of Terrorism

At the global level, the classical definition of terrorism and the causal factors bear the same roots as over the centuries. However, what is perceptually changing is the nature of terrorism and its tools due to multifarious factors. The new millennium is ushering many scientific revolutions. Simultaneously, the demise of the former Soviet Union (FSU) has brought in reconfigurations in international alignment, coupled with the proliferation of WMD technology. For example, there are no more (few?) communist sponsors for Leftist movements.[3] There is yet another phenomenon of the revival of societal and religious fundamentalism tending to culminate towards the theory of civilisation related clashes.[4] This in turn is causing neo-religious fanaticism, which is transcending state boundaries and polarising nations based on religious cultures. (The same philosophy can be traced to the times of Ismailis-Nizari, who operated from 1090 to 1275 with the view of Islamist extremists, and spread purified version of Islam)[5] There is yet another linkage to this phenomenon, i.e. the challenge to nations for maintaining their strategic autonomy. This is causing an organisational backlash by a religious community[6], casing accentuation of ad-hoc radical fundamentalism like the attack by the Islamic group on the World Trade Center. However, this phenomenon does not hold theoretically when applied in areas other than West Asia and Asia. The new millennium, which has been blessed by a *'Revolution in Military Affairs' (RMA)*, is also augmenting the potential of the new *'High Tech'* terrorists. To properly understand the decisional calculus of terrorist groups, we must identify certain core issues and attributes. Is there a particular attribute common to all terrorists groups, or are there significant variations from one group to another? If it can be determined that many or all terrorist groups actually share a basic hierarchy of wants, a general strategy of *'Counter-WMD-Terrorist Operations' (CWMDTO)* can begin to be shaped. Alternatively, if significant variation in preference orderings can be detected between terrorist groups, myriad strategies of an individually tailored nature will have to be identified. A panorama of global terrorism hotpots and their analysis will show the pattern giving the existing gradation of terrorist infested continents.[7] Globalisation is making WMD terrorism as a looming threat in today's society,[8] necessitating mock response practice. (Even cyber-terrorism is being categorised as a potential next millennium threat...?) A fugitive Osama Bin-Laden is still a lurking threat not only to USA but all countries, which supported USA in their war against terrorism.

The American policy of dealing with terrorism or states sponsoring terrorism like Libya, Syria, Iraq, Iran, etc is much akin to the policies of Hindu rulers quoted in all our mythologies, especially that of Lord Krishna who was known for being wily. The old Indian policy of dealing with an errant king was based on *Sam, Dhan, Bhed, Dand,* which if translated would stand for polite coercion, lure with goodies, breaking with treachery and ultimately the *Dand* or punitive measures. Americans tried everything with Taliban and when all failed, they resorted to punitive measures. Their involvement in the ongoing terrorist attacks in the Asian region is already well known.

In fact, the Americans had already formulated a strategic assessment for international affairs in September 1997, which had already outlined the emerging threats.

STRATEGIC ASSUMPTIONS OF THE DEPARTMENT OF STATE (1997-2002)

International Terrorism

- U.S. officials, facilities, and citizens will remain high-priority targets of terrorists.
- International co-operation to combat terrorism will continue to increase.
- State support for terrorism will continue to decline, but the number of unaffiliated, ad hoc, and new terrorists will increase. Religiously motivated and sectarian terrorism will grow.
- The number of international terrorist incidents will continue to decline, but terrorists will seek to increase casualties and damage by using more lethal explosives.
- The danger that terrorists will employ chemical, biological, or nuclear material will grow.
- Terrorists will attack less-protected targets, including vulnerable communications systems and infrastructures.

Weapons of Mass Destruction and Destabilising Conventional Arms

- When the United States cannot fully deny to hostile states, the technology for weapons of mass destruction, it can retard the rate at which advanced technologies appear in their arsenals or deter their use.
- Uncertainty about the stability of Russia's military will persist, but Russia will continue to fulfill arms control and non-proliferation commitments.
- Arms control treaties have become increasingly complex and their requirements more intrusive. Negotiations and implementation require high expertise and long-term commitments to implementation and compliance.

International Crime

- Trans-national crime is undergoing a significant evolution, particularly with the appearance on the world scene of criminal organisations from Russia, Asia, and elsewhere.
- Increasingly, foreign criminals will seek opportunities in the United States and American criminals will seek opportunities abroad.
- Improving the criminal justice systems of foreign governments will contribute to their ability to control their own crime problems and to work with the U.S. on international crime issues.

Drug Trafficking

- In order to reduce the entry of illegal drugs into the United States, it is necessary to reduce foreign production.
- The supply of illegal narcotics from abroad responds to demand from the United States.

- Although foreign governments have an interest in counter narcotics co-operation with the United States, limited institutional capacity, along with social, political and economic factors – including corruption – will remain major constraints.
- The Western hemisphere will remain the major foreign source of illegal drugs with the Mexican-U.S. border and Puerto Rico as major entry points.

Source: United States Strategic Plan for International Affairs, U.S. Department of State, September 1997.

DIALECTICS OF WMD TERRORISM : CHANGING NATURE

- Nature of terrorism and its tools due to various multifarious factors.
- Scientific revolution, demise of the former Soviet Union.
- Proliferation of weapons of mass destruction (WMD) technology.
- Revival of societal and religious fundamentalism tending to culminate towards the theory of civilisation related clashes causing Neo-religious fanatism transcending state boundaries and polarising nations based on religious cultures.
- Challenge to nations for maintaining strategic autonomy.
- 'Revolution in Military Affairs' is also augmenting the potential of the new 'High Tech' terrorists may be...towards WMD capability.

The topic of terrorist acquisition and use of mass destruction weapons appears a remote possibility to those who are not aware of the unfolding realities of the future threat. However, those who study warfare and terrorist behaviour, weapons proliferation, and national and international security matters, there is concern of a great magnitude.[9] In 1989, a scholar on terrorism, Robert H. Kupperman, gave a foreboding assessment when he wrote, "Speculation about whether terrorist groups would ever dare to use extreme weaponry such as nuclear explosives or biological, chemical or radiological agents that can inflict mass destruction is often dismissed as sensationalist. It is argued that the lack of availability of nuclear materials and the universal horror surrounding the use of chemical or biological weapons would deter their use. The unfortunate reality is that the materials for such weapons have proliferated widely, that the expertise required is actually within their grasp, and that horror is the name of the terrorism game".[10]

The nature of terrorism is in fact fast changing due to the following factors :

- Ideology and religious revivalism.
- Desire for more impact on targeted population.
- Technology availability including WMD/WMDR.
- Globalisation.
- States applying terrorism as a tool of military strategy and causing asymmetric warfare.

Fig. 3.2: WMD Attack

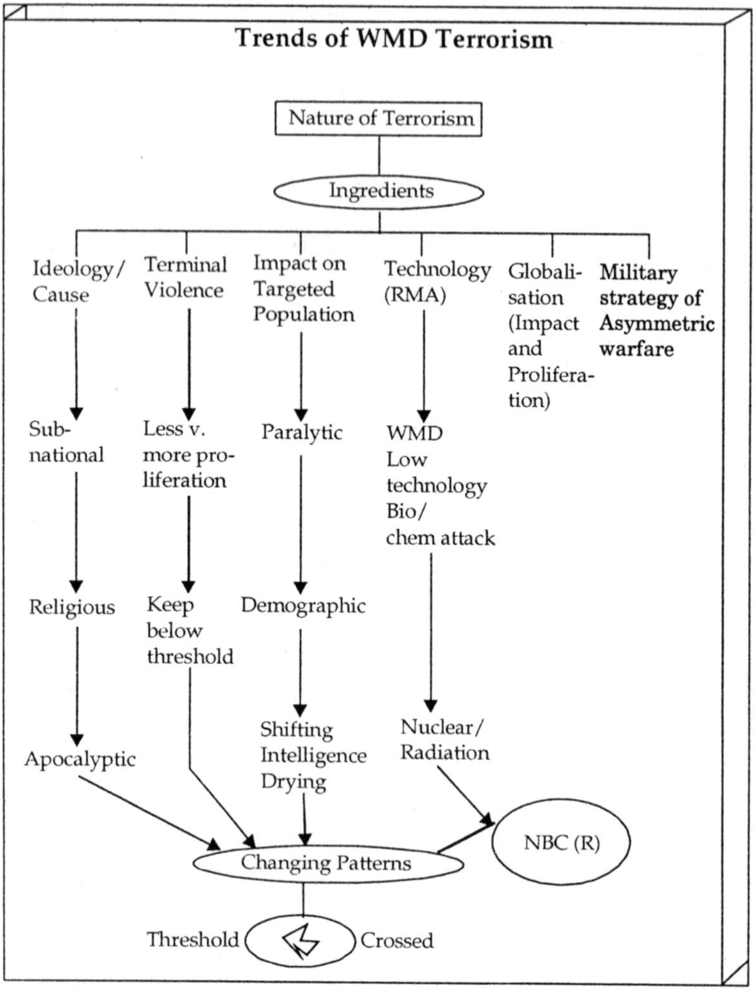

The inter connectivity of each of these factors is as shown in Fig. 3.2, showing the changing patterns, which one fears may cumulatively result in terrorists crossing the conventional threshold to the WMD level causing devastation.

This trend got validated very soon, after Aum Shinrikyo's poison gas attack in Tokyo in 1995, when rapt media coverage ensured that policy makers and the public could hardly avoid it. Much of what was said had doomsday overtones. For example, Walter

Laqueur stated that some terrorists "almost certainly will" use WMD, and a Harvard study accentuated the country's vulnerability to unconventional terrorism attack, concluding that several thousand could perish in a bio-terrorist attack[11] and many could meet similar fate in case of a chemical attack. The tools that terrorist applied earlier were of the conventional variety as they had to keep their popular support intact.[12] Minimum casualty has been their forte.[13] As Brian Jenkins' well-known saying goes, "terrorists want a lot of people *watching*, not a lot of people *dead*." They could rationalise their use of violence, holding the moral high ground over the targets of their acts.[14] Terrorists, it seemed, observed certain ethical boundaries. In the words of one student of terrorist behaviour, *"terrorism has traditionally used relatively unsophisticated weapons in a limited number of ways to inflict relatively little damage."*[15] Another authority on terrorism offers the reminder that terrorism "Is not about killing. It is a form of psychological warfare in which the killing of a small number of people convinces the rest of us that we are next in line." Even though terrorists did some shocking things, scholars could ascribe an element of predictability to terrorism. For this analogy many can still argue that the common terrorist will not cross the threshold of WMD terrorism unless it is supported by a state for political reasons. According to one count, in the twentieth century only twelve times did terrorists cause more than one hundred casualties with a single event or related series of attacks.[16] But with the shocking attacks on America giving undue credence to the theory that terrorists don't believe in mass killing is bound to boomerang. Now the targeted and vulnerable countries should go on the premise that the terrorists are capable of any heinous and dastardly acts with any excuse.

Terrorist expert Walter Laqueur has stated that some terrorists "Almost Certainly Will" use WMD. But B Jenkins says, "terrorists want a lot of people watching, not a lot of people dead".

INDIAN SUBCONTINENT AND BEYOND

A glimpse at the current terrorist movements in Asia and especially around the Indian subcontinent/South Asian region becomes necessary to get the true perspective of the dynamics of terrorist movements in this region, especially in the post-cold war scenario, which has unlocked sub-national fundamentalism, due to the infrastructure so created and its successful application in defeating a super power, like the erstwhile USSR.

In the Central Asian Region (CAR), there has been a cultural, social and religious revivalism of Islam, as people wanted to demonstrate their separateness from communism.[17] (There are 30 million Muslims north of Afghanistan border) There has been a revival of funds, Koran's litterateur and mullahs from Saudi-Arabia (Wahabi group), Iran (Iran Revolutionary Guard) and Pakistan to spread their version. The result was the mushrooming of mosques (From 80 to 1000) in Uzbekistan, beginning of *'Theological Schools'* in Azerbaijan and armed clashes (August 2000) with Kyrgyz soldiers. In Tajikistan, the Islamic forces have played a destructive role in the ongoing civil war. Fergana Valley continues to be an Islamic stronghold and the Islamic rebel forces are proliferating in Uzbekistan, Krygistan and Tajikistan,[18] although there appears now a backward movement due to the declared global war against terrorism. The CAR is linked to the Sunni 'Taliban' from the South and padded towards the West by a Shia Iran. Clearly one can identify an intra-civilisational fault line here. Though, this is a debatable issue. Markaz-Dawa-Ul-Irshad is a religious organisation based in Muridke (30 miles North of Lahore), which is Pakistan's largest jehadi organisation[19] Its militant wing is Lashkar-e-Taiba (covered subsequently). The other militant organisations, which are also operating here, perceive success at Kashmir as the first phase of their Jehad campaign. ISI facilitates procurement of weapons[20] for them. The hypothetical question, which arises now is, will it also mean transfer of WMD technology? There is a civilisational fault line also in the minds of the Taliban. The destruction of the statue of Buddha at Bamiyan can be considered noting less than cultural terrorism. The Taliban and all other such groups, indicate a Pan-Islamic agenda of intolerance. Advent of technology, proliferation of WMD (especially from FSU) and the civilisational divide would only usher in a period of WMD terrorism, the ultimate danger. Kemal Matinuddin has explained Taliban' as a "Transient phenomenon to a more stable arrangement, or at worst a nightmare to the western world and a problem for their neighbours".[21] Although post WTC, the Taliban looks decimated and its leaders are on the run to evade the dragnet of America, terrorist groups are capable of reviving and resurging with some other names to continue its barbaric activities against the targeted countries.

When Taliban was ruling in Afghanistan, it had emerged that the Afghanistan-Pakistan-South Central Asian (A-P-S) zone is the Islamic cauldron, which has intra-civilisational and inter civilisational faultlines, i.e., Shia versus Sunni, Islam versus Sinic; Islam versus Orthodox and Islam versus Hinduism. This zone, therefore, could have been graded as world's civilisational melting pot, where frictions could generate hotspots.

Looking specifically at South Asia and India in particular, the terrorist movements have all been affected by modernity. In Sri Lanka, the LTTE secessionist movement always had the potential of WMD technology.

Looking eastwards, in Cambodia, the Khmer Rouge has been disbanded in 1998. However the terrorist movement, Morco Islamic Liberation Army in Philippines, has the Islamic hue. In Thailand, a strong military offensive against Muslim separatist of new Pattani United Liberation Organisation in cooperation with Malaysia has been carried out. The Shan guerrillas in Myanmar and the Uighars in Xinjiang province of China have all shown upward mobility. The focus of contemporary guerrilla and terrorist groups is to acquire sophisticated weapons and explosives to kill more people. The international community continues to develop preventive and protective measures against mass casualty attacks, especially against CBRN attacks.[22]

Beyond doubt the turning point in terrorism in the Twentieth Century has been the Afghanistan imbroglio, which had been officially funded and polarised into a radical Islamic group to fight against the then Soviet Union. The Frankenstein so created had become cancerous and amoebic, causing Islamic Revivalism.[23] Further, as per perception of Jessica Stern, a religious based group is more likely to use a WMD. A similar view has also been shared by Leonard Weinberg and William Eubank.[24] The post '9-11' events have almost proved this theory to be true. Let us analyse the perspective threat holistically.

Any threat analysis basically has three determinants; status of non-state players, proliferation of WMDs and thereafter the philosophy and strategy of such groups in enacting a world terrorist act. Summaries and various case studies have been sprinkled in the content to bring in realism and suggest counter-measures. The study of Aum Shinrikyo is mentioned time and again so as to bring out certain lessons and a model for response. If one analyses the scientific training, formulae, and production know how, required by WMD oriented terrorist, it would be simply possible. According to some accounts, any individual who excelled in high school chemistry class has enough knowledge to make poison gas. All chemical reactions are not alike, however, and introductory chemistry classes rarely work with the extremely toxic chemicals involved in the synthesis of warfare agents. Some advanced knowledge is needed to produce such agents without incident and with minimal personal risk. Expert opinion therefore weighs heavily in favour of graduate-level chemistry or a graduate degree in organic chemistry would be essential to make Sarin or nerve agents.

In the aftermath of Aum's attack, there has been an ongoing debate about the future of WMD terrorism. Some have questioned the likelihood and some have shown threat everywhere. Analysis of terrorist trends should therefore become the foundation for any such assessment. At the outset, one is drawn to the notion that the threat of WMD terrorism is indeed rising primarily as a result of certain factors, analysed hence; namely, proliferation of WMD technology; the decline of traditional, politically-motivated terrorists groups and the rise of extreme ideologies[25] with a religious base. The form of international terrorism is also fast changing. New groups are emerging motivated by 'apocalyptic millennialism' redemptive fanaticism, or racist/ethnic hate.[26] Yet another pattern, which is discerning in terrorist formatting is loose mission oriented groupings, like in the case of World Trade Center bombings, which are difficult to trace[27] making retaliation impossible, which otherwise could have worked as a deterrent. Yet another aspect is irrationality, which appears to be a more rational methodology in the logic of terrorist violence, especially with regard to religiously motivated WMDs. On the other hand, there are some other relevant truisms about terrorism: one is that, terrorism is a 'weapon of the weak'; another is that 'terrorists want a lot of people watching, not a lot of people dead'. Both truisms, if they were true across the board, would indicate the risk of WMD terrorism as low. Nevertheless, on 20 January 1999, the President of the United States said that he has been persuaded by the intelligence agencies to believe that it was highly likely that a terrorist group would launch or threaten to launch a bio or a chemical attack on Americans within the next five years.[28] Beyond doubt the Aum Shinrikyo cult has upset the conventional wisdom of government control over WMD as well as the series of Anthrax attacks in the post '9-11' period. As Amy E. Smithson, Research Associate Stimson Center, New York, has reiterated that such kind of a threat is plausible.[29]

In fact, in South Asia, the situation is much more acute. If at all no statement on this regard is being made, it is more due to lack of a strategic vision and the lack of realisation of an emerging threat, of NBC terrorism in the most volatile region of the world, whereas in the western world the realisation has already come. Following the November 1995 Senate hearings on global proliferation of WMD and possible implications for terrorist activities, government agencies started coming out of the woodwork to assert their capabilities and missions pertaining to unconventional terrorism response. In the late 1990s Washington was awash with cabinet officers and elected officials issuing warnings about the problem:

(a) "The acquisition, proliferation, threatened or actual use of WMD by a terrorist group or individuals constitutes one of the gravest threats to the United States", observed Federal Bureau of Investigation Director Louis J. French."[30]

(b) "Perhaps most worrisome, we see in the last year are the growing indications of terrorist interest in acquiring chemical, biological, and nuclear weapons".- Central Intelligence Agency Director George J. Tenet."[31]

(c) "The potential for a chemical or biological weapons attack against the United State represents one of the principal national security threats to our country in the 21st century", said Senator Jon Kyl (R-Arizona).[32]

(d) "The WMDs are proliferating due to many reasons. Terrorists are also acquiring all kinds of technology. The day is not far when the world will be terrorised by WMD related blackmail".

In the mid 1980s and before, the idea of WMD terrorism was considered a remote possibility. The post 1990 period has seen global growth in terrorism perpetrated by groups that cannot be pigeon-holed as nationalist separatist, left wing, right wing, religious or any of the typologies that were effective in describing varieties of groups. In the past, several groups have been reported as making efforts to use nuclear weapons. Of late, newer groups have come with tendencies of using newer weaponries including WMD.[33]

The basic tools of a terrorist have been mostly conventional in nature till date, with the aim of catching public attention. Politically based terrorism is largely defined as an insurrection or an insurgency against an established government. The line tends to get blurred depending on specific tasks, motives and means used.[34]

There has been a whole range of speculation of the utilisation of a WMD tool in the sub-continental scenario by various government agencies and autonomous bodies of late. There appears to be lot of ambivalence and contingencies remain nebulous as yet. However, specifically in South-Asia itself one can identify two basic and distinct analogies; one is the evolving 'Pan-Islamic Terrorism' (PIT) theory in which a sort of an Islamic consortium[35] has formulated, more due to religious affinity and the other is the 'Ethnic-Secessionist Terrorism (EST)' type, like found more, due to ethnicity and the post-colonial momentum of nationhood.[36] The first theory could easily extend to touch the extreme end of WMD violence, which can even be validated due to proliferation through the FSU (explained later). However, these facts have many perceptions at the global level. Hoffman feels that the terrorists will not get the technological know-how. On the contrary the CIA report and even perceptions as given in the Presidential Directive 59, warns of the impending danger. Nevertheless, most of the assessments and appreciations are based on intangibles rather than some concrete data and empirical formulas. Thus, there is a case and tendency for one to work on bottom lines and worst-case scenarios.[37] (Nevertheless, the vast extent of literature and laboratories so found in the post '9-11' attack testify the analogy).

The terrorists (who could use WMDs, more in the South Asian context), broadly could be further classified into four categories. The first could be of the independent type with no political motives but self-aggrandizement and an 'apocalyptic millennialism' tendency. They may not always have a linkage with any particular theory, as enunciated above. The other could be of the 'sub-nationalistic type' within the ambit of the theory of EST. Movements in the North-East part of India/LTTE movement in Sri Lanka with a clear cut political agenda; the third could be of the 'quasi fundamentalist-political' type aligned more within the theoretical bounds of PIT. (Indigenous terrorists groups in J&K part of India. The fourth could be the purely 'Heterogeneous Fundamentalist State Sponsored 'type (The Taliban or the various terrorist groups as operating at the behest of Pakistan, who is the initiator of a proxy war in the subcontinent).These would be discussed in more details subsequently and their WMD tendencies identified. Most of the operational principles as relevant in the subcontinent to back a successful terrorist strategy would depend on the enunciated principles given below. This would enable in critically identifying the threats and their principles and thereafter drawing a counter-terrorist strategy, so as to curtail the WMD threat.

Principles of Successful Terrorism

- *Maintain* a viable and sustainable *political aim*.
- *Maintain the momentum* of achieving the objectives (cause panic in local population and their simultaneous isolation from government forces).
- *Indirect approach* in achieving the political objectives could become a *key strategy*.
- *Control population dynamics* by a philosophy of *Negativism* by transforming population bases, which are favourable to the terrorists, i.e., *cause demographic imbalance* by sparking sectarian violence, etc. causing mass exodus of population.
- *Skillful manipulation* of tolerance threshold by sporadic violence (rather than allowing continuous events of violence which may actually trigger a higher scale of retaliation by the affected state).

- Maintain *politico-military* offensive with the help of *Grand Strategy*. The use of blackmail as a tool of terror could even extend to the spectrum of a WMD threat.[38]
- Have a wide scale of *psychological operations* both at the national and international levels by talking of human rights and highlighting the misdeeds of the government forces. Thereafter, work out an information war strategy.
- The *legal war* is an extension of terrorist strategy. This implies engaging the government troops in legal complexities. (This aspect becomes more significant, where legal cases take years and can even be influenced by power and money politics).[39]

The existence of the typical anarchic-ideologue who could also be[40] 'High-Tech' the *Shrinyoko type* wanting to cause global 'apocalypse' and ruling the world thereafter. They don't even require popular support. The existence of any such suspected group with a cult culture has yet not been reported in the South Asian context. The likelihood is also scant, due to lack of resources, technology and poverty.

However, one has to watch the PIT category with a religious zeal and fervour. The second category offers a unique legitimising force for violence, one that is increasing in importance as a justification. Probably this is the motivating force for an act of mass-destructive terrorism.[41] Such a divinely ordained sanction makes such terrorists absolutist or less constrained by secular morality. In fact there has been a renaissance of religion-based terrorism with a nationalist and separatist cause. Therefore, amalgamation of many factors has created a new model of terrorists. Their tools of application may range from the lower threshold level of violence to the highest spectrum so as to internationalise their cause as well as disallow the movement in fading away. They exploit the manipulation of events and information further due to the element of information technology. Therefore, these terrorists are causing a 'Revolution in Terrorist Affairs' (RTA) by absorbing and synergising the force multipliers of the Revolution in Military Affairs (RMA), Information Technology, changing world order and the dynamics of the post-cold war politics. They are having an unwritten state support, especially in the South Asian scenarios. Their linkages with narco-terrorism, illegal trade and arms smuggling all become a part of the overarching grand plan of furthering religious or Jehadi type motivations of expansion from East to West.

However, simultaneously there are centripetal movements within the sect to further unify and consolidate their religion in one sect only, rather than have a pluralistic variety. For example, the

Hizbollah is a pan-Islamic movement,[42] that seeks to create a single Islamic community and rejects the concept of Arab or Persian nationalism, thus causing unity in the Islamic community rather than accepting diversity. On the contrary, the conflict in Shia-Sunni divergence has to be seen in a different context.

The main, and larger, issue is of religious objectivity and domination over the other, viz., Islam vs Christianity or Hinduism. The impact of globalisation is yet another factor accelerating such groups towards seeking and establishing conformist attitudes, with a view to having a better future for their race. It is impossible to regard religious terrorists as apolitical[43]. The Jehadi type terrorists have got merged with political objectives of nationalism of expansion. (The case for the call of Islamic Jehad against India falls in this category). The other hue which such Jehadi motives has been able to achieve is a different political aim of reducing domination by particular country (the case being the Bin-Laden versus American objectives). One of the declarations of Laden testifies to the removal of American forces in Saudi-Arabia as a political objective. In fact, Juergensmayer suggests that by using a religious justification for violence, terrorism becomes overtly political: they break the state's monopoly and claim political independence.[44]

On the other hand, many analysts have argued that religious terrorism is really not a new concept. Rapoport has traced that before the 19th century, religious motivation was the main cause for terrorism;[45] its location, the nature of its institutional or human victims, or the mechanics of its resolution or its ramifications transcend national boundaries. Religion, obviously, gives the moral plank to the terrorist. The intensity and importance of the battle can be used to justify the levels of violence employed in its name.[46]

These groups of terrorists also have younger stock, which in their zeal have a higher temperament to resort to higher level of terrorism[47]. This kind of religious terrorism has further been transformed into a *Transnational type*[48] and is a threat to status quo borders.

The transformation of terrorism has therefore occurred from an intra-state phenomenon to an inter-state phenomenon trespassing legality of de-facto borders.[49] As the world becomes more globalised and more interdependent, terrorist groups too are becoming more transnational.[50] In fact, at least in the South Asian environment there appears to be a phenomenon of "Convergence in Terrorist Affairs" (CTA). The same is explained as enumerated below:

- Religious or even ethnic ideologies are becoming transnational. The religious/ethnic affinity of population across borders is trying to merge for common religious political aims.

- Structural changes in terrorist ideological thinking are being made to become concurrent to religious/ethnic affinities.
- Globalisation and revolution in information technology has caused a spurt in transnational terrorist networking. Coupled with this is the factor of newer versions of small arms weapons and proliferation of WMD material.
- Yet another phenomenon, which is influencing terrorism structure in the South Asian region is the *Regional Parallel Economies* phenomenon generated in the golden crescent region comprising Afghanistan, Pakistan and Iran, which produce opium. Afghanistan's opium production had phenomenally improved during the Soviet intervention years.[51] .

Convergence in Terrorist Affairs (CTA)

Yet another facet of religious terrorism, which has been identified is that, both religion and violence are inextricably linked, and its prime purpose is to direct violence outside the religious community, to avoid fratricide within the group. It is believed that violence is necessary to conquer violence, so that states of violence and non-violence are not unconnected conditions.[52] (Terrorism appears to be inextricably linked to this phenomenon in the South Asian context, in fact more relevant to the Pakistan-Afghanistan Jehad concept asking for greater land). These tendencies are therefore a malicious part of most of the world religions except a few in Girad's theory. The theory of religious martyrdom is yet another factor, which has recently transformed into suicide missions, thus changing tactics of terrorism. They may manifest in a future scenario, towards a higher level of violence—even going to the extreme of using WMD. In Islam, martyrdom is widely admired, especially if it is achieved attempting to defeat Islam's enemy. In the South Asian context, both the LTTE and the various terrorist groups operating in J and K have shown this extreme capability. Martyrdom is important for the likelihood of nuclear terrorism, as it will ensure successful execution of the mission. Gavin Cameron also agrees upon this in his analysis, although he also mentions the contrary in a larger context, as certain elements would also want their enemies to die rather than themselves. The example of 'Messianism and Millenarianism' is also quoted taking the world towards doomsday. Most messianic missions associate with the destruction of the old order and the birth of the new.[53] Bin Laden's appeal for Islamic Jehad points towards this direction. The destructive force of WMD makes them an attractive instrument for groups that hold such aims.

A number of signs indicate that the new generation of terrorists is an insane bunch just the sort who would consider employing any instrument of violence. Unlike mundane attacks employing guns and bombs, germs or gas attack is a guaranteed headline grabber with significant psychological impact.[54] Terrorists may resort to weapons of mass destruction for one or more reasons: (1) to massacre as many people as possible; (2) to incite the type of widespread panic that could bring down a government; (3) to establish a position of strength from which to negotiate their demands; (4) to enhance their ability to execute attacks anonymously; (5) to disrupt and significantly damage a society or an economy; (6) to copy state behaviour; or, (7) to copy other terrorists.[55] The second, third, and fifth reasons have long been associated with terrorist behaviour, and the first and fourth motivations came to the fore in several major bombings in the 1990s.

As explained by Amy Smithson, another possible reason for terrorist use of chemical or biological weapons is that some terrorists may be engrossed with the luridness of death via toxic poisoning or disease and fancy the idea of using what they regard as spy tools.[56] Terrorists might also select a biological or chemical agent to fulfill a biblical prophecy. They might select an agent that would incapacitate, rather than kill, a large number of people, as the Rajneesh cult did in September 1984.[57] Use of incapacitating agents offers the advantage of causing significant fear, but not crossing the line to mass killing. Finally, terrorists may seek chemical or biological agents to try to contaminate and stigmatise a certain piece of property, such as an important landmark or business.

Another change, witnessed since past ten years, is that terrorists no longer automatically claim credit for an attack. This post-modern terrorism's anonymity feeds on one of the chief characteristics of what is currently called bio-terrorism.[58] Ehud Sprinzak, has distinguished between four different types of terrorism[59]:

- Mass-casualty terrorism (World Trade Centre, New York).
- State-sponsored chemical or biological (CB) terrorist attacks.
- Small scale CB attacks.
- Super terrorism—the strategic use of CB. (Mass casualties)

The concept of *"Trans-National Criminal Organisations (TCO)"*, in view of the impact of globalisation and revolution in Information Technology is already causing an evolving phenomenon of a 'Revolution in Terrorist Affairs', due to the following 'high-tech' ingredients in terrorists skills and organisations in the priorities as given:

- Ability of global communications through satellites and Internet or the WAP technology. This would give them additional mobility and flexibility in future terrorist operations.
- Global network on sharing of intelligence by terrorists.
- Interdependence between various terrorist groups in training and conduct of operations.
- Arms and narcotics trade at global level.
- New religious fanaticism, which is also an emerging phenomenon.
- Proliferation of WMD technology and accessibility to them.
- Acquiring skills in cyber terrorism.
- Utilisation of a large knowledge base available on the Internet which will enable them to get educated.[60]

Structures of Terrorism: Indian Experience

Specifically, there are four geographical areas in South Asia where divisions can be made. Considering India as the central feature, the one in the West of India are terrorists of the religious secessionist type, the one towards the East and South are of the political-secessionist type; and the ones within the heartland of India could be termed as ideological types or the economically deprived ones. The chances of *millennium apocalyptic* type will be remote due to the factors already explained.

In the political-Islamic type category there are more than 20 groups. Most of these groups were operating in Afghanistan but now have been diverted towards the South (Kashmir) to fulfill a political-religious cause, whereas, towards North-East of India, these groups are more ethnic and secessionist in nature.

Status and Characteristics of Terrorists Organisations in South Asia (Are there any tendencies towards use of WMD?)

In analysing any realistic threat perception, it becomes imperative to study the characteristics and tendencies of various terrorist organisations in South Asia. What is their linkage with other worldwide terrorist organisations becomes another pertinent question. The main terrorist hotspots in South Asia are:

- Pan-Islamic related organisations operating in areas of Afghanistan, Pakistan and Kashmir. (Table)

TERRORIST OUTFITS

• Hizb-ul-Mujahideen	NSCN
• Harkat-ul-Mujahideen	ULFA, LTTE
• Lashkar-e-Taiba	NLFT
• Al Barq	ARIF
• Al Qaida	IMA
• Hamas	RPF
• Islamic Front	RSO
• K-2, etc.	

- Organisations operating in the heartland of India.
- Organisations operating in Southern India and Sri Lanka.
- Organisations operating in North East India, Bangladesh and Nepal.
- Other global terrorist networks having their worldwide influence including in South Asia.

Pan-Islamic Groups

There are two categories of organisations. One is the fundamental-political type and the other is the pure Jehadi-terrorist type. A cursory look at their objectives, organisations and motivations may give their genocidal tendencies to perform a WMD act. (only some important ones are being discussed).

Fundamentalist-Political Organisations

All Party Hurriyat Conference (APHC): It is a conglomeration of 23 organisations and was established in 1993 in Srinagar. It has parallel organisations. There are unconfirmed reports of Pakistan funding for opening up APHC all over the world.[61] Because of its indivisibility claim of Kashmir it serves the aspirations of the indigenous people of J and K. It is less likely to give any directions regarding acquisition of WMD as a terrorist tool. However, its linkage with Bin Laden can raise political connections towards WMD capability in a future scenario. Jamaat-e-Islami (J&K) forms a major constituent of the AHPC. This party propagates violent Jehad. If the violence level is endeavoured to be raised to draw attention then propagation of views for use of higher scale of violence, i.e., WMD cannot be ruled out completely, although of the chemical or biological type only.[62]

Jammu and Kashmir Liberation Front (JKLF): It is a student organisation raised in 1963 but now turned terrorist. Less likely to get involved with WMD terrorist activities.

Shure-e-Jehad (Jehad Council): It is a frontline Jehad organisation under the aegis of the Inter Service Intelligence (ISI) of Pakistan and established in April 1996. The purpose is to coordinate all terrorist activities. Its connectivity with Bin Laden cannot be ruled out as it forms a part of Bin Laden's global terrorist network.[63] Therefore, access to WMD technology and capability cannot be strictly denied in a long term scenario up to 2010.

T errorist Outfits

As is known, there are certain camps, which are training the Jehad war machine. (These are as per perceptions of the author). The terrorists outfits are discussed below:

• ***Hizb-ul-Mujahideen (HM) (Party of Holy Warriors):*** It is the terrorist wing created as a counter-weight to JKLF and pro-Pakistani outfit. The HM split into two factions headed by Yousuf Shah and Masood Sarfaraz, whose group further got split into two, to form Jamaat-ul-Mujahideen.[64] As per their existing trends, they neither have the WMD technology nor are carrying out training towards that end.

• ***Harkat-ul-Mujahideen (HUM):*** This organisation was created for providing Afghani refugees in mid-80s and later contributed to the Afghan Jehad. Its linkage with Bin-Laden is deep. There are reports (of interrogation), which reflect on their tendency.[65] Headquarters is located in Rawalpindi.[66] The supremacy of Islam and Jehad, where ever Muslims are marginalised is their mission.

• ***Lashkar-e-Taiba (LeT) (Army of the Pure):*** This group participated in the Afghan Jehad and surfaced in Kashmir in 1993. Headquarters is co-located in Muridke. Its ideology reflects pan-Islamisation by liberating Kashmir, Palestine, Bosnia, etc. It has a composition of 70-80 per cent foreign terrorists. It has a very close linkage with Bin-Laden and probably has been flourishing under his umbrella. The very fact that since Bin-Laden is building WMD capabilities, the chances of LeT undertaking WMD terrorism are maximum. Further, being a terrorist organisation, which has more foreign content, its use of WMD threat would not draw any flak for Pakistan. In fact, since they do not hold any territory, any retaliation by India, as part of a state's nuclear doctrine cannot be applied. (Now on the banned list but seems to be still operating).

• ***Al Barq:*** (Lightening Force) It propagates the theory of 'Implementation of the UN Resolution'.

• ***Islamic Front:*** It has very close links with the APHC and it is presumed that it has a tie up with Osama Bin Laden.

• The other miscellaneous organisations, which are operating are Hizbullah, Dukhtaran-e-Millat (women organisation), Muslim Mujahiden, Alfaran and Al Badr.

• Some terrorist organisations which have emerged are, K-2 Regiment (Raised by ISI), Peer Panjal Suran regiment, Black Commando, Mujahidin-E-Kashmir, and Sipahi-e-Sahaba.

• ***Al Qaida:*** Osama Bin Laden (OBL) is the head of this organisation, and is operating globally on US targets. The outfit comprises of Saudis, Yemenis and Afghanis. The organisation has built up a chemical laboratory, presumably with Iraqi assistance. There are reports of OBL possessing nuclear/radiological weapons.[67] (The speculation continues as the search for OBL also continues).

• ***HAMAS (Islamic Resistance Movement).*** This was formed in late 1987 as an outgrowth of the Palestinian branch of the Muslims Brotherhood. Various Hamas elements have used both political and violent means, including terrorism, to pursue the goal of establishing an Islamic Palestinian state in place of Israel. Loosely structured, with some elements working clandestinely and others working openly through mosques and social service institutions to recruit members, raise money, organise activities, and distribute propaganda. Hamas's strength is concentrated in the Gaza Strip and a few areas of the West Bank. It has engaged in peaceful political activity, such as running candidates in West Bank Chamber of Commerce elections. Hamas activists, especially those in the Izz-el-En al-Qassam Brigades, have conducted many attacks—including large-scale suicide bombings—against Israeli civilian and military targets. In the early 1990s they also targeted suspected Palestinian collaborators and Fatah rivals. As regards their strength, there are unknown number of hardcore members; tens of thousands of supporters and sympathisers. They operate primarily in the occupied territories, Israel. In August 1999, Jordanian authorities closed the group's Political Bureau offices in Amman, arrested its leaders, and prohibited the group from operating on Jordanian territory. It receives funding from Palestinian expatriates, Iran and private benefactors in Saudi Arabia and other moderate Arab states. Some fund raising and propaganda activity take place in western Europe and North America. The likelihood of this organisation acquiring WMD technology in a long time scenario cannot be ruled out.

Harkat-ul-Ansar and Al-Qaida have demonstrated interest to acquire WMD technology.[68] The Taliban and Afghanistan based foreign Islamic groups are catalysing terrorist groups in South Asia. The Afghanistan based groups and ISI are providing training and money to most of the South Asian groups.

North-East India

There are multifarious groups operating in the North Eastern part of India.[69] They all have an ISI link and operate from neighbouring countries and, thus, are transnational in some characteristics. Their coercion and motivation to use WMD as a tool of terrorism is not known but cannot be ruled out either.[70] In fact, their usage would be welcome to the ISI cause and its linkage to Pakistan, even ISI would be difficult to pin point. This would obviously give strategic flexibility to Pakistan and their designs.

LTTE

They fall in the category of being ethnic sub-nationalism. A case study of ' Liberation Tigers Tamil Elam' (LTTE) and their fight for ethnic sub-nationalism brings out many lessons for South Asia, which are unique. This movement had its origin in 1972 and is also an aberration of the post-colonial British era. Such groups have also been compared with the 'Shinrikyo' group, more with the view of showing technological prowess. Undoubtedly, in Asia, other than 'AUM', LTTE, have employed or have expressed an interest in acquiring chemical, biological, radiological and nuclear (CBRN) material technology through criminal organisations. Terrorist acquisition of strategic weapon systems is low probability - high impact challenge to contemporary states.[71]

Bangladesh - Bhutan - Maldives

Insurgencies in the North-East India and one in Bangladesh have been inextricably linked.[72] The Chittagong Hill Tract (CHT) insurgency although solved, still has the potential of re-appearing because of the ISI factor (In fact, one insurgent group, Rotingya Solidarity Organisation has been operating since 1990, in the CHT. It has close links with the NSCN, ULFA, BSF and NLFT and is termed as a blue chips Burmese Muslims insurgent group operating in Bangladesh)[73] and the parallelism causing the contagion effect in Bangladesh. However, extreme poverty, lack of technology and an extreme cause, would rule out any WMD threat. Similarly, both Bhutan and Maldives, have no record of any terrorist insurgent activities. (Although the ULFA hideout in Bhutan have been creating tensions).

Myanmar

In 1988, State Law and Order Restoration Council (SLORC) in Myanmar was formulated by the new military junta. The border area between Myanmar and India is a safe haven for all kinds of insurgents. After the Kargil war, ISI has stepped up its activities of recruitment.[74] Four major insurgent groups have been raised namely, i.e., Arakan Rohingya Islamic Front (ARIF), Itihadul Mujahideen of Arakan (IMA), Rohingya Patriotic Front (RPF) and Rohingya Solidarity Organisation (RSO) under control of ISI. They are all supporters of the Jehad concept of pan-Islamic kind.

Maoist Threat in Nepal

The Maoist movement in Nepal may be classified into four stages, viz., strategic inception stage, strategic confrontation stage, strategic consolidation stage and strategic domination stage. The early 1950s and 1960s was the inception stage when students and political activists with communist leanings were attracted to Mao's revolutionary ideas. Poor governance, rampant corruption, yawning gap between the "Haves" and "Have Nots" acted like tonic to the Maoist leaders. The 1970s saw the confrontation stage through strikes, bandhs, etc. The decade of 1980 was the consolidation stage when the guerrilla training was imparted to the cadres to fight the elected government. This phase also saw the procurement of arms and ammunition. The decade of 1990s was the domination stage when Maoist Guerrillas successfully fought pitched battles with the security forces and have been ruling the roost in many districts of Nepal.

For the last five years, Nepal has witnessed a rebellion by Maoist guerrillas who have pledged to overthrow the country's monarchy and replace its parliamentary democracy with a one party state. The rebels now hold about a quarter of the country, and have thousands of armed activists who have attacked police stations and government officials. The rebels are particularly active in remote areas of the West and Mid-West of the country and mostly carry out hit and run attacks on police and security force outposts. Some 2,000 people, mostly civilians, have been killed in the fighting between the Maoists and the state. After the massacre of most of the country's royal family, some analysts believe that the Maoists may hold the key to Nepal's future. Following the killing of a number of policemen the King proclaimed a state of emergency in the kingdom on 26 November 2001 and the Government sent the Royal Nepal Army into action against the Maoist.

The Maoist breakaway faction of Nepal Communist Party, gave a call for 'Peoples War' in February 1996. The Maoist are very active in 31 districts, with varying degrees of influence over 63 out of Nepal's 75 districts. The district of Rukum, Rolpa, Jajarkot, Kalikot, Pyuthan, Salyan and Gorkh in mid and western Nepal are the worst affected. A 'People's Government' was formed in Rukum District, mid-West Nepal, in December 2000. Rolpa District followed suit in April 2001. People's government was later established in all districts of mid-west Nepal and some districts in other regions. Since September 2000, Maoist guerrillas have been attacking police and security forces relentlessly.[75]

Among the 40 demands of the Maoists are wide scale land reform, break in ties with India, discontinuation of foreign aid and abolition of monarchy. Maoists political demands especially those relating to Indo-Nepal relations and India's security concerns have gained acceptance and support from the mainstream political parties. The 40 point charter of NCP (Maoist) demands include abrogation of all treaties with India, control of the open border between Nepal and India, closure of all Indian Army recruitment centres in Nepal and introduction of work permits to Indians in Nepal. The Maoists toned down their opposition to the new king, Gyanendra, after the Royal Nepalese Army allowed safe passage to their cadres in Holleri village in Rolpa district on July 12. The incident led to the ouster of Prime Minister G P Koirala. Soon after Deuba replaced Koirala, the insurgents agreed to hold talks with the government.[76]

Recently the government took a number of initiatives to curb the Maoist problem. They are :

- Addition of portfolio of defence minister to finance minister Mahesh Acharya.
- Appointment of Pradeep Shamsher Rana to the Acting Inspector-General of Police so that he can coordinate with the Chief of Army Staff General Prajwal S. Rana in anti-Maoist operations.
- Deployment of the army in 13 districts.
- Convening all party meetings and calling the insurgent for dialogue.

Other measures taken by the Government included :

- Allocation of additional funds for development of affected districts. Officials were, however, unable to undertake any major initiatives due to Maoist threats.
- Activation of special courts to try insurgents.
- An amendment in January 2001 to the Local Administration Act, which enabled setting up of a Chief Administrative Officer in each development region, along with a Security Committee comprising APF, Police, National Investigation Dept (NID) and locally deployed RNA.
- Integrated development and security package with RNA deployment was devised for the worst affected mid west districts.[77]

Highlights of the Maoists Movement

- Armed Maoist insurgents began fighting to establish a "Peoples' Republic" in Nepal in mid-February of 1996 and they are now active, even influential, in more than half of the country.
- Successive governments have failed to quell the rebellion, either with force or with expensive development spending in affected

areas.

- The rebels are fighting for a "People's Republic" with a shadowy underground leadership and thousands of well trained fighters.
- The Maoists propagate a line known as "Prachandpath" and describe it as the Nepalese adaption of the ideology of Peru's wholly indigenous Shining Path Maoists.
- In some areas of Western Nepal, Maoist cadres run a parallel government.
- Their avowed strategy is straight from Mao Tse Tung's writings–a peasant takeover in the countryside to surround and threaten the elite in urban areas, selective use of violence and re-education of civilians.
- The Nepal Communist Party (Maoist) used to be part of the country's democratic parliamentary system. Maoists fought alongside centrist parties and mainstream communists for the establishment of democracy in 1990. But a falling out over elections in 1996 lead to the first shots being fired in the People's War. More than 2,000 have died since then.
- Maoists demands are wide scale land reform, a break in the close ties with India, end to foreign aid and end of role for the Royal family.
- Lately, there have been indications that Maoists are flexible on some key points.
- The rebels usually attack the police, trying to demoralise an underpaid and badly trained force.
- Attempts to hold peace talks with the government failed in October amid confusion over the release of two jailed Maoist leaders. Both sides say they are still willing to talk.
- Deeply entrenched rural poverty and social inequality provide fertile ground for the rebellion. The Maoists are most successful in parts of the country with the worst development statistics. Life expectancy in the mid western area of Rolpa, a Maoist stronghold, is just 52 years, and per capita annual income is below $ 100.
- The Maoists fund themselves through bank robberies and collection of often involuntary donations.
- Weapons are purchased from the illegal arms market. So far, the Maoists do not have sophisticated arms; neither do their opponents, the police.

The Communist Party of Nepal Maoist (CPN-M) is making preparations to start a bloody movement in North Bengal, Sikkim and parts of Bihar, according to intelligence reports. The Maoists are trying to establish a nexus with the PWG which is trying to build a safe corridor from Bihar to Nepal. Breakaway faction of the CPI(M) in Darjeeling is also reportedly providing moral support to the Maoists. The open border between the two countries, links between separatist movements on both sides and a history of Nepal being used as a safe-haven by terrorists to launch attacks in India have got the intelligence agencies worried.[78] Maoist leaders are said to be in league with the PWG Naxalites of Andhra Pradesh. Their aim may be to spread Maoist ideology in all the coastal states from Andhra Pradesh to West Bengal encompassing Orissa, and Bihar. That they are being propped up by ISI needs no emphasis. The strategic alliance between Pakistan and China is food for thought in view of Chinese indirect abetment (through the ISI), especially when the Chinese are consolidating their strategic frontiers.

India and Nepal have agreed to coordinate their actions on the border to revent the flow of arms and assistance from the Indian side to the Maoist insurrection in the Kingdom. There is a strong recognition in New Delhi and Kathmandu of the grave threat the Maoist rebellion poses to both the nations and the subcontinent as a whole. For Nepal, it is a question of defending the present political order. And India cannot be secure with the rise of another extremist force in its neighbourhood.

The attacks on America in 2001 also had a reverberating impact in Kathmandu. As the world opinion turned hostile against terrorists, it is also believed that Prime Minister Deuba's (mis) calculations to use the global anger against Maoists back home misfired. With the global fight against terrorism remaining confined to Afghanistan and Iraq, and with India and Pakistan faced with the resulting fallout, Nepal's war against terrorism was all but forgotten. The talks between the government and the Maoists, before the attack on America, were making progress even if it was not at the pace the Nepali Congress Party wanted it to be. But the war on terrorism made the government suddenly think that it could do without any further concessions to the Maoists.

Although one can rule out usage of any kind of WMD weaponry by these rustics, one cannot close the option entirely; it is believed that their leadership is highly educated with some of the Maoists being engineers.

NAXALISM IN INDIA

The term 'Naxalite' is derived from the name of a place, Naxalbari, located in Darjeeling district of West Bengal. In 1967, when Mao-Tse-Tung launched his Cultural Revolution in China, a group of leaders broke away from the Communist Party of India (CPI) (Marxist) because the party had decided to enter government after general elections held in that year. Charu Mazumdar, Secretary General of CPI (Marxist-Leninist) was the leader of the group. The group swore by Mao's political ideas and believed that violent revolution was the only way to capture power and destroy the 'class enemies', i.e., landlords and government officials. To achieve this aim the breakaway leaders mobilised a force of about 15,000 peasants and an armed revolution was launched on 3 March 1967. The movement soon gained popularity amongst rural folk as well as urban populace. The movement always believed in violent methods to capture power. The government used the police to suppress this movement effectively albeit at the cost of thousands of innocent lives.[79]

People's War Group

The PWG is the pioneer in the Naxalite movement in Andhra Pradesh. Formed in 1980 by a communist leader, K Seetharamaiah, the group has about 1,100 underground and 5,500 over-ground cadres. It has 74 dalams and four military platoons. Each dalam consists of about 10 members. The group is reported to possess sophisticated weapons including AK-47 and landmines with which it has been targeting security personnel, politicians and senior police officers. The PWG has been waging an armed rebellion for the creation of a communist state comprising tribal areas of Andhra Pradesh, Maharashtra, Orissa and Madhya Pradesh. The group targets feudal landlords whom they hold responsible for the exploitation of the poor.

Maoist Communist Centre

The MCC took birth in the early seventies in Bahrogara (Singhbum District). Though many of the Naxalites were wiped out in police action that followed, some of the leaders managed to escape to Gaya and Aurangabad areas where they built up the bases. The MCC first struck terror on 29 May 1987, when it brutally massacred 42 persons belonging to upper caste Rajput families at Dalelchak-Baghauria village in Aurangabad district of Bihar. Next this armed outfit posing as the defenders of the rural poor struck again at Bara in Gaya district on 12 February 1992 and hacked to death 37 members of Bhumihars families. Since then the MCC has continued perpetrating violence and genocide in different villages of central Bihar, both against 'class enemies' and its rival Naxalite outfits.

People's Guerrilla Army

On 2 December 2000, various Naxalite outfits joined hands to float the first united army of the Nazalites, the People's Guerrilla Army (PGA), in Andhra Pradesh, Bihar, Jharkhand and Madhya

Pradesh. Formed on the lines of the New People's Army in Philippines and the People's Liberation Army of Peru, the Naxalite leadership claimed that the PGA would work alongside extremists of Kashmir, Assam, Nagaland, Manipur. The purported objective of the PGA is to counter the security forces offensive against Naxalites. In its first phase, the outfit is reported to have started separate branches in parts of Bihar, Jharkhand, North Telengana (Andhra Pradesh) and in the tribal belt of Dandkaranya, which include parts of Andhra Pradesh, Maharashtra, Madhya Pradesh and Orissa.

Naxalite Problem in Bihar

In Bihar over a dozen Naxalite groups operate. Their area extends to around 26 districts of central and south-western Bihar. The worst affected are the southern districts of Chatra, Gumla, Palamau, Lohardaga and parts of Ranchi and Hazaribagh districts. At many places in these areas, they run a parallel administration – ranging from tax collection from officials and contractors to holding people's court to resolve local disputes both civic and criminal and meting out justice in their own way.

The Naxalite problem in Bihar is a little complicated because it is riddled with caste dynamics. The problem has its roots in the agitations by tenants and labourers in 1970. Peasant movement is not a new phenomenon in Bihar. Mass organisations of peasants with communist leanings have been active in the state since the 1930s. Despite prolonged agitation the crucial issue of land reforms was never seriously addressed. These organisations have been influenced by the ideologies of Marx.

Private armies of the landlords such as the Ranvir Sena and the Savarna Liberation Front have been brutally massacring the dalits against whom they hold a grudge either for refusing to work on unacceptable conditions or for collaborating with Naxalites. The Naxalites, with their ideology of violence, also do not hesitate to retaliate by killing Bhumihars or Rajputs. This senseless and brutal attacks and retaliatory attacks has rendered many people homeless and made many children orphans.

The possibility of all the above mentioned groups having WMD tendencies is impossible.

MEASURES TAKEN TO COUNTER NAXALISM

- The Central Government and some of the affected state governments have initiated measures to combat the Naxalites. These include:
- Formation of a Joint Coordination Committee (JCC) of the governments of different states facing the extremist problem.

- Formation of a Joint Operational Command (JOC).
- Banning of Naxalite organisations.
- Effective surrender policies.
- Formation of special intelligence branches (SIB) to deal exclusively with extremism.
- Increased financial assistance from the Centre to the states.
- Covert operations (infiltration of Naxalite groups).
- Adoption of villages.
- Formation of grama raksha dalams by the police.

Bodoland Imbroglio

The Bodoland problem, the demand for an independent state, has been burning for many years. Many terrorist acts have been committed by the Bodos. The Bodoland accord led to the formation of Bodoland Autonomous Council (BAC) covering 23,000 square kms. However, the Bodo people wanted to include additional 513 villages within the BAC, which was not accepted. Over and above this, there were many flaws in the accord like: BAC boundary not demarcated: Santhal dominated areas were placed within BAC: the clauses relating to election, and financial powers not made clear. The point is that due to lackadaisical bureaucratic approach, no problem gets solved. On the contrary it gets complicated.

MISCELLANEOUS THREATS AND ASSESSMENT: SOUTH ASIA

In the subcontinent there are a full host of terrorist movements like the Sunnis versus Shiites in Punjab (Pakistan), Mohajir Guerillas in Sind, Islamic factions in North-Western Frontier Province, Kasrains, Lehgaries, Bozdars and Malghani in Baluchinstan in Pakistan. In India, other than the organisation in Kashmir or the North East, there are organisations in the hinterland like the Naxalites or various caste type war groups of Bihar or Bhuj. Of the 34 conflicts in Asia-Pacific region, 17 are located in South-Asia. Violent political conflicts could be active at a very low level or be dormant, but retain the potential to graduate to the level of a low-intensity conflict. The point is that the focus of contemporary guerrilla and terrorist groups is to acquire sophisticated weapons and explosives to kill more people.[80] The analogy should logically lead to acquisition of higher spectrum of weapon capabilities, may be WMD. But in reality, such a contingency is unlikely due to the necessity of basic sophistication in technology, which these groups will never be able to access and train for, in the Indian environment at least for many decades.

However, let us examine some more organisations, some of which are towards West Asia :

Palestine

(a) ***Abu Nidal Organisation :*** Split from Palestine Liberation Organisation (PLO) in 1974. Carried out terrorist attacks in 20 countries. Relocated to Iraq in December 1988. Has operational presence in Lebanon and several Palestinian refugee camps. Operates over a wide area, including West Asia, Asia, and Europe. Has considerable support from Iraq, Libya, and Syria (until 1987).

(b) ***Palestine Islamic Jehad:*** Same goal as HAMAS. Receives financial aid from Iran and limited assistance from Syria.

(c) ***Palestine Liberation Front:*** Receives support mainly from Iraq. Has also received support from Libya.

(d) ***Popular Front for the Liberation of Palestine:*** Marxist-Leninist group founded in 1967 as a member of the PLO operates in Syria, Lebanon, Israel, and the Occupied Territories. Receives safe haven and some logistic assistance from Syria.

Lebanon

Hizbullah. Radical Shia group, wants increasing political power; opposed to Israel, closely allied with and often directed by Iran. Operates in the Bekka Valley, Beirut, and Lebanon. Has cells in Europe, Africa, South America, North America, and Asia. Receives substantial aid and training from Iran and Syria.

Philippines

Abbu Sayyaf Group: Smallest and most radical of Islamic separatist groups. Some of its members have studied or worked in West Asia and developed ties with mujahideen in Afghanistan. Wants an independent Islamic state in some areas in Southern Philippines.

Algeria

Salafi Group for Call and Combat (GSPC): The most effective armed group in Algeria. Algerian government has accused Iran and Sudan of supporting them.

Spain

Basque Fatherland and Liberty: Aims to establish independent homeland based on Marxist principles in Northern Spain. Operates in the Basque autonomous regions of Spain and South-Western France. Received training in Libya, Lebanon, and Nicaragua. Also appears to have ties with IRA.

Egypt

(a) ***Al-Gama's al-Islamiyya:*** Egypt's largest militant group, active since the late 1970s. Rifai Taha Musa, a hard-line former member of the group, signed Osama Bin Laden's 1988 fatwa calling for attacks against US civilians. Primary goal is to overthrow the Egyptian government and replace it with an Islamic state. Has worldwide presence, including Sudan, UK, Afghanistan, Austria and Yemen.

(b) ***Al-Jehad:*** Active since the late 1970. Close partner of Al-Qaida. Goal is same as that of Al-Islamiyya. Wide network outside Egypt, including Yemen, Afghanistan, Pakistan, Sudan, Lebanon and UK.

Most of these terrorist organisations have been banned by the USA. The result of this would be difficulty in money laundering operations and thus expansion of their network. This in turn would also have an impact on their WMD capabilities or tendencies in a long-term perspective.

LIST OF ORGANISATIONS/INDIVIDUALS BANNED BY THE US

Organisations

(a) Al Qaida/Islamic Army;
(b) Abu Sayyaf Group;
(c) Armed Islamic Group (GIA);
(d) Harkat ul-Mujaheedin (HUM);
(e) Al-Jehad (Egyptian Islamic Jihad);
(f) Islamic Movement of Uzbekistan (IMU);
(g) Asbat al-Ansar;
(h) Salafist Group for Call and Combat (GSPC);
(i) Libyan Islamic Fighting Group;
(j) Al-Itihaad al-Islamiya (AIAI); and
(k) Islamic Army of Aden.

Individuals

(a) Osama bin Laden;
(b) Muhammad Atif;
(c) Sayf al-Adl;
(d) Shaykh Sai'id;
(e) Abu Hafs the Mauritanian;
(f) Ibn Al-Shaykh al-Libi;
(g) Abu Zubaydah;
(h) Abd al-Hadi al-Iraqi;
(i) Ayman al-Zawahiri;
(j) Thirwat Salah Shihata;
(k) Tariq Anwar al-Salah; and
(l) Makhtab Al-Khidamat/Al Kifah.

Other Organisations

(a) Wafa Himanitarin Organisation;
(b) Al Rashid Trust; and
(c) Mamoun Darkazanli Import-Export Company.

Analysis and Threat Perceptions of Terrorist Structure

In totality, the end of the cold war coupled with globalisation - porous boundaries, 'Information Technologies' revolution and the ongoing RMA has ushered in a new 'high bred' variety of terrorist or the third generation of terrorists (more applicable in the present context of western countries). The revival of religious fundamentalism (more Islamic trends have been seen) has added a new dimension of threat, which is transgressing geographical boundaries and re-configuring more towards religious affinity (applicable more so to Asia).

In the case of India and Pakistan both are facing the dual challenge of ethno-political and religious-fundamental-sub-nationalist groups.

There has been a transformation of the first generation terrorists (like in North-East India) to the second generation (like present in Jammu and Kashmir/Osama variety) who use high-tech weapons and satellite communication. The third generation may possess WMDs and even WMDR (like laser/cyber war weapons). Speculations indicate to even a fourth generation terrorist by 2050, which may employ inter-planetary asteroid collisions in space.

Proliferation and Feasibility of WMD Technology

FSU and Proliferation of WMD

International Relations on Trade Issues, National Security and International Affairs division testimony before the subcommittee on emerging threats and capabilities, Committee on Armed Services, (06 March 2000) narrated the US President's National Security Strategy, (October 1998) in which terrorism has been presented as one of the most potent threats to peace and US interests. An assessment of the danger can be estimated by analysing the data given below at the time when the Soviet Union collapsed. It had the following inventory of WMD:

- 30,000 nuclear weapons.
- 650 tons of weapon-usable nuclear material.
- 40,000 metric tons of chemical weapons.
- 2,500 systems (missiles and bombers) for delivering WMD.
- It also had thousands of scientists, engineers and technicians trained on these weapons.

The Congress at the urging of senators Nunn and Lugar, authorised DOD to establish Cooperative Threat Reduction (CTR) programme in 1992. In 1955, DOE launched materials, protection control and accountability programme to help secure FSU's weapons-usable nuclear materials. Unemployed scientists were diverted towards peaceful commercial projects to reduce available nuclear material.

Impact on South Asian Security

There are more than a score of terrorist organisations operating in South-Asia. The ones which are most active in the Kashmir-Afghanistan corridor are operating very close to the FSU and thus have natural land axes to pilfered fissionable material. The chances of their possessing about 10-kilogram Plutonium and about 100 kilogram of HEU are many due to the following reasons:

(a) Volatile and centralised leadership by Bin Laden who has clearly developed a global terrorist network. Further, his funding is very high, through various 'Pan Islamic' and 'Anti-American' agencies.

(b) The main area of Pan-Islamic Industry is located near the places of drug transit routes. Similarly the other terrorist groups which are operating in areas further South or East like the NSCN or the LTTE are less likely to obtain them through the unguarded land routes from the area of FSU.

The question is that, will nuclear leakage threaten South Asian interests? If there is a leakage of nuclear material, it will de-stabilise South Asia due to proliferation along this route because otherwise there are many effective counter-proliferation measures, which are in vogue or have been taken by other nations earlier. South Asia has de-facto two nuclear powers and on the external geographic perimeter it has more than five to six countries, which are nuclear powers or are nuclear capable. Any nuclear leakage obviously speeds up the programme of potential nuclear powers and even opens an avenue for terrorists (including state sponsored) to go nuclear, thus building the flashpoints further. Few instances and points are mentioned below:

(a) Traditional path to nuclear weaponisation is slow, difficult and expensive. This path is very difficult due to NPT and many other supporting regimes.

(b) Israel attacked Iraq's Osirak reactor. A similar military action through the UN is also a possibility against such rogue states.

(c) Nuclear leakage eliminates fissile material choke points.

(d) Simple WMDs are not difficult to be manufactured by terrorists. Even a weapon that is poorly constructed or is made of a large amount of lower-grade uranium can be effective according to K. Santhanam, Director, IDSA. However he cautions that there will be a degree of difficulty.

(e) *The Bin Laden connection with lost nuke of erstwhile Soviet*

Union has been well articulated in various articles and intelligence reports. "Osama Bin Laden web site and articles" written by Yossuf Bodansky says, 'Bin Laden has 20 nukes'.[81] (The utterances of certain Kashmiri terrorists give vague indications of some kind of training which was given only to the very selected lot).

(f) Bin Laden is reported to have spent well over three million dollars since 1996 in an effort to purchase a nuclear suitcase bomb from FSU.[82]

NUCLEAR TERRORISM

The danger of nuclear terrorism most often brings pictures of a city totally devastated and incinerated by a nuclear bomb. While the focus remains on the problems associated with stolen weapons-grade nuclear materials, particularly those emanating from the former Soviet Union, the greater threat may actually be an attack against a nuclear power plant.

Transport of dangerous nuclear material in the open may well turn out to be the Achilles heel of the nuclear industry, a prime target for terrorist theft.

The magnitude of a single attack could reach beyond 100,000 deaths and the immediate loss of tens of billions of dollars. The land and property destroyed would remain useless for decades and would become a stark monument reminding the world of the terrorist's ideology. With more than 100 reactors in the United States alone, if one is successfully destroyed, just threatening additional attacks could instill the sort of high-impact terror, which is being sought by a new breed of terrorists. (Web Site: Three Mile Island Alert Security Committee).

Beyond doubt, nuclear plants remain the 'Achilles Heel' in any nation's security. Imagine a terrorist attack on a nuclear plant supported by helicopters. Blackmail would be their strategy with no insurance guarantees. As per web site on *'Threats and Sabotage of Nuclear Material'*, the following is listed:

(a) World Trade Centre terrorists threatened to attack "nuclear targets" with 150 suicide soldiers.
(b) World Trade Centre terrorists training camp and mock assault on an electrical substation 30 miles from Three Mile Island.
(c) New Radio programme on nuclear plant terrorism via *"Real Audio"* (Select Program Archives-1/28/97) and "Art Bell Talk Radio".
(d) The "Truck Bomb" problem. A large bomb exploding off site can initiate a meltdown.

(e) Emergency declared at Three Mile Island when station wagons crashed into the plant and the intruder could not be found.
(f) The "Insider" problem and previous acts of sabotage.
(g) $10,000 reward for arrest and conviction of saboteur at the St. Lucie nuclear power plant on 14 August 1996.
(h) Was sabotage involved in the 1979 Three Mile Island emergency? Some of the original investigators suspected foul play.

Accordingly, the Report of the International Task Force on Prevention of Nuclear Terrorism offered the following short-term recommendations for the protection of nuclear facilities:

(a) Denial of access to nuclear facilities should be the basic consideration in protection against sabotage.
(b) Thorough vigilance against the insider threat is needed.
(c) Guard forces should be thoroughly trained and authorised to use deadly force.
(d) The basic idea used for designing physical protection of nuclear plants should be reviewed to ensure that it accurately reflects the current threat.
(e) Power reactors should be protected against vehicular threats.
(f) Research reactors should have adequate security provisions against terrorists.
(g) Reactor safety designs should be re-examined to protect against an accident caused by terrorists.
(h) IAEA (International Atomic Energy Agency) physical protection guidelines should be reviewed and updated.
(j) Protection standards should be spelt out unambiguously.

In the aftermath of the Chernobyl disaster event the average person has become familiar with the meaning of "reactor – core meltdown." Such an event, in which a reactor deprived of its temperature-controlling coolant melts in its own heat and produces lethal clouds of radioactive gases, could be an objective of future terrorism. Significantly, as we shall see, incidents involving violence or threats of violence at nuclear facilities at home and abroad are already a matter of record.

In comparison with a low-yield nuclear explosion, a reactor-core meltdown and breach of containment would release a small amount of radiation. However, the consequences of such an event would still involve leakage of an immense amount of gaseous radioactive material that could expose neighbouring populations to immediate death, cancer, or genetic defects. To better understand the nature of the threat, we must first try to understand the fundamentals of nuclear reactors.

Essentially, these reactors may be characterised as giant tea-kettles that turn water into steam. The steam is piped to large turbines that turn generators. When a typical teakettle is operating at full power, the radioactivity in its fuel core can reach 17 billion curies, enough, in principle to kill everyone on the planet. Within the uranium fuel rods in the core, the fission reaction can unleash energy to drive the temperature above 4,000 degrees Fahrenheit – a temperature hot enough to melt through all protective barriers.

In assessing the dangers of nuclear power reactors, one of the reports said an extremely serious accident (which would closely resemble sabotage in its effects) to produce 3,300 deaths, 45,000 instances of early illness; 240,000 thyroid nodules over a 30-year period and 30,000 genetic defects over 150 years. Additionally, the economic loss that would result from contamination over an area of 3,200 square miles was estimated at $14 billion.

Radiological Weapons

Radiological weapons are not as widely understood as nuclear explosives, but they are equally ominous in their effects. Placed in the hands of terrorists, such weapons could pose a lethal hazard for human beings anywhere in the world. Even a world already dominated by every variety of weapons could not fail to recoil from such a prospect. Radiological weapons are devices designed to disperse radioactive materials that have been produced a substantial time before their desired effect. The targets against which terrorists might choose to use radiological weapons include concentrations of people on urban streets or at sports events, urban areas with a high population density as a whole, and agricultural areas. The weapons might be in the form of a plutonium dispersal device (only 3.5 ounces of plutonium could prove lethal to everyone within a large office building or factory) or devices designed to disperse other radioactive materials. In principle, the dispersal of spent nuclear reactor fuel and the fission products separated from reactor fuels would create grave hazards in any populated area, but the handling of such materials itself would be very dangerous to terrorists themselves. It is more likely, therefore, that would be users of radiological weapons would favour plutonium over radioactive fission products.

The threat of nuclear terrorism involving radiological weapons is potentially more serious than the threat involving nuclear explosive. This is because it would be easier for terrorists to achieve nuclear capability with radiological weapons. Such weapons, therefore, could also be the subject of a more plausible hoax than nuclear explosives. An institutional base for such cooperation has already been established and promoted in the mid-1980s specifically to allow super powers to coordinate against third party nuclear threats. U.S. should also encourage and assist its key allies for dealing with nuclear incidents.

Could Terrorists Build a Bomb?

Supply of fissile material is the key issue. With sufficient fissile material it is possible to build a backyard crude nuclear bomb working on the principle of 'Gun-Type' or the 'Little Boy Type;[83] and most probably it may require some kind of state sponsorship.

In sum, there is considerable public knowledge about relatively simple nuclear weapons and, thus, they are within reach of terrorists. In fact even a dead weapon or a fizzle yield could still serve the desired terrorist aim.[84] Beyond doubt, leakage of expertise can contribute to nuclear terrorism, as everything is available in the nuclear bazaar. This may have the following impact:

- State supported terrorists might be able to build more sophisticated devices. Through the leakage of expertise, terrorists may have in effect drawn the resources of the nuclear complex of former Soviet Union.
- The weapons can be delivered through missiles already procured by Pan-Islamic terrorist groups or even through clandestine infiltration operations, in the hinterland of India like Bangalore, Delhi or even in countries like Sri Lanka.
- Smuggling of fissionable material in India is not difficult at all, if the same is possible in the USA.[85]
- X-rays and metal detectors cannot defeat HEU.

The small sophisticated design is one with a diameter of about one or two feet and weight of about a 100 pounds or about 50 kgs. Approximately, very little fissile material is required. Conceivably oxide powder could be used or may be one might choose to go through the chemical operation of reducing it to metal. Such a process may take a few days and would require specialised equipment and techniques.[86] There are many views on the feasibility of such systems. In the scenario as obtained in the region such designs would require state support and individual groups may not be able to construct.

On the other hand, feasibility study of a crude design only confirms the simplicity with which such a weapon can be made by terrorists, who can pay exorbitant money or even blackmail a scientist for doing the task. Therefore one has to keep a watch rather than overrule the possibility completely.

Proliferation: Case Study of Pakistan

The existing nuclear export controls have their own loopholes and it is very difficult to prevent pilferage and proliferation. The following counter-proliferation measures exist :

- Non-Proliferation Treaty (NPT).
- Cartel Nuclear Supplier Group (NSG).
- Group of Experts Working under Wassenar Arrangement.
- The cornerstone of current nuclear exports is an agreement among the nuclear suppliers, with a view to subjecting themselves to audit through the above mentioned arrangements. However, these controls have really failed to check proliferation of dual-use items, which can thus be used for WMD weapons.
- Another aspect to the problem of leakage of NBC technology is the reality of a clandestine trade interconnected with drugs and arms dealing. The most famous case is that of Albrecht Migule, a West German businessman who shipped a nuclear plant to Pakistan in sixty-two truckloads and also provided a team of West German engineers to supervise its construction. (compiled from open literature). The facility processes natural uranium into easily gassified Uranium Hexa-Fluoride so that it can be enriched for possible use in nuclear arms. Thus, this programme as we look in retrospective was a critical building block in Pakistan's nuclear weapons programme (unlike many other smugglers), Migule was tried and convicted for exporting the $ 6 million plant to Pakistan in 1985. He was fined only $10,000 and an eight-month suspended sentence. This facility is presently operating in the town of Dera Ghazi Khan. Similarly in 1997, Dutch automobile transmission manufacturer provided hardened steel to Pakistan for high-speed centrifuge at Kahuta.
- The above mentioned has been visualised earlier. Recently, Pakistan has accepted the fact of proliferation by Abdul Quadir, the so-called father of Pakistan's nuclear bomb.

CHEMICAL AND BIOLOGICAL (CB) TERRORISM

Past Threat or Use of CB Agents

Contemporary terrorism is replete with examples of the threat and use of chemical and biological agents:

1974-American President Threatened

The "Alphabet Bomber" mailed a toxin material to a justice of the US Supreme Court threatening to kill the American President with nerve gas.

1978-Economic Losses

A Middle East terrorist group poisoned Israeli oranges with cyanide, resulting in severe economic losses to Israel.

1979-Bio-Attack Losses

In an accidental outbreak of anthrax amongst the local community of Sverdlovsk in former Soviet Union, only four to one milligrams of spores were released. This resulted in deaths between 400 to 1200 people.

1984-Making Toxin

The Parisian police arrested a member of the Baader Meinhof gang for growing a culture (Lostridium Botulinum) to produce Botulinum toxin in a home laboratory. The Rajneesh cult was accused of poisoning 750 people by contaminating salad bars with salmonella in restaurants, near Antelope, Oregon, to influence the outcome of local elections.

1984-Industrial Disaster

The accidental release of 30 tons of Methyl Isocyanate at the Union Carbide plant in Bhopal killed 6000 people and maimed another 10,000.

1991-Chemical Agents

German authorities foiled a neo-Nazi plot to pump hydrogen cyanide into a synagogue.

1992-Toxic Biological Agent

FBI arrested two persons of the Patriot Council in Minnesota for possession of less than one milligram of Ricin, a highly toxic biological agent.

1995-Chemical Attack

The Japanese Cult, Aum Shinrikyo, released sarin nerve gas in a Tokyo subway killing 12 and injuring 122 persons. Earlier, on 21 June 1994, seven people died and 200 were taken sick by sarin fumes in nearby town of Matsumoto. Evidence is now available that the members of the cult had undertaken a $.300 million-$1 billion research into the 0157:H7 variant of E. Coli. Cult scientists even visited Kikwit in Congo to obtain samples of the dreaded Ebola virus.

1996-Biological Terrorism

A former Aryan nation member was arrested in the US for

mail-ordering three vials of bubonic plague under a false lab code number.

In Scotland, during a genetic engineering experiment, a small quantity of the toxin E. Coli, was accidentally released. This led to an outbreak of food poisoning resulting in the death of more than a dozen people.

The sarin attacks in Japan by a group of religious fanatics have shown terrorists an easy way to attract an alternative media and government attention, with a relatively simple, easy to produce and difficult to control, act of terror through use of chemical agents with a very high SCCD factor.

Advances in chemistry and particularly the widespread use of toxic chemicals as herbicides besides the actual chemical themselves, their precursors, are also freely available. In 1996, an Austrian chemist was arrested for attempting to supply DFP (A weak nerve agent) in the black market. Chemical material would be easier to obtain, work with, adopt into weapons, hide and transport to the point of use. Compared with a fairly crude nuclear bomb, chemicals could well do more damage. Building a primitive nerve gas bomb basically involves little more than filling a large tank with a chemical agent to surround an explosive, which, in turn is linked to detonating circuit. Producing chemicals would impose safety and supply problems but none, which cannot be easily overcome. Chemical agents can also be used to contaminate water bodies such as ponds, lakes, and streams.

Covert use of these chemical agents may lead to mass destruction of civil population. These acts of terrorism could take either of the following forms:[87]

(a) A terrorist/religious fanatic group resorting to use of small-scale release of toxic chemicals to cause panic/damage to population or put pressure on the government.
(b) A group of organisations being supported by our adversaries in their secessionist/terrorist activity using relatively larger chemical weapons covertly either in depth areas to cause damage to civilian population or even in areas where downwind hazard affect the armed forces. Thus, if timed, at the time of operation, it can be used to great operational and tactical advantages.

Ron Purver, a strategic analyst for the Canadian Security Service, cautions that a number of hate and cult groups have also emerged threatening to use chemical and biological agents.[88]

Thus, these acts of terrorism, which may or may not be state sponsored, may lead to disasters varying in magnitude, depending upon the method used and their intention. Disasters could also be due to accidental release of chemicals from a chemical industry or leakage of vapours/ liquid during transportation of toxic chemicals. There is therefore a need to formalise response to a chemical disaster taking place due to either an accident in a chemical industry or occurring due to chemical terrorism. Terrorists may find one or a combination of any of the following to achieve their overall aim:

(a) Causing death, injury or incapacitation to either a selected segment of population or random.
(b) Threat of using chemical agents as a tool for political bargaining to obtain a favourable situation.
(c) Psychological effect as a result of above.
(d) Causing economic retardation for short period by selecting targets like trade/economic structures.
(e) Causing panic, rumours and thereby general turmoil amongst population and administrative machinery. Repeated use of chemical agents dispersed in time and space can lead towards discrediting of security forces and administrative set up.

WMD Measures

The use of WMD by ultra terrorists is a reality and cannot be ruled out. Intelligence gathering, strict domestic regulations, public and professional awareness are the key to deter terrorists and protect our society. In this regard, the Centre and States have a leading role to play by creating appropriate structures and mechanisms. Forewarned is fore armed.

As has already been narrated, blistering, choking, blood and nerve agents are all threats. However, the threat of biological terrorism is on the ascendance as revolution in biotechnology has been intensified. Biological weapons introduce a foreign bacteria or virus into an environment that is not prepared to defend itself from the intruder. Thus this foreign agent penetrates to kill plants, livestock, pets and human. These could be delivered in a most unobtrusive and innocuous manner, through the following means:

Inanimate Objects. In the Syrian Embassy in France, a man had approached a Syrian high official with a chemically coated Koran. The official could not suspect this innocent and faithful looking Koran.

Aerosol. It amounts to 'air spraying' with a pump or a gun. It can also be a *'hair spray'* type of device.

Projectiles. With the advent of the Internet, it is now possible to make home-made mortar rounds or even projectiles.

Umbrella Weapon. This weapon looking like an umbrella can shoot projectiles as tiny pellets made of n4ine-tenth platinum and one-tenth iridium.

The likely targets for such attacks could be:

Crowded Transit Places: In such public places the damage will be maximum due to gatherings at peak hours while the security may be minimum. These are:

(a) Railway stations, bus stands, underground shopping centres, cinema halls.
(b) Underground metros, subways and tunnels.
(c) Air-conditioned trains.
(d) Trade centres, stock exchanges, crowded market places, exhibition grounds like Pragati Maidan halls, etc.
(e) Centrally cooled large buildings.
(f) Areas of political power (Parliament house, secretariat and headquarters).
(g) Water supplies system and large reservoirs.
(h) Sabotage of hazardous and fire sensitive industries like the Bhopal Gas Plant, etc.
(i) Air-conditioned marketing plazas.

Biological Threats

Biological agents like toxins (such as Botulinum toxin or Ricin) or live pathogens (anthrax) are more potent on a weight-for-weight basis than chemical agents, since they replicate and multiply in their victims. According to biologists, there is a factor of about one million between the quantity of typical BW agents needed to kill a person and those of typical chemical agents.

High lethality and toxicity of biological agents is spectacular. Botulinal Toxin (BTX) has a mean lethal dose of a few tenths of a microgram. This equates to the lethality of nuclear explosion in terms of potential casualties caused. According to one estimate, half an ounce of BTX, which is more deadly than nerve gas, can be produced for about $ 500 per kilogram. According to informed sources, the comparative cost of production for inflicting large scale casualties by different weapon systems per square kilometre is as under:

• Conventional weapons	-	$ 600
• Nuclear weapon	-	$ 2400
• Nerve gas	-	$ 1800
• BW agent	-	$ 3

BW agents can attack even crops and livestock and this may appear as natural disasters. The present set up in India is inadequate to deal with such situations. They are dispersed at night and thus conceal the identity of the terrorist, while the cool temperature enhances the effectiveness of the biological agent. Ultra violet rays would only degrade its efficacy. Thus, there is a requirement of biological detectors to be placed at sea ports and international airports. Present RDX detection capability through sniffer dogs is not enough.

Some Observations on the Dangers

Chemical agents are easily available. They are easy to produce in a home laboratory by trained chemists especially in a country having a vast industrial base like India, China or even Pakistan. The UK and US have declassified and published the formula for VX nerve gas, a manufacturing technique similar to insecticides. The availability of toxic dual-purpose chemicals like phosgene and hydrogen cyanide, as well as toxic industrial chemicals like methyl isocyanate (which killed 6,000 people in Bhopal in 1984), makes the task of chemical terrorists easy. The ballpoint pen is chemically one step away from sarin.

Unlike BW, chemical agents are "controllable" and can be manufactured, purchased, stolen or obtained from foreign sponsors. Their effective dissemination is however very crucial. A rough thumb rule indicates that one ton (four 55 gallons drums) of agent is necessary to contaminate one square mile of territory. Nevertheless, this should not pose a serious problem to determined terrorists, since chemical agents can be effectively employed in confined spaces with much less quantities of agents. Crude atomizers and portable aerosol generators, like the one used for insecticide spraying, will disperse the chemical effectively.

As a result of the programme for de-nuclearisation in the former Soviet Union, there are about 500 metric tons of U-235 and 300 tons of U-239 from dismantled weapons that has to be disposed off. This is the equivalent of 60,000 nuclear weapons. There are also several reports regarding attempts to smuggle special nuclear materials like plutonium and lithium. The number of cases of illicit traffic in nuclear or radioactive materials more than doubled in 1994, to 124 from 56 in 1993 and 53 in 1992. Of these, 77 cases involved uranium and plutonium. A virtual 'nuclear black market' has come up.

The conventional view that construction of a nuclear weapon is beyond the capabilities of individuals and terrorist organisations is questionable. With the availability of smuggled fissionable nuclear material in the hands of 'scientist-terrorist', it may not be improbable to make a crude nuclear bomb. Students are expected to pay fees between $ 5,000 and $ 30,000 for a project.

The use of CB agents and cyber terrorism is not a question of "if", rather, it is matter of "when". In our context, the employment of micro mini nukes is still remote. However, the likelihood of a nuclear accident is relatively more real. In the interim, RDX, the Rolls Royce of all explosives, will continue to be the primary weapon. Meanwhile, attacks by cyber terrorists cannot be disregarded.

Proliferation of biological agents and use of biotechnology for military or terrorist purpose is an issue of concern. Such technologies will make warfare anonymous and essentially dangerous for human civilisation. The covert delivery of such systems would be very easy. Even terrorist carrying such agents cannot be detected by the current international detection systems at international airports. Therefore, a massive funding is required towards this end.

The most portentous application of such a warfare would be on the available water systems on earth. A focus on this issue is a must, as it would be the biggest challenge to humanity in the millennium.

The threat of poisoning water, advertently or inadvertently is only increasing. Some recent cases in this regard are:

(i) Cryptosporiduirn outbreak in Milwaukee, US, in 1993 - 4,00,000 casualties 111 fatalities.

(ii) Osaka 1996 - E. Coli infection in 1957 - 3 fatalities.

(iii) Bangladesh 1998- widespread arsenic poisoning from drinking water.

(iv) Sri Lanka Tigers 1980 - Group threatened to wage warfare against government by:

  (a) Sending qualified volunteers to bring material, cultures and infected water through snails to spread river blindness in canals and reservoirs.

  (b) Bring infected material and mosquitoes to spread yellow fever in Sri Lanka where the carrier was already present.

  (c) Poisoning of the army water supplies in northern and eastern Sri Lanka.

1991 - Canada. Authorities received a letter threatening to pollute supply of Kelowna town (Br. Columbia) with bacterial contaminant, apparently linked to the 1990-1991 Gulf War.

1996 - Gungxi Province, China. 200 students needed emergency treatment after the well serving the school's kitchen was intentionally contaminated with toxic chemicals.

1994 - Khmer Rouge Forces (Thailand). A dozen soldiers died after drinking water from streams and ponds poisoned by opposition forces.

Because pathogens are normally found in raw water sources,

epidemiologists would have problems detecting the difference between a natural and artificial attack. There are no tools to predict exactly what substance amongst the thousands of known toxins an attacker might choose. But the range of contaminants can be selected from the most toxic/infectious substances available because they can easily be diluted to very minute levels (less than 1 ppm) and still incapacitate or kill.

The point of entry of any contaminant to a water system is likely to have a major impact on any sabotage attempt. If the contaminant is introduced prior to the water treatment, it is more likely to be filtered and disinfected, thus eliminating most of it. If its entry is into the treated water, most organic and inorganic contaminants will be oxidised by the residual chlorine, and this depletes the residual chlorine. Detection might then occur because chlorine concentration levels are carefully monitored in public water supplies for potability.

A number of 'bio and chemical' agents are capable of surviving in treated (chlorinated) water, which includes some very potent ones, like anthrax, microcryptin, and cryptosporidium. Moreover contaminant can be injected downstream of the monitoring point. Bioengineering techniques can create chlorine resistant strains of organisms, or attempt micro-encapsulation techniques to defeat chlorinating and chlorine depletion monitoring.

Chlorine is the most widely used method of disinfecting water. Agents against which chlorine is ineffective include, anthrax, tularaemia, microcryptin, cyanobacterial toxins, saxitoxins, tricothecene mycotoxins, sporulated bacteria, bio-engineered strains, giardia and cryptosporidi. In fact, a scenario where the agent is added to the water distribution system along with the chlorine-neutralising agent is also possible. This would permit a wider range of agents. Other disinfection techniques are microfilteration, ozone and UV light.

Bio-threat Detection Capability

France's defense ministry has chosen Thales technology to enable its forces to detect a wide range of biological threats.

Operational systems for detecting biological threats will be developed and supplied by Thales Industrial Systems to the French armed forces following a contract announced early this year. Thales has been building on its expertise in defense against nuclear, biological and chemical (NBC) attacks since 1990.

Thales NBC protection systems are already operational in both France and Italy. Other European countries are expected to adopt the same sophisticated technology soon. Because Thales has adopted an open-architecture and modular approach in its systems that address NBC readiness, system capability can be easily upgraded. We can also start developing protection models on the same parameters. The post '9-11' strike was followed by many Anthrax attacks. The Americans have been alleging that the Russians have a very large bio weapons programme, which could proliferate into the hands of non-state actors.

The Anthrax Story

- Soviet Union has a sprawling biological weapons capability (Boris Yelstin signed a decree in April 1992 promising to comply with the convention).
- Ken Alibak (defected to US in 1992) reported that the Russian bio-plant employed 70,000 people. Among the achievements was development of anthrax, which is resistant to anti-biotics.

"Sheltered" Bio Analysis

As early as 1990, European countries began work on ways of shielding or sheltering an analysis vehicle from possible NBC contamination as its defense teams analyse the environment and determine the next decontamination steps to be taken.

Prospects for NBC Terrorism : Psychological Motivations and Constraints

Comprehensive analysis of the prospects for NBC terrorism deals with two aspects viz technological and psychological. Most of the research work available on the subject deals with the former like quoted in the study 'Nuclear Theft: Risks and Safeguards' by Mason Willriah and Theodore Taylor, prepared for the energy policy project of the Ford Foundation. The authors have provided rigorous material for the technology part but have failed to address the psychological part and motivations.

Brian Jenkins, a noted specialist, observes that historical record does not show that terrorists have tried to acquire WMD weapons and that they are housing a philosophy of mass destruction for their cause. But this conclusion is not realistic as there is lot of territory between irrationality and rationality leading to a 'Psycho-logic' phenomenon, which itself can be sub-categorised to individual psychology, group psychology and organisational psychology. The pressures on these groups externalise to justify their existence and

Fig. 3.3.

Motivations for Groups with Chemical and Biological Substances

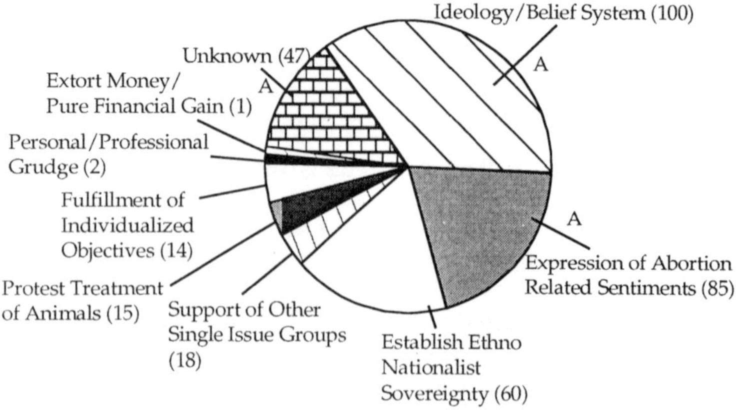

Source: WMD Terrirism by Amy Smithson and further developed with own perceptions.

to draw public gaze. If the terrorist group does not commit acts of terrorism it looses its meaning. However, the dichotomy remains that if the terrorist uses WMD as a means, it may lose its Robin Hood image and win public distaste and severe repercussions. Similarly, the WMD could be used more optionally as a blackmail mechanism rather than cause mass casualties. This aspect therefore should become an important ingredient to counter terrorist strategy. However, in the South Asian scenario, the Islamic Jehadi backed terrorist may find use of WMD more cost effective, provided it is used in a localised area or as a bargaining ground for blackmailing. The figure 3.3 above shows the perceptions of motivational level in a 360 degree arc. These impressions are transposed in consonance with Amy Smithson's (noted NBC terrorism research scholar with Stimson Research Centre, USA) ideas and work. As can be seen, the group, which is most prone, is 'ideological/ belief' type and the segment least prone is the 'personal/professional grudge' type. In the Indian subcontinent environment we have to be looking for the 'Ethno-Nationalist Sovereignty' type, who compose about 17 per cent of the segment.

Analysing the terrorism trends from the historical context and upto the modern era, brings out the fundamental truth that the basic nature and ingredients are same but in the post cold war era, there appears to be a partial transition to both fundamental type inter-civilisation and intra-civilisation clashes as well as the ongoing ethnic sub-nationalistic movement, more so due to the impact of post-colonial dynamics in this region. Moreover, the impact of globalisation and the 'RMA', is causing the phenomenon of 'RTA', which may well suggest possibility and use of WMD.

With empowerment of citizens, rising aspirations, the suffusion of consumerism and easy availability of dual-use technology, we are going to see the emergence of "techno-terrorists", who will resort to sophisticated means of violence to hurt society by use of WMD. Nuclear terrorism and the use of chemical and biological agents are commonly bracketed as weapons of mass destruction. To this can be added cyber terrorism and eco-terrorism.

One can amplify this aspect further, as the concept of no war in its classic Clausewitzian form becomes increasingly irrelevant. We are going to experience greater frequency in sub-conventional forms of conflict. In the event war does occur, the adversary could resort to the use of WMD through terrorists and information warfare weapons. It is in order for an adversary to employ covertly hired terrorist organisations or even its Special Forces as force multipliers, to support attacks during the command and control and critical infrastructure destruction phase, the purpose being to cause strategic dislocation. For example, the efficacy of terrorism as a state instrument may fetch more results than conventional high technology. (For instance, critical analysis of conventional operations in Kosovo have opened the debate of relevancy and method of such operations. These may have been less catastrophe oriented had they been planned by employing cyber, information, and covert terrorist operations, even hired, who would have pin pointedly addressed and neutralised command and control structure without collateral damage including loss of life).

In the Indian subcontinental situation, Pan-Islamic religious groups who are state supported would develop 'affiliation' with such weapons. A general analysis by Amy Smithson, when transposed in the environment as obtained here would increase the possibility of the usage by such religious groups manifold. (Fig. 3.4).

Fig. 3.4.

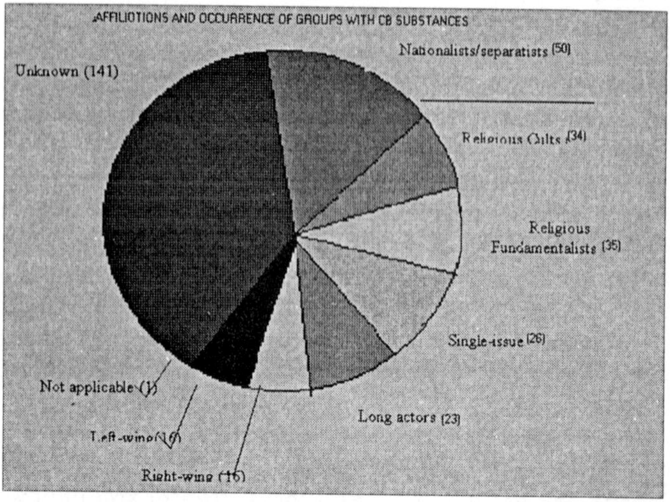

Source: WMD Terrorism by Amy Smithson. developed further with own perceptions.

Global Terrorism: Hotspots

"We see the rise of religious fanaticism millennial or apocalyptic cults and the potential for use of mass casualty weapons. Need for ever-largest bang being felt by terrorists, to get or maintain desired levels of publicity. Consequently, we worry considerably about the potential for terrorist use of NBC weapons. The Rajneeshis in Oregon, Aum Shinrikyo in Tokyo, and the Chechens in Moscow contribute immensely to these fears." (Table 3.1)

The views of likelihood of WMD terrorist attacks in the near future are as tabulated :

Use of WMD Terrorism: Views of Experts

- Robert Kupperman (1997)—High Consequence, Low probability.
- Brian Jenkins (Rand 1982)—Emerging scenario of WMD terrorism.
- Jeffrey D. Simon (Rand Dec 1989)—Most likely Bio-Terrorism
- Yonah Alexander, Phil Baum and Rapheal Denziger— "Terrorism, Future Threats and Responses", possible.
- Jeremiah Denton—"International Terrorism: the Nuclear Dimension", possible.
- Paul Leventhol, Yonah Alexander (eds)—Preventing Nuclear Terrorism: Report of the International Task Force and Prevention Nuclear terrorism, possible.

Table 3.1: Global Terrorism Hotspots

	Geographic Location		*Level of Terrorism*			*Remarks*
Place	*Country*	*Location*	*Extreme*	*High*	*Moderate*	
Algeria	Algeria	Africa	✔	—	—	
Somalia	Somalia	Africa	✔			
Sudan	Sudan	Africa	✔			
Doula/Yaounde	Cameroon	Africa	✔			
Lebanon	—	West Asia	✔			
Iraq	Iraq	West Asia	—	✔	—	Kurdish Rebels
Afghanistan	Afghanistan	Central Asia	✔			Taliban/OBL WMD tendency.
Jaffna	Sri Lanka	South Asia	✔			LTTE Cadres
Kashmir	India	South Asia	—	✔		JKLF, Mujahideens-Pakistan, etc. sponsored WMD tendency
North Eastern States	India	South Asia	—	—	✔	NSCN(IM), NSCN(K), ULFA, BODO groups.
Myanmar	Myanmar	South East Asia	✔		✔	
Indonesia	Indonesia	South East Asia	—	—	✔	

(Contd.)

Place	Geographic Location		Level of Terrorism			Remarks
	Country	Location	Extreme	High	Moderate	
Kosovo	Yugoslavia	Europe	✓	—	—	Most extreme. Even if the war stops, the KLA would become more active. WMD tendencies
Venezuela	Venezuela	South America	—	—	✓	
Chechnya	CAR	Russia	✓	—	—	WMD Tendencies
Colombia	Colombia	South America	—	—	✓	
North America	America	America	—	—	—	Under terrorist threats from Islamic groups. Use of NBC/ WMDs cannot be ruled out.

Note: The gradation of terrorist infested continent is Africa, Asia, Europe and America. However, Pan-Islamic 'Ultra Terrorists' armed with NBC – WMD are gathering to threaten America in the new millennium.

Empirics of Nuclear Leakages

Finally an empirical analysis has been carried out to ascertain the leakage of WMD material and their impact. At this instance a case study of FSU/Russia has been carried out to drive home the point of pilferage/ loss and the exact cause of potential danger:

Lots of effort have been put recently to ensure plugging of leakage. The total stockpile is given below:

- Total estimated stock of plutonium (PL) – 200 tons—Can make 40,000 bombs.
- Total estimated stock of HE-uranium-800-1,200 tons—Can make 40,000-50,000 bombs.

The sources of leakage are as given below:

- First Leakage Source – Russian stockpile – controlled by MOD of nuclear weapons (15,000-2000 developed weapons)
- Second leakage source-controlled leakage source—stockpile of – Russian weapons grade Ministry of Fissile Material Atomic Energy growing. Extracted (MINATOM) from destroyed weapons and produced at Atomic Plant (dismantling 1,000 weapons per year).
- Third leakage controlled by source – MINATOM has custody of an enormous amount of Fissile Material produced by nuclear reactors .
- Fourth Leakage – research institutes – other/agencies.[89]
- Note: Second category-most pilferage prone due to lack of infrastructure.

Now let us recount six instances of leakage[90] and their impact:

1. Lunch Case (Scientific Production Association	Employee (1992)	Stole 3.7 Pounds HEU
2. Murmank (shipyard)	Russian Navy Officer (1993)	Stole unused nuclear submarine fuel
3. Tengen (Germany)	Counter Feiter (1994)	5.56 gms of Super grade PL
4. Landshut (Germany)	Sting ops (1994)	0.8 gms of HEU
5. Munich	Airport (1994)	Pu239
6. Prague	Scientists (1994)	6 Pounds HEY

- If 3000 weapons are being dismantled at the rate of upto four sites per year, and if every weapon has an average 10 pounds of PL and 30 pounds HEU, another 15 tons of PL and 45 tons of HEU are being added every year. Add to MINATOM'S fissile material stockpile, which amounts to 75 tons of PL or 625 tons HEU.[91] (Transportation, connecting the Russian nuclear installation is a complicated transportation system). This is a huge number and requires super management.

As discussed there could be eight reasons as to why nuclear leakage will only worsen:

- Disorder in Russia.
- Widespread criminalisation in Russian society.
- Coherence and effectiveness of public institutions has broken.
- Size and complexity of Russians nuclear infrastructure.
- Out of stockpile maintained each year about 10 per cent returned to installation, through rail network that links the facilities to the Russian archipelago.
- Economic plight of individuals is forcing them to get into this lucrative trade.
- Dismantlement of nuclear plants.
- Erosion of Soviet security system.

The point is that, it may not really be possible to seal loss or theft of such material, which can go into the hands of non-state players and terrorists. In the situation as prevailing in the Afghanistan-Pakistan-Kashmir corridor terrorists, or to be more precise, Osama's men or groups may be already in possession of such dangerous material. That is what should be a global worry.

WMD Threat : Indian Experience

In the Indian experience of WMD threats, one cannot rule out a 'State sponsored terrorist threat'. Some of the scenarios that one can build are:

- ***Scenario 1: Nuclear Blackmail.*** Terrorist have placed a 'suitcase nuke' somewhere in Delhi or Bombay and pass an ultimate that in case India does not vacate Kashmir by a set time, it would explode the same through a suicide bomber.
- ***Scenario 2 : Nuclear Strike by Terrorism.*** In this scenario, there may not be any blackmail but an actual strike, with a threat of more strikes, unless India complies.
- ***Scenario 3 : 'CB' Strike.*** In this scenario *'CB'* cocktail is used in the forward line against SF as a tactical weapon or used in civil areas as a strategic weapon, causing psychological dislocation of the civil government.

The government in turn should anticipate any of these scenarios and design their counter-strategy, on the lines as articulated below.

The draft 'Indian Nuclear Doctrine' already lays down, as per para 10, that the fundamental purpose of Indian nuclear weapons is to deter the use and threat of use of nuclear weapons by any (state or entity) against India and its Forces, and that India will not be the first to strike but will respond with punitive retaliation should deterrence fail. This would imply that if any entity or the state, i.e., non-state players undertake such a strike, then it would be deemed that the state, which is supporting these non-state players, would be held responsible. Therefore, this clause is self-explanatory. However, an amplification may be required whenever, the existing draft nuclear doctrine is reviewed. Therefore, logically, for scenarios 2 and 3, India should respond with a commensurate punitive strike. However, for scenario 1, India should invoke nuclear deterrence in toto, and express further that the known camps of not only the non-state players will be struck but also the state, which is abetting these groups. The provisions of the UN to react and intervene in such scenario should also be spelt out in various counter-terrorist conventions.

References and Notes

1. Prepared statement before the Senate Judiciary Committee and select intelligence committee, 105 Congress 2nd session 22 April 1998. USA.
2. "Message of the Secretary of Defense", in *Proliferation: Threat and Response* (Washington, DC: US Department of Defense, November 1997), III. Cohen's op-cd on the topic was equally ominous. "A plague more MONSTROUS than anything we have experienced could spread with all the irrevocability of ink on tissue paper. Ancient scourges would quickly become modern nightmares". William Cohen, "Preparing for a Grave New World", *Washington Post,* 26 July 1999.
3. Jessica Stern, *The Ultimate Terrorist* (USA : First Harwood University Press, 2000), p. 6.

4. Samuel Huntington, *Clash of Civilization and the Making of the World Order* (New York: Touchstone 1997): see also, Samuel Huntington, Clash of Civilisations, *Foreign Affairs* (Summer 1993).
5. Jessica Stern, n. 3, p.15.
6. Bin-Laden has been demanding withdrawal of American forces from Saudi Arabia. This has given him an alibi to mobilise pro-Muslim support against the Americans.
7. Brij Mohan and AKL Vats, *Global Armegeddon: Emerging Challenges in the New Millennium* (New Delhi : Comcare International Publishers), p. 151.
8. In America there have been more than 600 mock practices, which have been carried out. In India too, there has been an effort in this activity. The civil defence organisation under the Home Ministry is also carrying out plans for mock ups.
9. For instance, the Chiefs of Staff Committee (India) in 1995 had perceived the emergence of a NBC terrorist threat. Similarly, way back, in a 1979 conference Robert Kupperman characterized the prospect of terrorists using chemical, biological, or nuclear weapons as a "high consequence, low probability event." Kupperman's presentation, entitled "Government Response to Mass-Destruction Threats by Terrorists," can be found in *On Terrorism and Combating Terrorism*, ed. Ariel Merari (Frederick, Md.: University Publications of America, 1985), p. 157. See also, Brian Jenkins, ed. *International Conference on Terrorism and Low-Level Conflict* (Santa Monica, Calif.: RAND, 1982); Jeffrey D. Simon, *Terrorists and the Potential Use of Biological Weapons,* Report R-3771-AFMIC (Santa Monica, Calif.: RAND, December 1989); Yonah Alexander, Phil Baum, and Raphael Danziger, "Terrorism: Future Threats and Responses," *Terrorism* 7, no. 4 (1985), pp. 367–410; Bernard Stewart, ed. "State-Sponsored Terrorism: The Threat and Possible Countermeasures," *Terrorism* 8, no. 3 (1986), pp. 253–313; Jeremiah Denton, "International Terrorism: The Nuclear Dimension," *Terrorism* 9, no. 2 (1987) : pp. 113–124; D.V. Segre and J.H. Adler, "The Ecology of Terrorism," *Survival* XV, no. 4 (July/August 1973), pp. 178–83; Paul Leventhal, Yonah Alexander, eds. *Preventing Nuclear Terrorism: Report of the International Task Force on Prevention of Nuclear Terrorism* (Lexington, Mass.: Lexington Books, 1987); Louis René Beres, *Terrorism and Global Security: The Nuclear Threat* (Boulder, Colo.: Westview Press, 1987).
10. Robert Kupperman and Jeff Kamen, *Final Warning: Averting Disaster in the New Age of Terrorism* (New York).
11. Walter Laqueur, "Post Modern Terrorism," *Foreign Affairs* 75, no. 5 (September/October 1996): 34; Richard A. Falkenrath, Robert D. Newman, and Bradley A. Thayer, *America's Achilles' Heel: Nuclear, Biological, and Chemical Terrorism.*
12. For a succinct overview of the roots of terrorism, see Walter Laqueur, *The New Terrorism: Fanaticism and the Arms of Mass Destruction* (Oxford: Oxford University Press, 1999), 8–48. Quoted passage from page 43. According to Laqueur's count, the Red Brigades alone committed approximately 14,000 terrorist acts within a ten year timespan. A more in-depth treatment of the topic can be found in Walter Reich, ed. *Origins of Terrorism: Psychologies, Ideologies, Theologies, States of Mind* (Washington : DC: Woodrow Wilson Center Press, 1998). According to one count, only twelve times in the twentieth century did terrorists cause more than one hundred casualties with a single event or related series of attacks. In 1993,

for instance, ten bombings in less than three hours in Bombay caused 235 casualties. Richard A. Falkenrath, "Confronting Biological and Chemical Terrorism," *Survival* 40, no. 3 (Autumn 1998): 52.

13. When the terrorist record is examined in its totality, it reveals that 20 per cent of the incidents have involved fatalities and in most of those instances the death toll was one or two. Brian M. Jenkins, "Understanding the Link between Motives and Methods" in Brad Roberts (ed.) *Terrorism with Chemical and Biological Weapons Calibrating Risks and Responses',* p. 45.
14. Jenkins, "Understanding the Link," in *Ibid.,* p. 46.
15. Philip B Heymann, *Terrorism and America : A Commonsense Strategy for a Democratic Society* (Cambridge, Mass : MIT Press, 1998), p. 8.
16. Brian Jenkins, n. 13.
17. Poonam Mann, "Fighting Terrorism : Indian and Central Asia" *Strategic Analysis,* Vol. XXIV, No. 11, (February 2001).
18. Bakaeyev Askar, 'International Security and Strategic Environment in context of Problems of Southern and Central Asia', Second Indo-Central Asian Seminar, organised by Institute of Defence Studies and Analysis September 11-12, 2000.
19. Poonam Mann, n. 17, p. 2040.
20. *Ibid.,* p. 2038.
21. Lt Gen (Retd) Kamal Matinuddin, *The Taliban Phenomenon: Afghanistan 1994-1997* (Karachi: Oxford University Press, 1999), p. 217.
22. Rohan Gunaratna, 'Terrorist threat target Asia' , *Janes Intelligence Review,* July 2000 : www.Janes.com, p. 39.
23. Jessica Stern, n. 3, p. 7.)
24. In an article, 'Terrorism and Shape of Things to Come' (Future of Terrorism) p. 1.
25. Francis. H. Marlo, WMD terrorism and US intelligence Collection, *Terrorism and Political violence,* Vol. II, No. 3 (Autumn 1955), pp. 53-71.
26. *Ibid.,* p. 55.
27. Alex P Schemed, "Terrorism and the Use of Weapons of Mass Destruction: From where the Risk?", *Future of Terrorism,* p. 106.
28. *Ibid.,* p. 107.
29. Ashton B. Carter, John M. Deutch and Philip D. Zelikow, *Catastrophic Terrorism: Elements of a National Policy,* Stanford Harvard Preventive Defence Project No. 1, No. 6 (Stanford Calif., Stanford University; Cambridge, Mass: Harvard University, 1998).
30. Statement of FBI Director Louis J. French, US Senate, Committee on appropriations, Special Bill on counter terrorism, 105th Cong, 1st Sees, 13 May 1997 (Washington, DC: US Government Printing Office, 1998), p. 16.
31. Testimony of George J. Tenet, US Senate, Select Committee on Intelligence, *Hearing on Current and Projected National Security Threats,* 105th Cong., 2nd scss., 28 January (Washington, DC: US Government Printing Office, 1998), p. 14.
32. Senator Jon Kyl, prepared statement before the Senate Judiciary Committee and Select Intelligence Committee, 105th Cong, 2nd sess., 22 April 1998.
33. Gavin Cameron, *Nuclear Terrorism* (NY : Macmillan Press), pp. 13-14.
34. For example, a terrorist organisation with a clear cut political aim of accession and who have an inner discipline, code of conduct and even a uniform to wear

may fall in the category of being called 'Insurgents'. See definition in Army general service publication, Vol. II, p. 3.

35. Bin-Laden appears to be the focal point of the evolving Pan-Islamic terrorist movements world over. Bin-Laden had made an open statement of launching a jehad against India and even threatened America, calling them an infidel. The Taliban which was created by the CIA to fight the Russian invasion of Afghanistan is now providing the crucible/base for the development of such world wide Islamic movements. Pakistan's claim over Kashmir is now projected by utilisation of such terrorist groups by them.
36. The problem of Naga independence can be traced to the statement of Nehru and Gandhi who had said that their case for independence will be considered later. The sessionist movements within Punjab had similar historical linkages of promised independence.
37. The Indian army has similarly worked on a response mechanism in a worst case scenario. The various civil defence organisations/Intelligence Bureau have thus been initiated into making some kind of a plan.
38. The hijacking drama of an Indian Airlines plane ended with India succumbing to terrorist blackmail of blowing the aircraft lest their demands are met. The aircraft was commandeered to Kandhar in Afghanistan. A similar scenario cannot be ruled out in future. However this time it may be a WMD threat of blowing up a city with a nuclear (suitcase type) bomb, unless the state does not concede to the demands of territory or some great strategic objective, not comprehensible now.
39. In Assam any military operation is swiftly followed by initiation of court cases by ULFA etc, against violation of human rights.
40. Gavin Cameron, n. 33, p. 73.
41. *Ibid,* p. 15.
42. Magnus Ranstorp, *Hizb'allah in Lebanon: The Critics of the Western Hostage Crisis* (London, Macmillan Press 1997). p. 55.
43. Bruce Hoffman, 'The Contrasting Ethical Foundations of Terrorism in the 1980s" *Terrorism and Political Violence,* Vol. 3 (July 1989), p. 398.
44. Mark Juergensmeyr, "The Logic of Religious Violence", in David C. Rapaport (ed.), *Inside Terrorist Organisations* (London: Frank Cass and Company Limited, 1988), p. 183.
45. Rapoport, 'Fear and Trembling', p. 659.
46. Ranstorp, "Terrorism in the name," p. 44.
47. The explanation of the concept of Madrasas for training jehadis is an apt example. Such type of terrorists will not only be more educated but would have both technological and cultural combine to use a higher scale of weapon. Read Ranstorp.
48. Edward Nicholas "Transnational Terrorism." He defines 'Politics of Terrorism' as: "The use or the threat of use, of anxiety-inducing extra- normal violence for political purposes by any individual or group, whether acting for, or in opposition to, established government authority, when such action is intended to influence the attitudes and behaviour of a target group wider than the immediate victims and when through the nationality of foreign ties, its perpetrators."
49. Ajay Darshan Behera, 'Transnational Terrorism: Analysing the Political and Social Economic Undercurrents', Asian Security Seminar held under the aegis of IDSA, New Delhi, 28-30 January 2001, pp. 2-3.

50. *Ibid.*, p. 4.

51. Ivelaw L. Griffith. "From Cold War Geopolitics to Post-Cold War Geonarcotics", International Journal.

52. Gavin Cameron, n. 33, p. 79.

53. *Ibid.*, p. 96.

54. B. David, "The Capability and Motivation of Terrorist Organisations to Use Mass Destruction Weapons", in *On Terrorism and Combating Terrorism,* n. 9, p. 147.

55. The use of biological agents to attack a country's livestock or agricultural sector is particularly useful for the final objective. Listing the first five reasons, the 1999 Catmore panel report, 9 11, Mentioning the first two reasons, as well as the final two. Falkcuratio, Newman, and Thayer, *America's Achilles' Heel,* n. 11, pp. 202-13.

56. Tucker and Sands, "An Unlikely Threat", pp. 49-50; Falkenrath, Newman, and Thayer, *America's Achilles' Heel,* pp. 202-13.

57. One biological weapons expert, Jonathan R Tucker, observed that "The prominent role of plagues (including anthrax) in the Bible suggests that millenarian groups could potentially resort to biological weapons to help bring about Armageddon". "Bioterrorism: Threat and Response", pp. 298-99. On page 292 of this essay, one can find comments on the known agents generally as riot control agents. The most commonly known and used riot control agent is tear gas, but other such agents can cause vomiting, salivation, and burning pain in the cyes, skin, and mouth, among other effects. See Frederick R. Sidell, "Weaponry and the Casualty", Frderick K. Sidell, Emost D Takafuji and David K. Franz (ed.) (Washington, DC: Office of the Surgen General, US Department of the Army, 1947) pp. 307-74.

58. Alex P. Sctimid, "Terrorism and the use of Weapons of Mass Destruction: From Where the Risk," *Future of Terrorism,* p. 108.

59. Centre for Strategic and International Studies, *The Nuclear Black Market* (Washington DC; CSIS 1996) p. 4.

60. The internet is already providing the knowledge for making a crude nuclear bomb, which can be made by school children. A discussion on this aspect with Abdul Kalam has confirmed the same possibility.

61. www.WMDterrorism.com

62. The issue has been debated in the security circles and the view appears to be validated. However what will take time is the understanding of technology.

63. Interviews carried out with certain persons. (Primary source of information).

64. Interviews and various reports substantiate this trend.

65. Extensive study has been carried out about their thinking and training. This is a group which in a futuristic scenario may get training in WMD terrorism.

66. There is yet another assessment that these groups may be trained by ISI for nuclear, biological and chemical related tasks.

67. www.wmd terrorism.com Internet report.

68. *Ibid.*, p. 39.

69. The author has operated in counter-terrorist operations in most of the North Eastern part. He has interrogated more than hundred of these insurgents/ terrorists. Most of them have shown linkage to ISI and that many were trained in Afghanistan.

70. Perceptions of prominent Defence analysts have been taken in this regard. Although this may only materialise after a decade or so.
71. Rohan Gunaratna, 'Terrorist threat target Asia' , *Janes Intelligence Review,* (July 2000), www.Janes.com.
72. Syed M. Ibrahaim,' Insurgency in the Chittgang Hill Tracts of Bangladesh' *Aakrosh,* Vol. 3 No. 9, October 2000, p. 37.
73. Nilesh Bhagat, 'Turbulance in Myanmar', *Aakrosh,* Vol. 3, No. 9, (October 2000), p. 82.
74. *Ibid.,* pp. 82-87.
75. Lt. Gen. RK Jasbir Singh, *Indian Defence Yearbook 2002,* p. 212.
76. *Ibid.,* p. 213.
77. *Ibid.,* p. 215.
78. *Ibid.,* p. 216.
79. *Ibid.,* p. 218.
80. Rohan Gunaratna, n. 71, p. 39.
81. Yussuf Bodansky is the Director of the Task Force on Terrorism and unconventional Warfare of the US Congress as well as the world terrorism analyst with the Freeman Centre for Strategic Studies (Houston). In addition the author has interviewed many terrorists, with the courtesy of DG Prisons, Jammu, India. Some of them have mentioned of selective training to selected people.
82. Yussuf Bodansky ("Bin Laden, the man who declared war on America" p. 328) and his followers are very serious about the use of chemical and biological weapons in future terrorist strikes. Already in summer 1998 senior field commanders of the Islamic Front were aware of the availability of chemical weapons and specific contingency plans for their use. This was confirmed by Ahmad Salamah Mabruk, a prominent commander of Zawahiri's Islamic Jehad, who was captured in Azerbaijan and extradited to Egypt in September 1998. Mabruk told his interrogators that bin Laden's World Islamic Front against Jews and Crusaders, of which Islamic Jihad is a member organisation, "has biological and chemical weapons which it intends to use in operations against US and Israeli targets." In April 1999 Mabruk's information was independently confirmed by another Islamist commander based in Western Europe. According to this commander, "these weapons [of mass destruction] have been purchased from East European states and the former Soviet Union" since 1996. The commander stressed that these weapons are already operational and that "plans had been drawn up to distribute quantities of these weapons to elements belonging to the [Islamic] Front in several states for use when necessary against U.S. and Israeli targets in the event of the failure to carry out operations against these targets through the use of explosives and conventional weapons."
83. On required assembly velocities in a gun bomb using HEU see Robert Serber, *The Los Alamos Primer: The First Lectures in how to build on Atomic bomb* (Berkeley: University of [California Press, 1992) pp. 56-57. Also refer to 'Avoiding Nuclear Anarchy' Graham. T. Allison & others, pp. 56-57. In this connection Dr K Santhanam says that though a very crude system can be assembled, it would require some kind of state sponsorship. May be as available in the Indian sub continental environment.
84. For a discussion of the illegal flow of criminal activity across international borders, see Transnational Crime: A new security crime"

in IISS, *Strategic Survey, 1994-1995,* pp. 25-33. The institutionalisation of organised crime is discussed in Phil Williams, "Transnational Criminal Organisations: Strategic Alliances", *Washington Quarterly*.

85. *Ibid.,* pp. 57-72.
86. Paul Levinthol-Yonah Alexander, *Preventing Nuclear Terrorism* published by DC Heath and company/Lexingtar, Massachusetts/Toronto.
87. n. 5, p. 3.
88. n. 7, p. 4.
89. Gratiam T Allison, Owan R. Cote, Jr. Richard A. Falkonrath, Steven E. Miller, *Avoiding Nuclear Anarchy* (Cambridge, Massachusetts, 2001), pp. 21-22.
90. *Ibid.,* pp. 24-26.
91. Own estimates.

Four

The Theory of Counter Strategy to Terrorism (Including WMD)

It is a known fact that from early 1970s Pakistan had organised terrorism through ISI, mainly against India. This support got diverted towards Afghanistan after its occupation by the erstwhile USSR. This created a great *'strategic'* advantage in India's favour, but concurrently, it also helped improve the *'ISI'* terrorism structure against Afghanistan with CIA help. When the erstwhile USSR withdrew from Afghanistan in 1989-1990, the *'geo-strategic'* situation took a volte-face, as Pakistan could now divert the American funded terrorist structure towards India. This in consequence, made a spurt of increased terrorist activities in Kashmir from the 1990s onwards till date. However, the *'post-Taliban'* situation in Afghanistan again turns the lever partially in India's favour, however, this advantage can be offset by Pakistan if they develop mutual working relationship with the new government in Afghanistan.

The importance of Afghanistan to Pakistan is manifold. It not only gives Pakistan strategic depth from the North, but is also a conduit between CAR-Karachi route[1], which great powers will always try to secure. Yet another interesting emerging factor, which has to be kept in mind is the PRC effort of manoeuvreing and leading the trans-Asian axis from an anti US bloc stretching from the Eastern shores of the Mediterranean through South and Central Asia to the Western rim and shores of the Pacific. In this configuration, again, Pakistan appears to be the *'Focal Point'* bringing together Iran and PRC.

India's recent strategic treaty with America for escorting and protecting ships passing through the Indian Ocean up to the Malacca Strait serves strategic interests and obviously, may be in contradiction to the designs of the poor state of other players in the region.

Therefore, one has to examine the grand view of this Central and South Asian (CASA-R) region, which is emerging as an area of contest. Further, if one examines intrinsically the geo-political and geo-strategic dynamics of this region, there emerges two wheels of power, India and Pakistan, both of whom are equally necessary, for domination of *'CASA-R'*

Any nation, which wants to maintain control of the globe, will have to have secured energy power. The oil of CAR thus becomes the *'Vital- Asset'* for tomorrow's dominance and super power status. The ferry of these oils cannot be secured unless three things happen. Afghanistan is stabilised, Pakistan remains an ally and the Indian Ocean passage is secured. Thus one can say that anyone who influences these wheels enjoys strategic gains. And, therefore any great power will have strategic compulsions of maintaining a *'Dual Nation Theory'* in this CASA-R or the Asia-Pacific region.

Looking specifically towards Pakistan's agenda of sponsoring terrorism, India would have to thus evolve a counter-terrorism strategy, which becomes an algorithm and a product to this overall geo-political and geo-strategic reality. With this backdrop, India has few options in forcing the smaller wheel in realigning its rotational path, which does not include the trajectory of terrorism.

First, it could be a total war scenario in which territorial victory is bargained for closing the terrorist shops. But this may involve international intervention due to the nuclear factor. The international intervention, if can be turned in India's favour, may suite the cause. Obviously, then American opinion on the legal status of Kashmir becomes important. This in turn can be leveraged if these powers consider India as a bigger wheel of containment against China vis-à-vis Pakistan. This again is a story of perceptions and can be challenged and debated.

The other option can be that the victim state organises terrorist networks against the perpetrating state. For this even the victim state creates a financial mechanism, in which mercenaries are created by money power and supported by the Security Forces. In fact, this should be a policy against the sponsoring state, who when its sees that the cost is unaffordable, would be forced to bargain.

The third option could be a more pro-active option in which the victim state seizes the simmering neutrality in parts of the sponsoring state either by a politico-military strategy or by multiple *'Salami'* type shallow operations, may be only in disputed/soft areas, as a whole. This may necessitate re-structuring some Army formations as *'Hi-Tech'* and elite troops. Further, the hot pursuit option so permissible under the principle of *'drost de Voisinage or nachbahrrecht'*[2] be exercised by the victim state.

The fourth option for the victim state is to bear the present proxy war with restraint and maintain the image of being a soft state, devoid of strategic thinking. A state, which is boxed and punished from all directions, viz., Kashmir, North East against China, Myanmar, Bangladesh and Nepal. It remains an inward looking state with policies of vote winning. It tries to solve a *'strategic problem'* with a tactical approach and countering these swarming of bees resultantly having material and human loss as a recurring feature.

Yet another bizarre option, which can emerge, is the centrifuging and trifurcation of the perpetrating state due to natural tribal, fratricidal and sectarian violence. Now this may not be good as a week and broken state would pose direct intervention in this region. But, it may also disorganise the perpetrating state in organising, terrorism against India the victim state.

Therefore, in summation India will have to take the option as per the flux and dynamics of the powers, both internal and external. The option of being 'Pro-Active', may be ideal which will pay the best dividends as it will be revolved on Pakistan-India basis, because, the thresholds would remain within the confines. In fact, by this method, India would be able to turn the plank. Even the use of long range rockets to hit these camps in conjunction with own limited Special Force teams operating in such areas be considered. Based on this broader framework and policy, a deliberate theory of a counter-strategy be knitted and operationalised. Most of the basic laws for dealing with inspired secessionist movements or pseudo guerrilla operating like terrorists is same. These have been re-emphasised or re-thought as obtained in the environment under discussion, as given in following paragraphs highlighting the fundamentals again.

To begin with let us define the theory of a counter strategy. Obviously, this would have to be worked out in relation to the adversary's strategy. There could be many shades and perspectives to this. However, here, we would adopt the perspectives under discussion. One can therefore define it as: *A pro-active or reactive policy or a plan which not only annuls the adversary's strategy to achieve a political aim, but also forces the adversary to become defensive by compulsion of coercive diplomacy, international alliance, economic vulnerability, legality and conventions and military riposte capability.* Ultimately the exercise is to make a counter manoeuvre making the adversary's position untenable, militarily or politically. The foundation and philosophy of any such strategic counter stroke is based on the fundamental principle since ages, as enunciated by Chanakya in *Arthashastra:* "Your neighbour is your natural enemy"

It implies all the more in a situation where your neighbour transcends the environment to cross border terrorism, therefore, extending the argument further - one has to evolve a counter doctrine to consolidate one's frontiers by securing extra national boundaries. He further linked the approach to the combination of military capability and diplomatic finesse. Chanakya wrote that outcome and aim of any strategic manoeuvre should ultimately result in victory. As Liddell Hart said, 'To create a better state of Peace'. The aspect of diplomacy combined with manoeuvres assumed great dimensions. Chanakya's *raison d' etre* was that diplomacy backed by military superiority is bound to succeed. The analogy in this case, implies that by essence any counter-strategy backed by superior military capabilities will ensure neutralising enemy's strategy as well as put them on a negative disposition. The same can be comprehended by recollecting India's historical achievements. India was invaded by Alexander in 300 BC—India's slavery starts from here although for a short time. Chanakya soon evolved a counter-strategy and organised a *Putsch.* He not only captured Taxila but Afghanistan too. The Maurya empire thereafter ruled from Brahmaputra to Kandhar, by shear counter-strategy of reorganised military force. Here, the concept of strategic manoeuvre also explores areas other than military which when addressed indirectly would produce the same results of direct military action, but with surer results.

It is worth recollecting that during the Maratha-Mughal wars in the 16th century, the stratagem of using small raiding parties was practiced by the Mughals so as to prevent any concentration of forces under Shivaji by creating *constant terror* and disturbances in various parts of his kingdom[3]. The Mughals also carried out many sieges from time to time like that near Pune on 19 May 1665. To counter this siege warfare, Shivaji employed a counter-strategy of flexibility and harassed the Mughal siege by withdrawing where the enemy was strong and striking at his weak points. In the words of Khafi Khan, "The surprises of the enemy, their gallant successes, attacks on dark nights, blocking of roads and difficult passes and burning of jungle made it very hard for the imperialists to move about. The Mughuls lost many men and beasts"[4]. This counter-strike gave ascendancy to Shivaji over the Mughals. These historical punctuations only prove the fact, that a good counter-strategy policy towards a belligerent neighbour is likely to prove effective rather than giving no riposte or counter to the perpetrator, accept threatening rhetorics, which do not stand the test of real politicking. In this connection the factor of a moral or a just war still holds equal credence today, as was through the ages. Thus the relevance of a direct manoeuvre in the conventional modality as hither-to-fore would have to be understood. For easy assimilation a matrix on the same has been evolved, which can help in controlling outcome of the counter-strategy.

The enemy in an immoral war is in a position of inferiority, as he would not be able to appeal to world conscience, of public opinion or demand intervention by outside powers. In the post 11 September 2001 scenario any state linked with terrorism, obviously does not enjoy a high moral ground. An aggrieved nation, has the option of initiation of a military campaign with decisiveness to produce an *International fait accompli*. However, if matters drag, the weaker state also will be able to mobilise support and the whole operation will slide into the indirect strategy and cause a stalemate. So the conflict, planned as decisive will drag down in attrition and the deciding factor will be weariness. This then spells the defeat of direct manoeuvre.

A decisive counter-manoeuvre need not have troops in strength but have superior air and air mobilisation forces. Let us work out the definition of indirect counter-strategy: "Using the minimum of force and military resources, the art of maximum exploitation of the narrow margin of freedom of action left to us by nuclear or political deterrence in order to achieve the designed, frequently large-scale results". Indirect counter-strategy is therefore that in which a psychological effect is produced upon the enemy by the most direct methods, including, if necessary, prolongation of the conflict. One can further conceptualise and try to draw it into tangible equations by the following matrix:

If F = Material force, M = Moral force, T = Time, K = Co-efficient specific to local conditions, which will be constant for both sides, which may involve terrain, climate and ecology and further, if S = strategic counter-stroke, and if we are looking at it from the perception of a counter-strategy to terrorism, then the equation which gets evolved is $S = KFM \times T^2$, that is, if force level is less but moral factor or moral force level is high then the value of strategic counter-stroke is equal to the summation of the factors where the value of M becomes critical, in offsetting deficiency of force levels. Further, as time passes, the superior standing army benefits by square of time forcing the perpetrator nation to become flexible and ask to end the military stand-off. (This equation purely stands true, only for situations where state sponsored terrorism is being perpetrated by a neighbouring state). However, if one has to increase 'S' with increase in time over a long protracted period then, obviously,,value of T increases and one can reduce the value of 'F' relatively. However, if the factor of 'M' reduces then 'F' may again have to be increased. In totality, therefore, the key factor would be to maintain ascendancy of 'S' and thereafter negotiate a settlement with the other party being ultimately coerced into abandoning state policy of terrorism.

Further, both psychological action and Will is equally important. Thus, indirect strategy amounts to a tough form of negotiation. Let us elucidate again by drawing a matrix, in which various actions and counter-actions may result in losing the so important 'M' factor in handling this kind of war. 'M' on the side being terrorised and combined with elongation of 'T' by the economically superior side is the key element to success. Let us see the same schematically, in which the options already discussed earlier are debated.

Fig. 4.1.

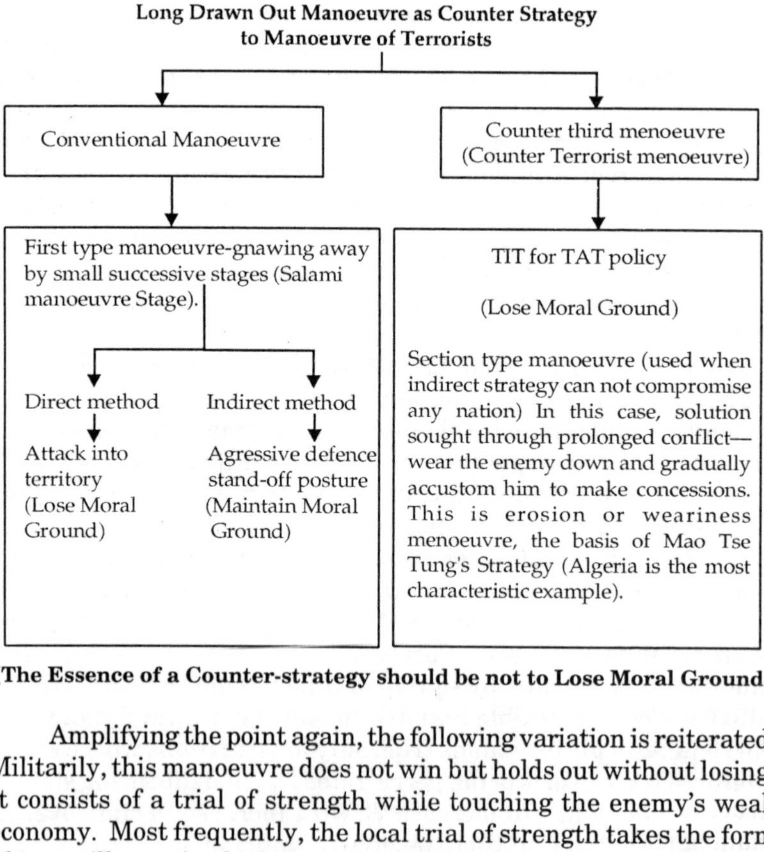

(The Essence of a Counter-strategy should be not to Lose Moral Ground)

Amplifying the point again, the following variation is reiterated. Militarily, this manoeuvre does not win but holds out without losing. It consists of a trial of strength while touching the enemy's weak economy. Most frequently, the local trial of strength takes the form of 'guerrilla war', which is a classic form of endemic conflict. The object of corresponding rules for pacification is to deny the guerrilla the 'Third Manoeuvre'. The defending side therefore tries to intervene by superior military forces and forces the perpetrating nation to change the policy of terrorism. The other nation bargains for negotiations. It should be noted that in this type of conflict one of the combatants, the side that initiated guerrilla war, has everything to lose, because for him the stake is total, which is seldom the case for the other side. The moral cards are also unequal unless the state being perpetuated also conducts the 'counter third manoeuvre' policy and reduces the value of 'M'. If one side puts forward demands which are at first sight unacceptable but which he refuses to discuss, he must go a long way with the weariness process and therefore be sure that he can hold out. If, on the other, he is aiming to cause his opponent to agree to open negotiations without prior conditions, negotiations can begin early, subject to the risk of having to resume the struggle, if the other side is not sufficiently weary. Nevertheless, the counter-strategy or manoeuvre has a powerful physiological lever to bring direct influence to bear upon the will of the opposing leader.

Now, let us discuss certain domestic measures, which the perpetrated nation should take in the infected zone. In this sequence further, as a counter-strategy and doctrine, one cannot rule out non-cooperation and disobedience movements which may prove effective against ruthless perpetrators. Therefore as a counter, involving the local population in the fight against the pseudo guerrilla is important on these lines. The aspect of active defence obviously should allow government sponsored organisations for village defence by harnessing ex-servicemen and creating territorial-military type forces. There is also a necessity for creation of 'Para Guerrilla Forces' so that any violence in counter-terrorist operations has no or reduced collateral which will deter non-cooperation movements. There is another aspect of re-structuring the mass base by giving key personnel certain economic benefits and pay packages and at the same time make selective arrests of some ring leaders. On the other hand the need is to create a charismatic leader, who is sympathetic to the state being terrorised.

Further, there is need for an organisational structure at the national, state and district levels and necessity of having a ministry of civil defence. Creation of councils and cells at various village levels would be a great help in countering the terrorist war. Resistance structure in residential areas should also be created. Extensive training and manoeuvres must be also organised on a yearly basis.

Now let us classify the various levels of a counter-strategy against terrorism (including WMD) in an environment where secessionists and guerrillas are using terrorism as their tool.

- International/global level action (Level 1).
- Regional and national level action (Level 2).
- State, operational and theatre level action (Level 3).
- Tactical level action (Level 4).

Each of the above mentioned levels would have varying shades of political, economic, legal, intelligence and military aspects. In summation, there will have to be a wholesome and comprehensive approach to the cancer of terrorism. Here, the focus will be more on the aspect of level 2, 3 and 4, which would be punctuated with the example of Kashmir terrorism now and then, for easy comprehension. At level 2 the basic counter-strategy would have to deal with the four basic components (discussed earlier) in the form of destroying the terrorists organisational structures, physical component of equipment and caches as well as lower their moral, by management of demographic and psychological warfare.

At Level 3, especially in a situation of proxy war, launched by the terrorists, a counter proxy war operational military strategy, which is demographic centric and which encompass all the aspects, is the best bet. The same is as shown in the diagram below:

Fig. 4.2: State/ Theatre/Operational Level - 3

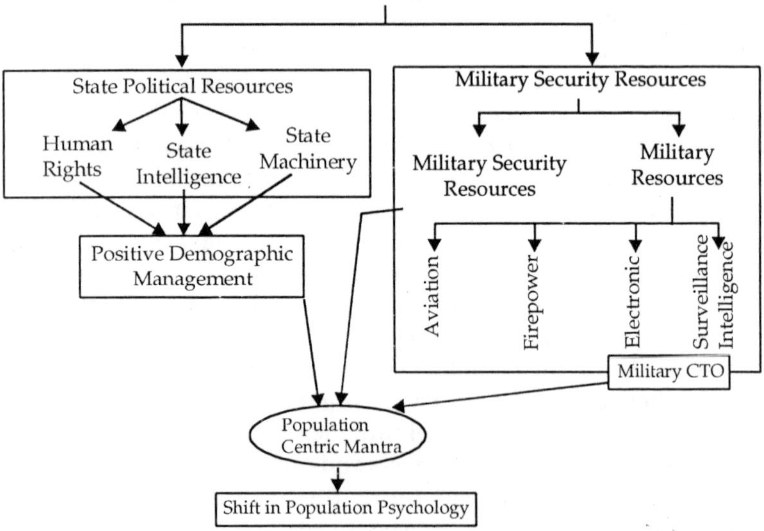

The basic theme should be to create synergisation at the state level of all the energies to thwart the aggressor's designs, by a

'Positive Demographic Management'. Simultaneously, development projects should enable positive assimilation of the population. Ultimately, the key to the overall counter-terrorism strategy is to blend the state political resources and the military resources in such a way as to blend and evolve a 'Population Centric Mantra', which can shift the population psychology. This mantra will be different for different environments. In most of these areas, the contours of this mantra should have simultaneity at all levels viz. demographic and development management combined with tactical military operation. However, where pure terrorism exists then in that case the only mantra is military action. Here it would be ideal to recall an old and a popular Sanskrit proverb "DANDAM DASHA GUNAM BHAVETH" which means the stick (punitive measures) will teach ten qualities (lessons).

Further, if one speculates that neo-terrorist warfare can be countered by military tactical strength alone, then one is mistaken. Even if troops are deployed in every inch of the territory, one may yet not be able to influence the population. On the other hand, the government would be heavily taxed in maintaining that heavy deployment posture. The Britishers during the 'Boer-War' came very close to this situation. Maximisation of security forces beyond a certain point does not lead to better results. Therefore, one can say with confidence that 'Neo-Terrorism' cannot be countered by military action alone. The worry becomes all the more, where the terrorists have easy access, to WMD material. (It is believed that Taliban, OBL/Al-Qaida groups are already in possession of some WMD).

Military action if combined with a counter-terrorist strategy focused to influence the population base can probably address the problem. A counter-terrorist strategy should encompass three major aspects, i.e., winning the hearts and minds of the population, economic benefit and controlled military action so as to give a sense of security to the people. Here we will focus more on the military strategy and tactics and build a model for action by the government forces. (Obviously the effect would be to disorganise terrorist networks and destroy their caches).

Normally the area of operation is very wide and therefore it is not possible to address all the hot spots simultaneously. Therefore it is better to divide the infected areas into the various categories and classifications. The so-called "Liberated Zone" or the area where there is easy movement and influence by terrorists be concentrated upon first.

Having identified the area, sufficient military, police, para military forces and political teams be concentrated and applied so as to re-establish control over the population. A suggested chronology of action should commence with elimination of political cells and reforming the population thereafter by civic action and education programmes followed by organising people into self-defence units. Simultaneously with the availability of transparent media, carry out subtle indoctrination. This may further involve, countering the ideological propaganda of the adversary and logically facilitating a better form of government and living to the population, coupled with controlled surgical type operation so as to eliminate the ringleaders of that area. Attacking the assets like arms and ammunition also make the terrorists dysfunctional. Over a period of a very short time the psychology of the population will shift in favour of the government forces, thus creating more intelligence and more terrorists being neutralised. This complete cycle in turn strengthens the governing regime, as elucidated in Fig. 4.3 below:

Fig. 4.3. A Model for Action by Security Forces.

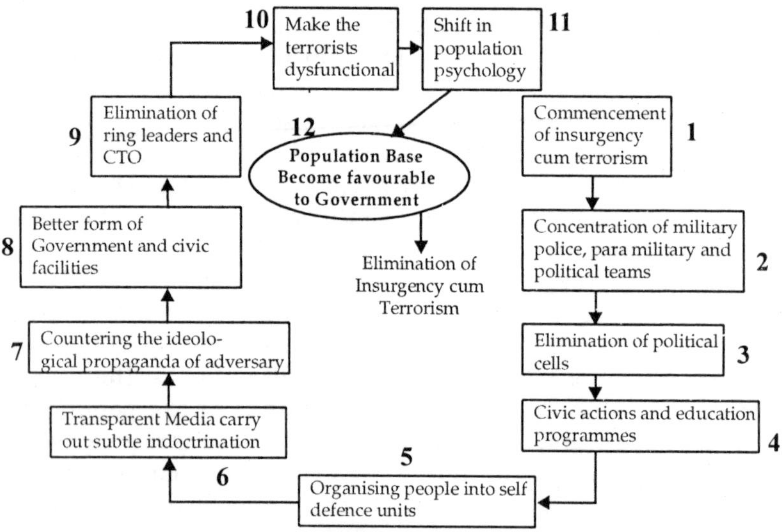

Legal provisions like prevention of terrorist ordnance should further strengthen the hands of the government machinery. Therefore, as can be seen, the re-establishment of domination in geographic area thereafter, in turn forces the terrorists to join battle with security forces so as to re-establish his area of influence. This in turn is violative of the principles of the terrorist operations and exposes them to elimination.[5]

Yet another aspect is the use of economy of force in case terrorism is being used as a political tool. One of indirect tools of the adversary is to make heavy deployment mandatory. This therefore should be avoided as part of counter-strategy and reduced deployment is offset by use of technology and air. These can be used to harass the invading terrorists and guerrillas. Simplicity of counter-terrorist operations ensures easier execution by multiple agencies and enables better coordination amongst the various agencies. Therefore it is an important guiding principle.

Fig. 4.4. Structure of Organisation (Theatre/State Level).

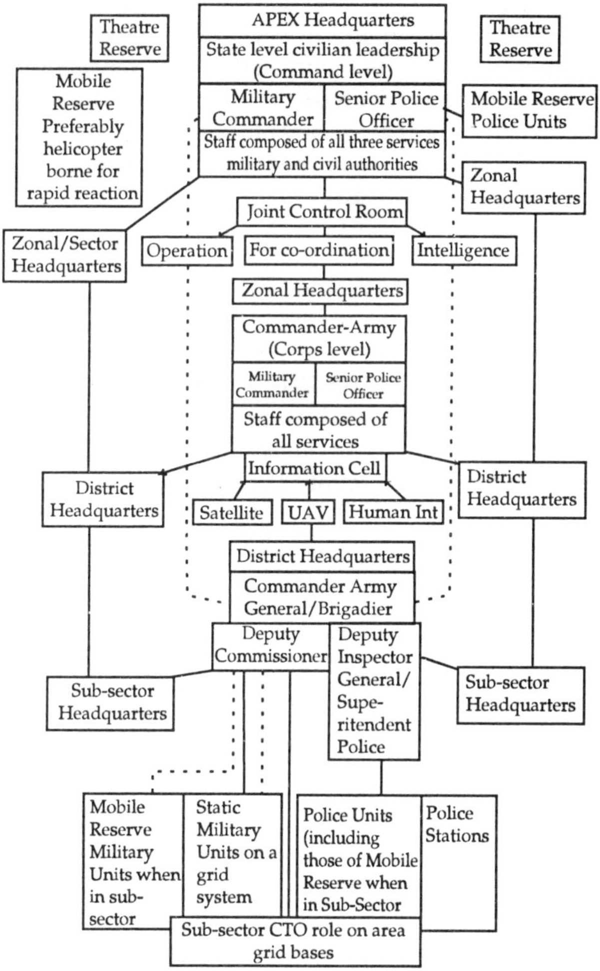

____________ Chain of Command for planning operations.

.... Chain of responsibility for executing operations.

Synergisation has to be ensured by creating force structures so as to amalgamate integration at the highest, theatre and tactical levels. As far as possible at the apex level the civilian leadership should chair all decision-makings but at the operational and tactical level only the military leader should coordinate the role of police, para military forces and civil administration for a particular operation. One of the suggested structures of organisation is given in Fig. 4.4.

At the operational level 'Joint Control Room' (JCR) should create an intelligence base of the terrorists and the population. Here both strategic and tactical operations should be planned with a future perspective. A joint counter-terrorist strategy should also emerge here as per the broader guidelines laid down by the Apex Headquarters. The JCR thereafter should disseminate their counter-terrorist doctrine to all the so called geographic based zonal headquarters, which could be many depending on the geography and cartography. Further, looking only at one such zonal headquarters, it should be under command a single point, which could mean a division or corps level military commander, who in turn should be assisted by other civil and police officials for CTO role only. At this middle level, there is a necessity of having an 'Information cell', which should have satellite, UAV and human intelligence connectivity. (The Intelligence part is discussed subsequently). Further, breakdown to sub-sectors would allow firmer control of tactical CTO.

It may be noted that Variation may be made in this organisation to suit prevailing conditions. In Jammu and Kashmir the organisation could be different to that in the North East.

Demographic and Geographic Categorisation

The major role of the JCR is to create the requisite demographic and geographic data base for macro counter-terrorist planning. A vast survey of many insurgencies and case studies of terrorism has revealed generally the demographic classification both of the population and the terrorist as per specifications in Fig. 4.5.[6]

Fig. 4.5: Demographic Classification of Population and Terrorists.

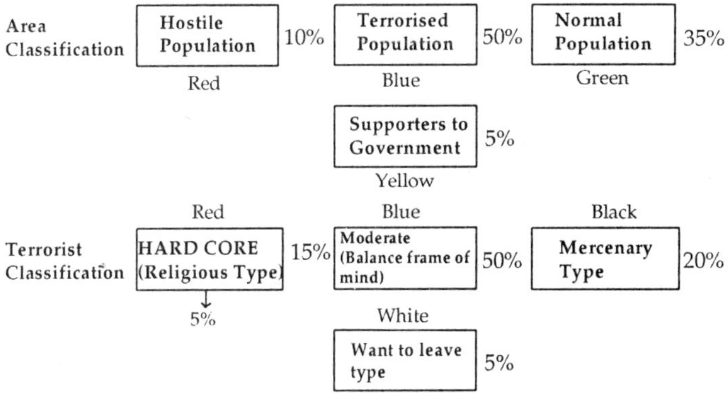

The analysis of the demographic segmentation should become the starting point, which a JCR, should consider in planning CTO. The approach in handling population in a 'Red Geographic Area' has to be different to that in 'Green' or 'Yellow' areas. Conjoint with this is the factor of the type of operating in that area viz Red, Blue, Black or White. The most dangerous situation is where there is a 'Red Geographic Area' with 'Red' category of terrorist. Sequence of tackling such an extreme situation (Almost like a liberated Zone) has to be more military oriented, although the basic philosophy of "Firmness with courtesy"[7] should be strictly adhered to in dealing with the local population. Under the umbrella of this overall strategy the tactical doctrine should follow the following steps. In blue or green areas certain steps suggested can be skipped:

(a) Deployment of the security forces jointly at the population base.
(b) Encircle the habitant area and follow it by typical "Cordon and Search" operation.
(c) During search focus on supply points and destroy cache's.
(d) Then sweep outside—driving the terrorists out of the population base.
(e) Carry enough military civic action teams so as to carry out medical camps and propaganda material for a successful shift in population psychology.
(f) It should be ensured that security forces live with equal hardships and help in their development projects to the civil population.
(g) Minimum troops should be on the show window and

maximum should remain out of sight once the cordon and search operation is over.

(h) Use helicopters and air support (slow flying aircraft) for carrying out the above-mentioned operations.

(j) Ensure sufficient population control measures to include identity card, selective curfew and controlling the distribution system of food supplies.

(k) In the end immediately organise intelligence teams in the population centres and formalise the same by way of payments and employment.

The impact of such an operation will change the texture of the demographic and terrorist classification, more in favour of the government forces. Similar treatment could be given to other (Red over Red) areas as found in the zone. If, for example, three such areas are to be tackled in a zone, then there is a requirement of synchronisation of the three operations at the JCR, so that there is an impact at the micro level. These operations should result in disturbing the terrorist beehive, and should be followed immediately by many minor tactical strikes by the local units.

Tactical Level

The basic concept is to fight a war on grid system of response and neutralisation. Terrorists-cum-guerrilla warfare organisation is functioning on the concept akin to a beehive. This implies that terrorists are like bees, which are based at a safe beehive, which is invisible because of being mixed up in the demographic base. Therefore, one of the choices for counter-terrorism operations is to shoot at every flying bee operating in the environment. This would require huge manpower and weapons. Because, if you shoot down one bee, yet another bee is created at the hive so it becomes an endless war, in which the troops get fatigued and frustrated in this vicious cycle. The other option is to identify the 'Hive' and smoke it down. But there may be a cluster of hives in a region. Even, if you have destroyed one hive, yet another may emerge parallel to it, due to external factors like the transportation of another hive from a hostile neighbouring state. Yet another option could be by changing the environment where bees cannot cross-pollinate due to removal of the breeding source. The Jehadis have been motivated and nurtured in Madarsas. Therefore, the best approach to stymie this bee like terrorist growth is to force the perpetrating state, to change its policy. The US in its war against terrorism is using this very option, in this region.

A combination of all options could be viable counter-strategy.

Obviously, the option of 'shooting the bees' is the worst option it is the least cost-effective option, whereas the option of controlling the breeding ground would be the best and optimum solution. Therefore, the priority of formulating a counter-strategy should be determined accordingly. Maybe the answer is a combination of all with a percentage ratio of 40:35:25 in the descending order of a policy, operational directive and tactical operations.

We now focus on the tactical option falling in the ratio of '25'. Let us retrace the terrorist-cum-guerrilla strategy being deployed in a 'Netwar' configuration based around population centres. This forces the defender to deploy widely, almost on a 'Grid System'. This obviously results in over consumption of troops. Thus, let us work on a strategy of lesser deployment tactically to conserve strength rather than dissipate, contrary to the grand strategy of the perpetrator. This is analysed in Fig. 4.6.

Fig. 4.6. Grid System of Deployment.

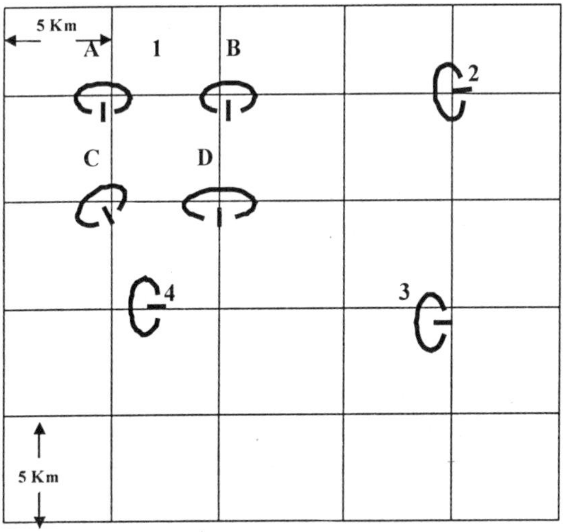

Conventionally, to dominate an area, security forces would be deployed as shown in A, B, C and D etc. To win this war, one should be able to do 1, 2, 3 and 4, etc thus magnifying influenced area to three-fold or in other words cutting down your force deployment by one-third. (For example, where a division level force is deployed you can reduce by a brigade. If one further extrapolates, where a corps is deployed, one can release a division at least). Let us see the mechanics and modus operandi of such an arrangement. For this to happen some basic technology and concept has to be developed. Let us call it the evolution of "Techno-Tactics" where technology application compensates for reduced deployment. The principle can be explained further on a grid system.

Let us assume that a company is deployed astride the centre or call it 0 (Zero). To enable it to influence the 'Area of Responsibility' militarily (ABCD) it is given more technology support by way of sensors, battlefield surveillance radars and advanced night vision devices. The security forces so deployed in
counter-terrorist role, where there is also some insurgency, should also have their organisation tailored to assimilate locals, not only to create intelligence but also to be able to neutralise the fear created by the terrorists in the population centres. It would be like 'Taking them out of the terrorist hook'. Financial benefit given in the form of pay and allowances would also assist in strengthening counter-insurgency operations at the grass root level. In the Indian scenario this can be addressed by minor modifications in the Rashtriya Rifles force structures; may be in every battalion, a platoon strength be recruited under the powers of the commanding officer directly from the population centres in rural areas where the unit is operating. This may have some disadvantages, but the benefits will outdo those disadvantages. This will also allow the operating security forces to expand areas of influence three-fold. In fact, lot of intelligence will flow from areas even where the forces are not deployed. Electronic intercept and direction finding must also be used to enhance situational awareness and accordingly be decentralised. It must also be given near real time satellite and 'Unarmed Vehicle' (UAV) connectivity for which a separate communication technique is adopted with organisations like DIPAC and the corps information centres. Due to availability of more night flying helicopters with night firing capabilities it is even possible to detect and neutralise them instantly. These helicopters could be decentralised in control at division level for better response. In fact, utilisation of technology as mentioned above could follow the sequence, once hard intelligence fructifies (shown by numbers marked serially in the Fig. 4.7).

Fig. 4.7.

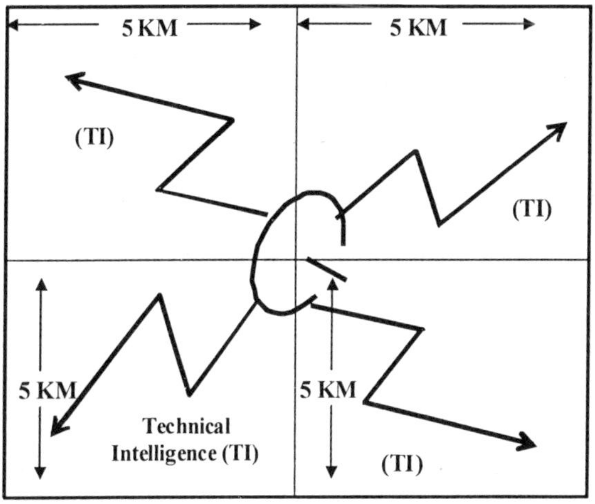

Following this cue, one can develop a tentative doctrine for counter-terrorism operations accordingly. The doctrine would be pre-emptive, reactive and pro-active.

Pre-emptive. If hard intelligence is obtained in anticipation due to electronic intercepts it could be utilised by ambushes or activating human resources in the area affected.

Reactive. If hard intelligence is obtained through any of the technical means, then the response and reaction is immediate and real time to neutralise the terrorist.

Pro-active. It would be possible by striking terrorists launch pads and camps available in the vicinity of the border. This would require a 'surgical strike' through employment of attack and utility helicopter in conjunction with laser guided precision munitions and Special Forces equipped with 'Combat Situation Awareness' capability. In a nutshell, the doctrine spells out the principles of employment of forces by synergising them. For example, it would mean creating a combat team in which the force mix could be the following:-

(a) Flight Attack Helicopters (AH) (2/3 helicopters).
(b) Flight Utility Helicopters (UH) (2/3 helicopters).
(c) Three squads of Special Forces (each squad having three to five men).
(d) One or two platoons of heliborne infantry mounted in utility helicopters.
(e) Team of Field Observation Officers (FOO) and Forward Air Controller (FAC).

Fig. 4.8.

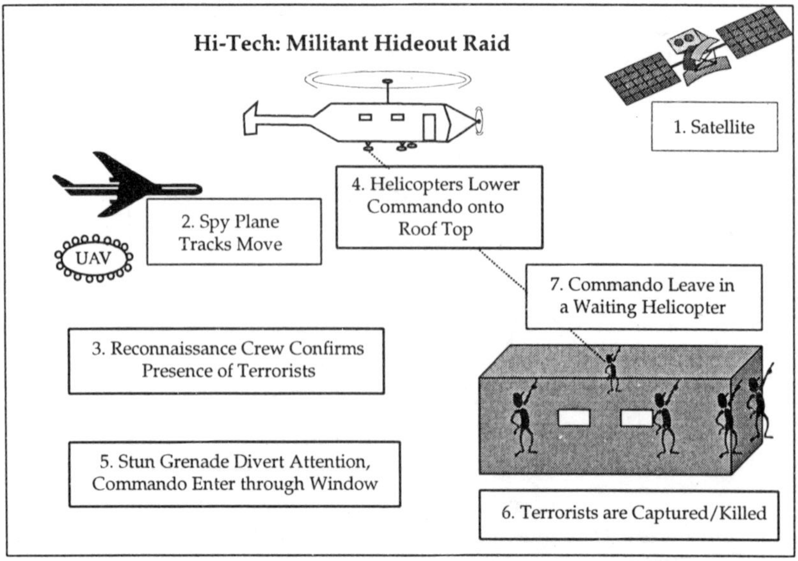

The tactical application is made by inserting special forces team first with FOO/FAC followed by induction of UH supported by AH. While infantry platoons neutralise the objective/terrorists, AH gives fire support augmented further through FOOs, who use laser designators and if required fighter aircraft strikes are guided by FACs. De-induction thereafter occurs within a very short time before the adversary can react.

Having understood the functional model requirement both at higher and tactical levels as a background, there is a deliberate requirement of evolving definitive concepts and doctrines against this 'third manoeuvre' or the CTO role. An analysis of casualties (own and terrorists) should be done to drive home the point of the necessity of evolving doctrines by developing a military pattern of activities, which can achieve the end state of fewer casualties by the security forces as compared to the terrorists. There is, thus, a case for developing statistical models, area and sector wise, comparing the encounters and the result. Some of the models that can be developed to draw out the ratios could be terrorists killed against own fatal casualties and against number of encounters and contacts. Some of the hypothetical models are shown.

Table 4.1: Analysis of Own Casualty

Year/Encounters	Own Fatal	Terrorist Kills
X+ 1 year	2.7 n	13 n
X+ 2 year	4.1 n	13.5 n
X + 3 year	2.2 n	29 n
X + 4 year	2.7 n	33 n
X+ 5 year	3 n	34 n

Fig. 4.9: No of Terrorists Killed Per Own One Fatal Injury.

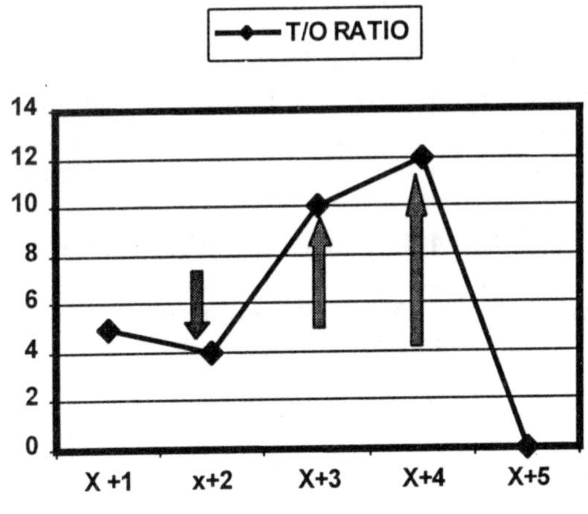

Table 4.2. Analysis of Encounters and Own Casualty.

Year	No of Encounters(E)	Own Fatal Casualty
X+1	7 n	2 n
X+2	6 n	4 n
X+3	8 n	2 n
X+4	12 n	3 n
X+5	N	5 n

Note: n denotes the numbers and their multiples in percentages.
x shows the years in continuation

Fig. 4.10: No of Encounters (E) Per Own One Fatal (F) Casualty.

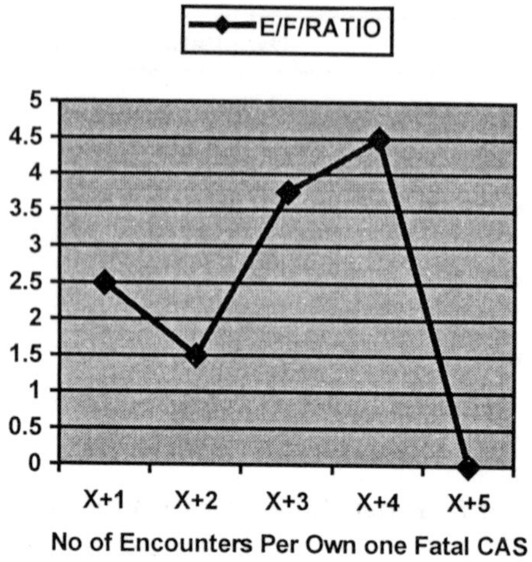

Similarly, an analysis can be done by drawing different curves, one for number of encounters and the other for number of kills. This can further help in identifying location of encounters and evolving and refining tactics for increasing kills in a particular sector.

Table 4.3. Analysis of Encounters.

Year	No of Encounters	Kills
X+1	6.8 n	13 n
X+2	5.9 n	15 n
X+3	8 n	33 n
X+4	12 n	35 n
X+5	0.3 n	1.4 n

Fig. 4.11. Analysis of Encounters - In a particular sector in J and K

YEAR	NO OF ENCOUNTERS	KILLS
1998	68	130
1999	59	147
2000	82	333
2001	124	348
2002	03	14

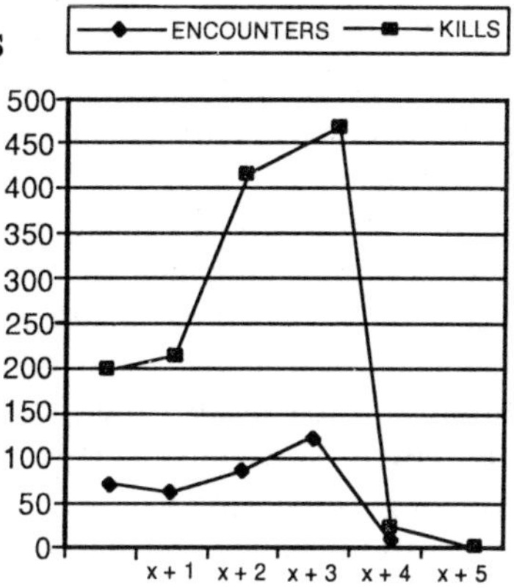

Table 4.4: Contact/Kill Profile 2001

Type	On LC	Inter Zone	Depth
Encounter	7.7 n	6.4 n	
Kills	128	171	25

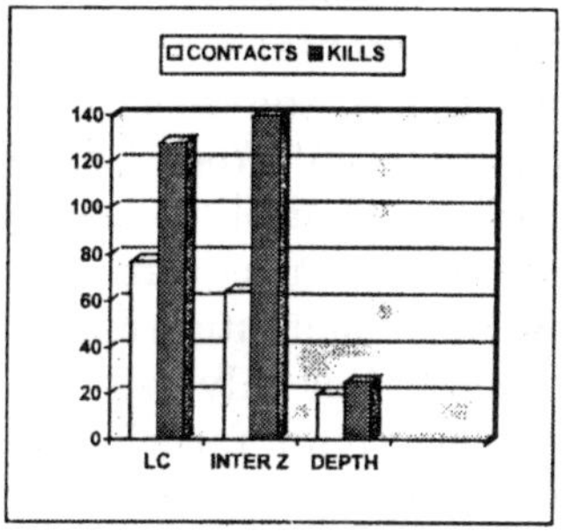

Based on all the above scientific and management based analysis one can reach a conclusion of evolving and refining concepts and doctrines from time to time.

Evolving Concepts and Doctrines (Against Third Manoeuvre)

The evolvement of concepts and doctrine should be carried out to cover short term (2000-2010) medium term (2010-2020) and long term (beyond 2020) scenarios. This will ensure mid course corrections necessitated due to changes in technological, security and strategic environment. All these concepts and doctrines would not be holistic without considering the reality of an intermix of the genesis of a 'Third Manoeuvre' as an important military strategy in achieving political and military goals. This strategy would therefore have to be meshed and dovetailed with the evolving concepts and technologies as discussed below. Any nation which can organise and exploit the adversary by such oriented terrorist-cum-guerrilla specialised forces with a combination of pseudo insurgencies would provide a low cost, protractive and pro-active option. Profound reforms of concepts, modes, and tactics in modern conventional operational doctrine are likely to be as discussed below.

Warfare will have more "jointness", be of smaller scale than World War II, be shorter in duration, involve deep attacks on rear areas which will change the definition of "battlefield dominance" to mobile or manoeuvre warfare through smaller specialised forces. Large quantities of high-tech weapons will accelerate a series of revolutionary changes in concepts, i.e., opposing sides may not necessarily face each other in battles. Instead, they will launch attacks hundreds or even thousands of kilometres away by fully employing air assaults and missile weapons, in conjunction with the 'Third Manoeuvre' through networked organisations if the environment permits.

Advances in simulation technology will improve deception warfare. Improvement of command decision-making will enable artificial intelligence simulation systems to mimic the commanding officers' mental activities and be extensively used in command activities in the near future. Peacetime military innovation will proceed to shift from the traditional formula of 'technology pushing' tactics to that of 'doctrine pushing'. That means the progress of military technology and development of weapons will be guided by thinking about future operations, including CTO and counter netwar concepts. Not only will "space forces" be created and expanded by even a "robot force", which will have to be deployed using multipurpose robots in future warfare. It will make 'Automated Battlefield' a reality.

Environment permitting, instability in border regions will be caused by adversaries, by indirectly organising pseudo insurgencies operating like guerrillas but networked with 'Hi-Tech' systems, who will create the 'Invisible Front' and tie down defender's combat troops. The Indian subcontinent is already experiencing the same.

There will be three main forms of long range strikes in the future: the first form is the one is which the air arm independently carries out long range strikes, the second form is one in which the long range strike combines with the long range rapid movement of troops transported by land and sea with the vertical airdrops of airborne forces, and the third form is five dimensional air, land, sea, space and electro-magnetic long range combat, combined with the 'Third Manoeuvre' causing the 'Invisible Front'. By striking at the "vital point" of the enemy's information and support systems one can at one blow paralyse the enemy and collapse his morale. Further, with the aid of electromagnetic waves, a virus can be injected from a long distance into the enemy's command and communication systems and into the computers of his aircraft, tanks and other weapons causing non-lethal destruction. This would cause WMDR effect, which can be used by the 'Neo Terrorist' who commit cyber terrorism.

The main type of military robot on active service or about to be put on active service in the armed forces of various countries of the world are vehicle emergency robots, mine laying robots, minesweeping robots, reconnaissance robots, transportation robots, electronic robots and driver robots. Later there will appear engineer robots, chemical defence robots, patrol robots, and even unmanned intelligent tanks, unmanned intelligent aircraft and other 'robot soldiers'. These robots can help in a big way in fighting CTO.

The main radiation weapons, i.e., laser, microwave, particle beam and subsonic wave possess enormous military potential. Direct Energy Weapon (DEW) refers to these weapons concepts based on lasers, radio frequencies, or particle beams.[8]

A variety of indications show that nano technological weapons could well bring about fundamental changes in many aspects of future military affairs. Nano technology will certainly become a crucial military technology in the 21st century. If the same were applied in conjunction with terrorist operations, they would be very effective. Terrorists may also start using DEW. DEW will be line-of-sight weapons, beam tracking, with almost the speed of light. Time of flight to the target would be essentially zero. A very high rate of fire from unlimited magazine with capability to be redirected. However, these suffer from the disadvantage of assessing soft kill probability as well as requirement for tracking the target and pointing the beam which tend to be quite stringent and thus may become difficult for the terrorists to use due to lack of sophisticated infrastructure.

The belief in qualitative superiority has major implications not only for how expectations are set for the performance of forces but also for how defence requirement priorities are defined. The new theory, emphasises modernisation and readiness as high priority, in it downgrade sustainability, on the premise that long wars no longer will be fought; future wars will be won through quality. The new theory should relax traditional standards for overpowering mass and thereby levies a requirement for smaller number of combat units. The future calls for an altered mix with more air wings and fewer division and ships. Greater emphasis will have to be on building qualitative excellence in strategy, doctrine, tactics, warfare and other areas, including the doctrine of netwars in which terrorist guerrilla type operations will pay handsome dividends.

There will be profound changes in the operational concept in the 21st century land operations because of the military revolution. It will be important to comprehend them correctly from the perspective of a successful CTO:

(a) Battle space will be extended to hundreds or several thousands of kilometres (partly due to the 'Third Manoeuvre', concept).
(b) The front and rear of the battlefield will be attacked simultaneously.
(c) The strategic rear area might be the first target of attack.
(d) Time and speed will have new meanings.
(e) Enemy C^4I^2 system and high threat weapons will be the main targets.
(f) Information attacks and firepower will be combined.
(g) The destruction of numerous enemy forces will no longer be the primary task.
(h) A network among various units of armed forces will be able to:
    (i) Carry out long range and accurate strikes.
    (ii) Every soldier will have the information and firepower support of the whole digital information network.
    (iii) Every unit will be in contact with the enemy force on the battlefield, and there will be no frontlines.

To this end, therefore, nations who sponsor terrorism and create pseudo-secessionism would be able to exploit terrorism as a tool of military strategy. They would even try to expand their strategic frontiers by these indirect approaches. The case of insurgencies in the Indian subcontinent including the Maoist guerrilla movement has to be seen from this realism. Logically, India should anticipate and counter these manoeuvres by a holistic counter-strategy against terrorism and pseudo-insurgencies.

Mastery of outer space will be a prerequisite for naval victory with outer space becoming the new commanding elevation for naval combat. Ships at sea will carry out anti-reconnaissance strikes against space satellites and other space systems. The side with electromagnetic combat superiority will make full use of that invisible killer mace to win naval victory. Future naval rivalry over "electromagnetic space" will be more important than land, sea and air space. The electromagnetic advantage will become the focus of rivalry between opponents. Naval C^4I^2 system will be the nerve centre and force multiplier in future warfare. The aspect of 'neo-terrorism' could imbibe these qualitative requirements to cause mass disruption.

The air battlefield will become decisively significant in future warfare due to growing significance of smart munitions, intelligent operational platforms and integrated automatic C^4I^2 systems. More stealth planes will be rushing into the air battlefields of the 21st century and stealth penetration bombing will be more commonly applied. The Air force must be capable of "taking down" the enemy's operational system by "striking the seams and ripping the fabric". The Revolution in Military Affairs will strengthen aerospace forces more than any other. Air power can start and stop operations easily which is definitely what military decision makers want to apply in today's conflicts, in which no one wants to escalate a conflict but everyone is eager to restrain the other. Because, an air force can achieve such a goal without escalating the conflict; it has more opportunities to be employed. Finally, air force must be linked to space force, and thus be used as one combined force to quell 'Neo-Terrorists' who may be denied similar facilities.

Information will characterise the whole process of combat. For example, the armed forces will use satellites, high altitude aircraft, helicopters and unmanned flying equipment to collect and process information and use digital communication techniques to transmit computer data within the information network. Future warfare cannot be carried out by a simple adjustment in the structure of the army but will be network formed by the land, sea, air and space forces, in conjunction with 'Third Manoeuvre' elements.

The information era will touch off a revolution in military affairs, just as the cannon in the 15th century and the machine in the past 150 years of the industrial era touched off revolutions. Information warfare will control the form and future of war. The following needs emphasis:

(a) Establish a strategic reconnaissance warning and air defence system.
(b) Develop information weapon system such as air defence weapons systems, offensive tactical guided missile attack systems, electronic warfare equipment systems and underwater mines laying system. These will give over the horizon high precision concealed, sudden defensive attack capability and a strong survival capacity, and make the enemy (Neo-Terrorists) terrified and worried providing an effective threat.

(c) Build information networks to bring all branches into a single combat network, which should then be inter-connected through United Nations for fighting the war against terrorism.

In all the contingencies and situations as mentioned above, the relevance of the concept of a 'Third Manoeuvre' or the so-called terrorist-cum-guerrilla type networked organisations cannot be denied. Reiterating the same, therefore one has to understand the total battlefield environment as enunciated above which will continue to give adequate space for carrying out asymmetric warfare and proxy wars during all the stages of a conflict (The Indian sub-continent in this context is an example where such movements are already existing and they should not be looked in isolation).

Now, let us take a 'WMD' perspective in a futuristic 'NBC' scenario where the terrorists may have the capability to use any of the agents. The above-mentioned teams are augmented with specialised 'NBC' defensive and detection equipment. Thereafter, the capability to 'Cap' the source of proliferation is also added by a 'Decontamination Team' which can also move by helicopters or surface means depending on the situation. In fact, there is a requirement of creating a 'Rapid Reaction Company' at the theatre level to handle 'NBC' threats or disasters. These could also be on the patterns as being practised in America (Dealt separately as part of Civil Defence Mechanism and Response). Integration of a civil defence plan to deal with such incidents also needs to be developed, both at the national and international levels. One such model at the UN, is depicted in Fig. 4.13.

This kind of approach would also be the most efficient method in handling areas where there are pure counter-terrorist operations, and where they can be only neutralised by military violence and not with the philosophy of winning the hearts and minds. A similar UN force could have tackled the recent American operation 'Anaconda' in Afghanistan.

Real-time detection of WMD, as in battlefield conditions, will seldom be possible within a democratic society. Any attempt to provide a nationwide civil defence programme, without evidence of

Fig. 4.13.

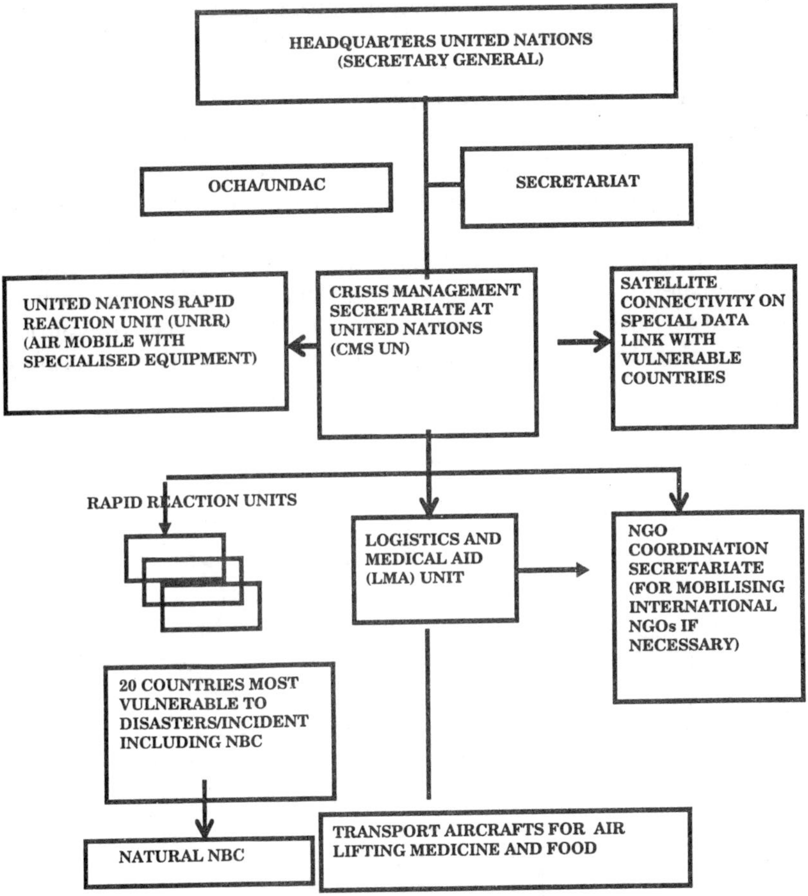

an imminent threat, would invite public indifference, misuse of equipment and even ridicule. Terrorists can however reconnoiter targets, monitor movements, infiltrate activists or liaise with dissatisfied employees. They can choose the timing, mode and place of their attacks, switching or delaying operations if necessary. Only the gathering of accurate and timely intelligence can blunt these advantages. There is a need to understand the aims, motivation and operational structure of the terrorists in question. Through surveillance of suspect groups and sources of dual-use technologies, national authorities can decrease the risks associated with use of weapons of mass destruction by terrorists. These risks include the acquisition or illicit manufacture and storage of agents, communications with state sponsors and the development and testing of dispersal systems. Data from electronic sources would be inadequate in seeking to pre-empt terrorist activity, and would probably have to be supplemented by surveillance of terrorist groups, the gathering of information from friendly governments and Interpol, and, where appropriate, joint initiatives and cooperation with transnational agencies in fighting this common menace. In fact, it is felt that there is a requirement of building an Intelligence structure in India akin to the one Israelis have for defeating cross border terrorism.

In fact, there is a requirement of a global plan towards counter-terrorism, as discussed in Chapter VI (Civil Defence Aspects). A global counter-terrorism strategy should spell out international commitments towards a joint global and integrated approach to combat terrorism. The generation of a counter-terrorism convention (CTC) akin to chemical weapons convention (CWC) is therefore mandatory. It could even start from pro-active NGOs, who were

Fig. 4.14.

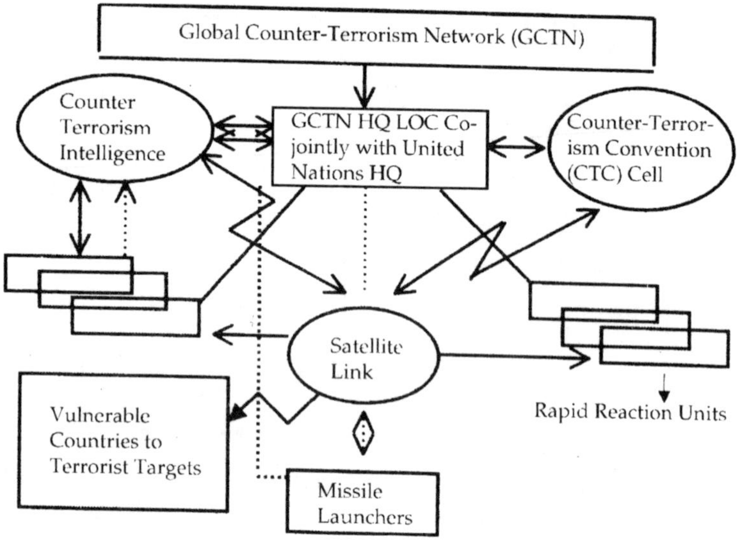

Note:

(a) Intelligence sharing to be done globally through dedicated satellite link.
(b) Rapid reaction units one for each continent. Jointly funded by United Nations.
(c) Missile launchers fired on targets on order from HQ GCTN.
(d) Dotted lines indicate command and control channel.

the main driving force behind the Landmine Treaties. A joint global effort may mean sharing of satellite facilities for communication and guidance of weapons against terrorist camps. (Akin to what was done by the USA to hit Osama Bin-Laden's hideouts). In a future scenario, when Fourth Generation Nuclear (FGN) weapons may be available, it may be possible to have an integrated joint strategy of using space and localised FGNs to neutralise world wide terrorists by targeting them and striking with precision to devastate their hideouts and even making them unusuable due to moderate radiation effects. A suggested global counter-terrorism network is shown schematically in Fig. 4.14.

This will have to get merged with the global civil defence network, covered in the subsequent part.

Further, there should be mock up exercises against terrorist WMD threats. One such model is discussed as follows:

There is definitely a national and international effort required towards formulating 'Mock Up' exercises against simulated disasters of all types including nuclear disaster, which may include terrorist attacks. One such exercise was done at 'Day Dag' Nuclear Power Plant, 40 kms. from Hong Kong. The results of this should be institutionalised in various emergency schemes. A suggested model for any such exercise in the post 2000 period should be constructed on the following lines:

(a) Exercise secretariat is created at the UN Headquarters, under the aegis of IAEA.
(b) Global talent is harnessed to create a simulation cell. This cell should be composed of specialist who can create artificial and natural (but man triggered), disasters, including the 'N', 'B' and 'C' types.
(c) Technical support group be formed to support the technical and scientific aspects.
(d) Co-ordination support group be created to maximise and co-ordinate efforts of various agencies including international support.
(e) Policy and Analysis Cell (supposed to set the exercise and should have factual data of earlier incidents, so that maximum lessons can be drawn) should be established. It would have a core of scientists to modulate data analysis.
(f) Threat assessment group, be formed to analyse the potential threats globally and thus help in formulation of counter-measures. Health hazards associated with the plume pathway and the ingestion pathway as assessed for contamination can also spread through trans-border movement of eatables and other consumer items. This may necessitate establishment of monitoring points and collection of sample readings.

(g) Evacuation/Sheltering Assistance groups be created and dovetailed with other national civil defence measures to produce maximum mitigation. Radiation contaminated area be avoided by helicopter survey and monitoring. The passage and route of evacuation be decided accordingly. (Use of potassium iodide as a means to counter-act against radiation is also moderated).

(h) Mobilisation of national and international air effort and naval effort becomes a pre-requisite to evacuation of population from contaminated inland areas of islands. It may become necessary to announce 'Sea Exclusive Zone' to risk exposures to refugees.

(j) Food anti-contamination action becomes a major effort and area of concern. Milk, leafy vegetables and livestock will have to be protected, as minuscule radioactive dust may settle on the food.

(k) Media and 'psy' management cells should be established and be proficient in announcing and disseminating basic individual and collective safety measures without assistance and concurrent to actions by all other agencies/ cells.

Space and CTO

In the War in Afghanistan, space technology emerged as an important force multiplier for supporting tactical operations. A case study of some important facets are as given below:

Application of the same in our environment would help us in real time location of at least large terrorist camps/movements, which then can be neutralised by a PGM which is navigated on the target through the sophisticated GPS satellite systems and in addition utilisation of navigational and guidance satellites. The information through these can be passed to the 'JCR' (apex level) and the 'Information cell' co-located with the zonal headquarters in the area of operations. Further, in case a 'National Intelligence Agency' is formulated and is also put under command of an Army Counter Terrorist Command, then the direct connectivity of satellites could be established between both the organisations simultaneously. 'DIPAC' kind of processing facility would then also have to be catered for at these organizations with the help of super computers giving instantaneous feedbacks. (There is a case for making a computer software, which can receive and decipher images of the terrorist through pre-packaged modules showing sensitivity to peculiarities of the terrorists like carriage of ammunition, type of dress and rations carried.

CASE STUDY 'Space' Enhances War on Terrorists

Quietly working through its service-level space components and computer network operations teams, US Space Command (USSC) has been a significant behind-the-scenes player in America's war on terrorism.

A Brigadier General and his staff, co-located with forward command centres, are providing space expertise to ensure that war fighters in the field get what they need from US military space resources. "They work for Gen Tommy Franks. They don't work for me. They're there to make sure he gets what he needs in terms of space and information operations support," said General Ralph E. Eberhart, Commander-in-Chief of US Space Command.

The mil-space community has chalked up "success stories in both process and product," he noted. "The supported Commander-in-Chief has been very complimentary, as have those who are out there on the tip of the spear. We're getting smarter all the time, and are providing more value added."

The command and its Air Force, Army and Navy components have refined military satellite communications procedures and augmented capacity with commercial resources, as necessary. Controllers at Schriever AFB, Colorado continually "fine-tune" GPS satellites to ensure that best possible navigation information is available for near precision GPS aided weapon deliveries in Afghanistan.

"I think that, over time, documentation will show how accurate these weapons have been (during) this conflict. We've set a new standard," for accuracy of ordnance such as the Joint Direct Attack Munition, Eberhart said.

Innovation by space troops has led to increasingly efficient use of bandwidth when downloading weather satellite data, enabling more frequent updates to terrestrial and space weather forecasts. Both are critical to the success of air strikes and Special Forces missions. Space "weather" refers to events such as solar flares, which can adversely affect communications, reconnaissance and navigation spacecraft.

Although he wouldn't discuss specifics, the General said that the USSC has supported counter-terrorism efforts through the Computer Network Operations Joint Task Force and the

Command's Joint Information Operations Centre. Their primary mission is to protect Defence Department information networks both domestic and deployed from intruders, but they also have a cyber attack capability.

"At the risk of challenging someone, we've seen no increase in activity (since September 11). Some of the (computer viruses and worms) that affected the commercial sector have just been a blip for us," Eberhart said. "Maybe it's because people are afraid to challenge us in this realm, because they know we're mad, and they're worried about the repercussions." *(Aviation Week and Space Technology)*

Intelligence Structure: Counter-terrorism *(An Israeli Case Study)*

> The King "... should divide the day as well as the night into eight parts . . . During the fifth, he should hold consultations with the council of ministers through correspondence and also keep himself informed of the secret reports brought by spies.... During the first one-eighth part of the night, he should meet the officers of the secret service.... During the seventh, he should hold consultations and send out the officers of the secret service for their operations."
>
> "The Duties of a King"—*The Arthasastra*
> Kautilya, Prime Minister, to Emperor Chandragupta Maurya (4th Century BC)

Every nation has its own intelligence apparatus with its own distinctive mythology. It was the English who coined the term 'intelligence' in the image of their unique temperament – a life style a code of behaviour that was pre-dominantly cerebral, based on the joining together of intelligence, insight and a broad knowledge of the facts, and the ability to put together all these elements to discriminating use.[9] The British created a vast empire from scratch and defended it almost effortlessly by the judicious application of the 'Divide and Rule' formula setting up their enemies one against the other so that the balance of power could be maintained with minimal use of force.[10] Handling terrorism requires a real time responsive intelligence apparatus, which would be discussed here.

The panorama unfolds in Asia between the seventh and fourth centuries B.C., when the Indians, the Chinese and the Persians succeeded in inventing and systematising strategic intelligence in three totally different ways and in deference to divergent ultimate objectives.[11] The Hindu wisdom that was well captured in the fourth century by Kautilya's *Arthasastra* for the benefit of the Maurya rulers had its ultimate and historically enduring sanction in sacred Hindu texts, which tell us that only divine surveillance can assure the deft management of cosmic and earthly affairs of state.[12] Trust in good espionage, for instance, reaches back to the Rigveda, where the spies of God Varuna are pictured seated around him while the deity holds court over the cosmic universe much as angels are often rendered in the Christian religious tradition.[13]

Historically, the British needed intelligence for Internal Security duties. Britishers always perceived a threat from Russia/ Central Asia to their Indian empire. Therefore, the complete orientation was towards the northerly direction. The first organised intelligence collection took place in British India in 1892-93. Major Gen Charles McGregor who was appointed as QMG of the Indian Army took over the Department of Intelligence. Earlier to this the Surveyor General of India located in Dehradun performed the functions of Intelligence gathering. The Indian structure, of course, has got also influenced by the MI-6 (UK). The existing intelligence structure in India has undergone some cosmetic changes since inception. The erstwhile Joint Intelligence Committee has been merged with the National Security Secretariat (NSCS), which is now permanent in nature and has a joint staff integrated from all agencies and departments. The various departments send direct reports to the NSCS, which meets at least once a fortnight. The existing structure is antiquated to a great extent, Arabs achieved strategic surprise against the Israelis in 1973. Kargil intrusion is another case in point. In both the cases, large-scale movements went undetected due to probably the larger picture of peace and predictability. However, if compared with 'Kargil', then both of them had the common infidel of 'Islamic forces.'

Before we formulate an Intelligence structure to fight terrorism, let us recapitulate lacunae so highlighted by the Kargil Review Committee. Kargil Committee Report has performed a yeoman service to the cause of Indian Intelligence. Never before the handicaps of the Indian Intelligence have been officially revealed to the public or a convincing case made out for urgent reforms. No outsider has been allowed in the past to look penetratingly into its ethos, culture, work styles and capabilities or to prepare a report card on its performance,

Nevertheless, the outcome of the Task Force, intelligence re-structuring should be considered a process of 'Evolution' due to the ongoing 'Revolution in Information Technology and Revolution in Military Affairs'. Thus, intelligence reorganisation should remain a 'Dynamic Constant' (DC) factor causing self-amends and corrections corresponding to the formulation of new paradigms of world order and the changing nature of warfare. The concept of integrating 'Corporate Intelligence' also needs consideration. If one traces the root of 'Intelligence' it can be traced to intelligence[15] and synergising the same with the national defence intelligence would not be constructive or net cost-effective, especially in the Indian subcontinent where economic backwardness precludes intelligent extravaganza.

Western Intelligence establishments have been practicing these virtues for quite some time. The many memoirs published there provide an index of the depth and pervasiveness of this phenomenon. Since 1948, the US Intelligence has been investigated by 12 Commissions - 7 Congressional and 5 Presidential. The profiles and charters of all the major intelligence organisations like the CIA and NSA of the USA and MI5, MI6 and CGHQ of the UK are public knowledge, being governed by the enactments of the concerned legislatures. Laws or executive directions at different levels for independent oversight have set up appropriate mechanisms.

Here, the focus would be to set intelligence structures which can address state sponsored terrorism. The Israeli Intelligence is presently one of the most effective structures available. Israel has given a very prominent stature to its intelligence organisation. It has been elevated to the level of a 'Service' (army/air force/navy) headed by a serving Major General and collects all strategic/ tactical intelligence and warning for war preparation. It prepares the National Intelligence Assessment and produces it to the National High Command (Knesset). The intelligence is more oriented in a bottom up approach. Distribution of intelligence structure is as given below:

MOSSAD—External intelligence.
SHABAK—Counter espionage.
LEKEM—Scientific affairs Liaison Bureau of the IDF.

The Israelis after the disaster of the Yom Kippur war have now included the Analysis Division with Mossad and Shabak, a lesson which India should absorb. In fact there is considerable overlap between various intelligence agencies. A comparison between the intelligence structure of India and Israel would bring out many important lessons. Both countries considerable overlap in the functions of their intelligence communities. However, the Mossad and the RAW are each other's counterpart in terms of function and character, and the IB in India can be considered as the equivalent of Shin Beth in Israel.

Both Israel and India arc parliamentary democracies with a considerably strong influence between their agencies and the policy makers. In its democratic aspect, India is arguably closer to the British model and has, at least in principle, more diffusion of power in the intelligence community. This similarity is of course merely procedural and being a democracy does not have a direct correlation with the structure of these organisations. Rather, there are other factors responsible for these differences:

(a) History obviously plays a very prominent role in determining these differences. Although both Israel and India became independent around the same time, as a state India existed much before Israel. Israel started the state building from scratch and the Jews of Israel built a state that suited their needs. Whereas in the case of India, a colonial state was left to them as the British abandoned that part of the empire. The white Sahib left the state apparatus and the brown Sahib filled the gap. Even to this day, the state of India has those manipulative and extractive features that reflect the legacy of colonial rule. Indian state institutions exhibit a higher degree of cultural inertia and much less innovation when compared to Israel, the creation of which is a direct result of marvellous intelligence operation and perhaps the biggest success story in the contemporary intelligence history.

(b) The officer elite in the Israeli intelligence is mostly western/modern, compared to the Indian elite, which is in the process of westernizing/modernizing. However, a point of similarity is that in both the cases there is a foreign culture superimposed on a local one, albeit differently.[17]

(c) Geography and strategic depth of the territory in Israel and India is radically different and perhaps it is the single biggest factor that differentiates Israel from rest of the organisations. Israel's land mass is thin and narrow, surrounded by its hostile Muslim neighbours whose wrath it acquired by dispossessing them of their soil. It was only after creating a de-facto credible nuclear deterrent (Officially Israel is NNWS) that its position has become relatively secure. Nonetheless, it is still dependent on deft and clever intelligence. In the field of comparative intelligence...Israel represents a special case of intelligence: A small country with considerable wealth ($ 7 million a day in foreign aid from the United States alone) spends a higher proportion of their national wealth on intelligence than most other countries. The very survival of Israel depends on good intelligence.

India, on the other hand, is secure by the Indian Ocean in the South and Himalayas to the East, left with part of its border along Pakistani and Bangladeshi territory to worry about. Its trepidation is more immediate and not as far-fetched as that of Israel. Israel monitors most of the world in an effort to obtain any piece of information that would complete an incomplete puzzle. In 1981, Israel took the possibility of a nuclear attack against it very seriously, a single one of which might have been enough to impair the whole state. The American intelligence indicated that Pakistan would have an atom bomb by 1982 and Iraq by 1983. The Uranium Oxide for the Pakistani nuclear reactor came from Niger via Tripoli leading the Israelis to conjecture that if Pakistan transfers just one bomb to Libya, Gaddafi might use it on Israel. The 1984 destruction of the Osirak reactor in Iraq is a logical step in the same direction to eliminate threat by a pre-emotive strike. The exact precision of attacking the targets was a result of first class intelligence.

(d) Lastly, another salient feature of difference that is instrumental in distinguihing between the Israeli and Indian agencies is the threat environment. The security predicament of Israel is primarily external[18], while that of India is also internal. The challenge to these and all intelligence organisations of the world is how to modify their structures to match the ever-changing process of intelligence. This itself varies with the physical environment, cultural moorings, available resources and need. These elements are much more efficiently integrated in the Israeli intelligence agencies than the Indian.

India's intelligence organisations have recently been restructured. One of the important elements of this structure is the creation of a Defence Intelligence Agency (DIA). This has become the apex body on all military matters where the intelligence pertaining to army, air force and the navy is synergised. Now coming specifically to terrorism, there is an urgent necessity of institutionalizing intelligence pertaining to terrorism so that 'Intelligence' can be used in a real time frame as a tool in counter-terrorist operations. (CTO).

What is required is an autonomous organisation or a field unit operating in states where terrorism is prevailing and also creation of a central national structure to coordinate the state intelligence as well as interact on real time basis with DIA (recently raised) with the ultimate aim of guiding the field forces (both military and paramilitary forces) into CTO. They could be organised as a special corps of three to four battalions operating and organised on theatre basis. Further, it is suggested that at least strength of a company (120 men) be employed in the district of operations. The company itself can have platoons and sections looking after area of responsibility of divisions or brigades respectively. These organisations should come operationally directly under the local military headquarters but also pass information to the corps headquarters working directly under the DIA. This autonomous organisation can in fact be called the 'National Intelligence Agency' (NIA) , which in fact becomes the executive arm of the DIA, which itself functions under the Army Counter Terrorism Command.

The modus operandi at tactical level could be on the following lines. Let us assume the operations of a company at a military corps level. The platoons would be organised on a grid system and not on the AOR pattern of the CT forces. They will cultivate sources within their grids and provide real time intelligence to the local military units, the local corps or the central corps at the apex, which will further coordinate with other intelligence organisations like RAW, IB, etc. These company groups would also obtain tactical intelligence in the immediate vicinity of the border from where terrorists are being launched. They will have separate and dedicated communication facilities and will be interconnected.

Presently, intelligence persons are attached to military headquarters and thus cannot operate with autonomy. This system will bring in professional competence. They will even have dedicated technical intelligence support like intelligence satellites or UAVs or even aircraft.

The overall concept is to create a mini 'Intelligence Arm' (Like the structures of Israeli Intelligence CFA/ISI or even Chinese organisations of which not much is known).

Army Counter-Terrorism Command

India is the only country in the world with more such a vast array of insurgencies and terrorist organisations, where the law enforcement agencies have not been able to contain these nefarious activities. There is thus a case for creating a national infrastructure for counter-terrorism. Ideally, this should be based on the existing army counter-terrorist network. In fact, an 'Army Counter-Terrorist Command' (ACTC) be created akin to the existing five army commands to deal with external threat. The role of this ACTC will be to be the all comprehensive national nodal agency for all counter-terrorist matters like computerised data box, supported by C^4 I systems for quick decision making and consequently employment of all types of heterogeneous SF so deployed in the area. The composition of such a headquarter should be a conglomeration of all services and agencies headed by a Lieutenant General of the Indian Army. Even the newly created National Intelligence Agency (NIA) should be able to have connectivity with this organisation, which should be under command the CDS. A holistic schematic diagram is as shown in Fig. 4.15.

The Research and Development cell would have elements from DRDO who will do research and CT equipment and the equipment cell will procure CT equipment from the world market till own R&D develops it, because technology versus manpower analysis definitely proves the importance of good technology in CTO role.

Technology Versus Manpower

In general, counter-terrorism operations have been directed with manpower orientation, as we continue to be trapped with the syndrome of creating combat superiority against terrorists by deploying more and more manpower, which yet falls short. Probably,

Fig. 4.15.

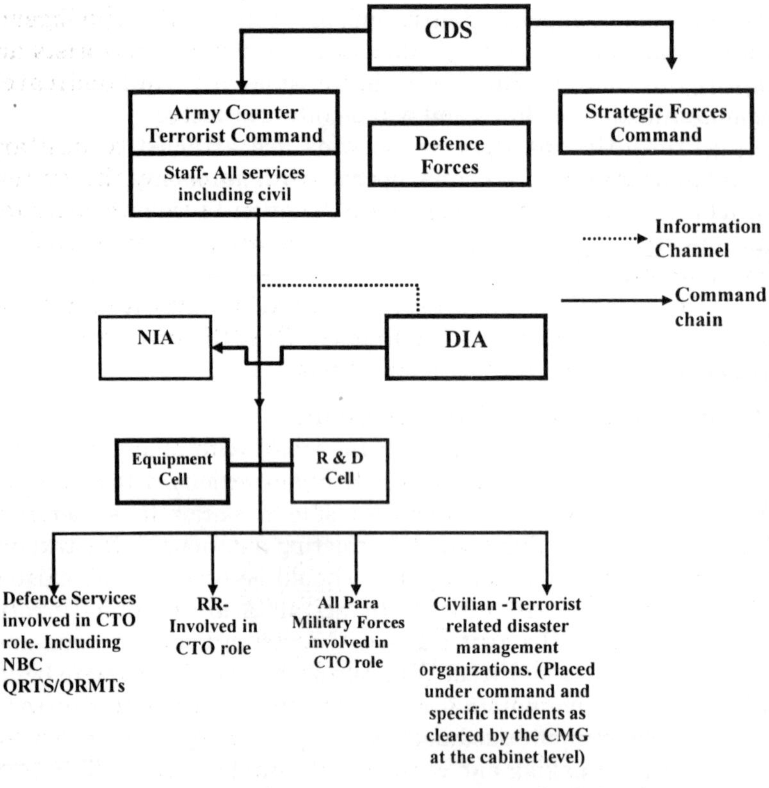

we continue to have the mindset of reacting with multiple units at a single point of terrorist incident. We continue to be trapped in a 'Low Technology Cul de Sac' as in the words of K.P.S. Gill, who further says that the bureaucrats perceive that uniformed persons are volunteers by profession and that they should not complain against privations, risks and hardship and must expect to be killed. Therefore, this problem can only be resolved if they are made to attend to at least state level coordination conferences and if they visit the forward units at least once a year to be more 'live' to the situation.

Further, with the transparency brought in by media, no army in a democracy can accept high casualty, as the concept of body count is a costly proposition for the government. To that extent India's capability to accept casualties has drastically diminished over the years. Kargil War is an illustration.

Fighting terrorism based on the principles of mass brings in the factor of human psychology. Fighting terrorism with numbers will *exponentially increase human error/reaction.* This is directly proportional to human rights violations. On the contrary, use of high technology for fighting insurgency is going to drastically reduce such violations. Consider the fact that one could incapacitate a terrorist in a crowd rather than kill in a scenario where collateral damage could do more harm to the cause of fighting terrorism. Hence payoffs in countering/reducing terrorism will be tremendous.

Normally in the armies of the developing world the working is based on a manpower intensive formula in which 'Numbers' is the key. This has crept up just because most of the conventional armies are manpower intensive with a large population support base. Other side is 'Technology', with vast advancement. The advent of new technology has vapourised the complete concept of battlefield and has changed the entire thinking, as already covered.. 'Technology' and 'Economics' are two key words on which the new theories are gaining dominance with technologically advanced weapon systems playing a major role. The entire battlefield scenario has shifted from man to the machine, with man behind the machine retaining some hold. Any army, which loses its men at very regular intervals, has the following fallouts:

(a) The first one is the morale of the troops, as every casualty erodes the confidence and morale of troops.

(b) The second fallout is the economic burden and the government losing a well-trained man on whom the government has spent a fortune. Lack of procurement of new technology is one of the reasons for such casualties.

(c) Social trauma is the third fallout.

Technology and Recent Wars

Gulf War. Operation Desert Storm was won by the coalition forces because of the use of latest systems like Tomahawk cruise missiles, stealth bombers and laser-guided bombs. This was the first high technology war wherein the ground forces were disseminated without actual ground fighting. The casualties on the coalition forces' side were amazingly low.

Kosovo. Like Gulf War, Kosovo too was a high technology war wherein the K4 forces dissipated the reasonably modern forces of Millosevic by sheer modern technology.

Kargil. Kargil was the other extreme wherein fighting was based initially on numbers and later on technology.

Afghanistan. Certain operations launched by the US forces have been won almost entirely by technology. Operation Enduring Freedom is a classic example as to how the latest technology in warfare can score over numerical superiority. The Americans used latest weapon systems to tame a rogue nation. The 'Daisey Cutters' became household name, in popularity next only to Osama Bin Laden, against whose forces they were used. Similarly during Operation Anaconda (17 days operation in the eastern parts of Afghanistan in Paktia Province), around 1000 US soldiers dropped to eliminate a stronghold of Al Qaida/Taliban. Ground action was minimal, thanks to array of high technology precision weapon systems.

Comparison of Operation Anaconda vis-à-vis conventional CTO in other armies of the world. This operation consisted of just about a battalion of US troops along with half a battalion worth of local friendly Afghan Forces. The operation started off with an air attack using latest technologies like laser guided bombers and bombs like 'Daisy Cutters'. There was minimal ground attack and according to US forces about 500-600 hardcore Al-Qaida terrorists were killed. Ground action was in the form of small team surgical strikes, dropped by choppers, equipped with night fighting capability and quick disengagement and ex-filtration by air.

Consider if some other developing nation were involved with this operation, it would have used nothing less than one to two divisions, without technological advancement. They wouldn't have used the air force as the Americans used. Moreover these conventional formated armies would have launched the attack in echelons, on the vast mountains, thus increasing fatal casualties as it was done in Kargil. It would have relied on time tested artillery and air which would have proved ineffective against the huge caves.[19]

Modern Developments. Some of the technology available, which can be made operational are :

(a) Modern development in technology includes accurate navigation with the help of global positioning system (GPS) based on satellites.

(b) Laser designators, which can help a soldier to quickly and accurately acquire a target.

(c) Image intensifiers or other night vision devices, which can turn night into day. Hologram aiming marks helps aim and shoot with pinpoint accuracy at night is possible.

(d) Light Kevlar bulletproof jackets and anti-mine shoes can provide a degree of protection on the battlefield.

(e) Induction with speed in any battlefield with the help of tilt rotor helicopters.

(f) Remotely piloted vehicles can help mapping the terrorist camps/caves.

(g) Satellites can pick up any infiltrating intruders and warn the forces, which can act immediately. In fact, software can be developed where thermal imagery of a terrorist can be continued due to his unique contents of weaponry and ammunition. Same is picked up by satellites and thereafter deciphered in real time through super computers.

(h) Special equipment like Hand Held Thermal Imagers (HHTI) can detect movement almost a kilometre away and can check infiltration to a large extent.

(j) Unmanned sensor, which can help a great deal in reducing fatigue to troops.

(k) In short information technology and digitisation serve to multiply intrinsic capabilities of the forces of yesteryears. It also provides the required cutting edge to the forces.

(l) Use of many weapons, which can incapacitate terrorists, should be preferably used where collateral damage to civilians is also to be avoided or where there is an 'IFF' problem with own forces. Use of 'sound weapons', which work on creating high frequencies, rubber bullets, sting weapons working on nano-technology and 'Super glues' type agents which can cause immobility to terrorists, should be considered. Use of rubber bullets and tear gas shells should also be institutionalised.

Technology and Doctrine

Some of the essential elements, which stand in relevance to counter-terrorism, are to establish a 'Technology Pushing Doctrine'.

Numerical superiority does not matter much if the forces are well equipped with the latest technology. A very fine and simple example is of Hand Held Thermal Imager (HHTI). It can detect any movement within a range of a few kilometres. Thus, instead of employing a large number of ambushes in a particular stretch, use of this vital equipment can help move a small force and intercept the infiltrators whenever and wherever desired. In fact even if the new equipment is costly on induction, it certainly turns out to be cheaper in the long run as valuable lives can be saved. India will continue to bear the brunt of terrorism in the years to come. It is imperative to undertake technological advancement. It entails a judicious and well thought of expenditure plan. It is unfortunate that although we require much needed weapon systems, the money is being underutilised and being surrendered to the tune of Rs. 5000 crores in the last fiscal year. It only suggests that defence procurement systems are time consuming and there may be a case for working on a 'Role-on Plan' rather than the annual budget. The utilisation of the fund is as important as allocation. On analysis of pros and cons of technological advanced weapon systems vis-à-vis numerical strength, technology overrules manpower or numerical strength to a large extent. The intangible payoffs of procurement of high technology include effect on morale, confidence in the organisation as well as self and considerable reduction in fatigue as surgical strikes even with small ambush parties will replace sitting throughout the night under adverse weather conditions.

Apart from the above cost, the other factors include loss of morale and above all the social trauma of loss of next of kin. High casualty also implies loss of volunteers to choose security forces as a career. With a casualty figure of say 500 deaths and 2000 wounded the cost comes out to 500 × Rs. 34 lakh = 170 crores. These figures are for those who are dead. If we add the figures of wounded it could come to Rs. 300 crores. For five years it would come to about 1500 crores.

Having seen the economics of a deceased soldier, we can formulate two things. Firstly, had the technologically advanced system been inducted the soldier might not have lost his life, thus saving a lot of money by the government. Secondly, the amount of money spent could have been saved had the Security Forces been given better equipment. Even if the casualties were reduced by 50 per cent the saving of Rs 85 crores would have been worth the cost spent on technology. In the present Low Intensity Conflict (LICO)scenario, it is clear that numerical superiority is not of much value. The ground on which the army is fighting does not necessitate much man-power. A suitable mix of numerical strength with high technology will defeat the small group operations of terrorist who themselves rely on high technology with rapid-fire lethal weapon systems.

If the strength in deployment is reduced by 50 per cent and corresponding reduction in casualty figures then the resultant saving will be considerable, both in short term and long term. In fact, if the prices of new equipment vis-à-vis the money spent on pay and allowances, pension and other allied allowances to a soldier are compared, it is seen that induction of new equipment in the armed forces will turn out to be cheaper and will have other allied effects. If the soldier has to retain his relevance on the modern battle-field, he has to look forward to information technology and digitisation as these act as tremendous force multipliers for the foot soldier (Same has already been now validated in the recent Iraq war). 'Long Term' and 'Short Term' gains of high technology include less casualties and more saving by the government, both in terms of human life and economics. It also includes high morale of troops, confidence in weapon systems and above all it imparts the required cutting edge vis-à-vis other armies of the world.

Future Concepts

In today's technologically advanced scenario there are lot of concepts that are gaining prominence the world over. These are the futuristic and technologically advanced soldiers who will dominate the battlefields of tomorrow. Pioneers in these futuristic battles are the Americans, with their new concept and designs. Apart from the Americans most European armies are continuously working at enhancing the capabilities of the foot soldier, i.e., the capabilities of technological advancement, which can make the soldier less vulnerable and more lethal. The Americans have gone much ahead on the road to digitisation of battlefield. The Advanced Projects Research Agency (APRA) of USA is working at a furious pace to convert their futuristic concepts into reality. Most advanced of these concepts is the American "Land Warrior", wherein every soldier will be equipped with laser designators, Global Positioning Systems, body vest computers, etc. Every such "land warrior" will be updated by V Sat communication to a command post and facilitating quick call for attacks on enemy forces and with lethal effect. Thus, this futuristic concept will change the entire battlefield scenario and convert the infantry man of yesteryears into a new individual who is more lethal and more effective. These futuristic concepts are some of the models on which we can think and modernise our own forces. This will go on a long way in increasing the efficacy of our soldier vis-à-vis the international and advanced forces. Such modernisation will also apply to fighting terrorism. Having seen and established the superiority of a small but advanced well-equipped force over a vast but technologically poor force, let us analyse how best this revolution can be completed in our forces. In reality, we are a force who has been fighting terrorism for over a decade with very little in terms of modern equipment and weapon systems. Small necessities of the battlefield like HHTIs and night vision have been procured of late, that too in inadequate numbers. We are still in the stage of converting from 7.62 mm calibre family of small arms to 5.56 mm calibre. The requirements of this vast army of ours are massive but the funds are low and the vision is blurred. In the emerging scenario there is a need to gear up for the future trends because it is only the modern and technologically advanced force, which can fight to win. To usher in a revolution there is a need to move in a logical sequence. Given the conditions of our economy and the mindset of the system, there is a need to look for a period of about two decades and that too in a very phased and a scientific manner with clear goals to be achieved. First we have to get our priorities right. Is it just creeping up to our neighbouring countries vis-à-vis arms superiority by purchasing weapons from international market or by looking ahead and instead of just catching up with our neighbours generate a process of expertise and research and development which will give a definite technology edge in the times to come? With a little foresight and vision, a judicious mix of distribution of funds for procurement of modern system from international market and developing the technology of international standards needs to be looked into.

Experts on terrorism have always upheld that terrorists have never succeeded in their objectives and that no state, big or small, has ever capitulated to their demands. The Irish terrorists have been at their job for the past 200 years. Both Jews and Arabs in Palestine have toyed with terrorism for the past 50 years without succeeding. The Basques in Spain, the LTTE in Sri Lanka and the Khalistani separatists in Punjab have all tried and failed.

Suggestions for combating terrorism is based on military doctrines though the general finding is that terrorism cannot be overcome by counter-terrorism, which has been universally accepted by informed observers. Some of the well-researched strategies on terrorism can be applied to our own experience in dealing with terrorism. There are many who believe that insurgency in the North East has lasted for the past 50 years because our security forces were insensitive to the feelings of the civilian population of these states. Whereas the insurgents never targeted non-combatants, we did not apply the same rule whenever we felt that the civilian population was harbouring or giving logistical support to the insurgents. To state that only repressive measures succeeded in ridding Punjab of terrorism would be erroneous. The only real answer to terrorism is not military counter-measures alone but winning the hearts and minds of people. The Punjab problem, in a way, ended only after the terrorists themselves became a bigger nuisance to the Jat Sikh farmers than the police.

One can advocate surgical, precise, offensive action against terrorists based on the element of surprise with an emphasis on discretionary tactical operations. One can draw on military science as propounded by Frederick the Great of Prussia who concentrated on the defeat of enemy but never on the physical destruction of non-combatants. Our army and paramilitary leaders now fighting Pakistan-inspired terrorism in Jammu and Kashmir should debate these principles.

In the end, the basic theme of such a global initiative would be based on mutual co-operation. Let us all fight disasters and terrorist wars together and not alone – as we all belong to this planet. The United Nations has already got a very fine track record in these accounts and, therefore, should become the mother organisation in handling global WMD terrorist incidents. Thus, there is also a necessity of global funding towards this end. Let us, therefore, analyse the aspect of budgeting for counter-terrorism.

Fig. 4.16.

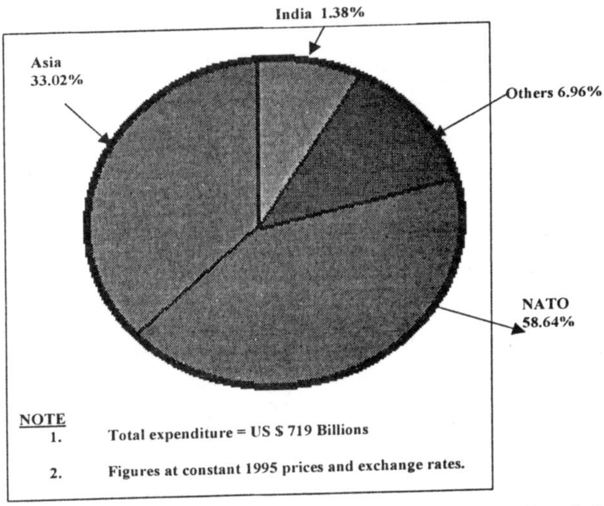

Source: Extracts from *Indian Defence Year Book 2002.*

Budgeting for Counter Terrorism

India's security concerns are multidimensional ranging from West to the East and the Indian Ocean towards the South. Very few nations are so located geo-strategically. In spite of this India's share in the world's defence expenditure has been wanting.

The total outlay of India's defence budget, Presently, works out approximately to 2.6 per cent of the Gross Domestic Product (GDP) of the Indian economy. There have been projections of a minimum requirement of 3 per cent GDP for a comprehensive and balanced arming of the defence forces with an eye to futuristic modernisation and tailoring organisations to meet newer threats like terrorism and asymmetric warfare or the so called 'Fourth Generation Warfare'. Unfortunately, India's defence expenditure as percentage of GDP has been wanting. (Fig. 4.17-the assessmrent is as per the author).

Fig 4.17

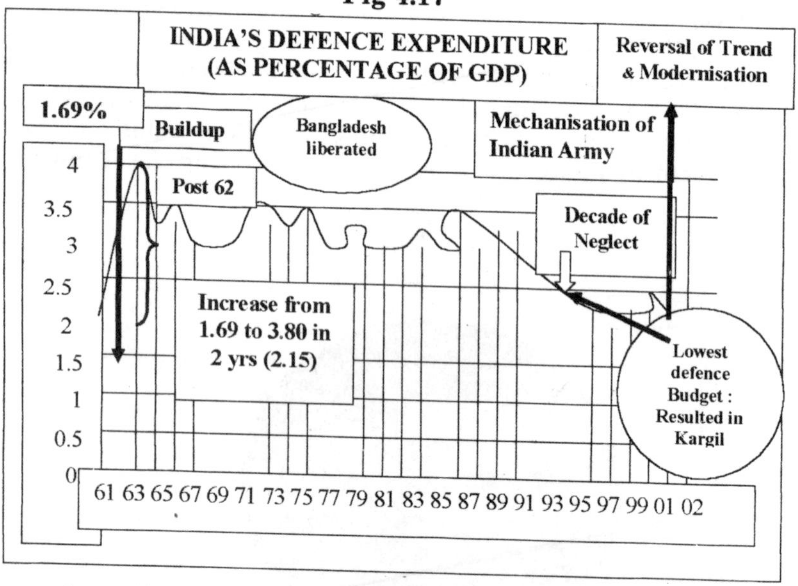

Actually in GDP terms, India's defence outlay is comparatively lower than that of China or Pakistan. A comparative analysis of the combat strength versus defence spending in regard to Asia military powers is tabulated in Fig. 4.18. The figure has been compiled from *Sipri* and *Indian Defence Yearbook.*

Fig. 4.18.

ASIAN MILITARY POWERS : 1999

Defence Forces In Thousand		Top Ten	Defence Spenders $ Billion (1995 prices)	
2935	China	1. Japan	51.2	
1240	Russia	2. Russia	22.4	
1100	India	3. China	15 ?	⇨ More than 3 % of GDP
1055	N Korea	4. S Korea	15.1	
672	S Korea	5. S Arabia	14.5	
639	Turkey	6. India	10.2	⇨ Less than 2.5% of GDP
587	Pakistan	7. Turkey	9.6	
518	Iran	8. Taiwan	9.3	
492	Vietnam	9. Israel	8.4	
476	Indonesia	10. Pakistan	2.8	⇨ More than 3.5% of GDP

While Pakistan's defence budget stands at $ 2.8 billion (4.7 per cent of its GDP), the Chinese outlay is estimated at $ 15 billion (more than 3 per cent of its GDP. However, there are enough reports to indicate that China has been fudging figures and this account and that their defence outlay could actually be much higher)[20]. The point to understand is that China is not attempting an across the board modernisation but identify certain key areas which will be developed to annul superior enemy capability (For example, like in the electronic magnetic spectrum). Therefore, it wants to combine technology with other asymmetric forms of warfare like use of special-forces or guerilla forces. Similarly, this may lay cost-effective approach to modernisation for India too, which should arm to build counter-terrorist strategy and procurement of weapons and equipment thereto, in the priority sectors.

Of late armies of the world have been revising their doctrines. Resorting to 'wide dispersal tactics' to enable forces to move rapidly through 'Small Windows of Opportunity' on a transparent battle zone where communication blackout will exist has been suggested in the military circles, and thereafter the talks of small unit operations of battalion and brigade commanders and small Special Forces. (See Chapter on "Modernisation Projects of the Army", *Indian Defence Year Book* 2002, New Delhi, Natraj Publishers, pp.

366-340). An analysis of this kind of force structuring also reflects the need for similar forces in counter-terrorist role. The raising of Rashtriya Rifle in this context needs understanding. The government has approved in principle a proposal to raise 30 new battalions of Rashtriya Rifles (RR) and that the overall strength by 2005 will be 60 such battalions.[21] Ironically, the RR battalions at present are clubbed with the Territorial Army (TA) and the National Cadet Corps (NCC) in the Non-Composition Table Part-1 of the government and therefore need an urgent integration with the army so that the concept of a unified command could fructify in real terms. But, this would mean sharing the impoverished army budget, which may then have to be raised, causing other ramifications. In totality the CT forces, mostly based on RR battalions will be about 1200 officers and 60,000 men, which actually would be equivalent to about seven divisions or two corps. In other words, if these forces are reorganized for conventional warfare, they would provide the cutting edge against Pakistan as far as troops combat ratio is concerned. On the contrary, if they are disbanded then an additional defence budget is available for modernisation. The geo-strategic and geo-political analysis confirms that insurgency and terrorist operations would continue at least for a decade, although they may get reduced due to the post 11 September 2001 scenario and the American objective of eliminating terrorism, wherever it is. Therefore, there is a case of maintaining the existing 41 RR battalions and not indulge in expansion to 60 RR battalions. This curtailment obviously would generate 575 crores initially and 545 crores towards annual maintenance.[22] Therefore assuming that for the year 2002-2003, funds allocation to the tune of approximately Rs. 1000 crores can be saved. This money can then be re-cycled towards modernisation of existing RR battalions and more cost effective procurement of equipment in consonance with the counter-terrorist strategy and doctrine. (Details are given in the chapter 'Modernisation of Paramilitary Forces and Police Forces' Indian Defence Year Book, pp. 399-414).

The army received Rs. 37,498[23] crores (up from Rs. 34127.22 crore) in the budget (2001-2002), which included budget for purchase of surveillance devices and unmanned air vehicles (UAV) from Israel for counter-terrorists operations. The irony is that due to systemic hurdles in procurement, Rs. 5,000 crores of the defence budget was surrendered. This much money was sufficient to equip the Army with counter-terrorist equipment, mainly, software packages and connectivity for satellite surveillance with a view to identify hideouts and group movements; purchase of additional UAVs, few attack helicopters, more sophisticated small arms including laser based systems, sensors, and hand held thermal imagers and more sophisticated signal equipment. The need for more and better Bullet Proof Jackets (BPJ) needs no emphasis for a soldier operating in the environment, either towards the North or North East of India.

The facet, which requires re-thinking in CTO, is the concept and cost of border management through paramilitary forces like Border Security Forces (BSF) and border fencing. Some aspects of analysis from various journals, like that of the *Indian Defence Review* have been used here.[24] The BSF has given a comprehensive modernisation plan to include latest surveillance and communication equipment, etc. The BSF has already modelled commando groups akin to the Kashmir police's 15 counter-terrorism Special Operations Groups (SOGs) who have been fighting terrorists since 1995. Similarly, the Assam Rifles which was created to fight insurgents in the North East was allocated additional Rs. 16 crores for the Financial Year 2001-2002 to enhance CTO capability. The force has a total of 32[25] battalions and one training centre, all deployed towards Nagaland, Manipur, Tripura and Assam. With the Naga problem coming within the framework of a solution, these forces can also be cut down in manpower but equipped with more modern surveillance equipment and also have satellite connectivity.

The Indo-Tibetan Border Police has about 25 battalions, four specialist battalions and three training centres. There is a proposal to enhance their strength by additional 35 companies, which actually needs to be reconsidered and instead they should be better equipped for surveillance, equivalent to the cost of raising 18 companies and get savings cost of 17 companies. This money saved, then can be effectively utilised in raising, may be just 4 specialised 'Hi-Tech' companies for CTO role, and may be another two specialised companies for managing high priority airports, (against terrorist action) and providing redundancy in the existing set up of the Central Industrial Reserve Force (CISF) for airport security. Similarly, the re-structuring of the Territorial Army (TA) should envisage downsizing and not enhancement. There is a scope of re-conversion of TA railways into regular infantry battalions, which again could be reduced to just four of them but better, equipped for CTO role. These could then be dovetailed in employment with RR battalions, which could then cause release of the troop deployment of the regulars.

As part of a defence strategy to check infiltration and cross-border terrorism, border fencing has been in progress since 1988 onwards. A total length of 452 kms. of flood lighting or fencing has been completed in Punjab; and 1048 kms. in Rajasthan. A plan exists for approximately Rs. 984 crores of fencing for North Eastern States in two phases (phase 1 is reaching completion). Similarly an amount of Rs. 86 crores (187 × 46 =8602 lakhs) at the rate of Rs. 46 lakhs per km in the Jammu region is under progress. As per feedbacks available on border fencing the effect has been positive. There is always scope of saving through better technology surveillance methods. It is proposed that surveillance on the border be planned by employing sensors and radars and many thermal imaging devices, which have proved very successful.[26] (The modus operandi of terrorist groups guided by the ISI, use UAVs to identify gaps in our deployment. Till today there is no counter-UAV strategy or weaponry. This needs to be addressed). If one does analysis of the cost of surveillance equipment required at least in the Kashmir region, one can easily see that the total equipment required in a strip of 200 kms length would not cost more than a few crores. (Approximately 4 crores as per current rate of thermal-imagers costing Rs. 10 lakhs per piece), as per the *Janes* series. Over and above this, the cost of maintenance of border fencing would be much higher than other surveillance. The answer probably is a mix ratio with only limited per cent of the area being fenced. Further, there is a misnomer of increase in defence budgeting every year. A case study of the 2002-2003 budget signifies the necessity of separate budgeting for CTO role and equipment.

The defence budgeting for 2002-2003 provided for Rs. 65,000 crores showing an increase of 14 per cent, which in actual fact was not more than 4 per cent of accretion. Because the negative factors of inflation, alteration in foreign exchange rates and incidental increments in running an organization, all pull down the overall actual availability of funds. Further, the 14 per cent increase so projected was also a result of skewed calculations by comparing with the revised estimates of spending for the previous year. On the other hand, if the comparisons are drawn between the initial provisions for both the periods under discussion, then the overall increase was just Rs. 3,000 crores which is just about 4.8 per cent or so. One may have to cater for other contingencies as well, reducing the total money by about 4000 to 5000 crores in the complete year. That left just about 60,000 crores, which was effectively reduced to just 50,000 crores due to unforeseen circumstance and systemic failure of procurement. Therefore in actual fact, there was a reduction in budget available. This particular case for the financial year 2001-2002/ 2002-2003, has just been argued with a view to drive home the point that there is scope for better financial management as the budget should actually be tailored to fulfill a phased blueprint of a future (at least 10 years plan) doctrine of warfare. While evolving such a doctrine, as discussed earlier, the reality of the type and nature of future wars cannot be overlooked. There is a need to develop a security doctrine to fight such threats and consequently do force structuring of defence forces so as to cater for this new dimension of warfare or the so called 'Third Manoeuvre', as analysed earlier. The existing system of budgeting leaves no scope for procurement of CTO equipment. In fact, what is required is again a holistic approach in organising various services for counter-terrorist roles. For example, an integrated approach is required between the army and the para-military forces, for border fencing and regarding requirement of surveillance equipment, and so on as all these organisations are working in the same available battle space. Therefore, factors of compatability, redundancies, dual function and cost-effective deployments have to be judiciously worked out. As a specimen, one can work on brick system of calculation; assuming the brick to be one major unit (infantry battalion) of the army or the para-military force. Each brick should have the following types of equipment for say, 1000 strength, which would mean a financial outlay as given below:

Table 4.5

			Price - Rs.
(a)	Hi-Tech small arms (AK 56)	-	5000 × 1000 = 50 lacs
(b)	8 Thermal Imagers		2 lacs × 8 = 16 lacs
(c)	12 sets of Sensors	-	22 lacs × 12 = 265 lacs
(d)	Bullet proof jackets	-	1000 × 10 = 1 lac
(e)	Radio communication 12 sets	-	12 × 25,000 = 3 lacs
			Rs. 334* lacs

Note: Costs obtained from Janes and other, open, sources. The costs may, therefore, vary by more than 50 per cent.* Between three to four crores approximately.

Based on this analysis, proportionate budgeting of various

forces needs to be modulated. For example, the army on its own may be having surveillance sensors for an area, where the BSF also buys similar equipment, causing unnecessary wastage. Thus, an integration in financial planning is required between the three Services of the defence forces and with the Ministry of Defence and Home. With the institution of Integrated Defence Staff (IDS) already in place, it is hoped that the Services' problems would be overcome. A similar mechanism would have to be evolved between the two ministries and finance be distributed accordingly.

Yet another theory, which requires instituting, is that the planning should be done with a 'Bottoms Up Approach' (BUA) by deciding the deployment, after which the equipment is decided and then the money is calculated cumulatively moving upwards. By this BUA almost 50 per cent of budget can be saved, as also the equipment would be effectively deployed successfully. In the current budget scenario as analysed above, for a particular year, there is actually no residual budget left for procurement of counter-terrorist system. The answer therefore, rests in a holistic and bottoms up approach whereby deployments for respective forces are worked out to specificity and the total budget is accordingly prioritised and coordinated between the MOD and MHA. Towards analysing the budget, a case study of US's bid on technology to fight terrorism is worth understanding.

US Bids on Technology to Fight Terror

(Case Study for planning of budget)

President Bush in his 2003 budget request to Congress had bid for $9 billion for the hi-tech arsenal as part of an additional $48 billion for the fiscal beginning October.

A Pentagon official said the budget will not increase overall troop strength from current levels. *Rumsfeld appears to be betting that better technology is the key to winning the war on terrorism. His budget request also includes $8.5 billion for missile defence and $68 billion for new weapons, including $5 billion for the US Air Force's new F-25 fighter.*

The behind-the-scenes battle over troop strength could surface when lawmakers question Rumsfeld about Bush's request for a $379 billion defence budget in 2003, up 14 per cent from this year. The increase would be the biggest since President Reagan's build up 20 years ago.

Before 11 September 2001, Rumsfeld wanted to cut troop strength and increase spending *on hi-tech weapons as part of a plan to "transform" the military into a lighter, more mobile fighting force for the 21st century*. The Service chiefs argued for more troops and weapons.

• ***Intelligence and Communications.*** At least $3 billion to improve intelligence gathering and computer networking.

• ***Unmanned Aerial Vehicles (UAVs).*** More than $100 million to buy missile-firing Predator drones like those used for the first time against the Taliban. Several hundred million dollars will speed production of Global Hawk, the long range UAV that also deputed in Afghanistan. Also stepped-up is the work on a stealthy, bomb-droping UAV.

• ***Army Future Combat System.*** Slated to make the tank obsolete, this combination of sensors, robots and remotely fired artillery would get more than $500 million.

• ***Space-based Radar.*** Officials have given top priority to developing a constellation of satellites that would track moving vehicles on the ground as well as aircraft.

(**Note** : From *USA Today; Army* magazine of December 2001 and also from CNN News of 10 July 2002).

Further, disaster management, organisations should also be dual roled and combined to take nuclear, biological and chemical disasters. Thus, again, there comes a requirement of integrated planning between MOD and MHA[27] for such dual and judicious employment. At least one company of BSF, ITBP and TA battalions be also trained and equipped to deal with such terrorist tasks at a very nominal cost of just Rs. 30 crores as second line or second response mechanism at the national level; but as first responders where they are directly tasked in a geographical area. This would be a better option than creating new structures, both, at Centre and State levels. For example, the National Capital Territory (NCT) plan of Delhi Civil Defence has demanded Rs. 500 crores for organising against a nuclear attack or disaster Delhi. (Details collected from various seminar and press reports in many newspapers). This is most uneconomical spending of the state money. What is required is to create first responders from home guards/ civil volunteers and supported by second responders from the central organisation, as already discussed. Therefore, again there is a requirement of a central agency, which can coordinate all such agencies of the MHA and MOD against NBC terrorist attacks or disasters[28]. There is, thus, a definite requirement of a separate ministry for disaster management, as it automatically becomes a money saver by harnessing and coordinating all the resources. In fact, it is also suggested that these resources, statewise, be also earmarked to help the army while fighting NBC terrorist incidents in forward areas of operations. Another aspect is the budgeting required for annual 'Mock up' practices against such terrorist WMD attacks. This obviously should get linked to international efforts and UN funding for such expenditures be bidded for. In fact, one cannot over rule, the concept of UN ' Quick Reaction Teams', against WMD terrorist attacks. These could be co-opted during national level exercises. Further, a 'SAARC—Anti Terrorist Fund' (SATF) is suggested, which should be included in the SAARC terrorist convention, recently agreed upon during the meeting Nepal in January 2002.

Further, let us re-examine as to out of the total outlay of defence budget of approx 65,300 crores (Anticipated to touch 68,000 – 70,000 crores for the year 2003-2004) what financial planning can be done for earmarking a common services budget purely for CTO roles, which will remain a threat at least for the next 10 years.

Fig. 4.19. Defence Budget : 2003-04.

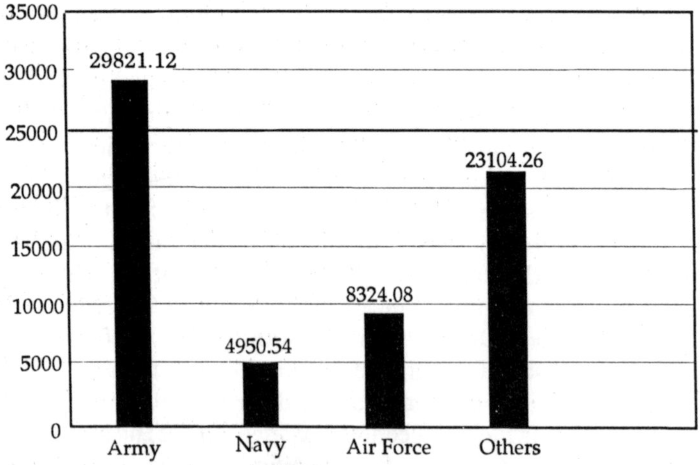

Total Defence Budget : Rs. 65300 Crores

Details taken from *Indian Defence Year Book*, 2002

As a rough estimate if one earmarks only 5 per cent of the budget for CTO expenditure as formulated in conjunction with MHA (to cater for CTO by BSF, Assam Rifles, etc.) and presided over may be by the 'CCEA', for control budget allocation. Thereafter, an integrated (MHA and MOD) Price Negotiation Committee (PNC) should centrally procure the systems. By this organisational synthesis, the end result achieved would not allow, in fact it would avoid, duplication compatibility of equipment and thus an overall economy saving.

Research and Development (R&D) Aspects

Presently, R&D is more oriented towards numerous mega projects, which involve highly sophisticated crew weapon or surveillance platforms costing thousands of crores. But since full scale conventional and classical battles are ruled out for some time such sophisticated weapons may never be used. What will definitely be required is the type of 'unrestricted warfare' or 'the skirmish battle' based on a concept of 'asymmetric warfare' or 'networked warfare' where predominance of 'infantry' elements like 'Special Forces' or 'Hi-Tech Soldiers' emerge. What is required is to equip the future combat soldier with the best equipment giving him 'invincible' capabilities. Such troops when employed in 'CTO' or any special missions would invariably succeed, due to better 'Combat Capability' at that point of decision. This point may be just 100 square metres (10 × 10 metres) or maximum 1000 square metres (100 metres x 10 metres). One can develop an 'Equipment Concept' based on the following contours:

(a) The equipment be designed to develop on eight key soldier capabilities.

(b) Camouflage and concealment, both during day and night. (Make them anti-sensor/ thermal in the night). Further the uniform be made of light weight molecular material that make the clothing change colours as per the environment.

(c) NBCR threat detection (against nuclear, biological, Chemical gases and radioactive fallout).

(d) Threat reduction (by bullet proof jacket and capability of fighting dirty, i.e. survivability in NBC environment).

(e) Real time automated medical treatment.

(f) Reduced logistics footprint (lightening the load of a fully equipped soldier by at least 10 kgs or so).

(g) A super helmet with 'Head and Display' capability for better combat awareness, and soldier-to-soldier connectivity. The option for satellite connectivity should also be there.

(h) Personnel weapons could be laser rifles and designators.

(j) Stun grenades or 'Stink' weapons in CT roles be also envisaged, to thwart suicide squads where civilians are also present.

(k) Hand Held Thermal Imagers (CT role) and IFF electronic gadgets fitted on the bolt of every soldier. In CT role differentiation can be made between friend and foe by an electronic matching or mismatching. It should also give your electronic and digitised location to the command element.

(l) Enhance mobility given to individual soldiers through spring boots or even small battery powered 'micro-flights', which can take off/ land in a small field (Ideal in CTO role).

(m) Soldiers be armed with miniaturised non-technology products including artificial 'Bees' which can be launched to target human beings without a specific combat dress. (Can target terrorists in a populated area).

Innovations in field could lead the way for better technology. The example of Punjab could be used for application in the scenario as obtained today.[29]

(a) Infra-red filter glass torch, which allows only infra-red relation to pass. (Toughened glass is coated with mixture of dyes, which only allow IR to pass and no visible light). It can be used on vehicles. If a heavier coating is done, it could be used to get a range of about 700 metres.

(b) Sound Multipliers, which could collect sound from a distance due to the parabolic effect of the reflector.

(c) Electronic Timer Detector, which can detect any concealed IED from at least 15 inches or so. It was actually developed for just Rs. 10,000, locally.

(d) Mobile tractors were constructed with three plates of tempered steel. This could be carried and installed anywhere. Looking at the above, keeping the necessity of fast improvisation, may this be an interim solution till more widely available and cost-effective technology takes its place. Some of the additional aids, which can be improvised are:

Some of the additional aids, which can be improvised are:

(a) ***IFF System.*** Suicide squads generally are successful because of the problem of 'Identification of Friend or Foe' (IFF). Thus, there is a necessity of a simplistic electronic device, which responds by matching of frequencies by the receiver held by the sentry. It could be developed on the basic principles of remote controlled bells, which are very light and can be strapped to a belt.

(b) ***Mobile Steel Bunker.*** This could be made by a combination of metal alloys and which are light. Some space could be kept between two skirting plates, which can then be filled with mud or sand or stones or wood as available in the environment. It could be made in three layers, which can be bolted in about a minute. These could be carried, during shallow search operations and erected at suspicious places. It can also be used at temporary sentry posts or at ALGs. It will increase SF tactical manoeuvrability as well as reduce own casualties.

(c) Use 'Tear Gas' and rubber bullets in neutralising terrorists, where civilians are present and where we do not want collateral casualties.

(d) Use incapacitating IEDs in front of areas, where static troops are deployed. Basically to prevent suicide attacks.

(e) Use very low-grade radioactive material of say only 10 Rads, (50 Rads is minimum dangerous dose for human being) lethality across the gaps, on the LOC. Therefore, elements, which cross over and get mixed up in nearby villages, can be detected through a 'Radio Meter', which responds to the radioactivity, which may emanate from the person. This could be done by a coordination and search operation or even while carrying out ambushes, establishing blocking position and also while tracking individuals.

(f) ***Chemical Detectors.*** Use lime or any other, non-hazardous chemical on infiltration routes along the LOC. By the technique as mentioned above, detection can be done through 'ACADA' or other chemical detectors.

(g) Poly-carbon shields of eight mm thickness can impede muzzle velocity of AK-47/56 Rifles and become lifesavers. It is a handy protective shield to be used during cordon and search operations, move in built up area and house-to-house searches.

(h) Side view mirrors be created by fixing two mirrors (size 12 × 12 inches) on a wooden frame at an angle of 60 degrees (one should be able to change angles with the help of a hinge) attached to a long pole. It will give enhanced visibility from a bunker or can be used during house-to-house search.

(j) Imagine a group of terrorists, when they encounter a squad of seemingly invisible warriors protected by armour, sensors and having superhuman capabilities. Once a CTO doctrine is developed, requisite weapons and equipment as mentioned above can be researched produced within a five years span, provided projects are given to the well established trade in the country.

(k) Develop systems like Mobile Isotopic Neutron Spectroscopy Systems (MINS), which can identify unknown objects. The technology works by bombarding an object with neutrons. The gamma rays that escape are then measured by a spectrometer, which identifies the bombarded object's chemical elements and their relative abundance. Specially developed software then compares the measurement against a database of substances whose chemical make-ups is known. This information provides the (MINS) operator with an identification of the object's contents within minutes. Other technologies including a holographic imaging system for airport screening, and hand held chemical/biological warfare agent detectors may also be considered.

(l) Anthrax decontamination foam, an early warning system to detect and identify chemical and biological aerosols released in public spaces and a national infrastructure simulation and analysis capability to provide the authorities with guidance on the potential impact of terrorist-related disasters.

References

1. 1990 onwards, the ISI has been carrying out covert operations to control the Kushka-Herat-Kandhar-Quetta-high way. Unfortunately, for Pakistan, due to the warlord rivalries, this actually could not occur.
2. Delupis, *The Law of War* (Cambridge: Cambridge University Press, 1987), p. 72.
3. Jadunath Sarkar, *Shivaji and His Times* (London: Longman Group Ltd, 1973), p. 110.
4. *Ibid,* pp. 117-18.
5. (Such a programme proved successful for General Papagos in Greece 1949, for General Briggs and Sir Gerald Temper in Malaya; by the War cabinet in Kenya against the Mau Mau and French in Nigeria in 1959-60. A similar example can be drawn again by the handling of insurgencies by the government forces in the North-East states (Mizoram and Nagaland since 1950) in India.
6. The Author had access to data on the demographic and terrorist classification, both in the North East and Kashmir. The data has been used statistically to produce these figures.
7. This assumption can be a presumption as a planning model for various actions in this work.
8. ***Laser Weapons***. These would employ an intense beam of coherent electromagnetic radiation at infrared (IR), optical, ultraviolet (UV) or X-ray frequencies.

   Radio Frequency (RF) Weapons. These would employ an intense beam of electromagnetic radiation at microwave or millimetre -wave frequencies.
9. Hesi Carmel (Ed), *Intelligence for Peace* (London: Frank Cass), p. 6, mentioned in the article, "The Man and his Time", written by Haggai Eshed.
10. *Ibid.,* p. 8.
11. Adda B Bozeman, *Strategic and Intelligence Statecraft* (London:Brassey's, 1992), p. 7.
12. *Ibid.,* p. 7.

13. *Ibid.*, p. 16.
14. *Ibid.*, p. 26.
15. Robert David Steele, "Private Enterprise Intelligence: Its Potential Contribution to National Security" (Internet: Intelligence Analysis as Assessment), pp. 1-2.
16. In-house efforts to carry out reforms get defeated. In 1988-89 a major effort was mounted to give a new face to the R&AW. Success was achieved in getting the scheme cleared by all the key departments including Personnel, Expenditure and Finance. Certain entrenched interests, however, had the final papers intercepted while they were in transit to the PMO, and lost. Soon, a new government was in office, which, predictably, had no desire to do anything in the matter. Similarly, the reforms, which the Kargil Committee has recommended, will not see the light of the day unless apolitical high powered bodies are structured to navigate them.
17. Factor that is responsible for shaping these organisations is culture. The ruling elite in Israel is of the Ashkenazi background, whereas the Sephardi Jews are considered second-class citizens whose contribution to the enterprise of state building is less than the Ashkenazim. The European Jews founded the Zionist movement, dominated it, and overwhelmed the long-existing Sephardi community in Palestine. They imposed their institutions and values on the politics, society and culture of the Yishuv (the Jewish community in the pre-1948 Palestine) and the State of Israel, assuming that the Jews from backward non-European areas would simply have to adjust to the established order. The Indians have been historically divided into various castes. Each caste as per Manu's code had a class of work to be performed like Kshatriyas, Shudras, etc. However, in post-independent India, the intelligence community seems to have been dominated by the Brahmins and thereafter the bureaucrats. This obviously has created a different functional ethos in both the countries and they appear to be divergent in nature in their performance.
18. Threat to Israel is external not only from across the borders but as on Islamic philosophy of terminating unauthorised existence of Israel and tyrannical practices of the Israeli state, accompanied by its gross violation of Human Rights. Read Harry Ellis, *The Dilemma of Israel*. US Interests in the Middle East Series (American Enterprise Institute for Public Policy Research, 1970), p.12 *and* 14. Jeffrey Richelson, *Foreign Intelligence Organizations* (Massachusetts: Ballinger Publishing, 1988), p. 191-194 and 196-197, 210, 222, 229. A rough typology that exists to understand structures of Intelligence systems can be divided into four categories: Federation, Confederation, Centralised and Decentralised types. The federation type organisation usually has its director appointed from within the Intelligence community (as in the case of the US), whereas the head of confederation-type comes from outside of the intelligence community (as in the case of UK). In the Centralized type, all intelligence functions are grouped under one chief (example: USSR, Turkey) and conversely, in the Decentralised one, all agencies work independently, accountable directly to the head of the state (example: Nazi Germany, Iraq). Read John Pike in *Federation of American Scientists* 1 December 1997. From the net - http://www.fas.org/irp/world Israel/mossad/20.
19. Operation Vijay of our forces was in strikingly similar conditions less the

caves, as OP Anaconda by the US Forces.

20. Chinese analysts calculate standing of nations by measuring 'comprehensive national strength by a dynamics, calculus process of measuring qualitatively and quantitatively key component or 'sub-systems' of a countries multi-layered national power system.
21. *Indian Defence Year Book 2002* (New Delhi: Natraj Publishers), p. 404.
22. *Ibid.*, p. 403.
23. Figures taken from *Indian Defence year book 2002*.
24. *Ibid.*
25. *Ibid.*
26. The author has experimented with Hand Held Thermal Imagers (HHTI), which give a range of detection of more than two kms of a human being at night.
27. HPC report on disaster management. The high powered committee constituted by the Prime Minister to review disaster management practices in the country has in its final report submitted to the Ministry of Agriculture on 8 October recommended a suitable legislation to define the respective roles of central and state governments in the event of a disaster and fix responsibility. The report contains a draft of the National Disaster Management Act and the State Disaster Management Act. Calling for an integrated multi-hazard approach to the disaster preparedness and mitigation, the report underlines the need for establishing a federal agency similar to the Federal Emergency Management Authority of the USA besides creation of an independent ministry – an umbrella organisation – exclusively for disaster management to co-ordinate the activities of various ministries (see table below). It has also been suggested that the Cabinet Committee on Disaster Management be made the highest decision making body (replacing the Group of Ministers) and the All-Party National Committee and the Working Group that fall under it be made permanent bodies so that a "secure" command and control mechanism is put into place. The report lays stress on training of personnel for which purpose it has suggested the setting up of a national institute for disaster management.

    Nodal Ministries for Managing Different Types of Disasters

Type of disaster/crises		**Nodal Ministry**
Air accidents	....	Civil Aviation
Civil strife	....	Home Affairs
Railway accidents	....	Railways
Chemical disasters	....	Environment
Biological disasters	....	Health
Nuclear accident inside Or outside the country	....	Atomic Energy
Natural disasters	....	Agriculture

28. It needs recollection that many aspects of disaster management have already been covered in the Eleventh Finance Commissions August 2000 Report. Their suggestion of creating a national force of 3,000 to 3,000 personnel anywhere in the country should also include NBC related terrorist attacks, causing expenditure control due to inherent coordination and dual tasking.
29. KPS Gill (Ed), *Terror and Containment, Perspectives of India's Internal Security* (New Delhi : Gyan Publishing House, 2003), pp. 195-198.

Five

Legal Aspects

> "And how, at the high level of elected member states of the UN, the *Human Rights Commission* has become a convenient platform for known terrorists and criminals not only to air their views but also to gain international recognition"
>
> Arundati Ghose (Former Ambassador and Permanent representative at the UN office in Geneva) mentioned in *Terror and Containment.*[1]

Let us now analyse the various legal aspects in this very important machinery for fighting the global war against terrorism, including WMD threats/incidents.

Internationally at UN level, regionally at SAARC level and at domestic levels various conventions, acts and ordinances have been passed to deal with crimes related with terrorism and steps that need to be taken by all states internationally and at domestic level to fight the same.

On 28 September 2001, the Security Council unanimously adopted a wide-ranging, comprehensive resolution with steps and strategies to combat international terrorism. The fight against terrorism was based primarily on Article 51 of the UN Charter, which empowers nation-states to use the right of self-defence against acts that threatens their existence. Adopted under chapter 7 of the UN Charter, the resolution is enforceable in respect of all its recommendations.

The UN members were asked to treat terrorist acts as criminal offences under their respective national laws. All countries were enjoined upon to refrain from providing any form of support, active or passive, to the financiers as also the actual and potential perpetrators of the terrorist crimes. The wide ranging areas where maximum stress was laid, are criminalising the provisions or collection of funds; directly or indirectly for terrorists or such like activities, individually or collectively; exchange of information regarding terrorist activities, their actions, movements of any such related information or material; the abuse of refugee status and the close connection between international terrorism and trans-national crime, illicit drugs, money laundering and illegal movement of arms, explosives, nuclear, chemical and biological and other deadly materials. It emphasized the need to enhance the co-ordination of national, sub-regional and international efforts to strengthen a global response to threat to international security.

The Indian Government feels that this resolution would be a stepping-stone for a regular monitoring by the UN Security Council of the state violating it. India has been demanding a comprehensive convention on terrorism. It is felt that the resolution will strengthen the international coalition against terrorism, which India has been advocating. The European council, while agreeing on the introduction of an "European arrest warrant" to facilitate the fight against terrorism, has also called for adoption of a common definition of terrorism.

The American strategic community, especially those dealing with counter-terrorism issues, for example Yossaf Bodansky already projected these emerging threats and the necessity for anticipatory defensive mechanism.

Consequently, at international level, new counter-terrorism measures were adopted by the Clinton administration way back in 1998. Therefore the apparatus which reacted in the 11 September 2001 scenario and the Anthrax attacks was able to do crisis management and damage control reasonably well. Some of the measures, which the Clinton administration had adopted. (Table 5.1)

Table 5.1
New Counter-terrorism Measures Adopted by the Clinton Administration

- Upgraded airport security.
- Improved bomb detections.
- Increased staff for the FBI to assess vulnerabilities in the physical infrastructure of the country and to expand technical capabilities to address nuclear, chemical, and biological threats.
- Better physical protection overseas for American troops, diplomats, and for diplomatic and trade offices.
- Expanded capabilities of U.S. attorneys and courts to handle additional workloads generated by counter-terrorism measures.
- Reinforcements of many U.S. federal buildings, particularly those occupied by law enforcement agencies.
- Contingency funds to respond to unanticipated events.
- Expanded efforts to detect illegal exports of relevance to WMD, to prevent nuclear smuggling, and to respond to nuclear incidents.
- Expanded efforts and improved co-ordination among intelligence collection agencies.

Before we talk of the many new legal measures, which have been formulated in the recent global war against terrorism, it would be better if we review the status of the existing conventions on terrorism. (Table 5.2)

Table 5.2
Status of Eleven Terrorism Conventions

- Convention on Offences and Certain Other Acts Committed on Board Aircraft-developed in 1963, entered into force 4 Dec. 1969.
- Convention for the Suppression of Unlawful Act Seizure of Aircraft (Hijacking Convention) – developed in 1970, entered into force 14 Oct, 1971.
- Convention for the Suppression of Unlawful Acts Against the Safety of Civil Aviation (Sabotage Convention) – developed in 1988, entered into force 26 Jan, 1973.
- Protocol for the Suppression of Unlawful Acts of Violence at Airports Serving International Civil Aviation – developed in 1988, entered into force 6 Aug. 1989 (for the United States: 18 Nov.1994).
- Convention for the Suppression of Unlawful Acts Against the Safety of maritime Navigation – developed in 1988, entered into force 1 March, 1992 (for the United States: 6 March, 1995).
- Protocol for the Suppression of Unlawful Acts Against the Safety of Fixed Platforms Located on the Continental Shelf – entered into force 1 March, 1992 (for the United States: 6 March, 1995).
- Convention on the marking of plastic explosives for the purpose of detection (Plastic Explosive Convention) – developed in 1991, not yet in force, awaiting one more signatory confirming ratification by that government.
- Convention on the Prevention and Punishment of Crimes Against Internationally Protected Persons – entered into force on 20 Feb. 1977.
- International Convention Against the Taking of Hostages—entered into force 3 June, 1983 (for the United States: 6 Jan. 1985).
- Convention on the Physical Protection of Nuclear Material—entered into force 8 Feb.1987.
- Convention for Suppression of Terrorist Bombings – opened for signature 12 January, 1998.

At regional and sub-regional levels various conventions have been made to fight terrorism. At the regional level, the SAARC Convention (Suppression of Terrorism) Act, is in existence. This is an act to give effect to the South Asian Association for Regional Cooperation and Convention on Suppression of Terrorism and for matters connected therewith or incidental thereto. Being aware of the dangers posed by the spread of terrorism and its harmful effects on peace, cooperation, friendship and good neighbourly relations which could also jeopardise the sovereignty and territorial integrity of states have resolved to take effective measures to ensure that perpetrators of terrorist acts do not escape prosecution and punishment by providing for their extradition or prosecution.

At national and domestic levels, there are other acts like the Anti-Hijacking Act and the Suppression of unlawful Acts against safety of civil aviation Act, that have been made in accordance with the Convention for the Suppression of Unlawful Seizure of Aircraft, on the 16th day of December 1970, signed at The Hague; and Convention for the Suppression of Unlawful Acts against the Safety of Civil Aviation, on the 23rd day of September, 1971, signed at Montreal, respectively. At domestic level to provide for speedy trial of certain offences in terrorist effected areas and for matters connected with it, the Terrorist-Affected Areas (Special Courts) Act is in existence.

Over a period, in spite of various international, regional conventions and national acts it was felt that people connected with terrorism and terrorist act were making use of certain procedural lacunae. It was felt that punishment for and measures dealing with terrorist activities required to be strengthened.

The Union Government was able to successfully institute the new 'Prevention of Terrorism Act' (POTA) (see appendix attached). The non-disclosure of information relating to terrorist acts has become an offence. The new legal framework intends to provide more teeth to the law enforcing agencies to effectively fight terrorism and fill the gap created by TADA. It will replace the criminal law (amendment) bill 1995 that was found to be too weak to tackle terrorism. It will define terrorist organisations, and make with holding information as an offence. A terrorist act has been defined as one that has been committed by using weapons and explosives or other methods to cause death or injury, damage to property, disrobed essential services and threatened the unity and integrity of the country. In addition, a need to streamline the powers of investigating agencies and special courts was felt. Though, this is a strong and a comprehensive document even then, it has some inherent drawbacks.

Certain organisations due to differences in ideology with the political parties in rule may become victims of political vindictiveness, which may disturb the basic roots of Indian democracy, that is secularism.

There is a definite need for stricter laws, while tackling terrorism but it is felt that by increasing the amount of fine along with other punishment may lead to corruption at various investigation levels. There is need to increase and enhance punishment and not the fine.

There is another factor of concern. Law and order is a state subject and one of the states has already announced that the State

Government would not implement the POTA even it is passed by the Parliament. There is a strong possibility that few others States may follow suit. This makes a virtual mockery of Parliament's authority.

With the enhanced power being given to investigating authorities, even an ordinary police officer, could make "victims" out of ordinary citizens. When it was first used, a Jammu family's property was attached.

It is public knowledge that Al-Qaida members have access to radioactive materials and could lethally employ them mixed with conventional explosives. There is a need to protect literature and materials concerned with weapons of mass distraction and prevent their smuggling in any way.

Conventions on Terrorism

In the post '9-11' situation, the Security Council passed an immediate resolution as discussed below. (Also attached as Appendix).

SECURITY COUNCIL RESOLUTION 1373 (28 SEPTEMBER 2001)

By resolution 1373 (28 September 2001) the council established a committee of the Council to monitor the resolution's implementation and called on all states to report on actions they had taken.

Under terms of the text, the Council decided that all states should prevent and suppress the financing of terrorism, as well as criminalise the wilful provision or collection of funds for such acts. The funds, financial assets and economic resources of those who commit or attempt to commit terrorist acts or participate in or facilitate the commission of terrorist acts and of persons and entities acting on behalf of terrorists should also be frozen without delay.

Reaffirming the need to combat terrorism by all means, in accordance with the Charter, threats to international peace and security caused by terrorist's acts, the Council expressed its determination to take all necessary steps to fully implement the current resolution.

Reaffirming the principle established by the General Assembly in its declaration of October 1970 (resolution 2625 (CCV) and reiterated by the Security Council in its resolution 1189 (1998) of August 13, 1998, namely that every State has the duty to refrain from organizing, instigating, assisting or participating in terrorist acts in another State or acquiescing in organised activities within its territory directed towards the commission of such acts.

"Acting under Chapter VI of the Charter of the United Nations", Decides that all States shall:

- Prevent and suppress the financing of terrorist acts;
- Criminalise the wilful provision or collection, by any means, directly or indirectly, of funds by their nationals or in their territories with the intention that the funds should be used, or in the knowledge that they are to be used, in order to carry out terrorist acts;
- Freeze without delay funds and other financial assets or economic resources of persons who commit, or attempt to commit, terrorist acts or participate in or facilitate the commission of terrorist acts; of entities owned or controlled directly or indirectly by such persons; and of persons and entities acting on behalf of, or at the direction of such persons and entities, including funds derived or generated from property owned or controlled directly or indirectly by such persons and associated persons and entities;
- Prohibit their nationals or any persons and entitles within their territories from making any funds, financial assets or economic resources or financial or other related services available, directly or indirectly, for the benefit of persons who commit or attempt to commit or facilitate or participate in the commission of terrorist acts, of entitles owned or controlled, directly or indirectly, by such persons and of persons and entitles acting on behalf of or at the direction of such persons;

Decides also that all States shall:

- Refrain from providing any form of support, active or passive, to entities or persons involved in terrorist acts, including by suppressing recruitment of members of terrorist groups and eliminating the supply of weapons to terrorists;
- Take the necessary steps to prevent the commission of terrorist acts, including by provision of early warning to other States by exchange of information;
- Deny safe haven to those who finance, plan, support, or commit terrorist acts, or provide safe havens;
- Prevent those who finance, plan, facilitate or commit terrorist acts from using their respective territories for those purpose against other States or their citizens.
- Ensure that any person who participates in the financing, planning, preparation or perpetration of terrorist acts or in supporting terrorist acts is brought to justice and ensure that, in addition to any other measures against them, such terrorist acts

are established as serious criminal offences in domestic laws and regulations and that the punishment duly reflects the seriousness of such terrorist acts;

- Afford one another the greatest measure of assistance in connection with criminal investigation or criminal proceedings relating to the financing or support of terrorist acts, including assistance in obtaining evidence in their possession necessary for the proceedings;
- Prevent the movement of terrorists or terrorist groups by effective border controls and controls on issuance of identify papers and travel documents, and through measures for preventing counterfeiting, forgery of fraudulent use of identify papers and travel documents.

Calls upon all States to:

- Find ways of intensifying and accelerating the exchange of operational information, especially regarding actions of movements of terrorist persons or networks; forged or falsified travel documents; traffic in arms, explosive or sensitive materials, use of communications technologies by terrorist groups; and the threat posed by the possession of weapons of mass destruction by terrorist groups;
- Exchange information in accordance with international and domestic law and cooperate on administrative and judicial matters to prevent the commission of terrorist acts;
- Cooperate, particularly through bilateral and multilateral arrangements and agreements, to prevent and suppress terrorist attacks and take action against perpetrators of such acts;
- Become parties as soon as possible to the relevant international conventions and protocols relating to terrorism, including the International Convention for the Suppression of the Financing of Terrorism of December 9, 1999;
- Increase cooperation and fully implement the relevant international conventions and protocols relating to terrorism and Security Council resolutions 1269 (1999) and 1368 (2001);
- Take appropriate measures in conformity with the relevant provisions of national and international law, including international standards of human rights, before granting refugee status, for the purpose of ensuring that the asylum seeker has not planned, facilitated or participated in the commission of terrorist acts;
- Ensure, in conformity with international law, the refugee status is not abused by the perpetrators, organizers or facilitators of terrorist acts, and that claims of political motivation are not

recognized as grounds for refusing requests for the extradition of alleged terrorists;

It is noted with concern of the close nexus between international terrorism and trans-national organised crime, illicit drugs, money-laundering, illegal arms-trafficking, and illegal movement of nuclear, chemical, biological and other potentially deadly materials, and in this emphasizes the need to enhance coordination of efforts on national, sub-regional, regional and international levels in order to strengthen a global response to this serious challenge and threat to international security;

It also declares that acts, methods, and practices of terrorism are contrary to the purposes and principles of the United Nations and that knowingly financing, planning and inciting terrorist acts are also contrary to the purpose and principles of the United Nations.

At this juncture, let us see as to what India's contribution in this field has been as India has been a victim of state terrorism for last almost 30 years. It had, therefore, been proposing an International Convention. India submitted a working document on 19 October 2000 to the UN General Assembly (see Appendix attached).

UN GENERAL ASSEMBLY, FIFTY- FIFTH SESSION, SIXTH COMMITTEE
Agenda Item 164, 19 October 2000

(Working document submitted by India on the draft comprehensive convention on international terrorism)

Through the draft, in order to take effective measures to prevent acts of terrorism and to ensure that perpetrators of terrorist acts do not escape prosecution and punishment by providing for their extradition or prosecution, and to that end had agreed as follows:

- (Article 2) Any person commits an offence within the meaning of this Convention if that person, by any person, unlawfully and intentionally, does an act intended to cause:
- Death or serious bodily injury to any persons; or
- Serious damage to a State or government facility, a public transportation system, communication system or infrastructure facility with the intent to cause extensive destruction of such a place, facility or system, or where such destruction results or is likely to result in major economic loss:

When the purpose of such act, by its nature or context; is to intimidate a population, or to compel a Government or an international organisation to do or abstain from doing any act.

• Any person also commits an offence if that person attempts to commit an offence or participates as a compliance in an offence as set forth in above paragraph.

• Any person also commits an offence if that person:

(a) Organises, directs or instigates others to commit an offence as set forth in the previous two paragraphs; or

(b) Aids, abets, facilitates or counsels the commission of such an offence; or

(c) In any other way contributes to the commission of one or more offences referred to in the previous paragraphs by a group of persons acting with a common purpose; such contribution shall be intentional and either be made with the aim of furthering the general criminal activity or purpose of the group or be made in the knowledge of the intention of the group to commit the offence or offences concerned.

• Each State Party shall adopt such measures as may be necessary:

• To establish as criminal offences under its domestic law the offences set forth in Article 2.

• To make those offences punishable by appropriate penalties, which take into account the grave nature of those offences.

• Each State Party shall adopt such measures as may be necessary, including, where appropriate, domestic legislation, to ensure that criminal acts within the scope of this Convention are under no circumstances justifiable by considerations of a political, philosophical, ideological, racial, ethnic, religious or other similar nature.

• Each State Party shall take such measures as may be necessary to establish its jurisdiction over the offences and shall cooperate in the prevention of the offences referred to in the Article 2.

• States Parties shall take appropriate measures, before granting asylum, for the purpose of ensuring that asylum is not granted to any person in respect of whom there are reasonable grounds indicating his involvement in any offence referred to in Article 2.

• Each State Party, in accordance with its domestic legal principles, shall take the necessary measures to enable a legal located in its territory or organised under its laws to be held liable when a person responsible for the management of control of that legal entity has, in that capacity, committed an offence referred to in Article 2. Such liability may be criminal, civil or administrative. Such liability is incurred without prejudice to the criminal liability of individuals having committed the offences.

• Upon receiving information that a person who has committed or who is alleged to have committed an offence referred to in Article 2 may be present in its territory, the State Party concerned shall take such measures as may be necessary under its domestic law to investigate the facts contained in the information. The required measures have been explained in this document.

• The State Party in whose territory the alleged offender is found shall, if it does not extradite the person, be obliged, without exception whatsoever and whether or not the offense was committed in its territory, to submit the case to its competent authorities for the purpose of prosecution through proceedings in accordance with the laws of that State. Those authorities shall take their decision in the same manner as in the case of any ordinary offence of a grave nature under the law of the State.

• Whatever a State Party is permitted under its domestic law to extradite or otherwise surrender one of its nationals only upon the condition that the person will be returned to that State to serve the sentence imposed as a result of the trial or proceeding for which the extradition or surrender of the person was sought, and that State and the State seeking the extradition of the person agree with this option and other terms they may deem appropriate, such a conditional extradition or surrender shall be sufficient to discharge the obligation set forth in the above paragraph.

• Any person who is taken into custody or regarding whom any other measures are taken or proceedings are carried out pursuant to this Convention shall be guaranteed fair treatment, including enjoyment of all rights and guarantees in conformity with the law of the State in the territory of which that person is present and applicable provisions of international law, including international human rights law.

• States Parties shall afford one another the greatest measure of assistance in connection with investigations or criminal or extradition proceedings brought in respect of the offences set forth in Article 2, including assistance in obtaining evidence at their disposal necessary for the proceedings.

• States Parties, which are not bound by a bilateral treaty or arrangement of mutual legal assistance, may, at their discretion, apply the procedure set out separately.

• None of the offences referred to in Article 2 and the acts which constitute an offence within the scope of and as defined in one of the treaties listed in Annexure 1 shall be regarded, for the purpose of extradition or mutual legal assistance, as a political offence or as an offence connected with a political offence or as an offence inspired by political motives. Accordingly, a request for extradition of for mutual legal assistance based on such an offence may not be refused on the sole ground that it concerns a political offence or an offence connected with a political offence or an offence inspired by political motives.

- Nothing in this Convention shall be interpreted as imposing an obligation to extradite or to afford mutual legal assistance, if the requested State Party has substantial grounds for believing that the request for extradition for offences set forth in Article 2 or for mutual legal assistance with respect to such offences has been made for the purpose of prosecution or punishing a person on account of that person's race, religion, nationality, ethnic origin or political opinion or that compliance with the request would cause prejudice to that person's position for any of these reasons.
- A person who is being detained or is serving a sentence in the territory of one State Party whose presence in another State Party is requested for purposes of identification, testimony or otherwise providing assistance in obtaining evidence for the investigation or prosecution of offences under this Convention may be transferred, subjected to the laid down conditions.
- The offences referred to in Article 2 shall be deemed to be included as extraditable offences in any extradition treaty existing between any of the States Parties before the entry into force of this Convention. States Parties undertake to include such offences as extraditable offences in every extradition treaty to be subsequently concluded between them. The other extradition conditions have been covered in Article 17 of the document.
- Nothing in this Convention shall affect other rights, obligations and responsibilities of States and individuals under international law, in particular the purposes and principles of the Charter of the United Nations and international humanitarian law.
- The activities of armed forces during an armed conflict, as those terms are understood under international law, which are governed by that law, are not governed by this Convention, and the activities undertaken by the military forces of a State in the exercise of their official duties, in as much as they are governed by other rules of international law, are not governed by this Convention.
- The State Party where the alleged offender is prosecuted shall, in accordance with its domestic law or applicable procedures, communicate the final outcome of the proceedings to the Secretary-General of the United Nations, who shall transmit the information

to the other States Parties.

• The States Parties shall carry out their obligations under the Convention in a manner consistent with the principles of sovereign equality and territorial integrity of States and that of non-intervention in the domestic affairs of other States.

• Nothing in this Convention shall affect other rights, obligations and responsibilities of States and individuals under international law, in particular the purpose of the Charter of the United Nations, international humanitarian law and other relevant conventions.

• Nothing in this Convention entitles a State Party to undertake in the territory of another State Party the exercise of jurisdiction or performance of functions, which are exclusively, reserved for the authorities of that other State Party by its domestic law.

• Any dispute between two or more States Parties concerning the interpretation or application of this convention, which cannot be settled through negotiation within a reasonable time shall, at the request of one of them, be submitted to arbitration. If, within six months from the date of the request for arbitration, the parties are unable to agree on the organisation of the arbitration, any one of those parties may refer the disputes to the International Court of Justice, by application, in conformity with the Statute of the Court.

THE SAARC CONVENTION (SUPPRESSION OF TERRORISM) ACT

At the regional level, luckily, the SAARC adopted a resolution on terrorism during the meeting at Nepal. (See Appendix attached). The description of important articles are discussed below:

• (Article I) Subject to the overall requirements of the law of extradition, conduct constituting any of the following offences according to the law of the Contracting State, shall be regarded as terrorist act and for the purpose of extradition shall not be regarded as a political offence or as an offence connected with a political offence or as an offence inspired by political motives —

- An offence within the scope of the Convention for the Suppression of Unlawful Seizure of Aircraft, signed at The Hague, on 16th December, 1970;
- An offence within the scope of the Convention for the Suppression of Unlawful Act, against the Safety of Civil Aviations signed at Montreal, on 23rd September, 1971;
- An offence within the scope of the Convention on the Prevention and Punishment of Crimes against Internationally Protected Persons, including Diplomatic Agents, signed at New

York on 14th December, 1973;

- An offence within the scope of any Convention to which the SAARC member States concerned are parties and which obliges the parties to prosecute or grant extradition;
- Murder, manslaughter, assault causing bodily harm, kidnapping hostage-taking and offences relating to firearms, weapons, explosives and dangerous substances when used as a means to perpetrate indiscriminate violence involving death or serious bodily injury to persons or serious damage to property;
- An attempt or conspiracy to commit an offence described in above sub-paragraphs, aiding, abetting or counseling the commission of such an offence or participating as an accomplice in the offences so described.

- (Article II) For the purpose of extradition between SAARC member States, any two or more contracting States may, by agreement, decide to include any other serious offence involving violence, which shall not be regarded as a political offence or an offence connected with a political offence or an offence inspired by political motives.

- The provisions of all extradition treaties and arrangements applicable between Contracting States are hereby amended as between Contracting States to the extent that they are incompatible with the Convention.

- For the purpose of this Convention and to the extent that any offence referred to in Article I or agreed to in terms of Article II is not listed as an extraditable offence in any extradition treaty existing between Contracting States, it shall be deemed to be included as such therein.

- Contracting States undertake to include these offences as extraditable offences in any future extradition treaty to be concluded between them.

- If a Contracting State, which makes extradition conditional on the existence of a treaty, receives a request for extradition from another Contracting State with which it has no extradition treaty, the requested State may, at its option, consider this Convention as the basis for extradition in respect of the offences set forth in Article I or agreed to in terms of Article II. Extradition shall be subject to the law of the requested State.

- Contracting States, which do not make extradition conditional on the existence of a treaty, shall recognize the offences set forth in Article I or agreed to in terms of Article II as extraditable offences between themselves, subject to the law of the requested

State.

• A Contracting State in whose territory a person suspected of having committed an offence referred to in Article I or agreed to in terms of Article II is found and which has received a request for extradition from another Contracting State, shall, if it does not extradite that person, submit the case without exception and without delay, to its competent authorities, so that prosecution may be considered. These authorities shall take their decisions in the same manner as in the case of any offence of a serious nature under the law of the State.

• For the purpose of above Article, each Contracting State may take such measures as it deems appropriate, consistent with its national laws, subject to reciprocity, to exercise its jurisdiction in the case of an offence under Article I or agreed to in terms of Article II.

• A Contracting State in whose territory an alleged offender is found, shall, upon receiving, a request for extradition from another Contracting State, take appropriate measures, subject to its national laws, so as to ensure his presence for purpose of extradition or prosecution. Such measures shall immediately be notified to the requested State.

• Contracting State shall not be obliged to extradite, if it appears to the requested State that by reason of the trivial nature of the case or by reason of the request for the surrender or return of the fugitive offender not being made in good faith or in the interests of justice or for any other reason it is unjust or inexpedient to surrender or return the fugitive offender.

• Contracting States shall, subject to their national laws, afford one another the greatest measure of mutual assistance in connection with proceedings brought in respect of the offences referred to in Article I or agreed to in terms of the Article II, including the supply of all evidence at their disposal necessary for the proceedings.

• Contracting States shall cooperate among themselves, to the extent permitted by their national laws, through consultations between appropriate agencies, exchange of information, intelligence and expertise and such other cooperative as may be appropriate, with a view to preventing terrorist activities through precautionary measures.

In addition to this, the summary of various other acts are given:

THE ANTI-HIJACKING ACT

Extent and application:

- This Act may be called the Anti-Hijacking Act, 1982.
- It extends to the whole of India and, save as otherwise provided in this act, it applies also to any offence there under committed outside India by any person.
- Whoever on board an aircraft in flight, unlawfully, by force or threat of force or by any other form of intimidation, seizes or exercises control of that aircraft commits the offence of hijacking of such aircraft.
- Whoever attempts to commit any of the acts referred to in this sub-section in relation to any aircraft, or abets the commission of any such act, shall also be deemed to have committed the offence of hijacking of such aircraft.
- For the purposes of this section, an aircraft shall be deemed to be in flight at any time from the moment when all its external doors are closed following embarkation until the moment when any such door is opened for disembarkation, and in the case of a forced landing, the flight shall be deemed to continue until the competent authorities of the country in which such forced landing takes place take over the responsibility for the aircraft and for persons and property on board.

Punishment for hijacking. Whoever commits the offence of hijacking shall be punished with imprisonment for life and shall also be liable to fine.

Punishment for acts of violence connected with hijacking. Whoever, being a person committing the offence of hijacking of an aircraft, commits in connections with such offence, any act of violence against any passenger or member of the crew of such aircraft, shall be punished with the same punishment with which he would have been punishable under any law for the time being in force in India if such act had been committed in India.

The Suppression of Unlawful Acts Against Safety of Civil Aviation Act

Extent and application:

- This Act may be called the Anti-Hijacking Act, 1982.
- It extends to the whole of India and, save as otherwise provided in this act, it applies also to any offence there under committed outside India by any person.

Offence of committing violence on board an aircraft in flight, etc.

- Whoever unlawfully and intentionally;
- Commits an act of violence against a person on board an aircraft in flight which is likely to endanger the safety of such aircraft; or
- Destroys an aircraft in service or causes damage to such aircraft in such a manner as to render it incapable of flight or which is likely to endanger its safety in flight; or
- Places or causes to be place on an aircraft in service, by any means whatsoever, a device or substance which is likely to destroy that aircraft, or to cause damage to it which renders it incapable of flight, or to cause damage to it which is likely to endanger its safety in flight; or

• Communicates such information which he knows to be false so as to endanger the safety of an aircraft in flight shall be punished with imprisonment for life and shall also be liable to fine.

• Whoever attempts to commit, or abets the commission of, any offence as above shall also be deemed to have committed such offence and shall be punished with the punishment provided for such offence.

Destruction of, or damage to, air navigation facilities—

• Whoever unlawfully and intentionally destroys or damages air navigation facilities or interferes with their operation in such a manner as is likely to endanger the safety of the aircraft in flight shall be punished with imprisonment of life and shall also be liable to fine.

• Whoever attempts to commit, or abets to commission of, any offence under sub-section (1) shall also be deemed to have committed such offence and shall be punished with the punishment provided for such offence.

THE TERRORIST-AFFECTED AREAS (SPECIAL COURTS) ACT (No. 61 of 1984)

Extent and commencement:

- This Act may be called the Terrorist-Affected Areas (Special Courts) Act, 1984.
- It extends to the whole of India except the State of Jammu and Kashmir.

Declaration of terrorist-affected area:

- If the Central Government is of the opinion that offences of the nature specified in the schedule are being committed in any area by terrorists on such a scale and in such a manner that it is expedient for the purpose of copying with the activities of such terrorists to have recourse to the provisions of this Act, it may, by notification.

- Declare such area to be a terrorist-affected area; and
- Constitute such area into a single judicial zone or into as many judicial zones as it may deem fit.

A notification issued as above in respect of an area shall specify the period during which the area shall, for the purposes of this Act, be a terrorist-affected area, and where the Central Government is of the opinion that terrorists has been committed in that area, from a date earlier than the date of issue of the notification, offences of the nature specified in the schedule on such a scale and in such a manner that it is expedient to commence the period specified in the notification from such earlier date, the period specified in the notification may commence from that date, subjected to the laid down conditions.

Establishment of Special Courts

For the purpose of providing for speedy trial of scheduled offences committed in a judicial zone, the Central Government may establish, by notification, a Special Court in relation to such judicial zone:

- Within such judicial zone; or
- If the Central Government having regard to the exigencies of the situation prevailing in such judicial zone considers it expedient so to do at any place outside such judicial zone but within the State in which such judicial zone is situated.

Notwithstanding anything contained as above, if having regard to the exigencies of the situation prevailing in a State, the State Government is of the opinion that it is expedient to establish in relation to a judicial zone, or in relation to two or more judicial zones in the State, an Additional Special Court outside the State, for the trial of such scheduled offences committed in the judicial zone or judicial zones, the trial whereof within the State:

- Is not likely to be fair or impartial or completed with utmost dispatch; or
- Is not likely to be feasible without occasioning a breach of peace or grave risk to the safety of the accused, the witnesses, the Public Prosecutor and the Judge of any or them; or
- Is not otherwise in the interests of justice.

The State Government may request the Central Government to establish in relation to such judicial zone or judicial zones an Additional Special Court outside the State and thereupon the Central Government may, after taking into account the information furnished by the State Government and making such inquiry, if any, as it may deem fit, establish by notification such Additional Special Court at such place outside the State as may be specified in the notification.

Procedure and powers of Special Courts:

- A Special Court may take cognizance of any scheduled offence, without the accused being committed to it for trial, upon receiving a complaint of facts, which constitute such offence or upon a police report of such facts.
- A Special Court may, with a view to obtaining the evidence of a person supposed to have been directly or indirectly concerned in, or privy to, an offence, tender a pardon to such person on condition of his making a full and true disclosure of the whole circumstances within his knowledge relative to in the offence and to every other person concerned in, or party to, an offence tender a pardon to such a person on condition of his making a full and the disclosure of the whole circumstance within his knowledge relative to in the offence and to every other person concerned whether as principal or abettor the commission thereof and any pardon so tendered shall, for the purposes of Sec. 308 of the Code be deemed to have tendered under Sec. 307 thereof.
- Subject to the other provisions of this Act, a Special Court shall, for the purpose of trial of any offence, have all the powers of the Court of Session and shall try such offence as if it were a Court of Session so far as may be in accordance with the procedure prescribed in the Code for the trial before a Court of Session.
- Subject to the other provisions of this Act, every case before an Additional Special Court shall be dealt with as if such case had been transferred under Sec. 406 of the Code to such Additional Special Court.
- ***Power of Supreme Court to Transfer Case:*** Whenever it is made to appear to the Supreme Court that an order under this section is expedient for the ends of justice, it may direct that any particular case be transferred from one Special Court to another Special Court.

THE PREVENTION OF TERRORISM ACT (POTA)—2001

The Extent and Application

- It extends to the whole of India.
- Citizens of India outside India.
- Persons in the service of Government, wherever they may be.
- Persons on ships and aircrafts, registered in India, wherever they may be.
- It shall remain in force for a period of 5 years from the date of its commencement but its expiry shall not affect the previous operation and application.
- Chapter1 of the ordinance covers the definition/meaning of certain standard words/phrases, unless the context dictates otherwise. Some of the important phrases are as follows:
- **Terrorist Act.** For the purposes of this subsection, 'a terrorist act' shall include the act of raising funds intended for the purpose of terrorism. The word 'terrorist act' can be defined as follows:

(a) With intent to threaten the unity, integrity, security or sovereignty of India or to strike terror in the people or any section of the people does any act or thing by using bombs, dynamite or other explosive substances or inflammable substances or fire arms or other lethal weapons or poisons or noxious gases or other chemicals or by any other substances (whether biological or otherwise) of a hazardous nature or by any other means whatsoever, in such a manner as to cause, or likely to cause, death of, or injuries to any person or persons or loss of, of damage to, or destruction of, property or disruption of any supplies or services essential to the life of the community or causes damage or destruction of any property or equipment used or intended to be used for the defence of India or in connection with any other purposes of the Government of India, any State Government or any of their agencies, or detains any persons and threatens to kill or injure such person in order to compel the Government or any other person to do or abstain from doing any act.

(b) Is or continues to be a member of an association declared unlawful under the Unlawful Activities (Prevention) Act 967, or voluntarily does an act aiding or promoting in any manner the objects of such association and in either case is in possession of any unlicensed firearms, ammunition, explosive or other instrument or substance capable of causing mass destruction and commits any act resulting in loss of human life or grievous injury to any person or causes significant damage to any property, commits a terrorist act.

(c) For the purposes of this sub-section, "a terrorist act" shall include the act of raising funds intended for the purpose of terrorism.

Proceeds of Terrorism

This shall mean all kinds of properties which have been derived or obtained from commission of any terrorist act or have been acquired through funds traceable to a terrorist act, and shall include cash, irrespective of person in whose name such proceeds are standing or in whose possession they are found.

Property

Means property and assets of every description, whether corporeal or incorporeal, movable or immovable, tangible or intangible and deeds and instruments evidencing title to, or interest in, such property or assets and includes bank account.

Punishment for and Measures Dealing with Terrorist Activities

- Whoever commits a terrorist act shall, if such act has resulted in the death of any person, be punishable with death or imprisonment for life and shall also be liable to fine and in any other case be punishable with imprisonment for a term which shall not be less than five years but may extend to imprisonment for life and shall also be liable to fine.
- Whoever conspired or attempts to commit, or advocates, abets, advises or incites or knowingly facilitates the commission of a terrorist act or any act preparatory to a terrorist act, shall be punishable with imprisonment for a term which shall not be less than five years but which may extend to imprisonment for life and shall also be liable to fine.
- Whoever voluntarily harbours or conceals, or attempts to harbour or conceals any person knowing that such person is a terrorist shall be punishable with imprisonment for a term which shall not be less than three years but which may extend to imprisonment for life and shall also be liable to fine. Provided that this sub-sections shall not apply to any case in which the harbour or concealment is by the husband or wife of the offender.
- Any person who is a member of a terrorist gang or a terrorist organisation, which is involved in terrorist acts, shall be punishable with imprisonment for a term which may extend to imprisonment for life or with fine which may extend to rupees ten lakh or with both.

• Whoever knowingly holds any property derived or obtained from commission of any terrorist act or has been acquired through the terrorist fund shall be punishable with imprisonment which may extend to imprisonment for life or with fine which may extend to rupees ten lakh or with both.

• Whoever threatens any person who is witness or any other person in whom such witness may be interested, with violence or wrongfully restrains or confines the witness or any other person in whom the witness may be interested, or does any other unlawful act with the said intent, shall be punishable with imprisonment which may extend to three years and fine.

• Any person in possession of certain unauthorised arm or explosive, etc., shall be punishable with imprisonment for a time which may be extended to imprisonment for life or with fine which may extend to Rs. ten lakhs or both.

• For the purpose of punishment mentioned above, the reference to "imprisonment for life" shall be construed as a reference to "imprisonment for ten years".

• Proceeds of terrorism held by a terrorist, or by any other person and whether or not such person is prosecuted or convicted under this ordinance, shall be liable to be forfeited to the Central Government or the State Government, as the case may be in the manner provided in the ordinance.

• The order of forfeiture made under this ordinance by the designated authority shall not prevent the infliction of any other punishment to which the person affected thereby is liable under this ordinance. However, where any claim is preferred or any objection is made to the seizure of any property on the ground that such property is not liable to seizure, the designated authority/special court, before whom such property is produced, shall proceed to investigate the claim or objection, provided no such investigation be made where it is considered that the claim or objection was designed to cause the necessary delay.

• Failure to furnish the information called for whom any agency, or deliberately furnishing false information shall be punishable with imprisonment for a term, which may extend to three years or with fine or with both.

Terrorist Organisation

• For the purpose of this ordinance an organisation is a terrorist organisation if it is listed in the schedule or it operates under the same name as an organisation listed in the schedule. The central government may by order, in the Official Gazette, add an organisation to the schedule, remove an organisation from the schedule or amend that schedule in some other way, once it believes that the organisation is involved in terrorism. An organisation shall be deemed to be involved in terrorism if it:

(a) Commits or participates in act of terrorism.
(b) Prepares for terrorism.
(c) Promotes or encourage terrorism or is otherwise involved in terrorism.

• However, an application may be made by the organisation or any other person affected by inclusion of the organisation in the schedule or terrorist organisation to the central government for exercise of its power to remove that organisation from the schedule.

• A person commits an offence if he belongs or professes to belong to a terrorist organisation. A person guilty of an offence under this section shall be liable, on conviction, to imprisonment for a term not extending ten years or with fine or with both. This sub-section shall not apply where the person charged is able to prove that the organisation was not declared as a terrorist organisation at the time when he became a member or began to perform to be a member and that he has not taken part in the activities of the organisation at any time during its inclusion in the schedule as a terrorist organisation.

• A person commits an offence if he invites support for a terrorist organisation and the support is not, or is not restricted to, the provisions of money or other property. Also a person commits an offence, if he arranges, manages or assists the arranging or managing a meeting he knows is to support a terrorist organisation, to further the activities of a terrorist organisation or to be addressed by a person who belongs or performs to belong to a terrorist organisation. Also, a person commits an offence if he addresses a meeting (meeting of three or more persons) for the purpose of encouraging support for a terrorist organisation or to further its activities. A person guilty of an offence under this section shall be liable on conviction, to imprisonment for a term not extending ten years or with fine or both.

• A person commits an offence if he invites another to provide money or other property, and intends that it should be used, or has responsible cause to suspect that it may be used, for the purposes of terrorism. Also a person commits an offence if he receives money or other property, and intends that it should used, or has reasonable cause to suspect that it may be used, for the purposes of terrorism. Also a person commits an offence if he provides money or other property, and knows or his reasonable cause to suspect that it will or may be used for the purpose of terrorism. In this section, a reference to the provision of money or other property is a reference to its being given, lent or otherwise made available, whether or not for consideration. A person guilty of an offence under this section shall be liable on conviction, to imprisonment for a term not exceeding fourteen years, or with fine or with both.

Special Courts

Some of the important provisions are as given below :

- The Central or State Government may, by notification in the Official Gazette, constitute one or more special courts. However, Special Courts constituted by the Central Government will have priority jurisdiction over the Court constituted by the State Government. A Special Court will be presided over by a Judge to be appointed by the Central/State Government with the concurrence of the Chief Justice of the High powers of a Court of Session (Sec 23).
- The proceedings under this ordinance may, for reasons recorded in writing, be held in camera if the special court so desires.
- A confession made by a person before a police officer not lower in rank than a SP shall be admissible in the trial of such person
- Interception of Communication in Certain Cases
- The provisions for interception of communication in certain cases have been covered in that
- A police investigation officer not below the rank of SP may make application for authorisation of interception of wire, electronic or oral communication to the competent authority.
- Evidence collected through the interception of wire, electronic or oral communication shall be admissible as evidence.
- Provisions for interception of communication in emergency have been catered for in the ordinance. Also measure for protection of information collected has also been incorporated in the ordinance.
- Interception and disclosure of wire, electronic or oral communication by a police officer except as otherwise specifically provided in section shall for such violation be punishable with imprisonment for a term which may extend up to one year and with fine up to Rupees fifty thousand.

Miscellaneous

- No court shall take cognizance of any offence under this Ordinance without the previous sanction of the Central Government or as the case may be, the State Government.

• Where a police officer arrests a person, he shall prepare a custody memo of the person arrested. The person arrested shall be informed of his right to consult a legal practitioner as soon as he is brought to the police station. Whenever any person is arrested, information of his arrest shall be immediately communicated by the police officer to a family member or in his absence to a relative of such person by telegram, telephone or by any other means and this fact shall be recorded by the police officer under the signature of the person arrested.

• The person arrested shall be permitted to meet the legal practitioner representing him during the course of interrogation of the accused person. Provided that nothing in this subsection shall entitle the legal practitioner to remain present throughout the period of interrogation.

• Nothing in this Ordinance shall affect the jurisdiction exercisable by, or the procedure applicable to, any court or other authority under any law relating to the naval, military or air forces or other armed forces of the Union.

• No suit, prosecution or other legal proceeding shall lie against the Central Government or a State Government or any officer or authority of the Central Government or State Government or any other authority on whom powers have been conferred under this Ordinance, for anything which is in good faith done or purported to be done in pursuance of this Ordinance. Provided further that no suit, prosecution or other legal proceedings shall lie against any serving member or retired member of the armed forces or other para-military forces in respect of any action taken or purported to be taken by him in good faith, in the course of any operation directed towards combating terrorism.

• Any police officer who exercises powers corruptly or maliciously, knowing that there are no reasonable grounds for proceeding under this Ordinance, shall be punishable with imprisonment which may extend to two years, or with fine, or with both.

• If the special court is of opinion that any person has been corruptly or maliciously proceeded against under this Ordinance, the court may award such compensation as it deems fit to the person, so proceeded against and it shall be paid by the officer, person authority of Government, as may be specified in the order.

• Notwithstanding any thing contained in any other law for the time being in force, the passport and the arms license of a person who is charge sheeted for having committed any offence under this ordinance, shall be deemed to have been impounded for such period as the special court may deemed fit.

Conclusion

Terrorism has spread Globally so much that it is no more a battle against any Nation, rather it has become a danger to the civilization and complete mankind. All the Nations of the World need to rise above their domestic compulsions and have to fight against this menace. With the terrorist organisations getting hold of radioactive materials and getting reach to Weapons of Mass Destruction the danger to human race has increased manifolds.

There are various international conventions to fight against terrorism as discussed earlier. The most significant of all has been the UN Resolution on Terrorism held on 28 Sep. 2001 where the UN Security Council approved a US Sponsored resolution that mandated the 189 members – nations to deny support and sanctuary to terrorist and their networks. It called for the immediate freezing of terrorists' funds and preventing movement of individuals and groups suspected of having terrorist connections, to crack down on training of terrorists, and to cooperate in any campaign against them, including one that involves the use of force. It is widely felt that mere existence of these convention does not solve the problem, today, there is a need to implement these on ground. Also, the various Acts and Ordinances at domestic level need to be strengthened to ensure that Weapons of Mass Destruction do not reach the hands of Terrorists and Anti National elements. All the states need to cooperate with each other in terms of various UN Charters and International Conventions on terrorism, rising above all political and domestic pressures in whatever form they may be.

In addition to these legal measures, there is yet another important facet in managing terrorist attacks, both conventional and WMD/WMDR oriented. These are discussed in the two subsequent chapters. (All the legal provisions are given as an appendix towards the end).

References

1. New Delhi: Gyan Publishing House, p. 89.
2. The acts detailed in this chapter have been excerpted from various books, the internet most, importantly from the United Nations sources.

Six

WMD Terrorism: Civil Defence and Response Mechanism

"I have been aware that governments have systematically lied to their population about the usefulness of shelters and it has been abundantly clear that civil defence is a matter of calculated fraud for profit. It has not been clear, until now, at least to me, that shelters have little to do with the danger against which they are theoretically constructed. It is not the fall out, but the vast firestorms, which render them futile. They represent more crematory ovens which will roast the pathetic hides from the bomb".

Sir Bertrand Russell
(British scientist and philosopher)

"Civil Defence is far from being, as some have represented it to be, a passive and supine thing - on advertisement of fear and a manifestation that we are pursued of the worst. On the contrary, a strong programme of civil defence is part of our deterrent posture, and a valid insurance".

Maj Gen Edward W Sawyer
US Army

"Civil Defence is a part of our total deterrence in the sense that the capacity to survive and recuperate, is calculated to deter the enemy from striking first, civil defence lends credibility to the nations nuclear arsenal".

General Lyman Lemnitzer
Commanding General-Allied Headquarters in Europe

Global Review and Imperatives for India

Disaster could be natural or artificial. Disaster could be an accident or an act of deliberation; the employment of WMD would fall in the latter category. Whatever the cause or purpose, it becomes imperative to pit the complete resources and assets, available to a state, to overcome the calamity. The globe is a fluid entity with assets that metamorphose invariably with time. These assets could be natural or artificial, these could be positive or negative or these could be related to civil defence or disaster management. What we as good human beings should pray for is a total national effort, under one umbrella having unity of command and single point reference. To obviate such disasters, we should pray for de-nuclearisation of the world where world stability depends on 'Inter-Dependence' and not 'Nuclear-Deterrence'. Let future working parameters for protection of human civilisation in the new millennium be, to fight hunger and darkness and not missiles and submarines, loaded with trigger alert weapon systems.The resurgence of the new Germany as an emerging leader of the fast uniting European Union (EU) is indicative by its vociferous nuclear stance for NATO, i.e. 'No First Use'. These equations get interlinked with the current ongoing US-Russia START II negotiations and other disarmament initiatives. The fact to highlight is that the highest civil defence measure is disarmament and arms control, as they address the root and not the trunk of the problem. The concept of 'Nuclear Weapons Convention' (NWC) is also enlarging and may engulf newer proportions of civility and nation states. Nevertheless, it is worth analysing the various civil defence and protective aspects as they strengthen the existing pillar of 'Nuclear Deterrence' and peace. The evolution of civil defence can be traced back to the Pentagon and the American 'Federal Civil Defence Act' (FCDA).

Earlier History

The origins of an International Civil Defence Organisation can be traced back to 1931, much before the Second World War. It was popularly known as Lieux de Genere International Association. It mooted a very genuine concept of creating Truce Areas where the non-combatant civilians and injured soldiers could seek refuge. The Headquarter soon shifted to Geneva, which began to be known as the Capital of Peace. This famous and nascent organisation rendered good services during the Spanish Civil War (1936), and Sino-Japanese conflict (1937) by creating Geneva-Zones. This theme got standardised on adoption of the Geneva Convention in 1949, the fourth convention of which laid out special protective measures for such helpless people. The Korean War also saw the establishment of a 'Lieu de Geneve'. However, it was only in 1958 that international status was given to this organisation, which was renamed as International Civil Defence Organisation. A series of world conferences were held in due succession with the aim of evolving newer codes of conduct and detection against radiation and other allied safety equipment. A wide range of issues were organised and institutionalised like:

(a) Organising records and studies centre.

(b) Establishment of Technical Commissions like the Shelter Construction Commission; International Disaster Assistance Commission and Disaster Medicine Commission.

(c) International meetings as symposiums and seminars.

(d) Establishment of neutral zones to preserve human life, art and culture.

(e) An International Disaster Aid Centre was also established in 1963.

USA

Certain steps were taken in the USA over the years:-

(a) **1948.** After World War II, an office of civil defence was established. Only a defunctionary lip service was given to this aspect.

(b) **1950.** Federal Civil Defence Act (FCDA) of 1950 was passed to organise an independent agency working under the Federal Government.

(c) A train accident was well attended by the FCDA popularising the concept.

(d) Dual responsibility of dealing with natural disasters as well as enemy attacks was delegated to the FCDA by the president.

(e) **1958.** National administration of civil defence and the office of civil and defence mobilisation was merged with the executive office of the President. Since then many amendments and improvements have come across this strong deterrent institution.

(f) **1960.** Review carried out by President John F Kennedy and secretary of defence was assigned major civil defence responsibilities, which included fall out shelters, warning and sanitation service.

(g) **1963.** Office of civil defence and mobilisation became office of 'Emergency Planning'.

(h) **1964.** Civil defence transferred to Army secretariat and thus started the joint civil military activities on this aspect. The Armed Forces, upon request may also assist the civil defence programme. Concept of mutual aid doctrine in civil defence took birth with the endeavour to integrate all national assets.

(j) Since then, the American civil defence organisation has been well established, with the cardinal principal of fast response and immediate aid to the victims.

Disaster Management: USA

The bulk of President Bush's request for 1.5 billion dollars to deal with bio terrorism goes for drugs and vaccine. More than 500 million dollars is for vaccine and 643 million for antibiotics. The actual plan to combat the disaster calls for stockpiling drugs and other emergency medical supplies, which can be rushed to site of attack in a few hours.

The plan, called the National Disaster Medical system in operated by Health and Human services office of Emergency Preparedness. It is an effort to respond to full range of problems that a task force warned would develop.

Each metropolitan medical response plan organizes local, federal and private resources to respond quickly and effectively to a massive problem. Specially trained responders, detection, protective, decontamination equipment, communication facilities and emergency transport are worked. However public health officials have been warning that the ability of such crisis teams will depend on earlier events when initially doctors and laboratories face cases.

In the beginning the Energy Department set up a response team called Nuclear Emergency Search Team (NEST). The FBI when given responsibility to counter the NBC terrorism came out with Domestic Emergency Search Team (DEST). Metropolitan cities have Medical Strike Teams. Even the Marine Corps have their own response team. Thus one can sum it up that US has recognised that there is a services problem. There is a Presidential Directive stating that responding to terrorists armed with WMD is the highest priority of US government.

Rapid Assessment and Initial Detection Teams

Besides this, the National Guard has Rapid Assessment and Initial Detection (RAID) Teams. The National Guard has equipped and certified nine WMD Civil Support Teams (WMD-CST) whose mission is to assist local first responder in determining the nature of attacks, provide medical and technical advice.

The mission of RAID and WMD-CST is to provide early assessment and initial detection of WMD, advise response teams, expedite employment of state and federal military support, liaison amongst all elements. There are 32 such teams located in 26 states. Each unit is co-located with Air National Guard aviation units to facilitate co-ordination of troop and equipment airlifts.

Training. The training is provided by Army Chemical School, and Defence Nuclear Weapon School. In addition to individual training requirements, the collective training too is given utmost importance. Fifteen months of rigorous training is imparted with special emphasis on:

(a) Nuclear, Biological, Chemical, radiological sampling, detection and decontamination.
(b) Functions of air-breathers and other protective equipments.
(c) Emergency communications.
(d) Co-ordination of civil-military operations.

Deployment

Equipment. Mobile analytical laboratory for field analysis of chemical/ biological agents and a unified command suite that has the ability to provide communications interoperability among various responders, advanced communications and automation equipment to assist and augment first response authorities, photoionisation detectors for identification of explosive and volatile substances.

Self-Containment. Each WMD-CST carries enough food and water to last for 72 hours. Each team moves out with its own detection and decontamination equipment, medical supplies and protective gear.

Interoperability. WMD-CST teams use commercial vehicles and predominantly civilian equipment for easy integration with civilian emergency management personnel.

Command and Control. Deployed teams automatically come under the authority of Incident Command System.

Response. Ready to deploy within four hours to anywhere within the area of responsibility.

Erstwhile USSR

The evolutionary steps in erstwhile USSR had been concurrent too, except that their protective measures and the thinking started much earlier, i.e., from the First World War period onwards. The difference is that unlike USA, it had to cater for war, on its own territories, being contiguous to hostile nations and being in Europe. The chronology of evolution of civil defence in the erstwhile USSR is highlighted.

(a) **1917-1930.** Thinking for protection against gas warfare had begun (protection given even to cattle and horses) as early as the First World War. The Russians had even established an institution for training chemical warfare officers, just after World War I, where chemical weapons were used for the first time on such a large scale.

(b) **1931-1953:** This was a period in which civil defence schemes took concrete shape especially against air raids, as enormous developments took place in military aviation. When the Germans opened the offensive on the Russian front, on 22 June 1941, there were only 14,000 civil defence workers. However, by August 1941, enough efforts were mobilised to reach a peak level of 50,000 workers. This could happen as they could take advantage of an already existing public organisation called 'Usuaviakhim' operating since 1927.

(c) **1953-Present Day:** The Russians first detonated the Hydrogen bomb in 1953. It is at this point of time that the Russians made incisive and radical changes in their protection and civil defence policies. The emphasis shifted to evacuation and dispersal, rather than to shelter construction, which was envisaged not to be cost effective. Their national training programmes were run by a national/volunteer organisation 'DOSAAF' (Volunteer society for cooperation with Army, Aviation and Fleet) for individuals in the age range of under 60 years. To cater against nuclear weapons, it has set up specialised units in civil defence, controlled mostly by the central government located at Moscow, under the Ministry of Internal Affairs. It is learnt, subsequently that it was brought under the Ministry of Defence. However, the current pyramidical structure is not clear, except that a shadow organisation is being maintained in peacetime, which blooms into a full-fledged force on orders.

Civil Defence Organisation: Other European Countries

A review of civil defence measures in Europe during the Cold War can draw maximum parallel to South Asian security environment today.

In the post Second World War scenario, it is Europe alone which has lived under a constant threat of war and use of nuclear weapons. During the Second World War, it was Europe again which was subjected maximum to the spoils of war. Thus, the growth of civil defence organisation took their roots here. It can be traced back to the Committee for Imperial Defence created in the year 1904 in Great Britain, which was followed up by a survey in 1925, for the maintenance of vital services. Other European countries like France, and Germany, had various civil defence measures instituted much before the Second World War. Very detailed orders were formulated on the organisational hierarchy, training, and policy for shelters. It is worth mentioning here, about yet another country, Sweden, whose preparation towards NBC civil defence measures is unparalleled and is today considered the best.

As a matter of fact the origins of civil defence in Germany can be traced back from 1923 to the present so as to protect the German industries against air attacks. The Civil Defence Corps (3,55,000) of Great Britain was authorised and placed under the Home Office by the Civil Defence Act of 1946. The Civil Defence Corps in France was authorised under an order of January 1959, which operated as part of the Paris Fire Brigade, and placed under the French Ministry of Interior. In Germany, the First Air Raid Precaution (ARP) law (LUFT SCHUT GESETZ) was passed on 26 June 1935, laying down a detailed structure for Civil Defence.

Historically, German Civil Defence organisations saved millions of lives, even when the bombardment of towns like Hamburg, Wilhemshafen, Cologne, Dusseldrof and Berlin, etc took place in 1945. Only 2 per cent of the city's population was killed. The post Second World War period and the tensions of the NATO—Warwaw cold war dynamics ushered in an era of phenomenal growth of the civil defence structures and various planning parameters in this part of Europe. For example, the legal, industrial and volunteer activity model is one of the best as found in unified Germany today. Their protection equipment is one of the best in the world. Here, the national administration of civil defence and the office of civil and defence mobilisation was merged with the executive office of the President, which made it a priority area with faster response.

Disasters and Civil Defence : South Asia

The nuclearisation of South Asia has added a new dimension to the already hazard prone environment. It faces different kinds of natural hazards. The problem is further accentuated as countries in this region are densely populated and are low-income economies making sustained efforts for economic growth. Recurrent natural disasters inflict setbacks to their efforts in development and aggravate poverty conditions in the region. The paradox lies in the civil defence efforts, which are not available for disasters. Such issues have to be dealt by SAARC.

The South Asian countries have diverse agro climatic regions, each subject to particular natural disasters. Long coastal regions are prone to cyclones; arid and semi arid regions to persistent droughts; the Himalayan mountain terrain and parts of the continental crust to earthquakes and landslides and the near perennial rivers of the region to periodic floods, especially in the North East part of the Indian subcontinent due to the swelling of the mighty Brahmaputra. The other major rivers of the region like the Ganga and Indus are also prone to flooding either due to heavy rains or due to fast melting of snow in the Himalayas. Floods occur with unfailing regularity in Pakistan, Sri Lanka, Bangladesh and Nepal too; while there are occasional flash floods in Bhutan. In India, more than 40 million hectares of land is flood prone. Pakistan has had five serious cases of floods in the past twenty-five years.

The coastal regions of India, Bangladesh and Sri Lanka are severely affected by cyclones arising in the Bay of Bengal. In the recent past, Bangladesh and India particularly have been ravaged by raging cyclones that have killed more than 6,00,000 people and damaged/destroyed property worth crores of rupees.

Moreover, the seismic disturbances are common all over the region. Nepal alone has experienced 23 major earthquakes between 1890 and 1975. Earthquakes of lesser magnitude also strike every year. Pakistan too has a long history of earthquakes. In 1935, an earthquake at Quetta killed 35,000 people. Around 56 per cent of India's total area is susceptible to seismic disturbances. India suffered from three major earthquakes recently in Maharashtra (1993), in Madhya Pradesh (1997) and Gujarat (2001) that have taken a massive toll of human lives and property. Bangladesh is also susceptible to occasional seismic disturbances though the magnitude of the disturbances here is of a considerably lower scale than the rest of the region.

Draughts are yet another phenomenon peculiar to the region due to the agro climatic diversity so prevalent. In fact, it is not uncommon for one part of a country to be experiencing droughts while a different part of the same country is reeling under the impact of floods. India is a classic case of "Ati Vrishti and Ana Vrishti". At times in some states there is embarrassing richness while in some others we see abject penury. Two-third of India comes under arid and semi arid regions and dry sub-humid conditions.

These areas are all prone to draughts. The western parts of India suffered from a major drought in 1987. The Pakistani states of Sind and Punjab are the country's drought prone areas, and there have been eight major droughts in Pakistan since 1947. Sri Lanka's northern and eastern parts also suffer from droughts occasionally.

Due to many environmental factors including deforestation, landslides are an increasingly common occurrence in the hilly areas of the region. Landslides cause extensive damage to roads, bridges, human dwellings, agricultural lands, orchards, forests, etc., resulting in loss of property as well as life. The degradation of hilly areas has also been increasing due to greater frequency of occurrence of landslides. In India alone, the cost of restoration works and associated economic losses due to landslides has been estimated conservatively at Rs 200 crores per annum. Frequency of disasters in Asian countries has been depicted extensively. It should be noted that India faces the largest number of disasters among the countries of South and Southeast Asia. The 'Malpa' landslide and Gujarat Earthquake in India are still fresh in our minds.

The collation of all these aberrations makes the relevance of Civil Defence contiguous to disaster management efforts in the South Asian context, all the more. Other than natural disasters, the region is well primed with military tensions. The threats range from Low Intensity Conflict (LIC) to conventional and nuclear war. Chances of usage of WMDs by terrorists are only increasing. Moreover, these areas except in the erstwhile Burma; never really came under focus during the Second World War, except setting up of a few ARPs under the British rule. Therefore, it hardly has any historical root. It requires rethink and rework now.

In India, it was only in October 1941 that the actual civil defence department came into being. Thereafter it was merged with Defence Department in 1943, only to be merged again with the Home Department in 1944. General Irwin laid the first blueprint for Civil Defence in India, however, in which no mention was made at all regarding threats against nuclear or thermo-nuclear weapons, Chemical or Bio-Warfare weapons. Again after the 1965 Indo-Pak conflict, a quantum improvement was endeavoured by India in encouraging a wider base of voluntary organisations, to include warden service, Horse-fire parties and communication services. The 'Home-Guards' concept of service in India took roots then and has matured since then, into an effective organisation, which has done well during various calamities. Let us also see the disaster management set up in India.

DISASTER MANAGEMENT IN INDIA

Any WMD terrorist act results in a disaster. Therefore it is necessary to recapitulate and analyse the existing disaster management structures.

Disaster management and civil defence should get invariably linked towards mutual substitution. Let us therefore analyse the set up in India for disaster management as all NBC related incidents would also require assistance from existing organisation.

(a) India is a parliamentary democracy with a federal structure dividing the nation into states, which are further administered through districts. The district administration is the focal point for field level organisations and implementation of contingency plans including disaster management. There are various district level mechanisms to tackle disasters, i.e., district relief committee and district control room. The district commissioner co-ordinates with all other government agencies like the armed forces or the para-military forces (Border Security Force, Central Reserve Police Force, Central Industrial Security Force, Indo-Tibet Border Police, Railway Protection Force, Assam Rifles, National Security Guard and the Home Guards).

(b) At national level, Ministry of Home Affairs (MHA) is responsible for man-made disasters and for natural disasters. Delegation of the nodal ministries is as tabulated below:

Table 6.1. Type of Disaster/Crisis and Nodal Central Ministry

Type of Disaster/Crisis	*Nodal Ministry*
1. Air Accident	Ministry of Civil Aviation
2. Civil Strife	Ministry of Home Affairs
3. Major breakdown of any of the Essential Services posing widespread protected problems	Concerned Ministries
4. Railways Accidents	Ministry of Railways
5. Chemical Disaster	Ministry of Environment
6. Biological Disasters	Ministry of Health
7. Nuclear Accident inside or outside the country which poses health or other hazards to people in India Natural Disasters	Department of Atomic Energy Ministry of Agriculture

(c) The Central Relief Commissioner receives information relating to forecast/warning of natural calamity from the Indian Meteorological Department (IMD) or from the Central Water Commission (CWC) on a continuing basis and keeps the Secretary, and through him the Home Minister and the Cabinet Secretary and the Secretary to Prime Minister and through them, the Prime Minister, the Cabinet and the "National Crises Management Committee (NCMC)" informed. He may, whenever required, also disseminate the information to different central government ministries/departments and the state governments for appropriate follow-up-action

Cabinet Committee

The Cabinet may set up a committee for effective implementation of relief measures in the wake of a natural calamity. The secretary in the Ministry of Agriculture acts as the secretary of this committee. In the absence of such a committee, all the matters related to the relief are reported to the Cabinet Secretary.

National Crisis Management Committee (NCMC)

Under the chairmanship of the Cabinet Secretary, the NCMC has been constituted in the cabinet secretariat. The other members of this committee include the Secretary to Prime Minister, Secretaries of Ministry of Home Affairs, Defence, Research and Analysis Wing and Agriculture Co-operation along with Director Intelligence Bureau and an officer of the Cabinet Secretariat. The NCMC gives direction to the Crisis Management Group as deemed necessary.

Crisis Management Group (CMG)

A group under the chairmanship of the Central Relief Commissioner comprising the senior officers from the various ministries and other concerned departments, reviews every year the contingency plans formulated by the Central Ministries/ Departments. It also reviews the measures required for dealing with a natural disaster and co-ordinates the activities of the Central Ministries and the State Governments in relation to disaster preparedness and relief and obtains information from the nodal officers on measures relating to the above. The Joint Secretary (National Disaster Management) and Additional Central Relief Commissioner is the convenor of CMG. The CMG has to meet at least twice a year.

At the State level, the State Relief Commissioner (or Secretary, Department of Revenue) supervises and controls relief operations through Collectors or Deputy Commissioners, who are the main functionaries to co-ordinate the relief operation at district level. The State Governments are autonomous in organising relief operations in the event of natural disasters and in developing the long-term rehabilitation measures. The State Government's efforts are supplemented by Central Government based on the recommendations of the Finance Commission. Fig. 6.1 gives the response structure, at state level, for disaster.

In India, under the present scheme, the defence forces only provide assistance on being requisitioned. Army's role has been phenomenal on this account. Ninety-five per cent of disaster related deaths worldwide occur in the developing countries. Because of its sub-continental dimensions, geographical situation and behaviour of the monsoons, India is exposed to various natural disasters like draught, flood, cyclone and earthquakes (24 states have been identified as disaster prone). In addition, the industrial and technological growth without adequate safeguards exposes the country to man-made or technological disasters like the Bhopal tragedy. Each time there has been a disaster, natural or manmade, the Army is invariably called in to help. And as always, the Army true to its motto of 'Service before Self' has swung into action with relief and rescue operations in double quick time, saving life and property. In the floods that devastated UP, Bihar, Orissa and Assam in July 1998, the cyclone that wrecked Gujarat in June 1998, and the earthquake in 2001, the Army provided invaluable round the clock assistance by rescuing marooned villagers, clearing blocked roads, providing medical assistance and restoring telecommunications on a war footing. The Army's role does not end with search, rescue and evacuation manoeuvres. It provides emergency health operations, rebuilds homes, rehabilitates the affected, and provides food and shelter for victims till the situation stabilises. Its organisational structure facilitates speedy and efficient response in dealing with disaster situations. As change is inevitable with new challenges, the Army now gears itself to handle these disasters even better in the years to come. The civil defence organisations at the state level are analogous to the pattern at the centre. The Directorate General of civil defence in India is responsible for co-ordinating and preparing the civil population in facing war created disasters. The demarcation of responsibilities for various categories of disaster has been done. The command

and control aspect is exercised through the bureaucratic channels of the respective ministries, and formulated into a National Crisis Management Cell (CMC) under the chairmanship of the cabinet secretary. The need is to have a closer interface with the Ministry of Defence and the Directorate General of Military Operations of the army to cater for faster response during requisitions by the civilian authorities. The recent setting up of the Headquarters Integrated Defence System (IDS) could meet this interface requirement more appropriately. These organisations at the local level should operate under an executive head, which is invariably the Deputy Commissioner/Magistrate.

Fig. 6.1.

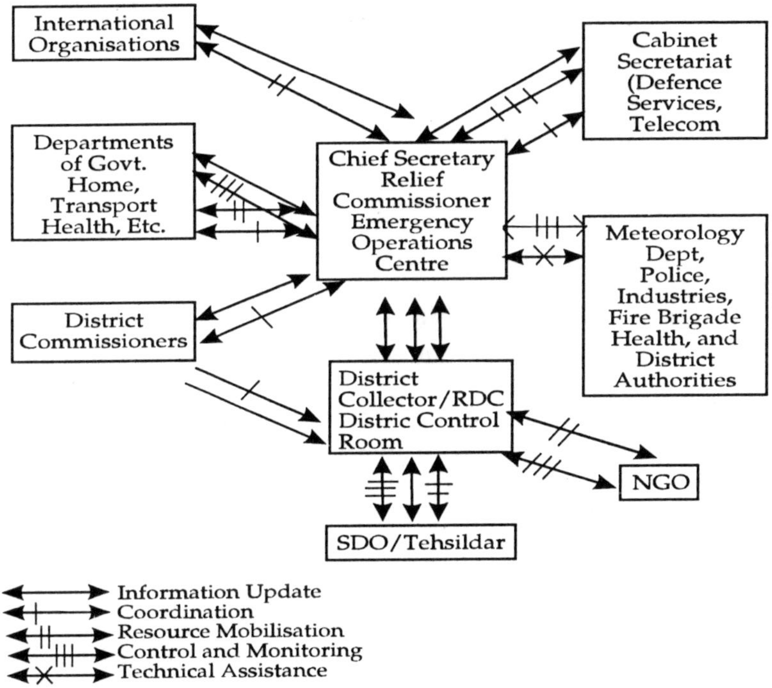

The above given organisational set up should remain the same even in the case of a WMD oriented disaster, except that any external aid from international organisations and from within the country should be catered for by establishing an Aid Coordination Cell.

ARMED FORCES IN DISASTER MANAGEMENT

The role of Armed Forces in disaster management in general and India in particular needs no emphasis. The Armed Forces, especially the Army, has been rendering yeomen service to the nation. The successive governments, be it central or state have been too quick to ask for army's help. However it is better for a layman to understand the advantage the Army holds vis-à-vis any other organisation, the principles in employing them, the shortcomings in them, and the shortcomings in the existing mechanism.

Suitability. The Army is ideally suited and has the capability to offer aid in any type of disaster. It is temperamentally capable because a soldier is naturally brought up to handle any crisis. The soldier has an inbuilt quality to endure hardship and danger. The Army as an organisation can respond to any crisis situation as it is equipped to cater for any type of eventuality. As far as infrastructure capability in concerned, the army has manpower, reliable communication equipment and the logistic support to combat any disaster.

Principles of Employment

This assumes tremendous importance as otherwise people are too ignorant about army or expect too much from them. Considering the inadequate knowledge of awareness officials, the principles of employment of using armed forces are listed below:

(a) Judicious use of armed forces.
(b) An army unit while operating in a disaster struck area continues to be under the command and control of their commanders.
(c) The requisition should be on task basis.
(d) Regular liaison and co-ordination.
(e) Advance planning and training.
(f) Integration of all available resource.
(g) No menial tasks.
(h) Early derequisitioning.

NBC/WMD Related Disasters. Although the overall responsibility of managing any major NBC/WMD related disaster is that of the Ministry of Home Affairs, the Army can be called upon to provide disaster support. It is inbuilt in the charter and role of the armed forces to provide aid during any calamity. Executive orders have been given by Army Headquarters to all the Command Headquarters to keep Quick Reaction Teams (QRTs), Bomb Disposal Units (BDUs) and Quick Reaction Medical Teams (QRMTs) based on available resources. The QRTs carry out the required reconnaissance and the QRMTs may be assigned the following jobs:

(a) Provide immediate first aid.
(b) Evacuate casualties.
(c) Carry out limited decontamination of casualties.
(d) Provide specific treatment.
(e) Evacuate casualties to earmarked hospitals.

Shortcomings

The shortcomings in the existing mechanism are far too many. Some of the basic ones are:

(a) There is no nodal agency. The Home Ministry should be the nodal agency.
(b) Community participation
(c) Lack of trained manpower.
(d) Response time.
(e) Inadequacy of documentation and data.
(f) Disruption of communication.
(g) Adhoc mechanism at State level.
(h) There is no institute to teach disaster management as a subject.

It is very easy to make a list of the shortcomings. But having had personal experience in many disaster related events, after observing (suffering) the shortcomings, the following are recommended:

(a) Comprehensive disaster management policy at national level.
(b) Home ministry to be the nodal agency.
(c) Separate organisation like Federal Emergency Maintenance Agency of the USA should be raised to combat disaster.
(d) Detailed local level plans and rehearsals.
(e) Community awareness and participation.
(f) Co-ordination with NGOs.
(g) Raising Territorial Army to combat disaster.
(h) Revamping the existing warning system.

The major lacunae are lack of wherewithal to meet future threats and challenges. Are we prepared to absorb a nuclear disaster like the Chernobyl incident? Are we prepared for quick response to protect our population Do we have any safety measures for such situations? A global survey has already depicted application of a variety of models. Moreover, with the proliferation of NBC related WMDs, any civil defence mechanism should be patterned to have the back up of the armed forces. The 'Netherlands Model', to this end, would provide the state of the art system. Let us analyse the same for its applicability in the Asian environment.

The Royal Netherlands Army (RNLA) is currently involved in NBC defence activities regarding civil defence, though only sideways, which is the prime responsibility of the Department of Home Affairs. However, military support and provision of assistance is rendered in case of terrorist action and in case of a disaster or severe fear for the development of such an event. Civil or judicial authorities can request military support. The decision on granting of aid is made by the Ministry of Defence. As a principle, all RNLA can be made availabile if not committed in more important duties. In case of extreme circumstances special disaster-relief units can be deployed. These latter units, however, have no special NBC defence capability. The only unit within the RNLA with specialist NBC defence capability is a NBC decontamination sub unit. The other RNLA unit has routine NBC defence tasks and equipment related to disasters and emergencies. Their capabilities are as listed below:

Nuclear Defence

(a) Dose Rate meter equipment for assessing dose rate range of residual gamma radiation and detection on beta and gamma radiation upto 3 MGY 9 cgy.
(b) External beta probe contamination can be measured.
(c) Individual protective equipment.

Chemical Defence

(a) Chemical detection and kit for identification.
(b) Chemical Agent Monitor (CAM) case for upgrading to broad spectrum monitoring.
(c) Special canister for protection against industrial chemicals (Type ABEKNO, class 2).
(d) During threats of expected terrorist attack, pyridostigmine tablets can be administered as prophylactic.

New Systems Under Development. The new systems under development are detection and monitoring at long ranges including those for biological weapons, known as 'BIDS'.

Organisational Attributes: Preview and Analysis of Protective Measures. All the above-mentioned evolutionary facts and the survey of international organisations – (USA, erstwhile USSR and the European countries) bring out lessons. The salient essence of these lessons is listed below:

(a) All civil defence organisations are legally tenable at national level by an 'Act', to assist in all types of disaster management.

(b) Ideally, Ministry of Home/Interior should handle such organisations, as it concerns the population of the country.

(c) Defence forces play a subsidiary role and only provide assistance on requisition. Defence forces should therefore be suitably tasked to remain abreast with current threat perceptions. This will obviously include 'NBC – WMDs' related incidents or disasters for which the armed forces would have to be suitably equipped and trained.

(d) Adequate funding and organisational thrust is necessary to make this organisation work.

Let us see the modus operandi of tackling Nuclear, Chemical and Biological related disasters. Out of this the, nuclear incident/ disaster would require fast mobilisation capability (preferably air based), of various specially tailored civil defence outfits, followed by detection and monitoring capability, which can build up, upon location/departmental resources, already deployed or getting deployed (For example, Department of Atomic Energy would have to cater for immediate disaster teams which would have mobile laboratories with scientists, decontamination and first aid facilities). The local medical teams may be in a position to have a faster response and thus may be the first to reach the disaster site and thus render crucial first aid and demarcation of area, before arrival of specialist civil organisations. Similarly, 'Chemical-Bio' related disaster/incident would be a frequent thing in times to come and would have to be tackled swiftly and smoothly. The pattern of tackling these emergencies as regards the armed forces, they could be the ones to reach the site immediately or build up on civil resources already deployed. Detection, monitoring and decontamination equipment would have to become a part of the armed forces team. Individual protective equipment against chemical and biological agents are already in vogue to include items like overall/garments, face let and mask, gloves and boots made of butyl rubber, which can operate in a contaminated environment at least for 24 hours.

All resources of the nation should be brought under one umbrella of the civil defence organisation under the Home Ministry, or preferably a Ministry for Disaster Management be created to include handling of specialised NBC disasters caused even due to terrorist actions.

Mobile collective protection measures and medical centres will be of help. These kinds of protection systems should be inflatable in which an air filtration unit can be fitted. For the walking wounded type of casualties, a series of body bags which envelope the upper torso should also be provisioned. Such teams should also have water filtration systems with them. For building and sustaining such an organisation, a philosophy needs to evolved on the following parameters:

(a) Civil Defence and disaster management effort be brought under one umbrella, preferably Ministry of Home Affairs.

(b) National budgeting and prioritisation.

(c) The principle of unity of command and single point reference in dealing with disasters/incidents ensured (may be by reorganisation).

(d) Civil Defence measures add to the deterrence capability, (where 'Nuclear Deterrence' is the plank and pivot of a national defence strategy). Thus, this aspect should get integrated to the nuclear doctrine.

(e) Due to the new emerging threats, philosophy of equipment development have made it mandatory for evoking techniques and the manufacture and procurement of NBC related safety and detection equipment too in a future scenario.

(f) All the above aspects be legislated by dejure formalisation and ratification in the parliament (techno-legal aspects).

(g) Communication technology (V satellite technology) network be utilised for networking and response.

(h) Creation of a 'Blue' book for better accountability.

Civil Defence Plan

The civil defence plan for any metropolitan city, say, New Delhi, Bombay, Madras or Calcutta should envisage the establishment of mobile columns in the adjoining towns at a distance of 50 kms or so. The object of mobile columns should be reaching the place of disaster at the earliest and render necessary assistance to the affected population. The mobile column should have the following detachments.

NBC Detachment. The nuclear detachment will undertake survey of the area for radioactivity and advise other teams of the mobile column for safe operation in the nuclear environment. It should also undertake decontamination operations to limit the extent of damage to men and material.

Rescue Detachment. The rescue detachment should undertake rescue operations to retrieve personnel trapped under debris and in damaged buildings.

Fire Fighting Detachment. The fire fighting detachment will deal with major fires, which are likely to develop as a result of the thermal effects of the nuclear explosion.

Fig. 6.2. Blast Damage From Gz For 20 Kt.

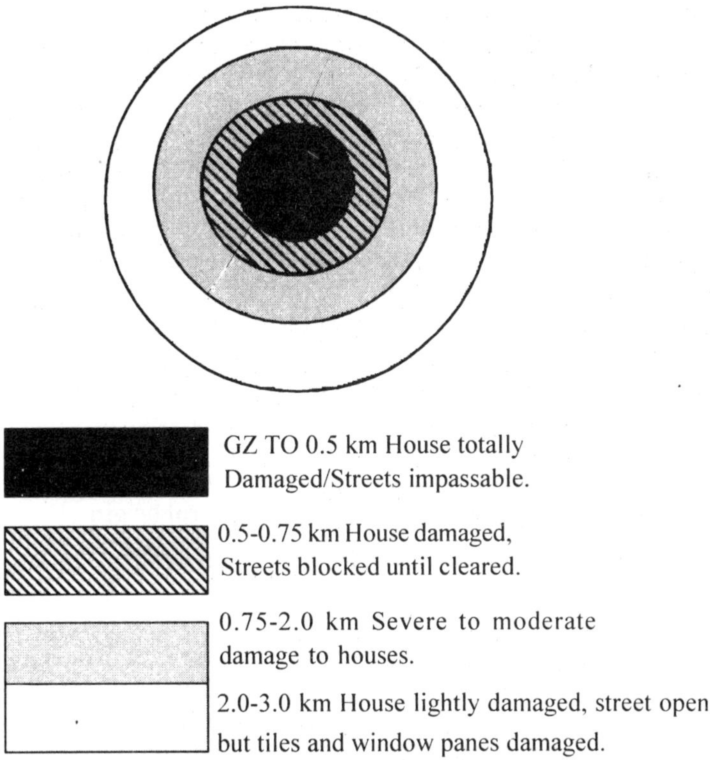

Communication Detachment. The communication detachment should ensure that lines of communications between the various detachments are maintained. The use of dispatch riders in NBC clothing is also envisaged.

Medical Detachment. The medical detachment renders first aid to the affected personnel and also to transport the casualties to hospitals and first aid post as necessary. This detachment also has the responsibility of disposal of the dead.

Administrative Detachment. The administration and training detachment will train the detachments for the intented role, and also perform the advisory role as required.

A model civil defence plan for a metropolitan city like New Delhi and the response mechanisms are given separately as appendices at the end.

Prognosis Post 2000: Fresh View Towards Globalisation

The globe continues to trot with the dangers of a nuclear war. In fact, it may not be incorrect to add, a 'Space War'. The 2000 millennium equipoise is slanted towards an Armageddon – may be a WMD in the hands of terrorists. Therefore, the very tenets of any civil defence type of organisation should be on the model of an 'International Department', as any global disaster has to be shared equally by all. This may necessitate intervention and legislation by the United Nations as a part of 'Conference of Disarmament' (CD) initiative. The most significant global effort made in recent times to mitigate effects of disasters is the launching of the IDNDR programme by the United Nations (This may have to be augmented for NBC related incidents).

The objective of IDNDR is to reduce through concerted international action, especially in the developing countries, the loss of life, property damage and social and economic disruption caused by natural disasters such as earthquakes, windstorms, floods, landslides, volcanic eruptions, wildfires, drought and desertification and other calamities of natural origin.

By the Year 2000, as per the Plan of the IDNDR, all Countries should have:

(a) Comprehensive national assessments of risks from natural hazards, with these assessments taken into account in development plans;

(b) Mitigation plans at national and/or local levels, involving long term prevention and preparedness and community awareness, and;

(c) Ready access to the global, regional, national and local warning systems and broad dissemination of the same.

The major conference of the IDNDR programme held in Yokohama (Japan) in May 1994 evolved a plan of action for disaster reduction called the Yokohama Strategy. It gives guidelines for Natural Disaster Prevention, Preparedness and Mitigation.

The plan of action is to be based on points like development of a global culture of prevention as an essential component of an integrated approach to disaster reduction, adoption of a policy of self reliance in each vulnerable country and community comprising capacity building as well as allocation and efficient use of resources, community participation in the disaster reduction process, and improved risk assessment, broader monitoring and timely communication of forecasts and warnings.

For the remaining part of the decade, the strategy called upon all countries to express political commitment to reduce their vulnerability through appropriate means. It also recommended that donor countries should increase the priority on disaster prevention, mitigation and preparedness in their assistance programmes and budgets.

It may even be clubbed with the prevailing concept of 'Nuclear Warfare Concept'. Thus the continuing Revolution in Military Affairs (RMA) should be channelised towards a positive end, for instance, the creation of a central helicopter/air based force (with air to air refueling capability); under global funding with state of the art equipment for detection, monitoring and decontamination. 'GPS' and space based systems should give real time information and navigation capabilities. These forces could be geo-strategically disposed with strategic communication tentacles and capability. Concept of 'Zones of peace' be also invoked globally akin to 'Zones of Truce' practiced earlier. May be they can be built on the lines of Nuclear Free Zones (NFZ). A survey of the Chernobyl incident proves that very little International help ever arrived. Only the innocent children and many innocent soldiers, who carried out the shoveling operations, were killed. Such like incidents can occur worldwide. Will our actions be tardy again? Will we point fingers at each other again? There is an urgent appeal to the United Nations, to initiate action for a 'Global Disaster Team' with the capabilities of air mobility, satellite communication, 'GPS' navigational capabilities, long range and short-range detection and identification of 'BC' weapons/bomb capability and an immediate capability for emergency decontamination. It may not be economical, for every country to organise such teams, thus let it be done centrally under the aegis of the United Nations and in direct control of the Secretary General, which would mean 'Kofi Anan' in today's context. These facilities can be superimposed on facilities being suggested. Though earthquakes are unpredictable hazards, monitoring of seismic disturbance helps to delineate hazard zones and also help in preparation of risk maps. Risk maps are then used to plan construction works and implement mitigation measures.

Several countries including India, which are threatened by earthquake hazard operated national and local networks for earthquake monitoring and surveillance. The first global network, known as World-wide Network of Seismic Stations (WWNS), was established in the early sixties. Later on, a few of these were converted to Seismic Research Observatories (SRO). Now a modern global network called Incorporated Research Institutes for Seism city (IRIS) has been established throughout the world. A suggested world level organisation is given below (See Fig. 6.3).

Fig. 6.3.

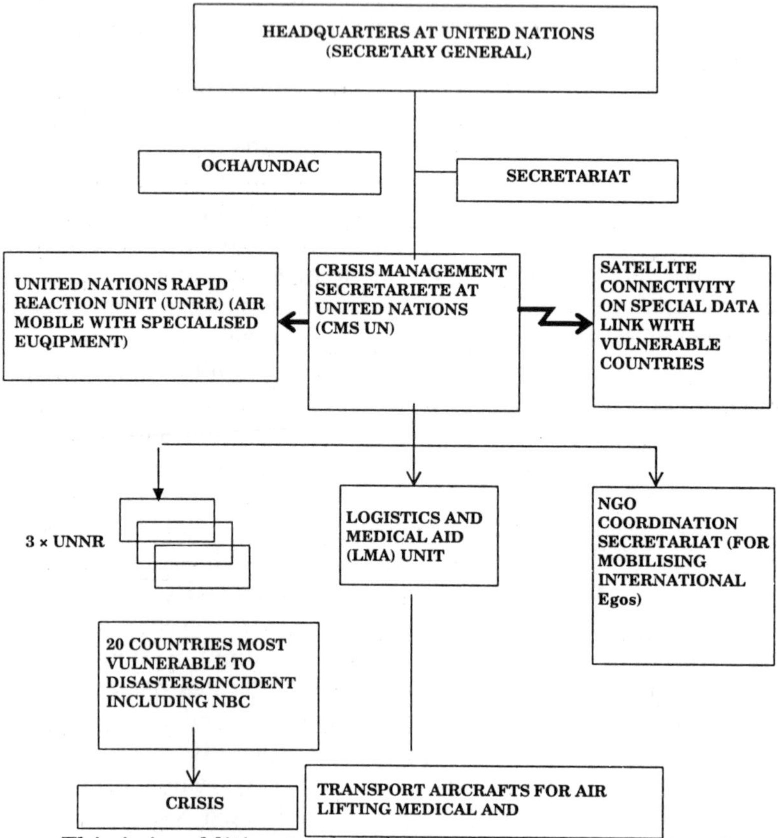

This is in addition to already existing systems to cater for a NBC related incident too.

(a) UNRR unit could be of approximate four specialist task forces each composed of 50 men to enable detection and decontamination duties.
(b) Global civil defence network be mapped and clearly disseminated. Existing monitoring stations for natural/artificial disasters be networked.
(c) IDNDR augmented for NBC related disasters.
(d) Exercise secretariat be created for mock up exercises globally to counter nuclear or other NBC related terrorist incidents.
(e) Existing organisation to be dovetailed, i.e., OCHA/UNDAC.

Note: Concepts and ideas taken during discussion of disaster management at Indira Gandhi National Open University and United Service Institution of India, New Delhi, 05-06 April 1999.

There is definitely a national and international effort required towards formulating 'Mock Up' exercises against simulated disasters of all types including nuclear disaster. One such exercise was done at 'Day Dag' Nuclear power plant, 40 kms. from Hong Kong. The results of this should be institutionalised in various emergency schemes. A suggested model for any such exercise in the post 2000 period should be constructed on the following lines:

(a) Exercise secretariate be created at the UN Headquarters, under the aegis of IAEA.

(b) Global talent is harnessed to create a simulation cell. This cell should be composed of specialists who can create artificial and natural (but man triggered), disasters, including the 'N', 'B' and 'C' types.

(c) Technical support group be formed to support the technical and scientific aspects.

(d) Co-ordination support group be created to maximise and co-ordinate efforts of various agencies including international support.

(e) Policy and Analysis Cell (supposed to set the exercise and should have factual data of earlier incidents, so that maximum lessons can be drawn) should be established. It would have a core of scientists to modulate data analysis.

(f) Threat assessment group, be formed to analyse the potential threats globally and thus help in formulation of counter-measures. Health hazards associated with the plume pathway and the ingestion pathway as assessed for contamination can also spread through trans-border movement of eatables and other consumer items. This may necessitate establishment of monitoring points and collection of sample readings.

(g) Evacuation/Sheltering Assistance groups be created and dovetailed with other national civil defence measures to produce maximum mitigation. Radiation contaminated area be avoided by helicopter survey and monitoring. The passage and route of evacuation be decided accordingly. (Use of potassium iodide as a means to counter-act against radiation is also moderated).

(h) Mobilisation of national and international air effort and naval effort becomes a pre-requisite to evacuation of population from contaminated inland areas of islands. It may become necessary to announce 'Sea Exclusive Zone' to risk exposures to refugees.

(j) Food anti-contamination action becomes a major effort and area of concern. Milk, leafy vegetables and livestock will have to be protected, as minuscule radioactive dust may settle on the food.

(k) Media and 'psychological' management cells should be established and be proficient in announcing and disseminating basic individual and collective safety measures without assistance and concurrent to actions by all other agencies/cells.

In the end, the basic theme of such a global initiative would be based on mutual co-operation. Let us not talk of fighting nuclear wars, but let us talk of saving this planet!

Seven

Atoms for War : ABC of Nuclear Toxicology Technology for Safety

(The Sudarshan Chakra: King of Weapons)

Historical Preview

Historically, application of science has been dual ended. The dynamite revolutionized the scientific application of explosive power. The atoms did the same. The roots of theory of atoms can be traced back to the epics of the great *Mahabharata* days, when the phenomenon of materialisation and de-actualisation could occur by the power of thought. Many analyses on this subject spin out many theories. In fact, scientists have already further split the atom into 'Hadrons', which, it is speculated could be further be traced to the source of light or light itself. Light itself is the creation of thought. Therefore, scientists have already started drawing linkages by announcing that where science ends, spirituality begins.

Can we therefore talk of a scientific invention where thought could be converted into tremendous energies, which could lift mountains and pave the way through oceans? The Indian epics and mythology speak of the Avtar of Lord Krishna, who could manipulate and control space and time. Even the weapons he fired were precision guided. He enjoyed celestial control of the cosmos. Thus, they would be the culminating point of science or may be spirituality. Here, the focus of the scientific explanations given below would be to encompass learning the characteristics of Atomic Energy. This part covers Nuclear Physics, Structure of Atoms, and the effect of a nuclear blast on humans and the environment and the related civil defensive measures.

Nuclear Threat : Technology for Safety

Nuclear weapons are strategic weapons and are distinguished from the conventional weapons of war because of widespread and devastating nature of their effects. They can also be termed as conflict terminator and when enlarged in today's environment as a conflict preventor or as a deterrence mechanism to war. Nuclear weapons have been used twice in history, at Hiroshima and Nagasaki, thus we have a detailed idea of their effects against cities and civil population. These weapons have never been used, as yet, against troops in the field, but the likely effects have been assessed from the testing of weapons and by using various simulators. Although, we now have a fair knowledge of the effects on equipment and the physical and physiological effect on men; but we have no experience of the effect on morale, which we can safely assume to be detrimental and severe. The safety of civil population is an important national imperative to key security planning. In this context civil defensive measures become a prime area of responsibility in national governance.

Only the best civil defence organisations (including NGOs) that are well trained and confident in their equipment will be fit to fight on after a series of such nuclear strikes. To assume impossibility of such an event is being impish especially in an India-Pak scenario, which hangs on a razors' edge, fumed by ethno complexity and the dynamics of the Afghan imbroglio. Besides Pakistan, many other countries now have the capability of manufacturing nuclear weapons. Amongst our neighbouring countries, China and states of Central Asian republics are nuclear. In the West Asian continent, Israel is a covert nuclear power and Iran is fast approaching the nuclear status. There have been reports (statement of Scott Ritter, former Inspector UN Special Commission) indicating that Iraq had the capability of manufacturing two or three nuclear weapons but without the fissile material. Egypt has also staked claims of nuclear capability. North Korean capabilities in this field are well known too. Therefore, in such a hostile environments, immediate generation of protective measures at all levels is the need of the hour. As a first step, let us understand the effects of nuclear weapons, which will help us to survive in a NBC environment including fighting a terrorist attack or evolving a counter-terrorist security doctrine.

Effects of Nuclear Explosion

The comparison of the effects of bombs from the Second World War period to the present megaton range is shown in Fig. 7.1.

Nuclear explosions are characterised by an immediate, rapid and brief release of nuclear radiations, a rapidly developing fireball, which emits intense thermal radiations (heat and light) and gives rise to a powerful pressure pulse which travels out from the point of bursts known as shock or blast waves. Interactions of the nuclear radiations with the atmosphere result in a fourth output—the electromagnetic pulse (EMP). The EMP is a pulse of electromagnetic and

communications equipment like mobile phones and even the fireball rises rapidly and cools forming the familiar spreading

Fig. 7.1.

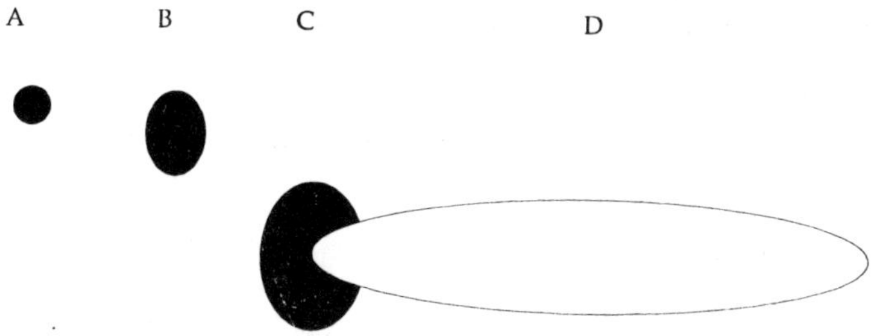

A- Lethal area from the blast wave of the blockbusters used in Second World War.
B- Lethal area from the blast wave of the Hiroshima bomb.
C- Lethal area of the blast wave of a 1-Mt bomb.
D- Lethal area for fall-out radiation from a 1-Mt bomb.

Source: *Effects of nuclear war on health services*, second edition, World Health Organisation.

mushroom shaped cloud with a column of smoke or dust called the stem. Without going into technical details of this process, the effects of nuclear explosion of concern to an individual are:

- Flash.
- Heat Wave.
- Blast and shock wave.
- Nuclear radiation's initial.
- Residual.
- Electromagnetic effects on equipment.

The energy released during the nuclear explosion can be roughly distributed in proportions as shown in Fig. 7.2.

Fig. 7.2. Energy Distribution.

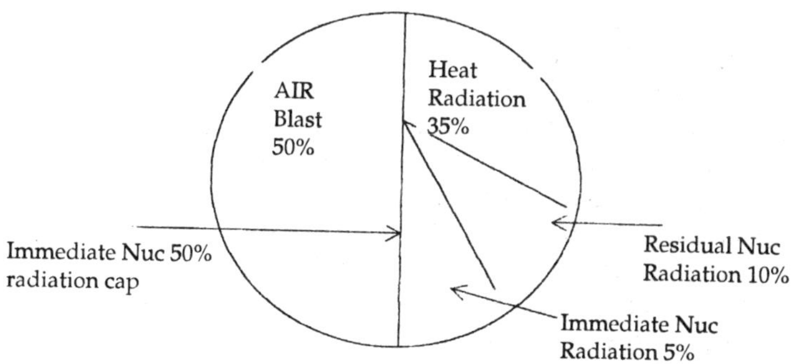

Energy Distribution

However, the effects on targets need not necessarily be in those proportions but will vary with yield of the weapon, distance from Ground Zero (GZ) and the height of burst, the effect of flash, heat, blast and radiation are explained below.

Flash

Eye Damage is More in Night than in Day

The intense flash from a nuclear burst affects vision well beyond the ranges at which heat burns occur. The flash effects can be divided into two parts as under:

- ***Dazzle.*** Dazzle or 'flash blindness' causes temporary loss of vision resulting from the brightness of the visible burst. It will only be of significance to personnel unaffected by other nuclear effects. As a guide, in daylight only those facing the burst are likely to be dazzled for about two minutes. At night dazzle will affect those facing the burst for about 10 minutes and those facing away from the burst for about three minutes.
- ***Eye Damage.*** Retinal burns occur when the eye lenses focus the fireball image onto the retina. Shallow burns heal completely. Deep burns lead to permanent blind spots, but the sight is not normally lost completely. It has been estimated that only two to three per cent of those dazzled will suffer retinal burns and only 0.1 per cent will suffer permanent blindness in one or both eyes.

Heat Wave

Heat Damage is Less on Foggy Days. Heat is the principal casualty-causing factor. It is likely that some 50 per cent of nuclear casualties will suffer burns due to exposed skin unprotected from the heat pulse and from charred or burnt clothing and/or local fires.

In a low airburst, 40 to 50 per cent of the energy released is in the form of light and heat. This energy travels with the speed of light and is absorbed by buildings, structures, people, plants and animals. For a 20 KT weapon approximately 80 per cent of the heat energy is absorbed within one second of the detonation. Weather conditions also play an important part on the effect of heat wave. For an airburst, a low cloud base will absorb some of the heat energy, whereas for a ground burst, it may reflect the heat waves and intensify the effects. The amount of attenuation of thermal energy by atmosphere depends largely on the visibility. Thus, thermal/heat effects will be greater on a clear day than a foggy day.

The amount of thermal energy delivered to a specified area (usually 1 cm^2) is often referred to as a thermal dose. Approximate thermal energies required for ignition of various materials is as under:

	1 KT	*1 MT*
• Naked skin	4 cal/sq. cm	6.5 cal/sq. cm
• Dark Wool Flannel	6 "	13 "
• NBC Suit	15 "	30 "
• Truck Canvas Canopy	15 "	30 "
• Dry Grass and Undergrowth	2/3 "	5/7 "
• Plastics	4/6 "	9/13 "
• NBC Suit	15 "	30 "

NBC Protective Clothing Gives Maximum Protection. It can be seen that at a given range a 1 MT weapon will deliver 1000 times more energy but will take longer to do so. Also a given thermal dose of 1 MT weapon will be delivered to a much greater range but in a much longer time and will do less damage. This can be exemplified by considering a man standing in the sun receiving a given amount of calories over a period of several minutes and the same man receiving that same total dose in a space of few seconds from a nuclear explosion. The first will produce a healthy tan while the second will produce burn injuries. That is why the thermal dose for same effect on a material, increases with the increase in the yield and also NBC protective clothing gives maximum protection from burns.

For a 20 KT weapon, second-degree burns will be caused up to a distance of 3700 m from GZ on naked skin and up to a distance of 2300 m when the skin is covered with normal clothing. Dry vegetation will catch fire up to a distance of 4000 m from the GZ. For a 1 MT weapon second-degree burns may be caused up to 1900 m.

Effects of thermal energy go beyond the immediate flash burns. Fires are caused by the thermal radiation that ignites the materials released by blast wave. The numerous fires thus initiated could spread and form one massive fire known as firestorm. A firestorm generates a column of rising hot gases that suck in fresh air from the periphery of the fire causing winds of speed up to 160 km an hour, burning combustible materials inside the firestorm, which produces carbon dioxide thus asphyxiating those who may have sought shelter there.

Blast and Shock Wave

High Air Burst Causes More Damage by Blast than Low Air Burst. The most destructive effect of a nuclear explosion on the living organism and human habitat is caused directly or indirectly by the blast wave. The detonation creates a shock front of very high pressure that propagates outward crushing and sweeping every thing in its path. Arrival of the shock wavefront at a point away from the explosion is experienced as a sudden devastating and shattering blow followed by hurricane type winds.

Blast wave follows a schematic pattern. Initially the pressure rises very sharply at the moving front and falls off towards interior region of the explosion. This is the positive phase of the blast wave and is called the static overpressure (in excess of atmospheric pressure), which decays as it travels away from the GZ. After a short time, the pressure behind the front falls below the surrounding atmosphere and the negative phase of the blast wave is formed called under pressure. During the negative phase, a partial vacuum is produced and the air is sucked in towards the opposite direction of GZ instead of being pushed away. The duration of overpressure of 20 KT weapon is approximately 1-2 seconds and that of a 1 MT weapons is 2 to 4 seconds. The negative phase is somewhat longer in duration than the positive phase and its peak under pressure is small in comparison to that of the overpressure.

The height of the nuclear explosion above the surface has an important effect on the blast wave produced. For an airburst, the blast wave and its reflection from the ground combine to produce a higher overpressure than for a ground burst. See Fig. 7.3.

From the Fig. 7.3, it can be seen that the 5 psi overpressure, for 10 KT weapons, is up to approx 0.6 miles for ground burst and 0.95 miles for air burst at 2150 ft.

Damage due to Blast. Nearly all the direct damage caused by overpressure and dynamic pressure occurs during the positive phase of the overpressure. 5 psi overpressure is sufficient to destroy an ordinary frame house and 50-100 psi for the reinforced concrete structure.

Effects on Personnel. The primary effects of blast on a man is remarkably little. Eardrums may burst between 7-17 psi overpressure and damage to lungs and other parts of the body are caused at approximate 40 psi overpressure. But the wind effect on him is not to be dismissed, because at 40 psi, the wind speed should be approximately 400 miles an hour. Parts of the body might snap

Importance of Height of Burst on Blast Wave Static Overpressure

Fig. 7.3.

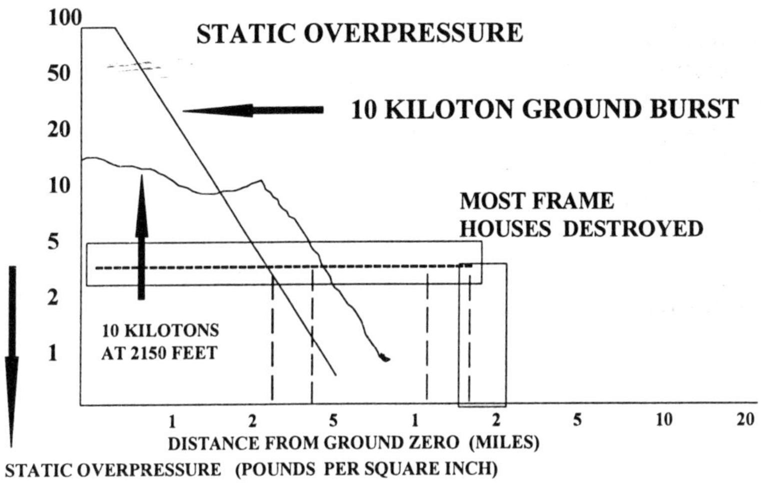

when the blast wave hits a man, but the main danger is from the secondary or indirect effects such as:

- The collapse of buildings shelters or the over turning of vehicles, trucks and cars.
- The impact of flying debris.
- Injuries caused to personnel by being picked up and flung by the winds against something stationary.

Damage to Assets. The damage suffered to assets, equipment and installation is likely to be due to antennas breaking off, cables getting stretched and severed, vehicle aircraft and other equipment overturned, buildings and shelters crushed or caused to collapse by the pressure changes, earthworks collapsed by the ground shock wave, supplies, equipment and weapons picked up and dispersed.

Ground Configuration. Pressure waves follow ground undulations, so terrain affords little protection from blast and shock, unless it is a hill or a mountain, which can provide sufficient depth. In a surface or near surface burst, 1 to 15 per cent of the released energy is transferred directly to the ground thus forming a crater and sending earthquake like tremors through the ground. This ground shockwave travels much faster than the blast wave in the air and to longer distances. This can cause damage to foundations of overground structures and even underground structures.

Skyscrapers are likely to collapse under 5 psi. Cities with basement constructions have an advantage.

Casualty Models

Many studies on various casualty models like the Princeton studies have confirmed that the existing models do not cater for super fires. Thus they have suggested a "Configuration model" which assumes that a circular mass fire would develop around ground zero and cause 100 per cent lethality for all these not within 2 kms of its edge. A comparison between conflagration and overpressure model predicts much higher casualties in the former. See Figs. 7.4 and 7.5.

Fig. 7.4.

CONFLAGURATION MODEL

Fatality rates from a 1 Mtr explosion at 2 km altitude: predictions of two casuality models

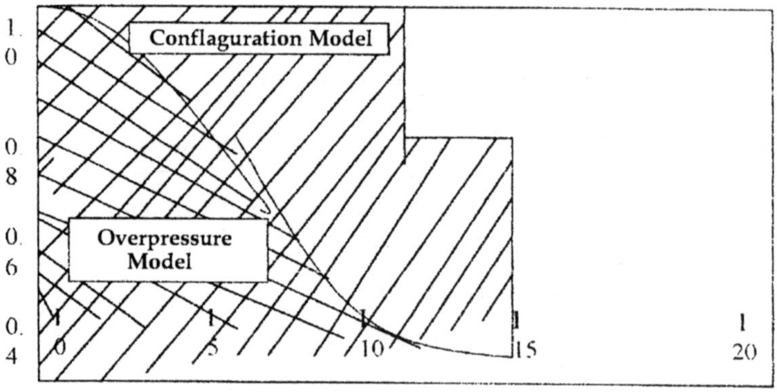

Source: *Effects of nuclear war on health and health services*, second edition, World Health Organisation, p. 114.

Nuclear Radiation

Radioactive Contaminated Area Becomes Quite Safe After 48 hours. Although radiation raises the most emotive discussion of any of the nuclear effects, it is not necessarily the most lethal. Indeed, taking a 20 KT airburst, an average of only 15 per cent of casualties would be caused by it. This figure may vary with the height of burst and the size of the yield. Various types of radiation are grouped under two main headings:

Initial Radiation. Initial radiation is defined as that radiation which is emitted during the first one minute of explosion. This radiation has more penetrating power than the other form of radiation.

Residual Radiation. Residual radiation is that which remains after one-minute post detonation. It essentially consists of neutron induced activity and fallout of radioactive material.

Fig. 7.5. Overpressure Model

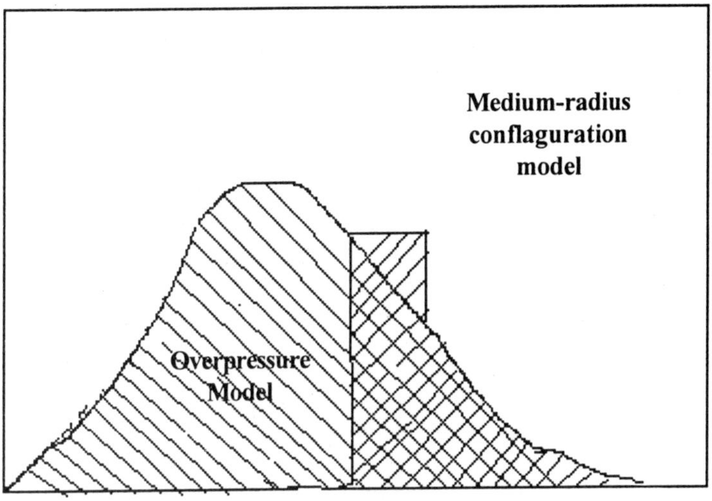

Initial Radiation. Initial radiation consists of alpha particles, beta particles, gamma radiation and neutrons. Alpha particles do not travel far and can be stopped by any obstruction, such as even a sheet of paper, and are thus of no significance. Beta particles are electrons, having a little more penetration power than alpha particles and can cause damages, in the form of a sort of burn to the skin called beta burns. These can be harmful in case ingested or if enters the body through a wound or a cut. Neutrons and gamma rays, which are neutral particles and electro-magnetic waves respectively, are the radiation casualty inflictors and can travel 2-3 km through air. Gamma rays can pass through dense materials such as metals and brickwork, but its intensity is reduced in so doing. Also, gamma rays are attenuated and scattered while passing through atmosphere. Due to scattering they arrive at a place from many directions. Most of the dose received will come from the direction of the explosion, but a considerable amount will also arrive by scattering effect. Neutrons have similar penetrating power as the gamma radiation and are also of great significance.

Residual radiation. As stated earlier, residual radiation consists of neutron induced activity and fallout. Neutrons produced during the explosion cause imbalance in the weapon material, the atmosphere and the elements they encounter. This produces induced radioactivity and the area beneath a nuclear burst becomes highly radioactive though for a shorter period. The fallout, as is well known occurs due to the earth particles sucked in the mushroom cloud during a ground or low air burst, which becomes radioactive and then falls on the ground in the direction of the wind in a specific pattern. Its military significance is the denial of ground it would cause or even a denial of transit through the ground. The actual radiation risk due to fallout can only be determined by 'radiological reconnaissance.' The rate at which radiation reduces or decays naturally is as under: -

- H + 1 hour 1000 rads/hour
- H + 7 hour 100 rads/hour
- H + 49 hour (H+2 days) 10 rads/hour
- H + 2 weeks 1 rad/hour

(Multiply time by seven and divide rate of dose by 10)

There are three important differences between the gamma radiation in the immediate and residual periods:

- The energy or penetrating power of residual radiation is less than that of the immediate. Protection provided by any material, therefore, will be greater against residual radiation than against immediate radiation.
- The emitters in the case of residual radiation are on the ground in the form of dust or water and can get inside the shelters unless action is taken to keep them out.
- The intensity of residual radiation is always decaying but may remain outside a shelter/trench for days or even weeks.

Radiation Dosage is Cumulative in Effect.

Radiation Measurement. The following are the units of radiation measurement:

Rad. The effect of radiation on a biological system, the whole or a particular organ is related to the amount of energy absorbed as a result of exposure to that radiation. The imperial unit used to express the biological effect of radiation is the rad. It is defined as the amount of radiation that will result in 100 ergs of energy being released in each gram of the irradiated material.

Gray. A new SI Unit (based on metric system) is currently being introduced and will replace rad. It is defined as the absorption of one joule of radiation energy per kg of absorbing material. A gray is equal to 100 rads or one centigray is equal to one rad.

Roentgen. The roentgen is the imperial measure of radiation exposure dose from gamma or X-rays. The roentgen and the rad are interchangeable in most circumstances and as a layman, one can take them as equal.

Indicators of radiation damage. The symptoms of radiation damage in personnel are usually described as 'radiation sickness'. Some or all of the following symptoms of this sickness are:

- Initial symptoms of headache, nausea, vomiting diarrhea and general malaise.
- A symptom free period with apparent recovery.
- The development of latent symptoms such as loss of hair and appetite, sore throat, fever, hemorrhages, prolonged incapacitation and/or death.
- Probability of death and reaction illness is shown in Figs. 7.6 and 7.7 assuming various dose values.

Fig. 7.6.

Probability of death (A) and radiation illness (B) as a function of the dose, assuming do values of 3.5 and 1.0 Gy (See text)

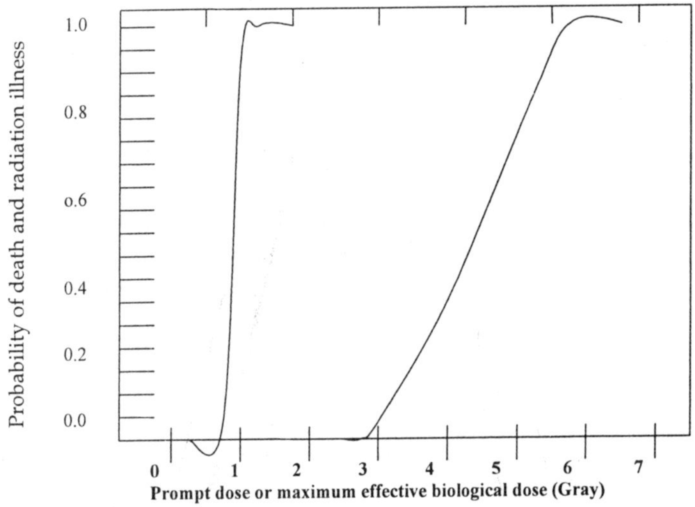

150 Rads and Below are Within Tolerance Threshold of Human Beings

Radiation Sickness. The living organism and human body has some ability to repair the damage caused by radiation but this may not be complete. In real radiation doses are cumulative in effect. The damage and symptoms, however, depend not only on the dose but also on the rate of dose received each time and the interval between exposures. Individuals are affected by radiation to different degrees so the radiation dose figures given in Fig. 7.7 should only be regarded as a guide:

Fig. 7.7.

Probability of death (A) and radiation illness (B) as a function of the dose, assuming do values of 3.5 and 1.0 Gy (See text)

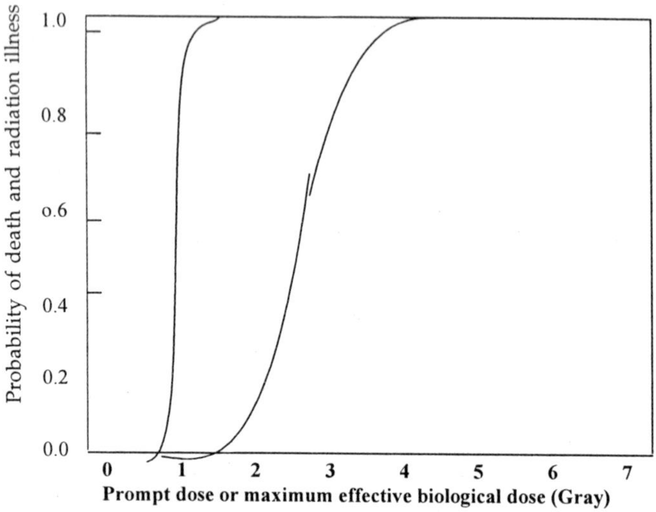

Source: Effects of nuclear war on health and services. Second edition, World Health Organisation, p. 128.

- Below 150 rads, no short term effect for human beings.
- From 150 to 450 rads, some incapacitation with death possible.
- From 450 to 800 rads, incapacitation and death most likely in the ensuing weeks.
- Above 800 rads, severe incapacitation and death certain.

Risk Factor. To provide rescuers with a guide to the doses to which human beings can be exposed without endangering their effectiveness, the doses that may be incurred in 24 hours on which current UK/US target analysis safety criteria are based, are as under:

*	Negligible risk (subject to a maximum of 75 rads in 30 consecutive days)	—5 rads
*	Moderate risk	—20 rads
*	Emergency risk for life saving	—50 rads (only to be taken operations)

It should be noted that these doses only apply in a crisis. In peacetime conditions very much smaller limits are laid down for the civilian population. An experiment on mice to guage mortality rate as a function of dose is shown in Fig. 7.8.

Fig. 7.8.

Acute radiation mortality of mice as a function of dose

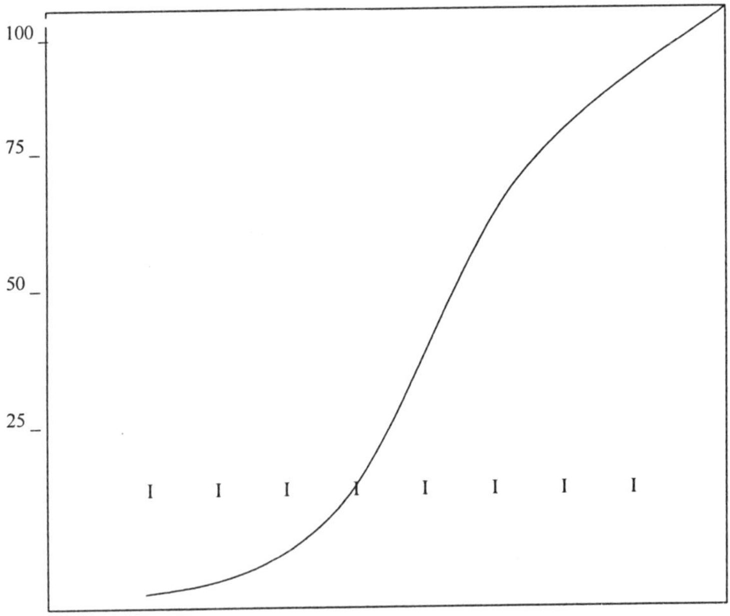

Source : Effects of nuclear war on health and health services, second edition, World Health Organisation, p. 89.

Electromagnetic Effects on Equipment

Valve type Communication Equipment has more survivability than microchips and electronics circuits

There are two main electromagnetic effects of a nuclear explosion. The first is EMP, which can damage electronic equipment and can cause changes in the electrical conductivity of the atmosphere and ionosphere. The second effect is called the Transient Radiation Effects on Electronics or 'TREE'.

EMP. During a nuclear explosion, EMP is generated by the emission of high energy gamma rays, which effect the atoms of the atmosphere so that electrons are liberated, leaving behind ionised atoms. This relative displacement of +ve and -ve charges produces an electrical field in the air and the ground. In spite of a short time of occurrence, it carries a considerable amount of energy. The effect of EMP on electronic equipment is fatal, however it is harmless to humans. The common civil population using mobile phones would become deaf. It is seen that valve type communication equipment has more survivability than microchips electronic circuits.

Fig. 7.9.

Diagram of Mobile Phone

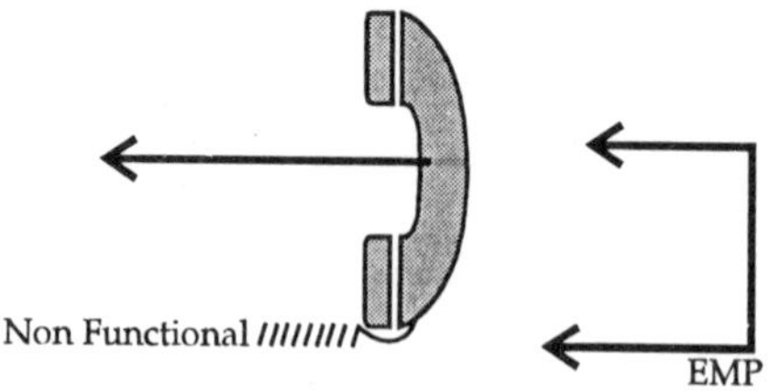

Types of Bombs

The various types of nuclear bombs/weapons used in modern warfare are summarised to be able to get a holistic view of the dangers of this weapon system and the urgency of enhancing the civil defensive measures.

Fission Weapons. These were the first kind to be developed and the only ones, which have been used but are now largely, obsolete. For fission explosion to take place the weapon must contain a minimum mass of uranium or plutonium isotope to allow a chain reaction to be maintained. This is defined as critical mass and would vary for different isotopes and combinations.

Two methods have been devised to initiate a fission process. In the first method, two sub-critical masses of fissionable material are brought together by a conventional explosive, called a gun barrel device. The second method makes use of the fact that when a sub-critical quantity of a fissionable material is strongly compressed it can become critical. The compression is achieved by means of a spherical arrangement of ordinary high explosive lenses, which create an explosion and compress the sub-critical material to a smaller critical mass.

In a very short span of time, roughly half a microsecond after the first neutron is initiated, so much energy is released due to chain reaction that extremely high temperatures and pressures are reached. Consequently no casing can hold or contain the exploding mass and the fissionable material begins to expand rapidly, which causes it to become sub-critical and thus the chain reaction soon ends. Thus in a fission weapon, an appreciable portion of the original material is unconsummated and forms part of radioactive fallout. Due to engineering difficulties, generally fission weapons do not exceed 500 KT in power (i.e., equivalent to 500,000 tons of TNT).

Fission weapons are of two types and the difference is solely based on engineering or design aspects. These are as follows:

(a) **Gun Type System.** This has already been explained earlier. Weapons where two fissile sub-critical hemispheres are joined or one is shot at another are called gun type systems. It was this mechanism which was used in the bomb which was dropped on Hiroshima. There are a few disadvantages of this system such as limitation in the yield, inefficiency and less economy. See Fig. 7.10.

7.10. Fission-Gun Type.

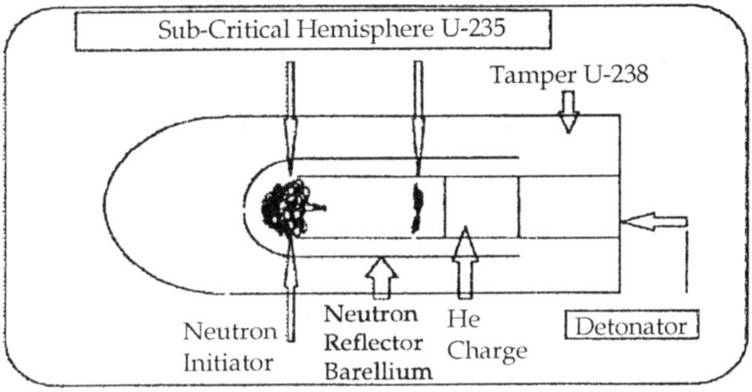

(b) **Implosion System.** The gun type system is inefficient. In order to nullify the disadvantages of the gun type system, a complex implosion type weapon was evolved in which a solid or hollow sphere of fissile material is compressed by means of a special HE Charge, called HE lenses, to about twice its normal density thus making it super critical (Present technologies allow compression to the ratio of 1:600). This allows very economical use of fissile material. Another advantage of this system is that plutonium 239 can be used as a fissile material which was not possible in the gun type system. As a matter of interest, the Pokhran peaceful nuclear explosion was an implosion device. See Fig. 7.11.

Fusion Type. (Thermonuclear) For a thermonuclear explosion, very high temperatures and pressures must be attained to achieve a fusion reaction. This is brought about by atomic trigger or by a fission reaction. It is possible to initiate fusion by combining lithium deutride compound with a small fission device (Fusion - lithium deutride compound + small fission device). See Fig. 7.12.

To Electric Exploder

However, unlike fission weapons, there is no limit, except the convenience of delivery, to the size of a fusion weapon, and the largest known to be tested had the yield of 65 MT. This type of weapon is regarded to be 'clean' because of small fission fragments and large fusion energy.

Fig. 7.11.

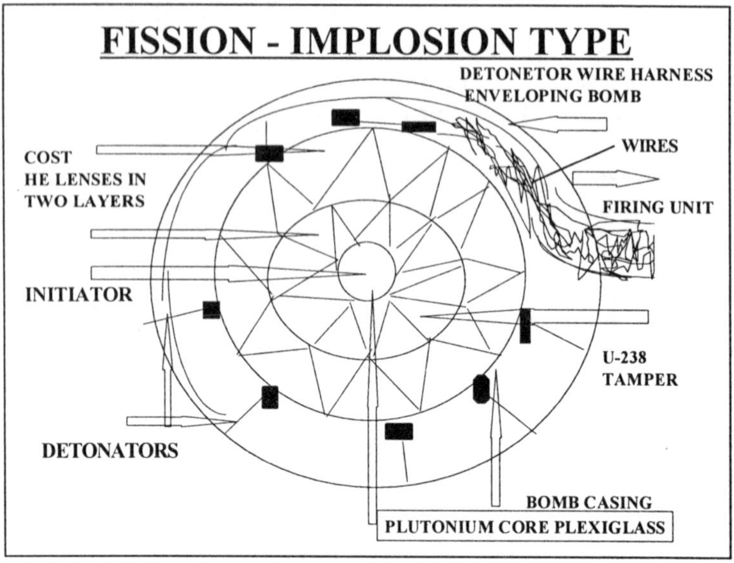

Fi g. 7.12.

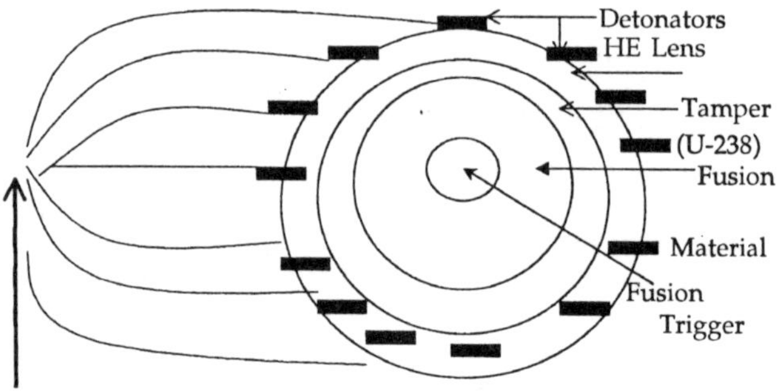

Fission-Fusion-Fission Weapon

This is a very common weapon in megaton range. It consists of the normal fusion weapon, which is surrounded by a layer of U 238. The very fast neutrons produced by fusion have sufficient energy to cause fission in U 238, which is otherwise stable. The large amount of fallout caused by the presence of uranium casing, lead to this weapon being described as 'dirty'. This type of weapon is generally used in high megaton range.

Fourth Generation Nuclear Systems (FGN)

Nuclear Technology is advancing and has already reached the status of breakthrough technologies. The effort is to miniaturise a nuclear device and localise its effects. The unfortunate part being, such superior technologies do not form part of disarmament negotiations. New simulation techniques do not require nuclear explosions being banned under CTBT. The ensuing FMCT debate does not talk of new techniques for allowing nuclear reaction. Fissile materials being considered under FMCT are plutonium and uranium, but not isotopes of hydrogen like tritium and deuterium, which allow thermo-nuclear action in a condensed form having a localised effect. As per nuclear research scientist, Andre Gsponer, located at Geneva, the future is bleak unless more scientifically advanced nations take the lead on disarmament. Laser Isotope Separation (LIS) technology is also revolutionising enrichment technology of a nuclear device radioactive elements. These are called fourth generation technologies.

Miniaturisation of nukes will revolutionise conventional warfare, as due to reduced kill areas, they will not be categorised as WMDs and so won't contradict any international law. They will fill the gap between conventional and nuclear weapons (In 1978 Andre Gsponer was one of the first physicist to alert that "CTBT is just an instrument legitimising possession and perfection of Nuclear Weapons by nuclear states").

Leaders in this technology are the P-5 nations, who are advocating CTBT. The other countries who are advanced in this technology are Germany and Japan.

Jean-Pierre Hurni who co-authored a technical report on FGN weapons rightly said—nobody can stop—Large Inertial Confinement Fusion (LICF) simulation facilities. And there is no stopping such programmes. Even Star Wars programmes have accelerated but under different names, like the 'Global Protection Against Limited Strikes' (GPALS) - is basically directed energy weapons. These are systems placed in space in ABM role. This obviously unbalances the balancing global deterrence concept. Further, imagine use of FGN Nukes in space to disable communication and other satellites of lesser capable nations.

Routes

The routes towards FGN explosion could be either through fission or fusion as explained below :

Fission. Yield generation is on sub-critical mode, which is not banned under CTBT. This mode is not suitable for high yield generation but is just adequate for 1 to 100 ton yields.

Fusion. Magnetic compression increases density of the fissile material and uses small anti-matter and lasers for ignition. The main charge could be deuterium and compressed Tritium.

Delivery Systems

There are many delivery systems evolved by various countries in the world. Each of them have their own advantages and disadvantages. These systems are based on a triad concept.

Deterrent Triad Concept

The deterrent triad concept calls for a triad of strategic delivery systems with different capabilities and operational characteristics to provide optimum survivability and offensive capability. Three delivery systems of this concept are explained in the succeeding paragraphs.

Manned Bomber. It is the oldest of the three elements, and despite some obsolescence still has a flexible payload and range, and can deliver with high accuracy and targeting flexibility right upto the last moment. It also has two unique assets in that it can be recalled at short notice and can return for use in another strike. On the debit side, it is vulnerable on the ground and in the air. It is also difficult to sustain manned bombers at high levels of generated alert for protracted periods.

ICBM. Second oldest of the triad elements, the Intercontinental Ballistic Missile is a land based weapon system, characterised by short flight times, ability to penetrate defences and to accurately deliver nuclear weapons of high explosive yield on to targets. Other credit features are the fact that it can retarget rapidly, can be quickly regenerated to full alert, and when protected in underground silos has high pre-launch survivability. However, with increasing capability of enemy ICBMs to destroy hard targets the survivability factor is decreasing.

SLBM. Most recent element is the 'Submarine Launched Ballistic Missile'. It is a sea based system offering its possessor the best combination of operational capability and survivability though at the expense of highly responsive command and control, and reduced accuracy of missiles. It has extremely low vulnerability to pre-emptive strikes, and is the strongest leg of the triad.

Missiles

Apart from the ICBM and SLBM being used as part of triad concept, a few more missiles, as part of delivery systems, are as follows:

- *Short Range Ballistic Missiles (SRBM)*. This has a range of only about 800 km.

- *Short Range Attack Missile* (*SRAM*). This is a stand off missile and is carried on manned bombers. This is being replaced by cruise missile.
- *Medium Range Ballistic Missile* (*MRBM*). This missile has a range between 800 to 2400 km. Examples are Pershing I or SS 20.
- *Intermediate Range Ballistic Missile* (*IRBM*). Has a range between 2400 to 6400 km, i.e., and intermediate between MRBM and ICBM.
- *Inter Continental Ballistic Missile* (*ICBM*). These are strategic missiles which can travel more than 8,400 kms. Their flight path is a parabola due to the gravitational pull on the trajectory.
- *Submarine Launched Ballistic Missile* (*SLBM*). These are fired from a submerged submarine, this is ejected through the water by gas pressure and its rocket ignites when it reaches the surface.
- *Air Launch Cruise Missile* (*ALCM*). This is a winged bomb, usually jet prepared, and is launched from a flying aircraft to give its jet engine a flying start. These are small; approximately 6 metres in length and after launch fly at a subsonic speed to the target. Because of smaller size, these are more difficult to detect and hence less vulnerable to anti- aircraft guns and missiles.
- *Ground Launched Cruise Missile (GLCM).* This is similar to an ALCM but is rocket boosted off a ground launcher so that it builds up sufficient speed for the jet motor to take over and sustain it in flight.
- *Submarine Launched Cruise Missile (SLCM).* This is another configuration of the cruise missile for underwater launch from submarine torpedo tubes.
- *Space Launched Missiles.* This is in the conceptual stage and would become tomorrow's strike weapons.

Pattern of Fallout and Protection

Factor Effects of a 20 KT Fission Bomb. Before we discuss fallout pattern of nuclear weapons, let us see the summed up normal effects of a 20 KT fission weapon when no other factors like terrain or weather are taken into account. The effect of radiation, burns or blast is proportional to the distance from the GZ and depends on the status of the target population or material, as per guidelines below:

Table 7.1

Effect	*Distance from GZ (m)*
• Radiation Deaths (Unprotected)	Upto 1200
• Radiation Deaths (Protected)	" 950

• Second Degree Burns (Naked skin)	"	3700
• Second Degree Burns (Uniformed)	"	2300
• Vegetation Fires (Dry vegetation)	"	4100
• Vegetation Fires (Green)	"	2200
• Trees Uprooted (Medium sized)	"	2650
• Concrete Bridges Damaged	"	530

Note: The distance for radiation deaths do not take into account either heat or blast effects.

Fallout Patterns

The battle for survival would hinge on fallout knowledge and predictions to guard the civil population from going to these areas. Idealised, Cigar shaped fallout patterns have been computed under the assumption of constant wind direction and velocity and stable weather conditions. This therefore gives life saving predictions to the civil defence organisations. The idealised patterns actually give poor guidance about the actual pattern of fallout distribution to be expected in a nuclear attack. Local wind fluctuations and precipitation will produce variations and hot spots.

Idealised Dose Contours - 20 KT Ground Burst

Danger Zone

For civil defence organisations, field commanders, it is imperative to know the danger zone of radioactive fallout after a ground burst so as to take prompt decisions and modify plans for movement of evacuation columns. The prediction of the danger zone will also enable to calculate the risk factor in so far as a particular township is concerned. The following data is necessary to calculate the danger zone: -

- GZ of the explosion.
- The yield of the weapon or the explosion.
- The direction and resultant wind speed.

Fig. 7.13 shows how to draw the predicted danger zone. From the ground zero, a circle is drawn whose radius depends upon the yield of the weapon. Then from the centre of the circle in the direction of wind, an arc of 40 degrees is drawn; 20 degrees on either side of the line showing wind direction. The length of zone II and I will depend upon both the yield (because higher the mushroom cloud, further the earth particles will travel) and the velocity of the wind.

Fig. 7.13.

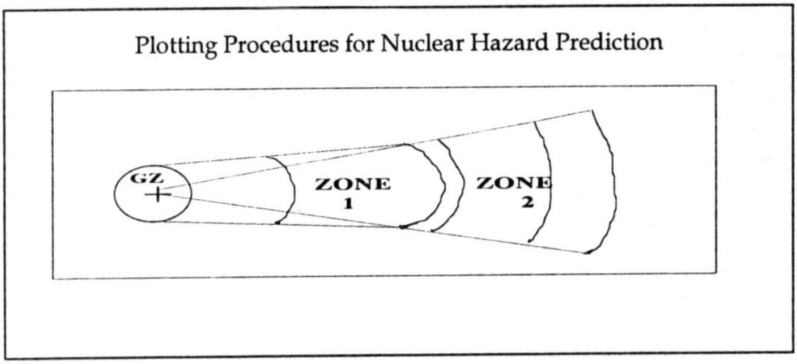

Prediction of Danger Zones

The required length of zones or the fallout around the GZ is pre-calculated depending upon the yield of the weapon and various wind speeds. Zone I is the area in which an unprotected person would receive a dose of 150 rads or more within a period consisting of the duration of the fallout and the following four hours. Consequently zone I is of immediate concern. Zone II is the secondary risk zone and the dose received by an unprotected person would be between 50 to 150 rads within a period of 24 hours. Outside zone I and zone II is the area where an unprotected person receives less than 50 rads within 24 hours. (Refer table below)

Table 7.2

Time of Stay	*Zone I Immediate Emergency*	*Risk*	*Zone II Secondary*	*Outside Zone I & II Risk negligible*
risk				
During fallout and following four hours	150 rads or more	less than 150 rads	-	
During the fallout And following 24 hours	-	50 rads or more	Less than 50 rads	

This procedure can be completed within five minutes of getting the required information from the Army units/strategic command and weather. As per the local civil defence scheme, relief operations can be planned and executed accordingly.

It must be kept in mind that this procedure is only followed for a surface or near surface burst and not for a pure air burst. This can roughly be made out from the stem of the mushroom cloud. In case of an airburst the stem would be white in colour, as no material would be sucked up in it, whereas for a surface or near surface burst the stem would be dark or black in colour.

The actual dose contours can only be drawn after carrying out reconnaissance of the area covered by nuclear fallout. Reconnaissance of the fallout area is carried out either by a vehicle fitted with special instruments or by helicopters, whichever is a faster means. Thus, there is a necessity of co-ordination with the Ministry of Transport and Civil Aviation for disaster management during such eventualities.

Mortality Rates

The biological effects of radiation (LD-50 Value) have been analysed in great details after the Hiroshima and Nagasaki strikes. The various models are as shown in Figs. 7.14 and 7.15.

Fig. 7.14.
Variation of the 50 per cent mortality distance with Age-solid curve : males, Dashed curve : females

Variation of the 50 per cent mortality distance with Age-solid curve: males, Dashed curve: females.

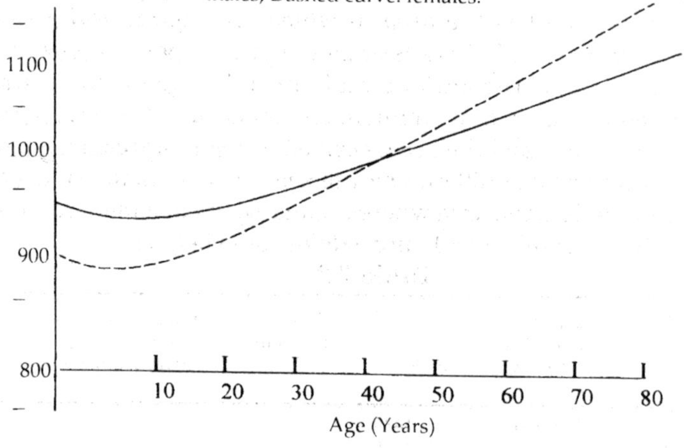

Mitigation of Nuclear Effects

Basic Consideration for Residual Radiation

The intensity of radiation can be reduced in one or both of the following ways:

Distance. Intensity of radiation decreases as the distance from the source of emission increases.

Shielding. Any material placed between the emitter and the target will reduce the intensity of radiation. The reduction depends upon the density and thickness of the material.

Protection Factor

Sand of Compacted Clay Provides Better Protection than Earth.

Fig. 7.15. Dashed curve : females

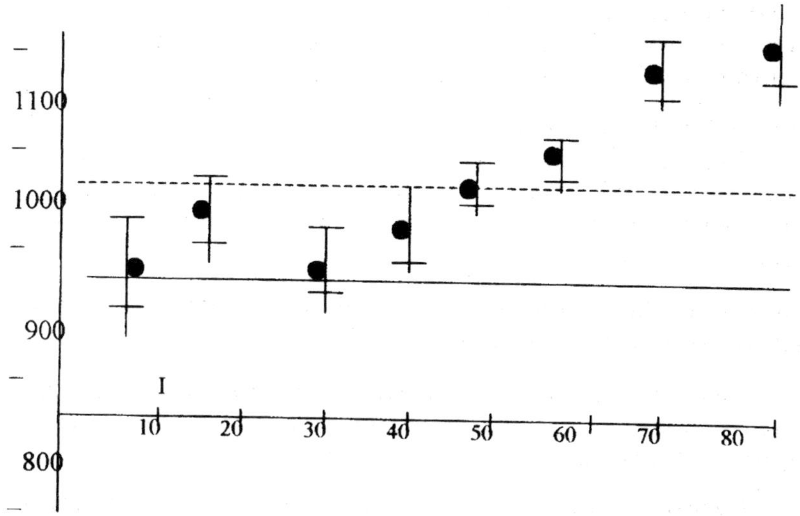

The quality of a shelter or a vehicle from residual radiation depends on its ability to reduce the outside intensities by both distance and shielding. The protection factor is a measure of this ability, which is:

$$\text{Protection Factor} = \frac{\text{Outside Dose Rate}}{\text{Inside Dose Rate}}$$

It is a ratio, a number without any label attached, the higher the number, the better the protection. For example, if the dose rate outside a shelter is 500 Rads/Hr and the dose rate inside is then the theoretical protection factors can be calculated in the absence of any radioactive matter.

The shielding values of earth cover for a hypothetical 1200 rads free-in-air dose is as under:

Table 7.3

Depth of Earth	*Protection Factor*	*Resultant Dose Rads*
Man in open	None	1200
Man in 4 foot deep open Fox hole	8	150
With 0.5 ft earth cover	12	100
With 1 ft earth cover	24	50
With 1.5 ft earth cover	48	25
With 2 ft	96	12.5

Note. The flat earth cover of an underground shelter provides much more protection than an equivalent thickness of cover on a similar above ground structure because the line of sight thickness is greater. Thus the requirement of underground collective shelters near population centres is a good option as a Passive Defensive Measure (PDM).

It is also interesting to note that sand of compacted clay provides better radiation shielding than earth because it is denser. Also, if earth or sand is damp it would have a better shielding against neutrons which are better absorbed by water.

Mitigation Techniques for Personnel

Taking into consideration all the effects of a nuclear weapon, certain nuclear weapon effect mitigation techniques have been evolved for personnel before, during and after a nuclear attack.

Recommended Protective Postures for Personnel before Attack, Individual Actions when Warned.

Protect your eyes - do not look at the fireball. Remember to cover eyes with your palms. Remove all types of eyeglasses to prevent subsequent injury from the blast wave.

Minimise exposed skin areas. Fatigues or thick clothing reduce thermal radiation on exposed skin by 50 per cent. Gloves protect hands. A scarf or hood can also cover effectively vulnerable areas of the head and the back of the neck.

Protect exposed skin areas. On warning, through the National Broadcast system, assume a position that protects your eyes and any exposed skin areas of the face arms or hands. Take position in trenches or shelters.

Keep clothes loosely fitted. Avoid direct contact of clothing with the skin such as around the shoulders, elbows waist and ankles. Thus avoid wearing tight pants/jeans and prefer to wear track suites or any loosely fitted clothes. Burns result from the conduction or heat from the hot fabric to the skin.

Wear headgear at all times. Caps can shield your face and eyes from thermal burns, protects your head from debris or impact with solid objects and provide limited radiation protection. Wear a scooter helmet if available.

Avoid black/dark colour clothing. Dark surface will absorb more thermal energy and may be burned more easily. Wear light colours.

Wear ear protection. Wear earplugs or headsets to protect your eardrums. Covering ears with cupped hands and opening your mouth after detecting the flash will also be adequate.

Do not wear the individual protection mask. It is black and made from rubber. Dark colours absorb thermal radiation, and rubber will melt or burn when heated.

Protection during a nuclear attack. An enemy nuclear attack will probably come without warning on a metropolitan city or on its suburbs. The first indication will be very intense light followed by extreme heat and hurricane like winds. The following individual responses must, therefore, be automatic and instinctive:

In the Open

- Immediately drop to the ground with the head towards the GZ. This action reduces blast injuries if a soldier is picked up by the blast wave.
- Protect eyes and exposed skin areas by covering the eyes and face with hands and by assuming a covered position in a shelter or a trench if possible.
- Protect ears by fingers or thumbs after covering the eyes with the palms to prevent eardrum rupture.
- Stay down after the initial shock wave. Wait for the winds to die down and the debris to stop falling before getting up.
- Count to five and you will stay alive. If blast wave does not arrive within five seconds of the flash you were far enough from the GZ and initial radiation exposure will not exceed 150 rads. Stay calm, check for injury, check for your friends and damage to property. Report on mobile phone or through any method about the damage to the city civil defence organisation headquarters.

In a Dugout Near Residential Area

- Get as low as you can and as fast as you can. Lie down on your back or curl up inside the dugout. Protect your eyes and ears as already mentioned.
- Remain in kneeling position in the trench until the winds have calmed and the debris has stopped falling.

In a Shelter or Building

- Dive for cover on seeing flash, drop to the floor and get under a desk or table.
- Dive out of the way of any windows or doors to avoid injury due to glass or wood splinters.

While Driving in Cars/Buses

- While sitting in the car always use a safety belt.

- Put your head down with hands on your eyes.
- Open the windows to avoid shattering of glass. However, once the blast effect is over, the windows are again closed to reduce effect of residual radiation.
- In buses, one can get under the seat.
- If possible, put air ventilation systems in the vehicle to ensure filtration of contaminated. Outside air (Incidentally it automatically provides filtration, also against normal pollution)

In Two Wheelers. On the detection of flash, dive from the vehicle to a face down, prone position. Dive in the direction of the flash to avoid the vehicle over turning on you due to blast.

What can be Done Immediately after a Nuclear Strike

Things to Remember

- Stay down under the cover until the debris stop falling. After 90 seconds, the greatest danger from heat, blast, initial radiation, and probably falling debris will be over.
- Stay calm, burns, injuries, dazzle and concern over radiation exposure may create panic.

Remember

- Blast winds will generally end in one to two minutes after the burst.
- Burns cuts and bruises are no different from conventional injuries.
- Dazzle is temporary and vision should return in a few seconds.
- If you have survived the blast, the chances of your being exposed to a lethal case of radiation are relatively small unless you are located in an early fallout area.
- Consider how best to secure and organise equipment, repair and reinforce positions, assist casualty and improve protection against possible fallout.
- Expect some initial dis-orientation as the blast wave may blow down and carry away many prominent and familiar terrain features such as trees and buildings.

Things to Do

- Beware of weakened structures and trees as they may fall down or collapse due to movement of heavy vehicles.
- Put out fires before they spread.
- Put right, overturned vehicles as soon as possible else coolant, battery fluid or lubrication oils may leak. Leakage of coolant

and oils will considerably increase the maintenance time to put the vehicle back to road for evacuation tasks.

- Stop and clean vehicles. Remove all sand or dust blown into the vehicle. Put ventilated filtration system, if provisions exist in the vehicle.
- Wear thick clothing to reduce effect of radiation.
- Look before you move. Inspect vehicles for damage and any debris that may have blown into the vehicle.
- Small debris is also a problem. Leaves and dust may be sucked into the intake of helicopters and the blower motor of collective protection equipment.
- Improve your cover, if possible, because this is still the best protection from the initial and delayed effects. Cover the openings of foxholes and shelters to prevent entry of fallout particles.

Action after the Fallout

- Keep monitoring radioactivity level.
- Keep calm.
- You can reduce the residual radioactivity by 30 per cent by clearing of fallout in an area of four metre radius around your shelter/trench and to 50 per cent by clearing out to 8 metres radius, with the help of shovels and buckets.
- Get inside the collective protection shelters, if available. The best civil defence measure would be to use collective shelters during the warning period and after the nuclear blast. This would thus require discussion of few design features for shelters and buildings. These shelters should also cater for biological and chemical threats.

NBC filter

NBC filters are designed to be fitted on collective shelter. Collective shelters are made to maintain an uncontaminated environment and allow smooth working without loss of efficiency for a sustained period. It becomes necessary to install 'NBC' filters as they are designed to protect the occupants of the shelter collectively from the effects of nuclear, biological and chemical weapons, making it unnecessary for them to wear NBC suits. For the safety reasons already referred to, two fitters are installed. Each comprises a filter assembly and ventilator assembly.

The filter assembly is housed in an airtight cabinet made of

2 mm-sheet steel with polychloroprene seals. Air Filtration takes place in three separate stages:

For the first, preliminary, filtration stage, a filter with galvanised-steel meshes is used. This element is not intended to provide NBC protection as such, its job being essentially to protect the main (aerosol) filter by trapping the coarse particles [diameter 10^{-6} m =um (micro meter)] and sparks. Its efficiency is about 70 per cent, as measured gravimetrically by the ASHARE method.

An aerosol filter is used for the second stage. This filter consists of sheets of folded paper (working area 4.5 m^2) made of sub-micron glass fibres. The filter is waterproofed, treated with fungicide and resistant to attack by bacteria. Its efficiency is stated to be 99.996% for 0.15 um particles. It should be borne in mind that bacteria measuring less than 0.3 um are not, as far as is known, dangerous to human beings. The filter is designed to trap fine dust and aerosols and its main applications are in the nuclear and biological fields.

Four vapour filters are employed for chemical protection. Each filter consists of a layer of activated carbon contained in sheet-steel box, the internal walls of which are coated with an elastic lining to prevent the contents from settling. It may seem surprising that the manufacturer has paid so much attention to this aspect of the problem, but many experts believe that, in a future conflict in central Europe, chemical weapons are more likely to be used than nuclear ones. Moreover, it has been widely reported that Soviet troops in Afghanistan have been using so called Yellow Rain, a mixture of mycotoxis, which persist, in the ground and is apparently fatal on inhalation or simply on contact with the skin.

The ventilation assembly comprises a high-pressure centrifugal fan driven by a 450 KW electric motor powered by a single-phase 220V/ 50Hz power supply and connected to the fan via a gearbox. If the fan to be driven manually by means of a detachable crank handle designed to be operated by two men, the unit must be earthed.

New Concepts

Nuclear Emergency Monitoring Cabin. This concept gives 'mobility' to the system as the monitoring cabin can be lifted by road, ship or helicopter for rapid deployment, into areas effected by radiation. Using lightweight but highly efficient layers one can maintain the weight efficiency ratio. The air filtration unit should be further detachable using light alloys as metal components. Latest carbon and metal technologies can be used to make the system light but robust.

Glass Fiber Reinforced Polyester. A honeycomb type of lightweight shelter is an effective design theoretically. The latest technologies of reinforced glass and allied elements in conjunction with some other alloys are worth conceiving and exploring. All such systems should be modular with add on facilities to ensure creation of structures as per size requirement. There is scope for research on the same by involving the large industrial houses, who have the capacity as technology to innovate. Thereafter, its utilisation by the military and civil defence authorities should be possible.

Inflatable rubberised (specially treated collective shelters which can shelter about 30 persons) should be developed. They should be utilised in a 'CB' contaminated environment. Therefore add one for airlock system and NBC filtration should be catered for.

Modification technology for giving protection against nuclear residual radiation and 'CB' weapons, in government buildings and residential housing be developed.

Therefore, there is a necessity of developing a whole 'collective protection systems' technology under one "Integrated Collective Protection Systems" (ICPS) analogy. The approach could be akin to the Integrated Guided Missile Project (IGMP) placed under the Ministry of Defence. The importance of a systems and serial manufacturing of such protective technology is mandatory in a future scenario. Developing nations in the world cannot forget the NATO bombings in Kosovo, Iraq and may be many others in the future. (Appendix F)

Table 7.4. Technical details of AMF80 Modules

Dimensions	*Model 1*	*Model 2*
Nominal diameter (m)	2.00	2.50
Internal diameter (m)	2.00	2.50
External diameter (m)	2.36	2.95
Wall thickness (m)	180	225
Useful length (m)	3.30	2.35
Weight per metre length (t)	3.22	4.93
Tolerances		
Internal diameter (mm)	# 10	# 10
Wall thickness (mm)	# 6.5	# 7.5
Materials		
Concrete	reinforced according to NFP. 16341	
Compressive strength (bar)	400	
Tensile strength (bar)	30	
Steel	drawn hot-rolled steel	
Tensile strength (kgf/mm^2)	55	
Elastic limit (kgf/mm^2)	50	
Elongation before rupture (%)	8	

Also available with a nominal diameter of 3.2 m.

In addition, a flow-rate meter fitted on each fan to check that the output does not fall below 60 m^3 a silencer is fitted to reduce the noise of the ventilator to a level acceptable for a period of about 48 hours (75 dBA, ice, the equivalent of a normal conversion).

Conclusions and Prospects

It must be noted that the shelter structure is designed to undergo deformation and yet remain airtight even in an event of powerful explosions nearby. It can only be damaged by a direct hit (the armoured doors are designed to withstand, without damage, the shock wave from a 1-kiloton nuclear warhead detonated at a distance of 150 m).

The shelter's modular design enables the user to build his shelter according to his specific needs. Being easy to assemble, dismantle and reassemble with a small team using conventional equipment, the AMF80 could even be moved to another site during the course of a battle. The fact that the cylindrical elements are available in several different diameters extends its range of applications still further, to air force ground hangers, for instance.

A high degree of chemical protection has been provided and the shelter's effectiveness against biological weapons exceeds 99.99 per cent. The shelter has been designed particularly to provide protection against enhanced-radiation weapons, and the thickness of concrete, combined with one metre of earth, is sufficient to attenuate fast neutron by a factor of 10 (increasing to 10 if the shelter is covered instead with 1.5 m of earth).

Chemical Threats : Save the Population Techniques (Chemistry of Chemical Astra)

> "To quell the Japanese resistance man by man and conquer the country yard by yard might well require the loss of a million American lives and half that number of British. Now all this nightmare picture has vanished. In its place is a vision-fair and bright it seems – of the end of the whole war in one or two violent shocks. Moreover, we should not need the Russians."
>
> — ***Capt BH Liddell Hart***

History of Chemical Warfare

The later half of nineteenth century saw the advent of Chemical Warfare (CW) agents as the Chemical industry developed during this period. The First World War saw the usage of CW agents by the French troops against the Germans in a major way at Some, in the battle of Frontiers of August 1914. In the period between the two world wars, there have been many allegations of the use of CW agents.

Surprisingly, no army during Second World War used chemical weapons; though they were equipped and trained for its use. In fact, Germany produced the nerve agents, a class of highly toxic chemical warfare agents in 1936, even before the Allies. It was in 1938 that the Germans decided to build a facility for the production of nerve agents. The first lot of Tabun was manufactured in 1943 and small quantities of Sarin in 1944. A third and still more effective nerve agent named Soman was at the laboratory stage at the end of the World War II. It was inexplicable as to why the Germans did not resort to the use of chemical weapons during World War II. Probably, the main reason was the fear of reprisals as they were convinced that the Allied troops also had supplies of nerve agent munitions.

A group of still more toxic nerve agents, the V agents, were developed in the U.K. in the 1950s. Also, it was during this period that the interest in non-lethal incapacitating chemical warfare agents developed.

The problems associated with the storage and destruction of out-dated chemical weapons led to the development of binary weapon system. A binary system contains two relativity harmless compounds placed separately in a warhead. The compounds automatically mix once the binary weapon is released by the delivery system, resulting in the formation of highly toxic chemical warfare agent with subsequent dispersion. The USA developed binary weapons for the two nerve agents, sarin and VX.

The post Second World War has seen proliferation of Weapons of Mass Destruction (WMD). In the 1960s, numerous reports appeared that chemicals were used in several armed conflicts. Mustard gas was said to have been used during the Yeman War (1963-1967). While herbicides and teargases were employed on a large scale in Vietnam War (1961-1970). In 1970, the USA accused communist troops of the use of Trichothecenes (Yellow Rain) in Laos, Kampuchea and Afghanistan. During 1980 –1988, the Iran-Iraq conflict has seen the use of chemical weapons. Furthermore, Iraq attacked the Kurdish rebels in their own country with CW agents. During the Gulf War (1991), Iraq explicitly threatened the Allied troops with the use of chemical weapons. Chemical weapons have become available to an increasing number of countries during the last few decades as a result of wider chemical industrial base or by choice. There have been more than 36 allegations of the use of CB weapons in various incidents since World War II, as enumerated below:

Table 7.5. Allegations – Use of CBW

Year	*Countries of Alligations*	*CW Agents Used*
1974 – 81	Laos by Laos and Viet Forces	Mustard, Irritants, Nerve and Mycotoxins
1978 – 81	Kampuchea by Viet Forces	-do-
1978 – 81	US Covertly in Cuba	Sugar Cane Rust, Swine Fever, Dengue Gases and Poisoning Water
Feb 79	Sino – Viet War (Both)	-do-
1979 – 81	Afghanistan (Soviets) Also Mujahideen	Nerve Type of Agents
Nov 80	(By Iraq)	-do-
Iran In 13 Countries		-do-
1982	Kampuchea, Laos and Iran	-do-
1985	In 6 Countries	-do-
1986	In 9 Countries	-do-.
1987	Vietnam, Iran, Iraq, Libya (Chad)	-do-
1988	Iran, Iraq, Angola, Ethopia	-do-
1989	In 5 Countries	-do-
1990/91	Gulf War	Iraq (Gulf War Syndrome Developed)
1992	Yugoslavia, Mozambique, Armenia	-do-
Mar 95	By Aum Shinrikyo Cult in Japan	Sarin

Allegations – Production of CBW

Countries	*Year of Production*
China	Has a Vast Chemical Industrial Base and enough Intelligence Report Point Towards CB Programmes. (China Has Not Declared Chemical Weapons Under the Provisions of CWC.)
India	Declared Its Weapons Under Provisions of CWC.
Iraq	More than 1000 Tonnes–American Led Allied Forces Have Tried to Destory Production Facilities In 1990-91 and 1998-99.
Iran	1000 T/Yr (Jdw – 14 Aug 96).
Libya	Constructed Underground CW Production Facility at Tarhunah Near Tripoli. (International Herald Tribune – 08 April 96).

Pakistan	Production Facility at Desto (Pakistan Has Also Not Declared any Chemical Weapons Under the Provision of CWC.
S. Africa	Possibly Continuing with a Secret CBC PGME started in 1980.
Sudan	Tomohaule Attach on Chemical Industry by America in 1999.
N. Korea	Can Produce 4500 T/Yr (Jane's Int Review August 96).
Russia	Western Media Allegations of a Very Advanced CBW Programme.
Syria	Constructing CW Production Facility at Aleppo.
USA	Declared its Facilities Under the Provisions of CWC.
Possibly	Egypt, Iran, Iraq, Libya and Syria Maintained BW PGMES (– 1 August 96).

(*Source:* Extracts taken from *Jane's Defence Weekly* and own assessment).

Iraq Crisis. The genesis of USA's antagonism against Iraq is basically rooted against allegations of preparing Chemical Weapons of mass destruction (WMD). Inspectors, belonging to the Organisation for Prevention of Chemical Weapons (OPCW) on ground verification have reported the same. Due to the non-compliance by Iraq, by not giving full access to these inspectors to all sites, the Americans have in return responded with missile and air bombardments. In reality, America wants to eliminate any future threat by Iraq on the American continent.

Threat to Nations in South Asia. Terrorism in India and other South Asian states will stay in times to come. There are more than 50 terrorist groups operating in this region. The backing of Pakistan's ISI is well known. They are likely to get in more funding and thus more sophisticated weapon systems. Chemical bombs or detonator systems can be very effective. The case of Tokyo's Sarin attack in the subway is an indication of India's vulnerability to such techniques.

Fundamental Characteristics of Materials. An effort has been made to put the scientific data in a 'non-science' manner to allow simplistic understanding of the fundamentals.The physical properties of substances are those which change the characteristics temporarily, i.e., the changes are reversible and the substances return to their original state once the factors inducing the changes are removed. Colour, texture, state of aggregation, solution, volatility and vapour pressure are some of the important physical properties. On the other hand, the changes brought about in substances on a permanent basis where they cannot be reversed and the composition of substances entirely changes are termed as chemical changes, characterised as chemical properties. All substances possess characteristic physical and chemical properties through which they can be detected and identified. Some of the important physical properties which one comes across often are mentioned below.

Table 7.6. Physical Properties

1.	Physical State	A chemical substance may be a gas, liquid or solid.
2.	Boiling Point	The temperature at which, under a given condition of pressure, a pure liquid and its vapour are in equilibrium. In practice, boiling points are referred to standard atmospheric pressure (760 mm of Hg) and those determined at any other pressure are qualified by a mention of the pressure at which they are recorded.
3.	Melting Point	The temperature at which the solid and liquid state of a substance coexists in equilibrium. Melting point is usually referred at normal pressure, 760 mm of Hg.
4.	Density	The mass of substance per unit volume. A mass of one-gram occupying a volume of one cubic centimeter has a unit density, $\rho = \frac{\text{Mass}}{\text{Volume}}$
5.	Vapour Pressure	The pressure at which a liquid and its vapour are at equilibrium at a given temperature. Vapour pressure is expressed in mm of Hg at specified temperature.
6.	Volatility	The weight of vapour present in a unit volume of air at a specific temperature under equilibrium condition between the vapour and it's liquid or solid. The unit of volatility is mg of vapour per cubic meter (mg/ M^3) at specified temperature.

Types of Chemical Reactions

The classical theories regarding compound formation by Dalton, Avogadro and Gay Lussac are generally empirical and do not meet the requirements of explanation for the formation of several types of compounds. The basic concept of valence as the combining capacity of an element holds good still, but certain anomalies develop for complicated compounds. In order to explain the compound formation, one has to resort to the structure of the atoms, electronic configuration and valence shells, etc. But it is sufficient to say that a compound is formed due to rearrangement of molecule electrons in valence shells of the combining atoms. Depending upon the type of rearrangement of electrons, various types of chemical reactions occur. Some of the important chemical reactions are discussed below:

Chemical Combination. When two or more elements chemically react (combine) under given experimental conditions, the reaction is known as chemical combination. For example, simple combinations like those between carbon and oxygen. It's irreversible till date.

$$\underset{\text{Carbon}}{C} + \underset{\text{Oxygen}}{O_2} \longrightarrow \underset{\text{Carbon dioxide}}{CO_2}$$

Chemical Decomposition. When a compound reacts to give rise to several products under given experimental conditions, the reaction is known as Chemical Decomposition. For example, lime stone on heating gives calcium oxide and carbon dioxide.

$$\underset{\text{Calcium carbonate}}{CaCO_3} \longrightarrow \underset{\text{Calcium oxide}}{CaO} + \underset{\text{Carbon dioxide}}{CO_2}$$

Electrolysis. The decomposition of a compound to its products by the use of electricity and the collection of the products at the two electrodes (anode and cathode) is known as electrolysis. For example, electrolysis of water gives hydrogen (–) and oxygen (+) as gases.

$$\underset{\text{Water}}{2H_2O} \longrightarrow \underset{\text{Hydrogen}}{2H_2} + \underset{\text{Oxygen}}{O_2}$$

Electrolysis can also be utilised in the production of organic compounds as in Kolbe's reaction.

Addition Reactions. Reactions in which generally two reactants combine to yield a single product and one of the reactants is an unsaturated compound is known as addition reactions. Double and triple bonded organic (having double bonds or triple) compounds exhibit additions as their characteristic reactions.

$$\underset{\text{Ethylene}}{CH_2{=}CH_2} + \underset{\text{Hydrogen}}{H_2} \longrightarrow \underset{\text{Ethane}}{CH_3{-}CH_3}$$

(saturated compound single bond)

Substitution Reactions. These reactions generally occur with saturated organic compounds in which the carbon atoms have satisfied valences and generally hydrogen is substituted by other elements or groups, i.e., single bonded organic compounds undergo these reactions. For example,

$$\underset{\text{Methane}}{CH_4} + \underset{\text{Clorine}}{Cl_2} \longrightarrow \underset{\text{Methylchloride}}{CH_3Cl} + \underset{\text{Hydrochloric acid}}{HCl}$$

Hydrolysis. A reaction involving the use of water as a reactant to bring about decomposition in the presence of acids or bases is known as hydrolysis. Here a large excess of water is generally used (unlike other reactions where stoichiometric quantities are employed). For example, hydrolysis of sarin, a nerve agent gives methyl phosphonic acid.

$$\underset{\text{Sarin}}{CH_3P(O)OCH(CH_3)_2F} + H_2O \longrightarrow \underset{\text{Methyl phosphonic acid}}{CH_3P(O)(OH)_2}$$

Oxidation and Reduction Reactions. In simple terms, oxidation reactions involve addition of oxygen to a molecule. Its use has however, been considerably widened to cover many processes similar to oxidation such as chlorination and other processes of combination with strongly non-metallic elements which add electrons readily. In fact, the term oxidation in its broadest sense means-simply a chemical reaction whereby one or more electrons are removed from one or more of the atoms of a substance. It is, of course, most frequently accompanied by a simultaneous process, whereby another substance gains the electrons and thus undergoes reduction. For example, sulphur mustard is readily oxidised with bleaching powder (generating chlorine) to its sulphoxide derivative.

$$\underset{\text{Sulphur Mustard}}{S(CH_2{-}CH_2{-}Cl)_2} + \underset{\text{Bleaching Powder}}{Ca(OCl)Cl} \longrightarrow \underset{\text{Mustard Sulphoxide}}{O{=}S(CH_2{-}CH_2{-}Cl)}$$

Finally, the knowledge on physical and chemical properties of materials will be helpful for not only a better understanding of various materials but also to appreciate the safety measures to be taken during their handling.

Human Physiology and Biochemistry

The science that deals with the normal functioning of the body is known as physiology, which is a tripod science of physics, chemistry and anatomy. Biochemistry is that branch of science which explains the functions of the body on a chemical basis akin to a chemical laboratory reaction. Biophysics is the study of ions moving across biological membranes. Physiology involves analyses of dynamic interrelationships that exist among cells, organs and tissues. The cell is the smallest functional unit and it is itself composed of organelles. Cell membrane that surrounds the cell is a remarkable structure and is semipermeable allowing few substances to pass through but restricting others. A nucleus is present in eukaryotic cells. The nucleus is made up (in large part) of chromosomes, the structure that carries a complete blueprint for all the heritable and individual characteristics of a species. The ultimate units of heredity are the genes on the chromosomes, and each gene is a portion of the DNA molecule. Mitochondria are relatively solid bodies, granular, rod-shaped, which remain scattered throughout the cytoplasm. They contain RNA, DNA and certain enzymes. The enzymes present in the mitochondria help in oxidative phosphorylation and are the site for formation of adenosine triphosphate (ATP) which is the high energy producing molecule in the cell. Apart from these, other organelles and structures like Golgi apparatus, Endoplasmic Reticulum, lysosomes, peroxisomes, microfilaments and microtubules are also present in the cell, each one of which has a definite function.

Physiological Systems

Different types of cells organise into tissues which in turn form different organs of the body. In order to understand the functions of different tissues/organs, it is convenient to divide them broadly into the following systems :-

Haemopoetic System. It consists of blood in which there are cellular elements dispersed in a fluid called plasma. The main functions of blood are transport of respiratory gases, hormones, nutritive materials and drainage of waste products.

Reticulo-Endothelial and Lymphatic System. Reticulo-endothelial system (eating with the help of skin) consists of reticulum cells, endothelial cells and wandering cells. The main functions of these cells are phagocytosis, formation of anti-body and formation of and destruction of RBC. The lymphatic vessels are thin walled channels containing valves so that the lymph can flow in one direction only and constitute the lymphatic system. (unidirectional).

Circulatory System. This system consists of heart and blood vessels (artieries, veins and capillaries). The pure blood from the lungs is carried through pulmonary veins to the left atrium and through atrioventricular opening to the left ventricle, from where arises a big artery known as aorta. The left ventricle contracts and the pure blood is pumped out of the aorta. The aorta and its arterial branches which break up into capillaries carry the pure blood to the entire body. The impure blood from different regions of the body is carried by the veins provided with valves into the right atrium, which sends the blood to the right ventricle and the cycle is completed. In an adult the heart beats at a rate of 72 beats per minute.

Respiratory System. Respiration is gaseous interchange between an organism and its environment, comprising all the processes by which the cells are supplied with oxygen and relieved of carbon dioxide formed during oxidation of metabolites.

Digestive System and Metabolism. This system deals with digestion, absorption and utilization of food taken by the mouth. The process of digestion is carried on with the help out enzymes present in the gastrointestinal tract. The end products of digestion are mostly absorbed from the intestine and help in growth and repair of tissues and in the liberation of heat and energy.

Nervous System. The nervous system is the most important organisation controlling and integrating the different bodily functions. The activities of the nervous system are dependent upon a complex interplay of numerous dynamic interactions and regulatory reactions. The nervous system operates through two main systems namely, the central or somatic nervous system and the autonomic nervous system composed of sympathetic and parasympathetic nerves.

Central Nervous System. The central nervous system (CNS) consists of cerebrum, cerebellum brain stem and spinal cord. The ability to think logically, to learn from past experiences and to communicate appropriately are the unique qualities of man which can be attributed to the development of highly-specialised central nervous system. Drugs and chemicals may either stimulate or depress the CNS. The drugs and chemicals can affect the nervous system in the following ways :

- They may act directly on neurous and modify the neuronal functions.
- They may act reflexly by sending afferent impulses to the CNS via the chemoreceptor, baro-receptors or peripheral nerves and thereby eliciting psychic, somatic or visceral responses.
- They may affect the nutrition and oxygen supply of the CNS by altering its blood supply or affecting its metabolism.

Autonomic Nervous System (ANS). The autonomic nervous system is also called visceral, vegetative or involuntary nervous system. Both the CNS and autonomic nervous system (ANS) can be considered as analogous to an elaborate system of telegraphy wherein numerous wire connections in the form of neurons bring information from both internal and external environments. The information received, decoded, decisions are made by various centres in the CNS and specific instructions are sent out to various peripheral tissues to produce appropriate responses. The reaction pattern could be psychic as are manifested in a change in emotions, thought and attitude. It could be somatic as demonstrated by various types of body movements or autonomic, as indicated by changes in respiration, circulation and visceral functions.

Nerve Transmission. The flow of information within and between neurones is conveyed by electrical and chemical signals. Transient electrical signals are particularly important for transferring information rapidly and over long distances. These electrical signals such as receptor potentials, synaptic potentials and action potentials are all produced by temporary changes of the current flow into and out of the cell that drives the electrical potential across the cell membranes away from its resting value. Ion channels embedded in the cell membrane control current flow into and out of the cell. There are two types of ion channels in membrane called gated and non-gated channels. Non-gated channels are always open and are not influenced significantly by extrinsic factors. They are primarily important in maintaining the resting membrane potential and the electrical potential across the membrane in the absence of signalling activity. Gated channels, in contrast, can open and close. Most gated channels are closed when the membrane is at rest and their probability of opening is greatly enhanced by the change in membrane potential, ligament binding, or stretch of the membrane.

Toxicology

Toxicology is the study of adverse effects of chemicals on living organisms and toxicologists are those who identify toxic chemicals and establish safe levels of exposure. It is very essential for a toxicologist not to scare the gullible world by reporting that every chemical is toxic. He should establish threshold levels for these chemicals for safety purpose.

Areas of Toxicology

Descriptive toxicology deals with testing of toxicity of chemicals for safety evaluation. The descriptive toxicologist conducts a battery of tests on experimental animals and extrapolates the data to humans and the environment for the evaluation of the risks posed by the chemicals.

Mechanistic toxicology deals with the mechanism of adverse effects caused by the chemicals. These studies are very essential for identifying less toxic alternative chemicals and for the development of antidotes.

Regulatory toxicology deals with the safety and risk evaluation of all chemicals for safe human usage.

Routes of Entry of Toxic Chemicals. There are three major routes of entry of toxic chemicals: oral, dermal and respiratory. A chemical or a drug may induce adverse toxic effects through the oral route by accidental overdose or in a suicidal attempt. The drug or the chemical can be absorbed into the system through the gastrointestinal tract. Absorption through the dermal route is very common in case of pesticides, paints, cosmetics, etc. The respiratory route or inhalation is one of the major routes of entry for environmental pollutants and other agents that are air borne. For experimental purpose or for the administration of drugs, parental routes are used like subcutaneous, intramuscular, intradermal, intravenous, intraperitoneal. Generally, toxic chemicals induce greatest effect by the intravenous route. A descending order of effectiveness for the other routes are inhalation, intraperitoneal, subcutaneous, intramuscular, oral and dermal.

Hazard Evaluation. The main purpose of elaborate toxicity tests carried out on animals is to provide a database that can be used to assess the risk or for the evaluation of hazard in humans. Acute toxicity tests like the calculation of LD50 or LC50 may be very difficult to extrapolate to humans, but it gives an empirical idea of how toxic the chemical would be.

From the sub chronic and chronic toxicity studies on laboratory animals, one obtains the lowest-observed-effect-level (LOEL), also referred to as the lowest-observed-adverse-effect-level (LOAEL). No-observed-effect-level (NOEL) for the species is also obtained from the sub chronic and chronic toxicity studies, which is the highest dosage administered that does not produce any toxic effect. Due to inter-species differences and inter-individual differences, the animal NOEL is reduced 100 times less for human safety norms. In practice, it is better to find a 'safety margin' by dividing the animal NOEL by the daily consumption of a particular chemical.

Occupational Toxicology. The main objective is to fix a safety or permissible level of exposure to industrial chemicals for the workers and also for the general population in the vicinity of the industry. Threshold Limit Value (TLV) is a commonly used marker, which is that concentration of the airborne chemical for which the worker may be exposed day after day without any adverse effect. Another value used is time weighted average (TWA), a value for a normal 8 hour work day (56 hour work week), and short term exposure limit (STEL), a value for short period of time, usually 15 minutes.

From the foregoing discussion it can be concluded that understanding the toxic potentials of all the chemicals commonly used is very important for fixing safety levels and also for finding antidotes in case of accidental exposure.

Classification of CW Agents

The chemical warfare agents possess different characteristics and belong to various classes of compounds with pronounced physicochemical, physiological and chemical properties. They can be classified in the following manner.

Tactical Classification. This classification is based on persistency of the CW agent after dissemination as also its volatility. Three different classes of CW agents on this basis are:

Physiological Classification. This is based on physiological effects produced by the CW agents. Their action is due to ingestion through skin, mucous membranes or blood. This class consists of the following agents:

Blood poisons such as Hydrogen cyanide, cyanogen chloride.
Lung injurants such as Chlorine, phosgene.
Vesicants such as Mustards and Lewisite.
Irritants such as CS, CR, CN, Adamsite.
Nerve agents such as G and V agents.
Defoliants such as Calcium cyanamide, Aminotriazol (ATA).
Psychochemicals such as LSD, BZ.
Lethal toxins such as Trichothecenes, Ricin.

Chemical Classification. Based on structurally related behaviour of CW agents such as:
Organophosphorus compounds.
Organosulphur compounds.
Organofluorine compounds.
Arsenicals.

Characteristics of CW Agents. The physical and chemical properties play an important role in the employment of CW agents as also their physiological activity on the targets. A chemical substance must meet certain exacting requirements before it can qualify as a potential CW agent. These requirements may be logically considered in two groups (a) technical and (b) tactical. The technical requirements are those concerned with the problems of bulk production and utilisation in the various forms of chemical munitions; the tactical requirements are those based on the effects produced in the battlefield.

Technical Requirements. Since the technical requirements for chemical agents are common to all the classes, i.e., gases, smokes and incendiaries, these requirements will be considered without distinction as to the class of the agents.

Raw Materials. The raw materials for a chemical agent should be available from domestic sources. Foreign sources of supply may be cut off in war if control of the sea or intervening land areas is lost; domestic resources have to be exploited under those conditions.

Ease of Manufacture. No matter how effective a compound may be in the battlefield, if it is difficult to make, there is always a serious threat of failure of supply by import under war conditions. Simplicity in manufacture enables production in a single plant, thus avoiding unnecessary transfer of intermediates from one plant to another with the attendant confusion and difficulty of co-ordinating production.

Chemical Stability. An important general requirement for a substance to be used as a CW agent is the chemical stability under all conditions of shortage. Effective lacrimators like bromine compounds, otherwise suitable for chemical warfare, react with iron and steel containers and it necessitates special linings of lead or porcelain. The production of satisfactory linings may prove to be a formidable task and can detract from the value of the compound for war purposes.

Hydrolysis. If a compound hydrolysis easily, it not only greatly reduces its effectiveness in the field but also seriously complicates its storage and loading into munitions. Since water vapour is always present in the atmosphere, hydrolysable compounds must be completely protected from contact with air in storage and also special precautions must be taken in loading such chemicals into shells and projectiles.

Polymerisation. When a chemical compound polymerises, it usually changes into a substance, which has radically different physical and physiological properties. Thus, a chemical compound may be a very active lacrimator in one form, while its polymer will have no lacrimatory power at all, so that if polymerisation occurs after filling into munitions, such a compound will be useless in the field. For example Papite or acrolein is a rather powerful lacrimator in its primary form, in storage, however, it polymerises into a non-lacrimatory powder. Hence this substance was subsequently abandoned as a chemical agent.

Tactical Requirements. These are the characteristics that the agents must possess in order to meet the vast requirements of modern warfare/terrorism.

Multiple Effects. Many gases have more than one mode of action as for example chlorpicrin is a lacrimator and a lung injuring as that injures the lung and hence eyes and lungs need protection. Mustard has triple effects, being a vesicant, lung injurer and lacrimator combined, and is the most difficult to protect against and hence most useful tactical agent. In general, the more extensive the mode of action of a gas, i.e., the greater the number of physiological effects it produces, the more valuable it is from tactical point.

Toxicity. For the lethal and casualty producing gases, toxicity is the most important requisite. The more toxic the gas is, the more effective and efficient it is as a chemical agent. That is to say that same casualty results can be produced with less quantity of the agent and with shorter period of exposure, in proportion to the toxicity. This follows from Haber's generalisation that the toxic effect is proportional to toxicity time's exposure period, except that this is not an essential requirement of lachrymators.

Duration Effects. If the aim of a battle is to defeat the enemy by inflicting on him, not fatalities, but non-fatal casualties of long duration, then those agents producing lasting effects are the most efficient. Mustard is the most efficient chemical agent, which produces slow-healing wounds but is fatal in a small number of casualties only.

Speed of Action. Rapid action is one of the most important characteristic of an efficient agent. It refers to the speed with which the agent after dissemination, produces effects on the body.

Insidiousness. If a gas is insidious on action as it does not produce any warning of discomfort during the necessary period of exposure, it will exert its full casualty effect before counter-measures are taken. The more insidious the action of a gas, the greater is its surprise effect as well as tactical value.

Volatility. It expresses maximum concentration of a gas, which can exist in open air at any given temperature.

Penetrability. Other things being equal, the greater the power of a gas to penetrate the enemy's masks, protective clothing, and other means of chemical defence, the greater will be the offensive power and tactical value of the gas.

Invisibility. The gas can be most effective when used as a surprise. It is more difficult to detect a gas by senses.

Colourlessness. Next to visibility, gas concentrations are most commonly detected in the field, especially in the night, by the characteristic odour of the agent. When the odour is undetectable, the surprise is deadly.

Toxins

Toxins are poisons originally produced by living organisms. They are either low molecular weight substances (monomeric) or high molecular weight (multimeric) proteins. They have been grouped under chemical warfare agents irrespective of whether they are produced by living organisms or by chemical synthesis (artificial toxins). The latter differ from their natural counterparts in the mechanism of their entry and/or action. The 1975 Convention on Biological Weapons prohibits the development, production and stockpiling of biological agents and toxins. Two toxins namely, saxitoxin and ricin (CAS registry No. 35523-89-8 and 9009-86-3 respectively) have been included in Scheduled chemicals in the CWC.

Classification of Toxins. No standard classification has been validated for toxins, but they can generally be classified according to their producing organisms. A representative classification for some selected toxins is outlined.

Table 7.7

Group	*Producing Organisms*	*Toxins Produced*
Bacteria	Clostridium botulinum	Botulin A, B, C, D, E
	Clostridium tetani	Tetanus Toxin
Vibrio cholera		Cholera toxin
Anabaena flos-aquae		Anabaena toxin
Protozoa	Gonyaulax catenella	Saxitoxin (shell
(Dinoflagellida)	Gymnodinium brevi	fish toxin)
		Redtide toxin (Gbtx)
Fungi (mycotoxin)	Aspergillus flavus	Aflatoxin
	Aspergillus parasiticus	B1, B2, G1, G2
	Fusarium episphaera	Tricothecene
	Fusarium lateritum	Nivalenol
	Fusarium oxysporum	T-2 toxin
	Fusarium roseum	T-2 toxin
		Nivalenol,
		T-2 toxin
Plants	Ricinus (castor bean)	Ricin
	Abrus precatorius	Abrin
Coelenterata	Soft corals (palythoa)	Palytoxin
Mollusca	Saxitomus giganteus	Saxitoxin
Amphibia	Californian newt	Tarichatoxin
	(Taricha torosa)	Batrochotoxin
Columbian frog		
(Phyllobates aurotaenja)		
Reptilia	Chinese cobra	Cobrotoxin
	(Naja naja atra)	Crotoxin
	Rattle snake	
	(crotallus durixuss terrificus)	

First Aid Against Chemical Attacks

The best protection against a chemical attack is to wear the equipment consisting of the following :-

- Mask with air filter.
- Overall Protective Equipment (breathe through material through which chemical gases cannot pass).
- Gloves.
- Boots.

These equipments be centrally stocked and earmarked in warehouses in major/metropolitan cities. However, in a situation, where no equipment is made available, then following survival steps can be taken:

- Put wet towel on face and hankey on nostril to work as filter.

- Paste naked body with wet mut.
- Use polythene bags to cover clothes and body.
- Use atta/flour for decontamination.

Other than this, certain steps and medicines are required as a first aid, as spelt out below:

Injection Atropine Sulphate (2mg/ml) in 30ml VIAL.
For use against nerve agents.
Give 2mgm iv/im every 15 min till full atropinisation occurs.
Qty: 20 vials per kit.

Atropine Sulphate : Oily Eye Drops : 1% Sterile
For instillation in eyes in case of exposure to nerve agents and vesicants like Sulfur Mustard and Lewisite.
Qty : 20

Beclomethasone Inhaler (50 ugm/dose) 200 metered doses.
For use on exposure to irritants and vesicants.
To clean, remove the canister, rinse in antiseptic lotion, dry and reassemble.
Qty: One inhaler per kit.

Chlorinated Lime
For decontamination of clothing and surroundings.
Qty: Two tins hermetically sealed, total 500 gms.

Tab Codein Phosphate (10 mgm)
For relief of cough (unproductive) and pain. Dose 3 tabs × 8 hrly.
Qty: 300 tabs per kit.

Tab Diazepam (10 mgm tab)
For use on exposure to nerve agents.
Qty: 200 tablets per kit.

Inj Pralidoxime Methyl Sulphate (Pam): Contains 500 mgm/ml.
Give 500 mgm i.v. Repeat after 15 min if necessary for nerve agents.
Qty: 30 mk vials, 16 vials per kit.

Inj Prednisolone Acetate: (25 Kgm/Ml). Inj Methyl Prednisolone.

Give 25 mgm i.v./i.m. can be repeated every 6 hrs.
In case of exposure to sulphur mustard, phosgene and other irritants capable of causing ARDS.

Tab Pam (Methiodide): 1 gm fast release tab and 500 mgm slow release tablets.
Give 1 fast and 3 slow release tablets at a time.
Qty: Tube pack of 60 tubes each. Each tube containing 1 fast and 3 slow release tablets.

Inj. Sodium Nitrite: 3 mk or 3% sol.
For cyanide poisoning.
Qty: 36 amps.

Inj Sodium Thiosulphate: 50% of 50 ml in case of poisoning with cyanide and prophylactically against sulphur mustard.
Qty: 50 ml ampoules, 6 ampoules per kit.

Chloromycetin-steroid Eye Oint
Appy locally in case of exposure to Lewisite.
Qty: One Tube per kit.

Pad Gauze Surgical : Sterile (With Cotton Film Insert) 110 × 10 cms.
Qty: 42 packages per kit.

Pad Gauze Surgical: Individual: Disposable: Saturated With 70% Isopropyl Alcohol.
Qty: One pack per kit.

Needle Hypodermic Sterile Disposable 38.1 Mm, 18 Swg.
Qty: 100 needle per kit.

Scissors Bandage Universal 177.8 Mm.
Qty: One per kit.

Syringe Sypodermic 50 Ml (All Glass)
Qty: One per kit.

Tray Instrument Polypropylene
Qty: One per kit.

Fullers' Earth Buffer Bottles: For decontamination.
Read instructions for use on bottle itself.
Qty: 5 per kit.

Detection Paper For Chemicals: For detection of sulphur mustard, C and B type nerve agents.
Qty: 5 paper per kit.

Water Testing Kit NBC
Detailed instructions given separately.
Qty: One per kit.

Inj Bal (Dimercaprol) – 3 ml amps
For arsenal and heavy metal poisoning.
Qty: 36 amps.

(WARNING: These details are collated from open and available sources. No dosage be taken without authorised medical prescription)

Field Kit for the Detection of Poisons and Nerve Agents in Drinking Water

This kit can test the following poisons in drinking water at the maximum permissible limit laid down by W.H.O. The kit is provided with all the reagents/materials needed for 50 tests.

Table 7.8

	WHO Limits / ppm (particles per million)
• Nerve agent	0.1 mg
• Mercury	0.5
• Manganese	0.2
• Copper	1.5
• Cyanide	0.05
• Lead	0.1
• Arsenic	0.1
• Microbiological contamination	0.05

Before using the test methods, the following points may be noted:

- The sample of water should not be chlorinated.
    - It should be clear. If turbidity is observed, the same should be clarified.
    - The sample of water should be slightly acidic (ph 6 to 7). Distilled water may not been supplied, but deionized water may be used in lieu of distilled water. For the preparation of deionized water shake the sample of water (50 ml) with four scoopfull of (3) for a few minutes and allow the resin to settle down.

Test for Nerve Agents. Fill the sample in the glass bottle (with red dot) upto half level. Shake. Leave for five minutes. If water turns yellow it is free from Nerve agent. If the colour remains clear, water is contaminated with nerve agents.

Test for Mercury. Add gradually ten drops of the sample of water at the centre of the water, allowing one drop to be soaked completely before adding the next drop. After adding all the drops wait for two minutes. Appearance of brick red/orange colour will indicate the presence of mercury.

Test for Manganese. Put one tablets (9) at the centre of the filter paper and add ten drops of sample on the tabled slowly. A blue/blue green colour on the paper will indicate the presence of manganese.

Test for Copper. Put one tablet (10) on a piece of thick filter paper and add slowly ten drops of water sample on the tablet. Appearance of olive green colour will indicate the presence of copper.

Test for Cyanide. Take one ml distilled water in a test tube, add one tablet (11) and one tablet (4) together. Shake the test tube to make suspension. Add two drops of suspension on a square piece of filter paper. Now take 100 ml suspected sample of water in a polythene bottle; add one tablet (13) and two scoop of (2). Put the paper upside down directly on the mouth of the bottle. Wait for five minutes. A distinct blue green colour will appear on the paper facing the water, will indicate the presence of cyanide.

Test for Lead. Take 100 ml of the sample of water in the polythene bottle. Add one scoop of resin (91). Shake the bottle gently up and down for two minutes, then allow to settle the resin. Reject the supernatant liquid. Add another 100 ml sample and repeat as above till one litre of sample is extracted. Pour the resin on a piece of filter paper to remove the moisture, then take the resin in a test tube. Add one ml distilled water and one crushed tablet (12) and one tablet (7). Shake vigorously for 5-10 minutes. The solution will become turbid. Now take 5-10 crystals of (8) in a test tube, add 2 ml of water to make the solution. From this add 5 drops of solution over the filter paper where turbid solution has already been added. A distinct dark violet stain will develop which indicate the presence of lead.

Test for Arsenic. Take a piece of filter paper. Add two drops of reagent (5). Take 100 ml of the suspected sample of water in the polythene bottle. Add one tablet (6), shake the bottle for a minute then add one scoopful (2) immediately, put the filter paper in which reagent already added directly on the mouth of the bottle. A pink violet stain on the surface of the filter paper will indicate the presence of arsenic. Yellow stain has no significance.

Microbiological Contamination. Fill the Aluminium screw cap media bottle provided in the kit box with the water sample upto the upper level of the lable. Shake the bottle gently. After five minutes keep the bottle at room temperature preferably 30°C for 18 hrs. If water in the bottle turns jet black, will indicate that sample is highly microbiologically contaminated and unfit for drinking purposes.

BIOLOGICAL THREATS : CIVIL DEFENCE
(Anatomy of Biological Astra)

Environmental Health Aspects : A Must to Counter Bio-Agents

The emerging Bio-Warfare and bio-terrorism capabilities is a stark reality. The dangers of this are increasing rapidly. It is necessary to understand, the well-recognized hygiene and sanitation measures necessary to maintain the health of person in a social environment. This chapter is only intended to emphasize the lessons, which have been learnt in the past, usually the hard way.

Future defensive doctrines in an area of bio-contamination would lay stress on the importance of effective hygiene and sanitation in a biological operational environment. One of the responsibilities of all civil medical personnel is to prevent this and to ensure that standards are maintained even in the most difficult circumstances.

Accommodation

Trials have proved that the morbidity of an infective disease spread by the inhalation route can be significantly curbed by good ventilation. Attempts should be made to avoid overcrowding and unnecessary congregations. Stuffy, humid, smoke-filled atmosphere should be avoided. Closing doors and windows will not reduce the hazard from an aerosol cloud of biological agent. Thus, buildings which are sealed and air-conditioned would be prone to bio-attack. In general terms, the agents will thrive in still air and in the relatively higher humidity during the night. Brisk ventilation will disperse the agent and reduce effective doses. It may also assist to dehydrate the agent. Thus, buildings having airconditioners should be switched off or otherwise be made airtight.

Personal Hygiene

The life of most microorganisms is reduced by exposure to detergent/soap and warm water. Beards and clothing can harbour microorganisms and spores. Personnel should shave regularly, outer clothing should be exposed to sunlight when possible and underclothes washed or, better still, boiled. Spare clothing should be kept loosely wrapped in polythene bags.

Cooking

Fresh food only should be cooked and eaten while the food is warm. However, food which has been cooked and kept exposed to the air is an ideal culture medium for many biological agents. Although toxins can be disseminated by aerosol bombs, a more efficient method is to apply the toxin to ready-prepared food or to food, which requires no cooking for example fruit and salads. Every effort should be made to protect fresh edibles by keeping them in airtight containers. Meals should be prepared in small batches, (in hostels/hotels) preferably fried or boiled for at least 15 minutes. It should be remembered that the inside of thick clabs of meat or joints might not reach particularly high temperature even though the surface of the meat appears well cooked. Meat should be cut into small pieces before cooking. Condiments and sauces, if used, should be added to food before cooking and should not be used at table. Table salt and pepper should not be used while eating on the table.

Water

Local sanitation authorities should, wherever practicable, be familiar with the source and chain of supply of water to their location. The deliberate pollution of large reservoirs, with for example a toxin, is possible, but not practical because of unknown factors including dilution; degree of oxygenation; and filtration and disinfection methods. The safest source of water, in a biological and chemical operations environment, is deep artesian well of which there are many in India. The water must be filtered and chlorinated before use. A diatomaceous earth filter (kieselguhr) should filter all water used by hotels/hostels. A greater absorptive effect for chemical agents, and probably for biological agents, is achieved if activated charcoal powder is added to the kieselguhr in a ratio of one part charcoal powder to two parts kieselguhr. The water must then be chlorinated. Effective chlorinating remains the method of choice by which biological agents, but not toxins, may be rendered harmless in water. The deliberate addition of biological agents to water will produce far higher bacterial cell counts than may be found naturally, necessitating higher chlorinating levels to produce a safe supply; the rule should be to demonstrate 2 ppm of free chlorine in the water at the end of 30 minutes by the neutral red test. Thereafter, water should be vigorously boiled before drinking as tea or coffee, rather than as a cold drink.

Decontamination

Biological agents have the same susceptibility to modern disinfectants as naturally occurring micro-organisms. Static disinfectants should be used liberally on floors and work surfaces. Medical personnel should use a disinfectant bucket when discarding contaminated material (dressing, swabs, syringes, etc).

Quarantine

A biological agent attack on unprotected personnel in a large building complex is unlikely to infect everyone. Those individuals not affected must be identified, and a system of reversed quarantine implemented immediately. This will involve the use of full individual protective measures; provision of separate accommodation, which may need thorough disinfecting first; and provision of non-infected food and water. This group must have minimal contact with infected individuals, so they may continue with vital tasks and provide logistic support to the survival effort of the rest. Reversed quarantine cannot be applied to medical personnel but they should work in full protective clothing if they are symptom-free. It should be remembered that personnel with mild illness are as likely to transmit infection as those who are seriously ill.

Pest Control

The effective control of rodents and arthropods is a hygiene priority.

Protective Equipment

The civil defence measures working under the government should organize some protective clothing to be pooled and kept centrally for such contingencies. The army is also co-opted during such disasters. A brief on various types of clothing is explained.

NBC Clothing

The protective suit will protect against arthropod inoculation but some arthropods, such as lice, could get through to the body if clothing does not fit properly. Some micro-organisms (Brucella melitensis and Coziella burnettii) and all spores can remain on. It is preferable for this contamination to be on the discardable suits rather than on clothing. Several organisms can gain entry to the body through minute skin surface abrasions and cuts, a common problem of vigorous labour/sports activities; wearing the rubber gloves may provide protection.

Face Respirator

The face respirator protects against biological agent aerosols. The aerosol consists of a droplet of protective/nutrient medium in which clumps of bacteria are present. The respirator canister will protect the respiratory system against particles greater than 1-1.5 micron (um) size. This is not a simple function of the size of the filter pore but depends upon the production of turbulent airflow in the micro air stream of the filter. Although small in size, each aerosol droplet has a definite inertia, which causes it to impinge on the filter material as it attempts to negotiate the turbulent air stream. It is the formation of the turbulent air stream, which, in part, imposes the physiological load upon the wearer of a respirator. Aerosol droplet size is a function of the viscosity and density of the fluid and the method of aerosol production. While aerosol production itself is a simple matter, the production of droplets sufficiently small to defeat the respirator canister is not. For example, a Bernoulli high-pressure gas-driven nebulizer will produce water droplets of 5 um size; to achieve a uniform size of 1 um requires an ultra-sonic nebulizer.

Immediate Survival Drills (ISD)

The best personal protection against the consequences of biological agent attack is to wear full NBC protective garment. On the first suspicion survival drills (ISD) should be practised without delay. Therefore, there is a necessity of making these suits available in the market, as a civil defence measure so that various individuals can buy or few NGOs can organise control and procurement with government help.

Immunisation

This chapter is only intended to summarise the situation in the context of biological operations or attacks by terrorist or hostile nations. As advances in immunology are made, changes will be required.

Naturally Occurring Diseases

The effectiveness of certain vaccines against naturally occurring diseases, for example, smallpox and yellow fever raises the possibility of invoking a range of immunizations against biological agents causing diseases.

Many vaccines have been produced only to be discarded because of serious side effects or limited efficacy. Thus ongoing research and technological breakthroughs are expected.

Following a biological operations attack, the number of micro-organisms will be much greater than that occurring in a natural disease. This raised level of attack may overcome the resistance provided by immunization.

Immunisation is likely to be most effective for those personnel on the outer edge of an attack area where the number of micro-organisms has fallen to natural levels. Immunisation may also attenuate a disease process while not providing complete protection and it may protect secondary targets from transmissible disease. A continuing and comprehensive immunisation, which assumes the availability of a large range of vaccines, poses problems of vaccine inter-compatibility and causes an increase incidence of adverse reactions.

Two main factors to be considered are:

- A biological agent is less likely to be used if an effective vaccine exists against it.

- Most viral biological operations agents are members of large virus groups with many subtypes and strains showing minimal cross-immunity. A large repertoire of vaccines would be required and would need to be given well in advance of an anticipated attack. These factors discount the use of conventional vaccines as effective protective agents.

The routine use of an effective vaccine may deny that particular agent to an enemy unless further research is undertaken to overcome the protection provided by vaccination.

Toxins

In the case of protein toxins, immunity can be induced in some instances by vaccination with an inactivated form of the toxin (toxoid). It is possible that using a conjugate of the toxin with antigenic protein could produce immunity to other toxins, which are not proteins, although this is still in the research stages. The dropsy incident in India had been identified as due to toxic mustard oil.

Where long-standing vaccination programmes of proven efficacy are utilised to combat naturally occurring infectious diseases, which incidentally provide protection against potential biological agents, such programmes should be pursued with vigour. Specific programmes of immunisation against biological agents may not be practicable.

Identification and Diagnosis of Biological Agent Casualty

Until biological agent detection alarm systems are available, medical officers and their assistants are best placed to appreciate that a biological agent attack has occurred. Lot of research on this is currently being done.

Medical personnel should be alert to the possibility of biological agent attack at all times. An awareness of the threat is the first step in defensive and protective counter-measures.

Casualty Rate Patterns

Epidemics of naturally occurring inhalation infectious diseases tend to have a characteristic pattern of occurrences. Some patients will present similar symptoms and signs. There is then a respite before a larger group appears, then another lag, before further, greater numbers appear. The significant factor is not the actual number of patients, but the presence of very definite troughs at the beginning of the epidemic.

Following a biological agent aerosol attack, the pattern of casualty flow is quite dissimilar. A steady and increasing stream of patients will be seen. This is comparable to a naturally occurring outbreak of food poisoning. It is, however, unlikely that a biological agent attack will take place in isolation upon one military facility or unit. The simultaneous appearance of outbreaks in different geographical locations having a pattern should alert medical commanders to the probability of biological agent attack.

Medical officers should arrange for simple graphs of infectious (febrile) diseases occurrence. If a clear pattern emerges, warning can be passed to the higher authority. While this may not be feasible in the forward areas of the battlefield, it should be considered in rear areas and in static locations.

Signs and Symptoms

The aim of a biological operation is to kill or severely incapacitate. An illness, which produces a mild pharyngitis and a temperature of 98°C, is unlikely, in itself, to be evidence of a biological agent attack.

Medical officers should be alert to the sudden onset of symptoms, the appearance of high temperatures and any uncommon sign or symptom which is present in all the patients, for example, the severe headache of Q-fever; the diploma of botulism; the jaw pain of brucellosis The signs and symptoms of the diseases listed subsequently shows that the abrupt onset of high fever, headache, prostration and some degree of respiratory distress occurring simultaneously in a large number of personnel should be regarded with suspicion.

Biological agents are presented in pure form at high dose levels and the micro-organism used may cause an exotic disease of even a totally new illness. Attempts to reach a firm diagnosis on clinical grounds alone may not be productive. The warning and accurate reporting of the symptoms and signs may be of more value in alerting other units to the danger. The establishment of diagnosis is likely to require hospital laboratory facilities.

Non-specific Treatments

Precise diagnosis of biological agent casualties in NBC environment is likely to be difficult. Both casualties and medical personnel may be in full IPE; signs and symptoms are common to many diseases; and laboratory facilities may not be available. Treatment principles will therefore differ from those used in peacetime.

Palliative Treatment

Measures should be taken to lower temperature; relieve pain; maintain spontaneous respiration; and secure an intravenous access for IV fluids and the administration of drugs.

Antibiotic Therapy

In the context of biological operations, antibiotics must be given, even without a firm diagnosis. Most bacterial diseases and several of the rickettsial illnesses respond to antibiotics. The choice of drug depends on the clinical circumstances, but at the first echelon of medical care, one broad-spectrum antibiotic should be administered in full therapeutic doses parentally and, if possible, intravenously. The choice is between chloramphenicol and the tetracycline's, bearing in mind that Bacillus anthracites are not susceptible to chloramphenicol. The penicillin's and streptomycin should be reserved for later hospital use. Treatment of co-existing injuries should follow established principles.

Steroids

Parental steroids should not be used routinely and never without an appropriate antibiotic cover. However, if the patient is shocked and there are reasons to suppose that the biological agent attack has been a toxin rather than a micro-organism, intravenous hydrocortisone is justified in the absence of appropriate antitoxins.

General

The medical officer may be faced with many patients who are clearly dying, and if no diagnosis can be made it may be necessary to employ a pharmacological blunderbuss of combined antibiotic and steroid therapy. The critical factor would be whether a lethal or incapacitating agent has been used. If reports are received from the attacked location that personnel are already dying, then consideration should be given to using such treatment on all patients. Under certain circumstances, it may be desirable to give antibiotic treatment to exposed (potentially infected) personnel who have not yet developed any illness, as a means of preventing transmission and conserving manpower.

The Treatment Environment-Collective Protection

Collective Protection

In any future hostilities with likelihood of a contaminated environment it is envisaged that much medical treatment will take place in Collective Protection (colpro), shelters, where a clean treatment environment can be maintained.

The use of colpro equipment for patients with transmissible disease can only be considered if the colpro is not required for other patients. Patients could only be treated in colpro if the medical staff were in full protective clothing whilst outside as the colpro facility otherwise could become contaminated with biological agent.

Patients who have abrupt onset febrile illnesses or are prostrated and whose illness is thought to be the result of a biological agent attack should not be allowed into colpro used for other non-biological agent patients. They should be treated in an isolation ward by staff wearing full IPE until it is certain that the disease is non-transmissible.

Decontamination

It is beyond the scope of these analyses to consider the handling of conventional casualties in a biological operational environment. However, potentially contaminated outer garments should be removed as soon as possible by fully protected personnel, away from other patients. The casualty should then be placed in a casualty bag for respiratory protection and nursed in an isolated ward.

Decontamination of biological operations casualties may be achieved by washing the NBC protective over garments with a bleach or disinfectant solution: however, this will be time consuming and may be impractical. Staff who has been handling biological operations casualties must be decontaminated by washing with the strongest bleach or disinfectant solution available. The decontamination of biological agent casualties is under review. However, the persistency of the agent is high both on wet and dry surfaces, due to which decontamination becomes necessary. Lot of research for treatment has been done in developed nations, especially UK. The clinical summary facts have been collated from various open sources and are only indicative and not final.

Clinical Summary - Botulism

A lethal non-transmissible illness characterized primarily by nervous system symptoms including ptosis, visual difficulty and dry mouth, which may be followed by progressive paralysis and respiratory failure. An antitoxin is available but treatment is mainly supportive. The clinical summary is tabulated below:

Name of biological agent	Botulinum toxin
Common name of disease	Botulism
Usual means of natural spread	Food
Infective dose in air	0.2-1 mg (estimated)
Infective dose by ingestion (water or food)	1 mg (estimated)
Ease of secondary spread	None can occur
Effectiveness of vaccine	High
Incubation period	0.5-7 days
Mortality due to food	1.6-76% in outbreaks
Persistency of agent in the wet	not known
Persistency of agent on dry surfaces	not known
Identification time (Current PHLS method)	No established method

Clinical Summary – Bacillus Cereus Enterotoxins

A non-lethal, non-transmissible illness taking two forms, one characterised by vomiting and the other by diarrhoea. The illness is self-limiting and treatment is symptomatic. Clinical summary is tabulated below:-

Name of biological agent	Bacillus cereus enterotoxins
Common name of disease	Apparently, one type causes Diarrhoea, a second type causes Vomiting
Usual means of natural spread	Food
Infective dose in air	not known
Infective dose by ingestion (Water or food)	Low
Susceptibility population	High
Ease of secondary spread	None is possible
Effectiveness of vaccine	Not known
Incubation period	0-12 hours (diarrhoea) 1-6 hours (vomiting)
Mortality	Low
Persistence of agent in the wet	High
Persistence of agent on dry surfaces	High
Identification time (Current PHLS method)	18-48 hours (or rapidly by microscopy of sputum).
Additional comments	This organism forms spores which are notoriously persistent in soil and generally very resistant to natural hazards.

Clinical Summary - Anthrax

Pulmonary anthrax is a lethal, non-transmissible disease characterized by hemorrhage, mediastinitis and meningitis. Responds to antibiotics if given early enough. Clinical summary is tabulated as follows:

Name of biological agent	Bacillus anthracis
Common name of disease	Anthrax
Usual means of natural spread	Contaminated hides, bonemeal (most cases are cutaneous, and not serious, but occasionally fatal lung infections occur).
Infective dose in air	Uncertain (estimates range from 10 to 100 organisms)
Infective dose by ingestion (Water or food)	High
Susceptibility population	High in cold regions
Ease of secondary spread	Low
Effectiveness of vaccine	High
Availability of vaccine	Restricted
Incubation period	1-7 days
Mortality	25-100% (in cases with lung involvement)

Treatment

There are several anti-viral medicines already in existence, as explained below:

Acyclovir and BCDU (Bromo vinyl deoxuridine). These are effective against the herpes group of viruses, under experimental conditions.

PFA (trisodium phosphonoformate). This is a virus-inhibiting drug, which is also effective against the herpes group including herpes virus 1 and 2, Epstein Barr virus, human cytomegalovirus and Narek's disease virus.

Amantadine and Rimantadine. These appear to block the virus replication of influenza A virus. Rimantadine was used in the USSR during the 1977/78 epidemic; it appeared to reduce clinical signs and febrile responses. A reduced morbidity rate from 71 to 14 per cent was claimed and it is significant that the drug was given before exposure, or within the first 3 days, emphasizing that virus replication must be blocked at an early stage.

Ribavirin. This is a synthetic nucleotide, which inhibits the replication of both RNA (Ribo Nucleic Acid) and DNA (Deoxy Ribo Nucleic Acid) virus following its activation by phosphorylation by cellular adenosine kinase. Experimentally, it has inhibited influenza An abd B viruses, by inhalation of a drug aerosol. Ribarvirin appears to be active against the herpes group and arenaviruses (e.g., lassa fever). The activity of the drug appears to be less obvious against picorna, rhabdo- and arboviruses.

Interferon. Interferon's are glycoproteins, which differ in activity and stability according to the species of cell (fibroblast, leukocyte or lymphocyte) in which they are stimulated. The activity of interferon is complex, as it certainly depresses viral replication but also may inhibit cell growth and proliferation. This drug has shown itself to be effective experimentally against type 4 rhinovirus (again by nasal spray), Marburg, yellow fever, influenza B and Venezuelan encephalomyelitis viruses. The degree and type of activity of interferon against viruses would appear to be dose related; interferon itself may also be toxic in high doses.

Pre-treatment

Bacterial Agents

Generally, prophylactic antibiotics are undesirable in the absence of an actual or imminent biological agent attack because of the likelihood of adverse effects when used for more than a few days. For certain specialized military groups engaged upon vital, short-term military activities, a course of a prophylactic broad-spectrum antibiotic may be considered. A course of tetracycline, spetrin or possibly chloramphenicol used prophylactically could protect against, or attenuate, several biological agent induced diseases. Many antibiotics have been manufactured, tested and discarded for reasons of toxicity or because, in routine clinical practice, they were found to be no more effective than other antibiotics. Some of these, particularly those of the streptomycin group, have a very broad range of activity and could be useful in a biological operational environment.

Viral Agents

Instead of attempting to manufacture a range of vaccines against potential biological agents, it may be more practicable to consider immune-stimulating or immune-enhancing compounds. These compounds may be classed as specifically protective since they boost the humoral or cellular defensive responses of the host to the specific immune-gene stimuli, which are being generated by the replication of the viral agent. The immune-enhancing drug could be administered either during the few days following attack when immune-genie components are most abundant, or prophylactically in anticipation of an attack. The combined use of an immune-enhancing drug followed by a specific immune-globulin (if available) offers hope for the more specific treatment of viral biological agents. Two such immune-enhancing drugs are levamisol and the enzyme L-asparginase, both of which are relatively non-toxic in man and are immune-enhancing at low doses. Immune-enhancing drugs alone may attenuate a disease process without protecting against infection.

Warning and Detection of Biological Agent Attack

Data Processing

The pattern of occurrence of illness resulting from a biological agent attack is entirely different from a naturally occurring illness. Such patterns may be expressed mathematically and detected by computer after appropriate data processing.

Medical officers could provide daily information on an appropriate format of the occurrence of illness. Such data would be fed through software terminals to a central facility for analysis. Such a system has an obvious routine peacetime application and could replace the normal morbidity return. Preliminary field studies have taken place and a draft on general staff requirement (GSR) has been written.

Biological Agent Detection Devices

Theoretically, there are several methods by which organic matter may be detected in the soil and in air, including devices based upon gas chromatography, labelled gas exchange systems and chemiluminescence. Such systems have been used successfully in the Antarctic and on the planet Mars. The main problem, in the biological operations context, is to differentiate the biological agent attack from the normal background of organic matter.

XM-19/XM-2

The system consists of two devices, a XM-19 automatic biological agent alarm and a XM-2 air sampler. The air collector of the XM-19 continuously samples air at the rate of 1,000 litres per minute and selects particles in the respiratory size range for testing. Biological particles are detected in the device because haem-containing proteins catalyse the oxidation of luminol by sodium perborate which results in the production of measurable amounts of light. The detector sounds an alarm when the haem content of the air exceeds a certain level, and a co-located XM-2 is then activated to collect an air sample so that the suspect biological contaminant can later be identified at field laboratories specially equipped to perform rapid identification tests. The logic circuitry of the XM-19 allows biological attacks to be discriminated from naturally occurring biological particles. The device will only respond to bacteria and some rickettsia. This United States system has serious deficiencies and, in the present form, has been found unpractical.

FAST (Fluorescent Antibody Screening Technique)

A good deal of protection against biological agent attack could be obtained by continuously sampling the air and screening retrospectively for the presence of key biological operational agents, provided the identification could occur quickly enough to allow realistic prophylactic and therapeutic measures to be instituted. FAST is a system in which air samplers, operating continuously, have their accumulated aqueous samples of air removed for testing at regular intervals. These samples can be tested with fluorescent-labelled antibody reagents specific to the previously selected key biological operation agents. In an immunofluorescence test, taking up to one hour, portions of the sample would be divided into microscope slides, treated with fluorescent conjugates specific to the desired microorganisms and observed under a fluorescing hand-held McArthur field microscope. If candidate bacterial or rickettsial agents (or the larger viruses) are detected, plans for specific antibiotic therapy could be activated in time for casualties to be prevented among personnel who are in the incubation stage of the infection.

Samples could also be routinely collected from surfaces, for example vehicles and clothing, and screened by the same techniques as an aid to contamination control.

Future Developments

This section is intended to reflect current thoughts on some aspects of defence against biological operations. The ideas expressed may never be translated into practice. One development, which requires consideration, is casualty handling in a biological operations environment. Therefore there is a necessity to do research for developing Bio-Detectors or so called 'BIDS' systems. Western countries have made tremendous advancement. Equipment is under trials, which can detect Bio-agent from more than 20 kms. or so. In the South-Asian region, due to peculiar climatic conditions and prevailing health environment, such identification systems would have to be super-sensitive to a particular agent, lest it gets activated on wrong signals.

NBC Weapons and Terrorism

In this regard, the threat of use of NBC weapons by terrorists is looming in front of us. Therefore, understanding the terrorist psyche is very important to evolve a Global Counter-terrorist Strategy.

Eight

Conclusion

Terrorism has always existed since the beginning of human life. It is the evil, which co-exists with the good. Complete elimination and eradication may be a utopian view. But what is required is to promote activities and institutions, which may curtail breeding grounds for terrorist activities.

The modern era is seeing the transformation of a terrorist of a classical or conventional variety to a revolutionary variety or the so-called 'Neo-Terrorists', due to many factors especially the on going RMA. Further due to the prognosis of future wars being 'smaller wars' where the full-scale classical Second World War type military adventures may not be possible. This creates a 'Space' for fighting wars in the lower spectrum. These wars could be called 'LIC' or 'Asymmetric Wars' or even 'Proxy Wars', in the form of a 'Third Manoeuvre' satisfying coercive diplomacy.

Simultaneously in the post '9-11' scenario and America's resolve to eliminate terrorism globally, abetment of the same should logically not be encouraged by great powers to create leverages for bargaining or may be to extend their 'Strategic Frontiers'.

The Indian scene, is a typical example of Pakistan's effort to wrest Kashmir by a proxy war being fought through a 'third manoeuvre' architectured through complex and self-sustaining networks. India on its own has to revise its military strategy and cause changes in its operational and tactical doctrine to 'quell' this new warfare. Budgeting and synergisation become important factors in a holistic 'Counter-Strategy' to fight this war.

Our basic stratagem should be to shift out of the existing *linear syndrome* as a remedy and solution and *transcend to new non-linear paradigm*. In essence, our present strategy is inward looking and defensive. This be re-structured and re-aligned to include actions across the borders/LC (including AG PL) especially in the POK area. The relevance of this, at this point of time has to be seen, as the global effort to fight terrorism, continues unabated. Pakistan's proxy war cannot be addressed by own internal 'House Keeping'. Further, of late, some movements have been identified in POK, of their integration with the main Kashmir as against Pakistan's iron and suppressive rule without adequate freedom. In sum, the present aim should be therefore modified towards aim plus (to include POK). This obviously would also create more *strategic space* for negotiations and an ultimate solution between the two spectrums.* In a situation, where there is a stand-off between two armies, an 'Exit Policy' should be formulated and appreciated before any military manoeuvre. The stand-off, thereafter should be leveraged by the stronger asymmetric force to bleed the perpetuator of terrorism economically.

As suggested, re-explore facilitating of UNO as 'Watch Men' against specific terrorist acts in Kashmir. In view of the current trend, utilise this resource now for raising internationally on human rights violation by terrorists. The following be added in projecting our case. The moral cause of Kashmir being part of India should be propagated at the house door-step level. In addition an information war cell be created at all levels.

One has to comprehend the right perspective so that the counter-mil measures are cost effective and not repetitive. Therefore, re-learning and drawing linkages between military strategy and terrorism in J&K needs to be re-established as discussed in this book. India, (under UN observation?) be allowed to carry out full-scale millitary ops (akin to Americans). Presently, it is not possible due to negative politicisation caused by any collateral damage (due to civilian casualties). This syndrome should be broken, if necessary with UNO's presence. (Under American diktat?) Presently, many areas where it is known to us, that terrorists have infrastructure like bunkers, etc cannot be tackled because of political clout or representation in that area. (Many areas within Kashmir are literally called liberated zones). These be tackled with full millitary force co-opting UNO so as to neutralise any local political interference or distorted mileage in the international fora.

* (The earlier premise of squeezing Pakistan economically by the border deployment has already proved to be a misnomer, in view of heavy economic revival as reward for joining the international coalition against terrorism. Foreign exchange reserves have gone from $3.3 billion in September to $4.86 billion last month. Pakistan rupee has risen to 8 per cent against the dollar since September 11. Wall Street has pushed overall GDP growth projections from 2.6 per cent to as high as 3.1 per cent. Pakistan's trade deficit has dropped from $921 million in the second half of 2000 to $ 425 million in 2001. Its current account went into $1 billion surplus. It was in the red in 2000).

The abstracts as discussed above should clearly precipitate our perception of Pakistan's proxy war through a 'Netwar concept'. Therefore, there comes a need to develop a Counter-Netwar doctrine. Some of the aspects pertaining to this could be :

- Develop a 'Hi-Tech' tactical doctrine for ops against hideouts liberated zones/rd-opening/infiltration. The thrust could be to create 'Special Forces' from existing resources, which are area specific. These forces be organised in very small groups, but equipped with the latest 'State-of-the-Art' systems, including communications and laser designators for directing PGM fire. They could even have connectivity through carriage of satellite telephones and an electronic IFF. A doctrine be developed so that these can be employed in conjunction with existing RR battalions on a grid system as hither-to-fore.
- Additional release of surveillance equipments like sensors, HHTI, UAV and more frequent satellite coverage.
- Present 'DF' equipment pt has an error of 6×6 kms. Same be narrowed down to 1×1 km. error by better equipment.
- Use of AH/fighter aircraft and doctrine for neutralisation of terrorists be developed.
- In all RR battalions, Commanding Officer be delegated powers to do local recruitment in the AOR of at least one pl strength. This much strength ought to be suppressed during the raising/recruitment phase. However, subsequently during earmarking of a grid, the recruitment be done within the grid. This re-organisation will assist to separate the terrorist from the population. Validation of the same can be done on trial basis of a few battalions, before a policy is formulated.
- In many areas 'Hindus' are also working as 'OGW'/Guides due to the lure of money and being terrorised. Thus, the need to book them under POTA and also create more employment opportunities for them.

The policy of 'demographic shift' in certain high terrorist infested areas be done on selective basis. This will separate the 'Fish from water' and thus enable their liquidation. A political demographic strategy for the same should be formulated in conjunction with MHA/MOD, at the apex level. Although, this would be a radical step, but on an experiment basis, a few places can be tried, in case the present level of terrorist activity does not die in the near future. Similarly there is a necessity of carrying out military action in so called 'Liberated Zones'; where terrorists have strongholds UNO be used as force-multipliers as SF carries out full scale CTO.

One should even consider opening 'R&D' cells with the field force to enable introducing technology in the field as per use or tactical requirements. Method of 'fast track' procurement should be institutionalised both at the field force and MOD level to reduce differential in technology vis-à-vis the terrorists.

One should think of originating a 'Border Area Action Plan' to enable good governance and wean away locals from supporting terrorists. In lot of areas Gujjar-Bakarwal community should thus be assimilated towards positivity.

There is yet another dimension of the possession of WMDs by terrorists. Measures of counter-proliferation and establishing counter-terrorism conventions at the UN level, continental and regional levels become very important to this end. The other aspect of WMDRs as a philosophy has also to be understood. In fact the '9-11' attacks all fall in this category due to mass disruption, which occurred.

A WMD terrorist attack can cause mass destruction akin to the first atomic bomb on Hiroshima or a lesser degree through employment of radioactive material or even the 'Bio-Weapons', which is known as the poor man's atom bomb. Therefore, one has to re-structure disaster management drills and responses, globally as well as within nations. In India's case a beginning has been made towards such contingencies.

In finality, one can procrastinate, that it may not be really possible to eliminate the cancer of terrorism completely. Therefore, what we have to work on is to enhance the capability of 'Conflict Containment' as the duality of the law of nature will allow both evil and good to co-exist. We therefore will have to work at global level collectively, so that we can manage this evil, which should not be allowed to raise its head or be utilised as a tool of military strategy and political leverage. It should not be allowed through a strong UN mechanism to be able to follow the policy of 'State terrorism' or the so re-defined 'Neo-terrorism' philosophy, which may encompass the utilisation of the ongoing RMA including proliferation of WMDs, which may mark the beginning of the end of civilisation. Thus, the *mantra* should be to reverse the current dynamics of a new 'RTA' by addressing the root causal issues of economic and educational deprivation combined with the reduction of civilisational and ideological differential. The Indian experience should become the laboratory, where all these factors have thrived. In fact, in addition to the Afghan imbroglio this zone has emerged as the epi-centre of global terrorism. The answer therefore is to de-legitimise the case in Kashmir at a global level, so that the seed of the evolving 'Neo-Terrorism' is uprooted forever.

In totality and summation there is a need to evolve a re-vitalisation plan akin to the European Marshall Plan after the Second World War which was with a view to contain communism. In this case, a plan be evolved in which the triangle of terrorism between Afghanistan–Pakistan and POK is stabilised through an economic-adrenalin package for re-construction, education (including at Madarsas) and developmental projects causing mass employment opportunities through UN mechanism for counter-terrorism. The total aim being to contain and isolate terrorism from this region, so that it becomes extinct over a period of time.

Appendix A

THE PREVENTION OF TERRORISM ORDINANCE

(No. 9 of 2001)

Promulgated by the President in the Fifty-second Year of the Republic of India.

An Ordinance to make provisions for the prevention of and for dealing with, terrorist activities and for matters connected therewith.

WHEREAS Parliament is not in session and the President is satisfied that circumstances exist which render it necessary for him to take immediate action.

NOW, THEREFORE, in exercise of the powers conferred by clause (1) of Article 123 of the Constitution, the President is pleased to promulgate the following Ordinance:-

Chapter I
Preliminary

- • This Ordinance may be called the Prevention of Terrorism ordinance, 2001.
- It extends to the whole of India.
- Every person shall be liable to punishment under this Ordinance for every act or omission country to the provisions thereof, of which he is held guilty in India.
- Any person who commits an offence beyond India which is punishable under this Ordinance shall be dealt with according to the provisions of this Ordinance in the same manner as if such act had been committed in India.
- The provisions of this Ordinance apply also to:
- Citizens of India outside India.
- Person in the service of the Government, wherever they may be; and
- Person on ships and aircrafts, registered in India, wherever they may be.
- It shall come into force at once and shall remain in force for a period of five years from the date of its commencement, but its expiry under the operation of this sub-section shall not affect:-
- The previous operation of, or anything duly done or suffered under this Ordinance, or
- Any right, privilege, obligation or liability acquired, accrued or incurred under this Ordinance, or
- Any penalty, forfeiture or punishment incurred in respect of any offence under this Ordinance, or

- Any investigation, legal proceeding or remedy in respect of any such right, privilege, obligation, liability, penalty, forfeiture or punishment as aforesaid. And any such investigation, legal proceeding or remedy any be instituted. Continued or enforced and any such penalty, forfeiture or punishment may be imposed as if this Ordinance had not expired.
- In this Ordinance, unless the contest otherwise requires:-
- 'Code' means the Code of Criminal Procedure, 1973:
- "Designated Authority" shall mean such officer of the Central Government not below the rank of Joint Secretary to the Government, or such officer of the State Government not below the rank of Secretary to the Government, as the case may be. As may be specified by the Central Government or as the case may be, the State Government, by a notification published in the Official Gazette.
- "Proceeds of Terrorism" shall mean all kinds of properties which have been derived or obtained from commission of any terrorist act or have been acquired through funds traceable to a terrorist act, and shall include cash, irrespective of person in whose name such proceeds are standing or in whose possession they are found.
- "Property" means property and assets of every description, whether corporeal or incorporeal, movable or immovable, tangible or intangible and deeds and instruments evidencing title to, or interest in, such property or assets.
- "Public Prosecutor" means a Public Prosecutor or an Additional Public Prosecutor or a Special Public Prosecutor appointed under section 28 and includes any person acting under the directions of the Public Prosecutor.
- "Special Court" means a Special Court constituted under section 23.
- "Terrorist Act" has the meaning assigned to it in sub-section (1) of section 3, and the expression "Terrorist" shall be construed accordingly:
- "State Government", in relation to a Union Territory, means the Administrator thereof;
- Words and expressions used but not defined in this Ordinance and defined in the Code shall have the meanings respectively assigned to them in the Code.
- Any reference in this ordinance to any enactment or any provision thereof shall, in relation to an area in which such enactment or such provision is not in force, be construed as a reference to the corresponding law or the relevant provision of the corresponding law, if any in force in the area.

Chapter II
Punishment for, and Measures for Dealing with, Terrorist Activities

- • Whoever:-
  - With intent to threaten the unity, integrity, security or sovereignty of India or to strike terror in the people or any section of the people does any act or thing by using bombs. Dynamite or other explosive substances or inflammable substances or firearms or other lethal weapons or poisons or noxious gases or other chemicals or by any other substances (whether biological or otherwise) of a hazardous nature or by any other means whatsoever, in such a manner as to cause, or likely to cause. Death of, or injuries to any person or persons or loss of, or damage to, or destruction of, property or disruption of any supplies or services essential to the life of the community or causes damage or destruction of any property or equipment used or intended to be used for the defence of India or in connection with any other purpose of the Government of India. Any State Government or any of their agencies, or detains any person and threatens to kill or injure such person in order to compel the Government or any other person to do or abstain from doing any act:
  - Is or continues to be a member of an association declared unlawful under the Unlawful Activities (Prevention) Act, 1967 or voluntarily does an act aiding or promoting of any unlicensed firearms. Ammunition, explosive or other instrument or substance capable of causing mass destruction and commits any act resulting in loss of human life or grievous injury to any person or causes significant damage to any property, commits a terrorist act.

Chapter III
Terrorist Organisations

- • for the purpose of this ordinance an organization is a terrorist organization if:-
  - it is listed in the Schedule, or
  - it operates under the same name as an organization listed in that Schedule.
- The Central Government may by order, in the Official Gazette:-
  - Add an organization to the Schedule:

- Remove an organization from that Schedule:
- Amend that Schedule in some other way:

- The Central Government may exercise its power under clause (a) of sub-section (2) in respect of an organization only if it believes that it is able to prove.
  - That the organization was not declared as a terrorist organization at the time when he became a member or began to profess to be a member; and
  - That he has not taken part in the activities of the organization at any time during its inclusion in the Schedule as a terrorist organization.
- • A person commits an offence if :-
  - He invites support for a terrorist organization, and
  - The support is not, or is not restricted to the provision of money or other property within the meaning of section.
- A person commits an offence if he arranges, manages or assists in arranging or managing a meeting which he knows it:-
  - To support a terrorist organization.
  - To further the activities of a terrorist organisation, or
- To be addressed by a person who belongs or professes to belong to a terrorist organization.
- A person commits an offence if he addresses a meeting for the purpose of encouraging support for a terrorist organization or to further its activities.
- A person guilty of an offence under this section shall be liable on conviction, to imprisonment for a term not exceeding ten year or with fine or with both.

Chapter IV
Special Courts

- • The Central Government or a State Government may, by notification in the Official Gazette, constitute one or more Special Courts for such area or areas, or for such case or class or group of cases, as may be specified in the notification.
  - Where a notification constituting a Special Court for any area or areas or for any case or class or group of cases is issued by the Central Government under Sub-section (1), and a notification constituting a Special Court for the same area or areas or for the same case or class or group of cases has also been issued by the State Government under that sub-section the Special Court constituted by the Central Government, whether the notification constituting such Court is issued

before or after the issue of the notification constituting the Special Court by the state government, shall have, and the Special Court constituted by the state government shall not have, jurisdiction to try any offence committed in that area or areas or, as the case may be, the case or class or group of cases and all cases pending before any Special Court constituted by the State Government shall stand transferred to the Special Court constituted by the Central Government.

- Where any question arises as to the jurisdiction of any Special Court, it shall be referred to the Central Government whose decision in the matter shall be final.
- A Special Court shall be presided over by a judge to be appointed by the Central Government or as the case may be, the State Government, with the concurrence of the Chief Justice of the High Court.
- The Central Government or, as the case may be, the State Government may also appoint, with the concurrence of the Chief Justice of the High Court, additional judges to exercise jurisdiction of a Special Court.
- A person shall not be qualified for appointment as a judge or an additional judge for a Special Court unless he is, immediately before such appointment a sessions judge or a additional sessions judge in any State.
- For the removal of doubts, it is hereby provided that the attainment, by a person appointed as a judge or an additional judge of a Special Court, of the age of superannuating under the rules applicable to him in the service to which he belongs, shall not affect his continuance as such judge or additional judge.
- Where any additional judge or additional judges is or are appointed in a Special Court, the judge of the Special Court may, from time to time, by general or special order, in writing, provide for the distribution of business of the Special Court among all judges including himself and the additional judge or additional judges and also for the disposal of urgent business in the event of his absence or the absence of any additional judge.
- A Special Court may, on its own motion, or on an application made by the Public Prosecutor and if it considers it expedient or desirable so to do, sit for any of its proceedings at any place, other than its ordinary place of sitting.

  Provided that nothing in this section shall be construed to change the place of sitting of a Special Court constituted by a

State Government to any place outside that State.

- Notwithstanding anything contained in the Code. Every offence punishable under any provision or this ordinance shall be triable only by the Special Court within whose jurisdiction it was committed or, as the case may be, by the Special Court constituted for trying such offence under section 23.
- if having regard to the exigencies of the situation prevailing in a state:-
    - it is not possible to have a fair, impartial or speedy trial or
    - it is not feasible to have the trial without occasioning the breach of peace or grave risk to the safety of the accused, the witness, the Public Prosecutor and judge of the Special Court or any of them, or
    - it is not otherwise in the interests of justice.

The Supreme Court may transfer any case pending before a Special Court to any other Special Court within that State or in any other State and the High Court may transfer any case pending before a Special Court situated in that State to any other Special Court within the state.

- The Supreme Court or the High Court, as the case may be may act under this section either on the application of the Central Government or a party interested and any such application shall be made by motion, which shall, except when the applicant is the Attorney-General of India, be supported by an affidavit or affirmation.
- When trying any offence, a Special Court may also try any other offence with which the accused may, under the Code, be charged at the same trial if the offence is connected with such other offence.
- If, in the course of any trial under this Ordinance of any offence it if found that the accused person has committed any other offence under this ordinance or under any other law, the Special Court may convict such of such other offence and pass any sentence or award punishment authorized by this ordinance or such rule or, as the case may be under such other law.
- When a police officer investigating a case requests the Court of a Chief Judicial Magistrate or the Court of a Chief Metropolitan Magistrate in writing for obtaining samples of hand writing, finger prints, foot prints, photographs, blood, saliva, semen, hair, voice of any accused person, reasonabl

suspected to be involved in the commission of an offence under this ordinance, it shall be lawful for the Court of a Chief Judicial Magistrate or the Court of a Chief Metropolitan Magistrate to direct that such samples be given by the accused person to the police officer either through a medical practitioner or otherwise, as the case may be.

- If any accused person refuses to give samples as provided sub-section (1) the court shall draw adverse inference against the accused.
- • For every Special Court, the Central Government or, as the case may be, the State Government, shall appoint a person to be the Public Prosecutor and may appoint one or more persons to be the Additional Public Prosecutor or Additional Public Prosecutors.
- A person shall not be qualified to be appointed as a Public Prosecutor or an Additional Public Prosecutor or a Special Public Prosecutor under this section unless he has been in practice as an Advocate for not less than seven years or has held any post, for a period of not less than seven years, under the Union or a State, requiring special knowledge of law.
- Every person appointed as a Public Prosecutor or an Additional Public Prosecutor or a Special Public Prosecutor under this section shall be deemed to be a Public Prosecutor within the meaning of clause (u) of section 2 of the Code, and the provisions of the code shall have effect accordingly.
- • Subject to the provisions of section 49, a Special Court may take cognizance of any offence, without the accused being committed to it for trial, upon receiving a complaint of facts that constitute such offence or upon a police report of such facts.
- Where an offence triable by a Special Court is punishable with imprisonment for a term not exceeding three years or with fine or with both, the Special Court may, notwithstanding anything contained in sub-section (1) of section 260 or section 262 of the Code, try the offence in a summary way in accordance with the procedure prescribed in the Code and the provisions of sections 263 to 265 of the code, shall so far as may be, apply to such trial.

Provided that when in the course of a summary trial under this sub-section it appears to the Special Court that the nature of the case in such that it is undesirable to try it in a summary way, the Special Court shall recall any witness who may have been examined and proceed to re-hear the case in the manner provided by the provisions of the Code for the trial of such offence and the said provisions shall apply to and in relation to a Special Court as they apply to and in relation to a Magistrate :

Provided further that in the case of any conviction in summary trial under this section, it shall be lawful for a Special Court to pass a sentence of imprisonment for a term not exceeding one year and with fine which may extend to rupees five lakh.

- Subject to the other provisions of this Ordinance, a Special Court shall, for the purpose of trial of any offence have all the powers of a Court of Session and shall try such offence as if it were a Court of Session so far as may be in accordance with the procedure prescribed in the Code for the trial before a Court of Session.
- Subject to the other provision of this ordinance, every case transferred to a Special Court under section 25 shall be dealt with as if such case had been transferred under section 406 of the Code to such Special Court.
- Notwithstanding anything contained in the Code, but subject to the provisions of section 299 of the Code, a Special Court may, if it think fit and for reasons to be recorded by it, proceed with the trial in the absence of the accused or his pleader and record the evidence of any witness. Subject to the right of the accused to recall the witness for cross-examination.
- Notwithstanding anything contained in the Code, the proceedings under this Ordinance may, for reasons to be recorded in writing, be held in camera if the Special Court so desires.
- A Special Court if on an application made by a witness in any proceeding before it or by the Public Prosecutor in relation to such witness or its own motion, is satisfied that the life of such witness is in danger, it may, for reasons to be recorded in writing, take such measures as it deems fit for keeping the identity and address of such witness secret.
- In particular, and without prejudice to the generality of the provisions of sub-section (2) the measures which a Special Court may take under that subsection may include:
    - The holding of the proceedings at a place to be decided by the Special Court.
    - The avoiding of the mention of the names and addresses of the witness in its witnesses are not disclosed:
    - The issuing of any directions for securing that the identity, and address of the witness are not disclosed;
    - A decision that it is in the public interest to order that all or any of the proceedings pending before such a court shall not be published in any manner.

- Any person who contravenes any decision or direction issued under sub-section (3) shall be punishable with imprisonment for a term which may extend to one year and with fine which may extend to one thousand rupees.
- The trial under this ordinance of any offence by a Special Court shall have precedence over the trial of any other case against the accused in any other court (not being a Special Court) and shall be concluded in preference to the trial of such other case and accordingly the trial of such other case shall remain in abeyance.
- Notwithstanding anything in the Code or in the Indian Evidence Act, 1872, but subject to the provisions of this section, a confession made by a preson before a police officer not lower in rank than a Superintendent of Police recorded by such police officer either in writing or on any mechanical or electronic device like cassettes, tapes or sound tracks from out of which sound or images can be reproduced, shall be admissible in the trial of such person for an offence under this ordinance or rules made there under.
- A police officer shall, before recording any confession made by a person under sub-section (1) explain to such person in writing that he is not bound to make a confession and that if he does so, it may be used against him.
- The Confession shall be recorded in an atmosphere free from threat or inducement and shall be in the same language in which the person makes it.
- The person from whom a confession has been recorded under sub-section (1) shall be produced before the Court of Chief Metropolitan Magistrate or the Court of a Chief Judicial Magistrate along with the original statement of confession, written or recorded on mechanical or electronic device within forty-eight hours.
- The Chief Metropolitan Magistrate or the Chief Judicial Magistrate, shall, record the statement, if any, made by the person so produced and get his signature or thumb impression and if there is any complaint of torture, such person shall be directed to be produced for medical examination before a Medical Officer not lower in rank than an Assistant Civil Surgeon and thereafter, he shall be sent to judicial custody.
- Where, after taking cognizance of any offence, a Special Court is of the opinion that the offence is not triable by it, it shall, notwithstanding that it has no jurisdiction to try such offence, transfer the case for the trial of such offence to any court having jurisdiction under the Code and the court to which the case is

transferred may proceed with the trial of the offence as if it had taken cognizance of the offence.

- Notwithstanding anything contained in the Code, an appeal shall lie from any judgment, sentence or order, not being an interlocutory order, of a Special Court to the High Court both on facts and on law.

Chapter V
Interception of Communication in Certain Cases

- In this Chapter, unless the context otherwise requires, -
  - "Electronic communication" means any transmission of signs, signals, writings, images, sounds, data or intelligence of any nature transmitted in whole or in part by a wire, radio, electromagnetic, photo electronic or photo optical system that affects inland or foreign commerce but does not include:-
  - The radio portion of a cordless telephone communication that is transmitted between the wireless telephone hand-set and the base unit;
    - Any wire or oral communication;
    - Any communication made through a tone only paging device; or
    - Any communication from a tracking device;
  - "Intercept" means the aural or other acquisition of the contents by wire, electronic or oral communication through the use of any electronic, mechanical or other device;
  - "Oral communication" means any oral communication uttered by a person exhibiting an expectation that such communication is not subject to interception under circumstances justifying such expectation but such terms does not include any electronic communication;
  - "Wire communication" means any aural transmission made in whole or part through the use of facilities for the transmission of communication by the aid of wire, cable or other like connection between the point of origin and the point of reception (including the use of such connection in switching station) and such term includes any electronic storage of such communication).
  - The Central Government or the State Government, as the case may be, may appoint an officer not below the rank of Secretary to the Government in case of State Government and not below the rank of Joint Secretary to the Government in the case of Central Government, to be the Competent Authority for the purpose of this Chapter.

- • A police officer not below the rank of Superintendent of Police supervising the investigation of any terrorist act under this ordinance may submit an application in writing to the Competent Authority for an order authorizing or approving the intercepting of wire, electronic or oral communication by the investigating officer when he believes that such interception may provide, or has provided evidence of any offence involving a terrorist act.
- Each application shall include the following information :-
  - The identity of the investigating officer making the application, and the head of the department authorizing the application.
  - A statement of the facts and circumstances relied upon by the applicant to justify his belief that an order should be issued, including-
    - Details as to the offence of terrorist act that has been, is being, or is about to be committed;
    - A particular description of the nature and location of the facilities from which or a place where the communication is to be intercepted.
    - A particular description of the type of communications sought to be intercepted; and
    - The identity of the person, if known, committing the terrorist act whose communications are to be intercepted.
  - A statement of the period of time for which the interception is required to be maintained, if the nature of the enquiry is such that the authorization of interception should not automatically terminate after the described type of communication has been first obtained;
  - A particular description of facts establishing probable cause to believe that additional communications of the same type will occur thereafter; and
  - Where the application is for the extension of an order, a statement setting forth the results thus far obtained from the interception, or a reasonable explanation of the failure to obtain such result.
  - The Competent Authority may require the applicant to furnish additional oral or documentary evidence in support of the application.
- • Upon such application, the Competent Authority may reject the application, or issue or order, as requested or as modified, authorizing or approving interception of wire, electronic or oral communications, if the Competent Authority determines on the basic of the facts submitted by the applicant that-

- There is a probable cause for belief that an individual is committing, has committed, or is about to commit a particular offence described and made punishable under section 3 and 6, of this ordinance.
- There is a probable cause of belief that particular communications concerning that offence may be obtained through such interception.
- There is probable cause of belief that the facilities from which, or the place where, the wire, electronic or oral communications are to be intercepted are being used or are about to be used, in connection with the commission or such offence, leased to, or are listed in the name of or commonly used by such person.
- Each order by the Competent Authority authorizing or approving the interception of any wire, electronic or oral communication under this section shall specify-
- The identity of the person, if known, whose communications are to be intercepted.
- The nature and location of the communication facilities as to which, or the place where, authority to intercept is granted.
- The period of time during which such interception is authorized, including a statement as to whether or not the interception shall automatically terminate after the described communication has been first obtained.
- • The competent authority shall immediately after passing the order under sub-section of section 38, but in any case not later than seven days from the passing of the order, submit a copy of the same to the Review Committee constituted under section 59 along with all the relevant underlying papers, record and his own findings, in respect of the said order, for consideration and approval of the order by the Review Committee.
- An order authorizing the interception of a wire, electronic or oral communication under the section shall, upon request of the applicant, direct that a provider of wire or electronic communication service, landlord, custodian or other person shall furnish to the applicant forthwith all information, facilities, and technical assistance necessary to accomplish the interception unobtrusively and with a minimum of interference with the services that such service provider, landlord, custodian, or person is providing to the person whose communications are to be intercepted.
- • No order issued under this section may authorize or approve the interception of any wire, electronic or oral communication for any period longer than is necessary to achieve the objective

of the authorization, nor in any event longer than sixty days and such sixty days period shall begin on the day immediately preceding the day on which the investigation officer first begins to conduct an interception under the order or ten days after order is issued whichever is earlier.

- The extension of an order may be granted, but only upon an application for an extension made in accordance with sub-section 37 and the Competent Authority making the findings required by sub-section (i) of section 38, and the period of such extension shall be no longer than the Competent Authority deems necessary to achieve the purposes for which it was granted and in no event for longer than sixty days at a time.
- Every order and extension thereof shall contain a provision that the authorization to intercept shall be executed as soon as practicable and shall be conducted in such manner as to minimize the interception of communications not otherwise subject to interception under this section and shall terminate upon attainment of the authorized objective, or in any event on the expiry of the period of said order or extension thereof.
- • An interception under this Chapter may be conducted in whole or in part by a public servant, acting under the supervision of the investigating officer authorized to conduct the interception.
- Whenever an order authorizing an interception is issued pursuant to this section, the order may require reports to be made to the Competent Authority who issued the order showing that progress has been made towards achievement of the authorized objective and the need for continued interception and such report shall be made at such intervals as the Competent Authority may require.
- • Notwithstanding anything contained in any other provision of this section, an officer not below the rank of Additional Director General of Police or a police officer of equivalent rank who reasonably determines that :-
    - An emergency situation exists that involves :-
    - Immediate danger of death or serious physical injury to any person.
    - Conspiratorial activities threatening the security or interest of the State, or
    - Conspiratorial activities, characteristic of a terrorist act, that requires a wire, electronic or oral communication to be intercepted before an order from the competent authority authorizing such interception, with due diligence, be obtained, and

- There are grounds on which an order should be issued under this section to authorize such interception.

May authorize, in writing, the investigating officer to intercept such wire, electronic or oral communication, if an application for an order approving the interception is made in accordance with the provisions of sub-sections (1) and (2) of section 37 within forty-eight hours after the interception has occurred, or begins to occur.

- In the absence of an order approving the interception made under sub-section (1), such interception shall immediately terminate when the communication sought is obtained or when the application for the order is rejected, whichever is earlier; and in the event of an application for permitting interception being rejected under sub-section (1) of section 38 or an application under sub-section (1) of section 42 for approval being rejected, or in any other case where the interception is terminated without an order having been issued, the contents of any wire, electronic or oral communication intercepted shall be treated as having been obtained in violation of this section.
- • The contents of any wire, electronic or oral communication intercepted by any means authorized by this section shall as far as possible, be recorded on tape or wire or other comparable device and shall be done in such manner as to protect the recording from editing or other alterations.
- Immediately upon the expiration of the period or order, or extension thereof, such recording shall be made available to the Competent Authority issuing such order and shall be sealed under his directions and kept in the custody of such person or authority as the Competent Authority orders, and such recordings shall not be destroyed except upon an order of the Competent Authority and in any event shall be kept for ten years.
- Applications made and orders issued under this section shall be sealed by the Competent Authority and custody of the applications and orders shall be kept in such manner as the Competent Authority directs, and shall not be destroyed except on an order of the Competent Authority, and in any event shall be kept for ten years.
- Notwithstanding anything in the Code, or in any other law for the time being in force, the evidence collected through the interception of wire, electronic or oral communication under this Chapter shall be admissible as evidence against the accused in the Court during the trial of a case.

  Provided that, the contents of any wire, electronic or oral

communication intercepted pursuant to this Chapter or evidence derived therefrom shall not be received in evidence or otherwise disclosed in any trial, hearing or other proceeding in any court unless each accused has been furnished with a copy of the order of the Competent Authority, and accompanying application under which the interception was authorized or approved not less than ten days before trial, hearing or proceeding.

Provided further that, the period of ten days may be waived by the judge trying the matter if he comes to the conclusion that it was not possible to furnish the accused with the above information ten days before the trial, hearing or proceeding and that the accused will not be prejudiced by the delay in receiving such information.

- • The Review Committee constituted by the Central Government or the State Government, as the case may be shall review every order passed by the Competent Authority under section 38.
  - Every order passed by the Competent Authority under section 38, or disapproved by the officer under section 42, shall be placed before the Review Committee, which shall be considered by the Review Committee within ten days after its receipt, to decide whether the order, was necessary, reasonable and justified.
  - The Review Committee, after examining the entire record and holding such inquiry if any, deemed necessary may, by order in writing, either approved the order passed by the Competent Authority or may issue order disapproving the same.
  - On issue of an order of disapproval by the Review Committee, the interception, if any, already commenced shall be forthwith discontinued and the intercepted communication, if any, in the form of tape, wire or other device shall, thereupon, not be admissible as evidence in any case and shall be directed to be destroyed.
  - Except as otherwise specifically provided in section 38, any police officer who—
  - Intentionally intercepts, endeavours to intercept, or procures any other person to intercept or endeavour to intercept any wire, electronic or oral communication.
  - Intentionally uses, endeavours to use, or procure any other person to use or endeavours to use any electronic, mechanical or other device to intercept any oral communication when:
    - Such device is affixed to, or otherwise transmits a signal through a wire, cable, or other like connection used in wire communication; or

- Such device transmits communications by radio, or interferes with the transmission of such communication;
- Intentionally discloses, or endeavours to disclose to any other person the contents of any wire, electronic or oral communication, knowing or having reason to know that the information was obtained through the interception of a were, electronic or oral communication in violation of this Chapter.
- Intentionally uses, or endeavours to use, the contents of any wire, electronic or oral communication, knowing or having reason to know that the information was obtained through the interception of a wire, electronic or oral communication in violation of this Chapter or
- Intentionally discloses, or endeavours to disclose, to any other unauthorized person the contents of any were, electronic or oral communication, intercepted by means authorized by section 38.
- Intentionally continues the interception of wire, electronic or oral communication after the issue of an order of rejection by the Competent Authority under this Chapter.
- Intentionally continues the interception of wire, electronic or oral communication after the issue of an order of disapproval by the Review Committee under sub-section (3) of section 45.

Shall for such violation be punishable with imprisonment for a term which may extend to one year and with fine up to rupees fifty thousand.

- • The Central Government and the State Government as the case may be, shall cause an annual report to be prepared giving a full account of –
  - The number of applications for authorization of interceptions received by the Competent Authority from the Police Department in which persecutions have been launched.
  - The number of such applications permitted or rejected.
  - The number of interceptions carried out in emergency situations and the number of approvals granted or rejected in such matters.
  - The number of prosecutions launched based on such interceptions and convictions resulting from such interceptions along with an explanatory memorandum giving general assessment of the utility and importance of the interceptions authorised.
  - An annual report shall be laid by the State Government before the State Legislature within three months of the completion of every calendar year.

Provided that, if the State Government is of the opinion that the inclusion of any matter in the annual report would be prejudicial to the security of the State or to the prevention or detection of any terrorist act, the State Government may exclude such matter from being included in such annual report.

- An annual report shall be laid by the Central Government before each House of Parliament within three months of the completion of every calendar year:

Provided that, if the Central Government is of the opinion that the inclusion of any matter in the annual report would be prejudicial to the security of the country or to the prevention or detection of any terrorist act, the Central Government may exclude such matter from being included in such annual report.

Chapter VI
Miscellaneous

- • Notwithstanding anything contained in the Code or any other law, every offence punishable under this Ordinance shall be deemed to be a cognizable offence within the meaning of clause © of section 2 of the Code, and "cognizable case" as defined in that clause shall be construed accordingly.
- Section 167 of the Code shall apply in relation to a case involving an offence punishable under this Ordinance subject to the modification that in sub-section (2) :-
  - The references to "fifteen days", "ninety days" and "sixty days", wherever they occur, shall be construed as references to "thirty days," "ninety days" and "ninety days", respectively, and
  - after the proviso, the following proviso shall be inserted, namely :-

    "Provided further that if it is not possible to complete the investigation within the said period of ninety days, the Special Court shall extend the said period up to one hundred and eighty days, on the report of the Public Prosecutor indicating the progress of the investigation and the specific reasons for the detention of the accused beyond the said period of ninety days :

    Provided also that if the police officer making the investigation under this Ordinance, requests, for the purposes of investigation, for police custody from judicial custody of any person from judicial custody, he shall file an affidavit stating the reasons for doing so and shall also explain the delay, if any, for requesting such police custody.

- Section 268 of the code shall apply in relation to case involving an offence punishable under this Ordinance subject to the modification that :-
- The reference in sub-section (1) thereof :-
  - To "the State Government" shall be construed as a reference to "the Central Government or the State Government",
  - To "order of the State Government" shall be construed as a reference to "order of the Central Government or the State Government, as the case may be" and
- The reference in sub-section (2) thereof, to "State Government" shall be construed as a reference to "Central Government or the State Government, as the case may be".
- Sections 366, 367 and 371 of the Code shall apply in relation to any case involving an offence triable by a Special Court subject to the modification that the reference to "Court of Session", wherever occurring therein, shall be construed as the reference to "Special Court".
- Nothing in section 438 of the Code shall apply in relation to any case involving the arrest of any person accused of having committed an offence punishable under this Ordinance.
- Notwithstanding anything contained in the Code, no person accused of an offence punishable under this Ordinance shall, if in custody, be released on bail or on his own bond unless the Court gives the Public Prosecutor an opportunity of being heard.
- Where the Public Prosecutor opposes the application of the accused to release on bail, no person accused of an offence punishable under this Ordinance or any rule made thereunder shall be released on bail until the court is satisfied that there are grounds for believing that he is not guilty of committing such offence :

Provided that after the expiry of a period of one year from the date of detention of the accused for an offence under this Ordinance, the provisions of sub-section (6) of this section shall apply:-

- The restrictions on granting of bail specified in sub-section (6) and (7) are in addition to the restrictions under the Code or any other law for the time being in force on granting of bail.
- Notwithstanding anything contained in sub-section (6), (7) and (8) no bail shall be granted to a person accused of an offence punishable under this Ordinance, if he is not an Indian citizen

and has entered the country unauthorised or illegally except in very exceptional circumstances and for reasons to be recorded in writing.

- No Court shall take cognizance of any offence under this Ordinance without the previous sanction of the Central Government or as the case may be, the State Government.
- Notwithstanding anything contained in the Code, no police officer
  - In the case of the Delhi Special Police Establishment, not below the rank of a Deputy Superintendent of Police or a police officer of equivalent rank.
  - In the metropolitan areas of Mumbai, Kolkata, Chennai and Ahmedabad and any other metropolitan area notified as such under sub-section (1) of section 8 of the Code, not below the rank of an Assistant Commissioner of Police.
  - In any other case not relatable to clause (a) or clause (b) not below the rank of a Deputy Superintendent of Police or a police officer of an equivalent rank. Shall investigate any offence punishable under this Ordinance.
- • Where a police officer arrests a person, he shall prepare a custody memo of the person arrested.
  - The person arrested shall be informed of his right to consult a legal practitioner as soon as he is brought to the police station.
  - Whenever any person is arrested, information of his arrest shall be immediately communicated by the police officer to a family member or in his absence to a relative of such person by telegram, telephone or by any other means and this fact shall be recorded by the police officer under the signature of the person arrested.
  - The person arrested shall be permitted to meet the legal practitioner representing him during the course of interrogation of the accused person:

Provided that nothing in this sub-section shall entitle the legal practitioner to remain present throughout the period of interrogation.

- • In a prosecution for an offence under sub-section (1) of section 3, if it is proved :-
  - That the arms or explosives or any other substances specified in section 4 were recovered from the possession of the accused and there is reason to believe that such arms or explosives or other substances of a similar nature, were used in the commission of such offence, or
  - That the finger-prints of the accused were found at the site of

the offence or on anything including arms and vehicles used in connection with the commission of such offence the Special Court shall draw adverse inference against the accused.

- In a prosecution for an offence under sub-section (3) of section 3, if it is proved that the accused rendered any financial assistance to a person, having knowledge that such person is accused of or reasonably suspected of and offence under that section, the Special Court shall draw adverse inference against the accused.
- No civil court or other authority shall have or, be entitled to, exercise any jurisdiction, powers or authority in relation to the matters referred to in section 19 and section 39 of the Ordinance.
- • Nothing in this Ordinance shall affect the jurisdiction exercisable by, or the procedure applicable to, any court or other authority under any law relating to the naval, military or air force or other armed forces of the Union.
- For the removal of doubts, it is hereby declared that for the purposes of any such law as is referred to in sub-section (1), a Special Court shall be deemed to be a court of ordinary criminal justice.
- The provisions of this Ordinance shall have effect notwithstanding anything inconsistent therewith contained in any enactment other than this Ordinance or in any instrument having effect by virtue of any enactment other than this Ordinance.
- No suit, prosecution or other legal proceeding shall lie against the Central Government or a State Government or any officer or authority of the Central Government or State Government or any other authority on when powers have been conferred under this Ordinance, for anything which is in good faith done or purposed to be done in pursuance of his Ordinance.

Provided further that no suit, prosecution or other legal proceedings shall lie against any serving member or retired member of the armed forces or other para-military forces in respect of any action taken or purported to be taken by him in good faith, in the course of any operation directed towards combating terrorism.

- • Any police officer who exercises power corruptly or maliciously, knowing that there are no reasonable grounds for proceeding under this Ordinance, shall be punishable with imprisonment which may extend to two years, or with fine, or with both.
- If the Special Court is of opinion that that any person has been corruptly or maliciously proceeded against under this

Ordinance, the court may award such compensation as it deems fit to the person, so proceeded against and it shall be paid by the officer, person, authority or Government, as may be specified in the order.

- Notwithstanding anything contained in any other law for the time being in force, the passport and the arms license of a person, who is charge sheeted for having committed any offence under this Ordinance, shall be deemed to have been impounded for such period as the Special Court may deem fit.
- • The Central Government and each State Government shall, whenever necessary, constitute one or more Review committees for the purposes of this Ordinance.
- Every such Committee shall consist of a Chairperson and such other members not exceeding three and possessing such qualifications as may be prescribed.
- A Chairperson of the Committee shall be a person who is, or who has been, a judge of High Court, who shall be appointed by the Central Government, or as the case may be, the State Government, so however, that the concurrence of the Chief Justice of the High Court shall be obtained in the case of a sitting judge.

Provided that in the case of a Union Territory, the appointment of a person who is a judge of the High Court of a State shall be made as a Chairperson with the concurrence of the Chief Justice of the concerned High Court.

- The High Courts may, by notifications in the Official Gazette, make such rules, if any, as they may deem necessary for carrying out the provisions of this Ordinance Relating to Special Courts within their territories.
- • Without prejudice to the powers of the High Courts to make rules under section 60, the Central Government may, by notification in the Official Gazette, make rules for carrying out the provisions of this Ordinance.
- In particular, and without prejudice to the generality of the foregoing power, such rules may provide for all or any of the following matter, namely,
- Regulating the conduct of persons in respect of arms the control of which is considered necessary or expedient and the removal of such persons from such areas;
- The entry into, and search of -
    - Any vehicle, vessel or aircraft; or
    - Any place, whatsoever,

Reasonably suspected of being used for committing the offences referred to in section 3 or section 4 or for manufacturing or storing anything for the commission of any such offence.

- Conferring powers upon-
    - The Central Government;
    - A State Government;
    - An Administrator of Union Territory under Article 239 of the Constitution.
    - An officer of the Central Government not lower in rank than that of a Joint Secretary; or
    - An officer of a State Government not lower in rank than of a District Magistrate.

To make general or special orders to prevent or deal with terrorist acts.

- The arrest and trial of persons contravening any of the rules or any order made thereunder.
- The punishment of any person who contravenes or attempts to contravene or abets or attempts to abet the contravention of any rule or order made thereunder will imprisonment for a term which may extend to one year or fine or both.
- Providing for the seizure and detention of any property in respect of which such contravention, attempt or abetment as is referred to in clause (e) has been committed and for the adjudication of such seizure and detention, whether by any court or by any other authority.
- Determination of the price of the forfeited property under subsection (2) of section 10.
- The procedure of making application under sub-section (3) of section 19.
    - The qualifications of the members of the Review Committee under sub-section (2) of section 59.

Appendix B

SECURITY COUNCIL RESOLUTION 1373

(28 September 2001)

Reaffirming is unequivocal condemnation of the terrorist acts that took place to New York, Washington, D.C., and Pennsylvania on September 11, the Security Council this evening unanimously adopted a wide-ranging, comprehensive resolution with steps and strategies to combat international terrorism.

By resolution 1373 (2001) the Council also established a Committee of the Council to monitor the resolution's implementation and called on all States to report on actions they had taken to that end no later than 90 days from today.

Under terms of the text, the Council decided that all States should prevent and suppress the financing of terrorism, as well as criminalise the wilful provision or collection of funds for such acts. The funds, financial assets and economic resources of those who commit or attempt to commit terrorist acts or participate in or facilitate the commission of terrorist acts and of persons and entities acting on behalf of terrorist should be also be frozen without delay.

The Council also decided that States should prohibit their national or persons or entities in their territories from making funds, financial assets, economic resources, financial or other related services available to persons who commit or attempt to commit, facilitate or participate in the commission of terrorist acts. States should also refrain from providing any form of support to entities or persons involved in terrorist acts; take the necessary steps to prevent the commission of terrorist acts; deny safe haven to those who finance, plan, support, commit terrorist acts and provide safe havens as well.

By other terms, the Council decided that all States should prevent those who finance, plan, facilitate or commit terrorist acts from using their respective territories for those purpose against other countries and their citizens. States should also ensure that anyone who has participated in the financing, planning, preparation or perpetration or terrorist acts or in supporting terrorist acts is brought to justice. They should also ensure that terrorist acts are established as serious criminal offences in domestic laws and regulations and that the seriousness of such acts is duly reflected in sentences served.

By further terms, the Council decided that States should afford one another the greatest measure of assistance for criminal investigations or criminal proceedings relating to the financing or support of terrorist acts. States should also prevent the movement of terrorists or their groups by effective border controls as well.

Also by the text, the Council called on all States in intensify and accelerate the exchange of information regarding terrorist actions of movements, forged or falsified documents; traffic in arms and sensitive material; use of communications and technologies by terrorist groups; and the threat posed by the possession of weapons of mass destruction.

States were also called on to exchange information and cooperate to prevent and suppress terrorist acts and to take action against the perpetrators of such acts. States should become parties to, and fully implement as soon as possible, the relevant international conventions and protocols to combat terrorist.

By the text, before granting refugee status, all States should take appropriate measures to ensure that the asylum seekers had not planned, facilitated or participated in terrorist acts. Further, States should ensure that refugee status was not abused by the perpetrators, organisers or facilitators or terrorist acts, and that claims of political motivation were not recognised as grounds for refusing requests for the extradition of alleged terrorist.

The Council noted with concern the close connection between international terrorism and organisational crime, illicit drugs, money laundering and illegal movement of nuclear, chemical, biological and other deadly materials. In that regards, it emphasised the need to enhance the coordination of national, sub-regional, regional and international efforts to strengthen a global response to that threat to international security.

Reaffirming the need to combat by all means, in accordance with the Charter, threats to international peace and security caused by terrorist acts, the Council expressed its determination to take all necessary steps to fully implement the current resolution.

The meeting, which began at 10.50 p.m. adjourned at 10.53 p.m.

Resolution

- The full text of resolution 1373 (2001) reads as follows:
- The Security Council, "Reaffirming its resolutions 1269 (1999) of 1999 and 1368 (2001) September 12, 2001.

"*Reaffirming* also its unequivocal condemnation of the terrorist attacks which took place in New York, Washington, D.C., and Pennsylvania on September 11, 2001, and expressing its determination to prevent all such acts,

"*Reaffirming* further that such acts, like any act of international terrorism, constitute a threat international peace and security,

"*Reaffirming* the inherent right of individual or collective self-defence as recognised by the Charter of the United Nations as reiterated in resolution 1368 (2001),

"*Reaffirming* the need to combat by all means, in accordance with the Charter of the United Nations, threats to international peace and security caused by terrorist acts,

"*Deeply* concerned by the increase, in various regions of the world, of acts of terrorism motivated by intolerance or extremism,

"*Calling* on States to work together urgently to prevent and suppress terrorist acts, including through increased cooperation and full implementation of the relevant international convention relating to terrorism.

"*Recognising* the need for States to complement international cooperation by taking additional measures to prevent and suppress, in their terrorist through all lawful means, the financing and preparation of any acts of terrorism,

"*Reaffirming* the principle established by the General Assembly in its declaration of October 1970 resolution 2525 (CCD) and reiterated by the Security Council in its resolution 1189 (1998) of August 13, 1998, namely that every State has the duty to refrain from organising, instigating, assisting or participating in terrorist acts in another State or acquiescing in organised activities within its territory directed towards the commission of such acts,

"Acting under Chapter VI of the Charter of the United Nations,

"* Decides that all States shall:

"* Prevent and suppress the financing of terrorist acts;

"* Criminalise the wilful provision or collection, by any means, directly or indirectly, of funds by their nationals or in their territories with the intention that the funds should be used, or in the knowledge that they are to be used, in order to carry out terrorist acts;

"* Freeze without delay funds and other financial assets or economic resources of persons who commit, or attempt to commit, terrorist acts or participate in or facilitate the commission of terrorist acts; of entities owned or controlled directly or indirectly by such persons; and of persons and entities acting on behalf of, or at the direction of such persons and entities, including fund derived or generated from property owned or controlled directly or indirectly by such persons and associated persons and entities;

"* Prohibit their nationals or any persons and entities within their territories from making any funds, financial assets or economic resources or financial or other related services available, directly or indirectly, for the benefit of persons who commit or attempt to commit or facilitate or participate in the commission of terrorist acts, of entitles owned or controlled, directly or indirectly, by such persons and of persons and entitles acting on behalf of or at the direction of such persons;

"* Decides also that all States shall;

"* Refrain from providing any from the support, active or passive, to entities or persons involved in terrorist acts, including by suppressing recruitment of members of terrorist groups and eliminating the supply of weapons to terrorists;

"* Take the necessary steps to prevent the commission of terrorist acts, including by provision of early warning to other States by exchange of information;

"* Deny safe haven to those who finance, plan, support, or commit terrorist acts, or provided safe havens;

"* Prevent those who finance, plan, facilitate or commit terrorist acts from using their respective terrorists for those purpose against other States or their citizens;

"* Ensure that any person who participates in the financing, planning, preparation or perpetration of terrorist acts or in supporting terrorist acts is brought to justice and ensure that, in addition to any other measures against them such terrorist acts are established as serious criminal offences in domestic laws and regulations and that the punishment duly reflects the seriousness of such terrorist acts;

"* Afford one another the greatest measure of assistance in connection with criminal investigation or criminal proceedings relating to the financing or support of terrorist acts, including assistance in obtaining evidence in their possession necessary for the proceeding.

"* Prevent the movement of terrorists or terrorist groups by effective border controls and controls on issuance of identify papers and travel documents, and through measures for preventing counterfeiting, forgery of fraudulent use of identity papers and travel documents

"* Calls upon all States to:

"* Find ways of intensifying and accelerating the exchange of operational information, especially regarding actions of movements or terrorist persons or networks; forged or falsified travel documents; traffic in arms, explosive or sensitive materials; use of communications technologies by terrorist groups; and the threat posted by the possession of weapons of mass destruction by terrorists groups.

"* Exchange information in accordance with international and domestic law and cooperate on administrative and judicial matters to prevent the commission of terrorist acts.

"* Cooperate, particularly through bilateral and multilateral arrangements and agreements, to prevent and suppress terrorist attacks and take action against perpetrations of such acts;

"* Become parties as soon as possible to the relevant international conventions and protocols relating to terrorism, including the International Convention for the Suppression of the Financing of Terrorism of December 9, 1999,

"* Increase cooperation and fully implement and relevant international conventions and protocols relating to terrorism and Security Council resolutions 1269 (1999) and 1368 (2001) ;

"* Take appropriate measures in conformity with the relevant provisions on national and international law, including international standards of human rights, before granting refugee status, for the purpose of ensuring that the asylum seeker has not planned, facilitated or participated in the commission of terrorist acts.

"* Notes with concern the close connection between international terrorism and transactional organised crime, illicit drugs, money-laundering, illegal arms-trafficking, and illegal movement of nuclear, chemical, biological and other potentially deadly materials, and in this emphasises the need to enhance coordination of efforts on national, sub-regional, regional and international levels in order to strengthen a global response to this serious challenge and threat to international security.

"* Declares that acts, methods, and practices of terrorism are contrary to the purposes and principles of the United Nations and that knowingly financing, planning and inciting terrorist acts are also contrary to the purpose and principles of the United Nations.

"* Decides to establish, in accordance with rule 28 of its provisional rules of procedure, a committee of the Security Council, consisting of all the members of the Council, to monitor implementation of this resolution, with the assistance of appropriate expertise, and calls upon all States to report to the Committee, not later than 90 days from the date of adoption of this resolution and thereafter according to a timetable to be proposed by the Committee, on the steps they have taken to implement this resolution:

"* Direct the Committee to delineate its tasks, submit work programme within 30 days of the adoption of this resolution, and to consider the support it requires, in consultation with the Secretary-General;

"* Express its determination to take all necessary steps in order to the full implementation of this resolution, in accordance with its responsibilities under the Charter;

"* Decides to remain seized of this matter".

Appendix C

UN GENERAL ASSEMBLY, FIFTY-FIVE SESSION, SIXTH COMMITTEE AGENDA ITEM 164, 19TH OCTOBER 2000 WORKING DOCUMENT SUBMITTED BY INDIA ON THE DRAFT COMPREHENSIVE CONVENTION ON INTERNATIONAL TERRORISM

The States Parties to this Convention

Recalling the existing international conventions, relating to various aspects of the problem of international terrorism, in particular the Convention on Offences and Certain Acts Committed on Board Aircraft, signed at Tokyo on September 14, 1963: the Convention for the Suppressions of Unlawful Seizure of Aircraft, signed at the House on December 16, 1970; the Convention for the Suppression of Unlawful Acts against the Safety of Civil Aviation, signed at Montreal on September 23, 1971: the Convention on the Prevention and Punishment of Crimes against Internationally Protected Persons, including Diplomatic Agents, adopted by the General Assembly of the United Nations on December 14, 1973; the International Convention against the Taking of Hostages; adopted by General Assembly of the United Nations on December 17, 1979; the convention on the Physical Protection of Nuclear material, signed at Vienna on March 3, 1980; the Protocol for the Suppression of Unlawful Acts of Violence at Airports Serving International Civil Aviation, Supplementary to the Convention for the Suppression of Unlawful Act against the Safety of Civil Aviation, signed at Montreal on February 24, 1988; the Convention for the Suppression of Unlawful Acts against the Safety of Maritime Navigation, done at Rome on March 10, 1988; the protocol for the Suppression the Unlawful Acts against Safety of Fixed Platforms located on the Continental Shelf, done at Rome on March 10, 1988; the Convention on the Marking of Plastic Explosive for the Purpose of Detection, signed at Montreal on March 1, 1991; the International Convention for the Suppression of Terrorist Bombings, adopted by the General Assembly of the United Nations on December 15, 1997; the International Convention for the suppression of the Financing of Terrorism, adopted by the General Assembly of the United Nations on December 9, 1999.

Recalling also General Assembly resolution 49/60 of December 9, 1994 and the Declaration on Measures to Eliminate International Terrorism annexed thereto.

Recalling further General Assembly resolution 51/20 of

December 17, 1996 and the Declaration to supplement the 1994 Declaration on Measures to Eliminate International Terrorism annexed thereto.

Deeply concerned about the worldwide escalation of acts of terrorism in all its forms which endanger or take innocent lives jeopardize fundamental freedoms and seriously impair the dignity of human being.

Reaffirming their unequivocal condemnation of all acts, methods and practices of terrorism as criminal and unjustifiable, wherever and by whomever committed, including those which jeopardise friendly relations among States and peoples and threaten the territorial integrity and security of States.

Recognising that acts, methods and practices of terrorism constitute a grave violations of the purpose and principles of the United Nations, which may pose a threat to international peace and security, jeopardize friendly relations among States, hinder international cooperation and aim at the undermining of human rights, fundamental freedoms and the democratic basis of society.

Recognising also that the financing, planning and inciting of terrorist acts are also contrary to the purpose and principles of the United Nations, and that it is the duty of the States Parties to bring to justice those who have participated in such terrorist acts.

Convinced that the suppression of acts of international terrorism, including those which are committed or supported by States, directly or indirectly, is an essential element in the maintenance of international peace and security and the sovereignty and territorial integrity of States.

Realising the need for a comprehensive convention on international terrorism.

Have resolved to take effective measures to prevent acts of terrorism and to ensure that perpetrators of terrorist acts do not escape prosecution and punishment by providing for their extradition or prosecution, and to that end have agreed as follows:-

Article 1

For the purpose of this Convention;

- "State or government facility" includes any permanent or temporary facility or conveyance that is used or occupied by representative of a State, members of government, the legislative or the judiciary or by officials or employees of a State or any other public authority or entity or by employees or officials of an intergovernmental organisation in connection with their official duties.
- "Military forces of a State" means the armed forces of a State

which are organised, trained and equipped under its internal law for the primary purpose of national defence or security, and persons acting in support of those armed forces who are under their formal command, control and responsibility.

- "Infrastructure facility" means any publicly or privately owned facility providing or distributing services for the benefit of the public, such as water, sewerage, energy, fuel or communications, and banking services, telecommunications and information networks.
- "Place of public use" means those parts of any building, land, street, waterway or other location that are accessible or open to members of the public, whether continuously, periodically or occasionally, and encompasses any commercial, business, cultural, historical, educational, religious, governmental, entertainment, recreational or similar place that is so accessible or open to the public.
- "Public transportation system" means all facilities, conveyances and instrumentalities, whether publicly or privately owned, that are used in or for publicly available services for the transportation of persons or cargo.

Article 2

- Any person commits an offence within the meaning of this Convention if that person, by any persons, unlawfully and intentionally, does an act intended to cause:
    - Death or serious bodily injury to any persons; or
    - Serious damage to a State or government facility, a public transportation system, communication system or infrastructure facility with the intent to cause extensive destruction of such a place, facility or system, or where such destruction results or is likely to result in major economic loss:

When the purpose of such act, by its nature or context; is to intimidate a population, or to compel a Government or an international organisation to do or abstain from doing any act.

- Any person also commits an offence if that person attempts to commit an offence or participates as an accomplice in an offence as set forth in paragraph 1.
- Any person also commits an offence if that person;
    - Organises, directs or instigates others to commit an offence as set forth in paragraph 1 or 2; or
    - Aids, abets, facilitates or counsels the commission of such an offence; or
    - In any other way contributes to the commission of one or

more offences referred to in paragraphs 1, 2 or 3 (a) by a group of persons acting with a common purpose; such contribution shall be intentional and either be made with the aim of furthering the general criminal activity or purpose of the group or be made in the knowledge of the intention of the group to commit the offence or offences concerned.

Article 3

This Convention shall not apply where the offence is committed within a single State, the alleged offender is a national of that State and is present in the territory of that and no other State has a basis under Article 6, paragraph 1, or Article 6, paragraph 2, to exercise jurisdiction, except that the provisions of Articles 10 or 22 shall, an appropriate, apply in those cases.

Article 4

Each State Party shall adopt such measures as may be necessary;

- To establish a criminal offences under its domestic law the offences set forth in Article 2;
- To make those offences punishable by appropriate penalties, which take into, account the grave nature of those offences.

Article 5

Each State Party shall adopt such measures as may be necessary, including, where appropriate, domestic legislation, to ensure that criminal acts within the scope of this Convention are under no circumstances justifiable by considerations of a political, philosophical, ideological, racial, ethnic, religious or other similar nature.

Article 6

- Each State Party shall take such measures as may be necessary to establish jurisdiction over the offences referred to in Article 2 in the following cases:-
    - When the offence is committed in the territory of that State or on board a ship or aircraft registered in that State.
    - When the alleged offender is a national of that State or is a person who has his or her habitual residence in its territory.
    - When the offence is committed wholly or partially outside its territory, if the effects of the conduct or its intended effects constitute or result, within its territory, in the commission of an offence referred to in Article 2.

- A State may also establish its jurisdiction over any such offence when it is committed.
    - By a stateless person whose habitual residence is in that State; or
    - With respect to a national of that State; or
    - Against a State or government facility of that State abroad, including an embassy or other diplomatic or consular premises of that State; or
    - In an attempt to compel that State to do or abstain form doing any act; or
    - On board a ship or aircraft, which is operated by the government of that State.
- Each State Party shall take such measures an may be necessary to establish its jurisdiction over the offences referred to in article 2 in cases where the alleged offender is present in its territory and where it does not extradite such person to any of the States Parties that have established their jurisdiction in accordance with paragraphs 1 or 2.
- When more than one State Party claims jurisdiction over the offences set forth in article 2. The relevant States parties shall strive to coordinate their actions approximately, in particular concerning the conditions for persecution and the modalities for mutual legal assistance.
- This Convention does not exclude any criminal jurisdiction exercised in accordance with national law.

Article 7

States Parties shall take appropriate measures, before granting asylum, for the purpose of ensuring that asylum is not granted to any person in respect of whom there are reasonable grounds indicating his involvement in any offence referred to in article 2.

Article 8

States Parties shall cooperate in the prevention of the offences set forth in article 2, particularly;

- By taking all practicable measures, including, if necessary, adapting their domestic legislation, to prevent and counter preparation in their respective territories for the commission, by whomsoever and in whatever manner, of those offences within or outside their territories, including.
    - Measures to prohibit in their territories the establishment and operation of installation and training camps for the commission, within or outside their territories, of offences

referred to in article 2; and
- Measure to prohibit the illegal activities of persons, groups and organisations that encourage, instigate, organise, knowingly finance or engage in the commission, within or outside their territories, of offences referred to in Article 2;

- By exchanging accurate and verified information in accordance with their national law, and coordinating administrative and other measures taken as appropriate to prevent the commission of offences as referred to in Article 2.

Article 9

- Each State Party, in accordance with its domestic legal principles, shall take the necessary measures to enable a legal located in its territory or organised under its laws to be held liable when a person responsible for the management or control of that legal entity has, in that capacity, committed an offence referred to in Article 2. Such liability may be criminal, civil or administrative.
- Such liability is incurred without prejudice to the criminal liability of individuals having committed the offences.
- Each State Party shall ensure, in particular, that legal entities liable in accordance with paragraph 1 above are subject to effective, proportionate and dissuasive criminal, civil or administrative sanction. Such sanctions may include monetary sanctions.

Article 10

- Upon receiving information that person who has committed or who is alleged to have committed an offence referred to in Article 2 may be present in its territory, the State Party concerned shall take such measures as may be necessary under its domestic law to investigate the facts contained in the information.
- Upon being satisfied that the circumstances so warrant, the State Party in whose territory the offender or alleged offender its present shall take the appropriate measures under domestic law so as to ensure that person's presence for the purpose of prosecution or extradition.
- Any person regarding whom the measures referred to in paragraph 2 are being taken shall be entitled to:
  - Communicate without delay with the nearest appropriate

representative of the State of which that person is a national or which is otherwise entitled to protect that person's right to, if that person is a stateless person, that State in the territory of which that person habitually resides;

  - Be visited by a representative of that State:
  - Be informed of that person's rights under sub-paragraphs (a) and (b).

- The rights referred to in paragraph 3 shall be exercised in conformity with the laws and regulations of the State in the territory of which the offender or alleged offender is present, subject to the provision that the said laws and regulations must enable full effect to be given to the purposes for which the rights accorded under paragraph 3 are intended.
- The provisions of paragraphs 3 and 4 shall be without prejudice to the right of any State Party having a claim to jurisdiction in accordance with Article 6, paragraph 1 (b) or 2 (b), to invite the International Committee of the Red Cross to communicate with and visit the alleged offender.
- When a State Party, pursuant to the present article, has taken a person into custody it shall immediately notify, directly or through the Secretary-General of the United Nations, the States Parties which have established jurisdiction in accordance with Article 6, paragraph 1 or 2, or if it considers it advisable, any other interested States Parties, of the fact that such person is in custody and of the circumstances which warrant that person's detention. The State which makes the investigation contemplated in paragraph 1 shall promptly inform the said States Parties of its findings and shall indicate whether it intends to exercise jurisdiction.

Article 11

- The State Party in whose territory the alleged offender is found shall, if it does not extradite the person, be obliged, without exception whatsoever and whether or not the offence was committed in its territory, to submit the case to its competent authorities for the purpose of prosecution through proceedings in accordance with the laws of the State. Those authorities shall take their decision in the same manner as in the case of any ordinary offence of a grave nature under the law of that State.
- Whatever a State Party is permitted under its domestic law to extradite or otherwise surrender one of its nationals only upon the condition that the person will be returned to that State to

served the sentence imposed as a result of the trial or proceeding for which the extradition or surrender of the person was sought, and that State and the State seeking her extradition of the person agree with this option and other terms they may deem appropriate, such a conditional extradition or surrender shall be sufficient to discharge the obligation set forth in paragraph 1.

Article 12

Any person who is taken into custody or regarding whom any other measure are taken or proceedings are carried out pursuant to this Convention shall be guaranteed fair treatment, including enjoyment of all rights and guarantees in conformity with the law of the State in the territory of which that person and applicable provisions of international law, including international human rights law.

Article 13

- States Parties shall afford one another the greatest measure of assistance in connection with investigations or criminal or extradition proceedings brought in respect of the offences set forth in Article 2, including assistance in obtaining evidence at their disposal necessary for the proceedings.
- States Parties shall carry out their obligations under paragraphs 1 in conformity with any treaties or other arrangements on mutual legal assistance that may exist between them. In the absence of such treaties or arrangements. States Parties shall afford one another assistance in accordance with their domestic law.
- States Parties, which are not bound by a bilateral treaty or arrangement of mutual legal assistance, may, at their discretion, apply the procedure set out in annex II.

Article 14

None of the offences referred to in Article 2 and the acts which constitute an offence within the scope of and as defined in one of the treaties listed in Annex I shall be regarded, for the purpose of extradition or mutual legal assistance, as a political offence or as an offence connected with a political offence or as an offence inspired by political motives. Accordingly, a request for extradition or for mutual legal assistance based on such an offence may not be refused on the sole ground that it concerns a political offence or an offence connected with a political offence or an offence inspired by political motives.

Article 15

Nothing in this Convention shall be interpreted as imposing an obligation to extradite or to afford mutual legal assistance, if the requested State Party has substantial ground for believing that the request for extradition for offences set forth in Article 2 or for mutual legal assistance with respect to such offences has been made for the purpose of prosecuting or punishing a person on account of that person's race, religion, nationality, ethnic origin or political opinion or that compliance with the request would cause prejudice to that person's position for any of these reasons.

Article 16

- A person who is being detained or is serving a sentence in the territory of one State Party whose presence in another State Party is requested for purposes of identification, testimony or otherwise providing assistance in obtaining evidence for the investigation or prosecution of offences under this Convention may be transferred if the following conditions are met:
  - The person freely gives his or her informed consent; and
  - The competent authorities of both States Parties agree, subject to such conditions, as those State Parties may deem appropriate;
  - For the purpose of this article;
  - The State to which the person is transferred shall have the authority and obligation to keep the person transferred in custody, unless otherwise requested or authorised by the State from which the person was transferred;
  - The State to which the person is transferred shall without delay implement its obligation to return the person to the custody of the State from which the person was transferred as agreed beforehand or as otherwise agreed, by the competent authorities of both States;
  - The State to which the person is transferred shall not require the State from which the person was transferred to initiate extradition proceedings for the return of the person;
  - The person transferred shall receive credit for service of the sentence being served in the State from which he was transferred for the time spent in the custody of the State to which he was transferred.
- Unless the State Party from which a person is to be transferred in accordance with this article so agrees. That person, whatever his or her nationality, shall not be prosecuted or detained or

subjected to any other restriction of his or her personal liberty in the territory of the State to which that person is transferred in respect of acts or convictions anterior to his or her departure from the territory of the State from which such person was transferred.

Article 17

- The offences referred to in Article 2 shall be deemed to be included as extraditable offences in any extradition treaty existing between any of the States Parties before the entry into force of this Convention. States Parties undertake to include such offences as extraditable offences in every extradition treaty to be subsequently concluded between them.
- When a State Party which makes extradition conditional on the existence of a treaty receives a request from another State Party with which it has no extradition treaty, the requested State may, at its option, consider this convention as a legal basis for extradition in respect of the offences set forth in Article 2. Extradition shall be subject to the other conditions provided by the law of the requested State.
- States Parties which do not make extradition conditional on the existence of a treaty shall recognise the offences referred to in Article 2 as extraditable offences between themselves, subject to the conditions provided for by the law of the requested State.
- If necessary, the offences set forth in Article 2 shall be treated, for the purposes of extradition between States Parties, as if they had been committed not only in the place in which they occurred but also in the territory of the States that have established jurisdiction in accordance with Article 6, paragraphs 1 and 2.
- The provisions of all extradition treaties and arrangements between States Parties with regard to offences set forth in Article 2 shall be deemed to be modified as between States Parties to the extent that they are incompatible with this Convention.
- States Parties which, pursuant to paragraph 2 of this article, have agreed to consider this Convention as a legal basis for extradition in respect of the offences set forth in Article 2 may consider utilising the procedures set out in Annex III.

Article 18

- Nothing in this Convention shall affect other rights, obligations and responsibilities of States and individuals under international law, in particular the purposes and principles of the Charter of the United Nations in international humanitarian law.

- The activities armed forces during an armed conflict, as those terms are understood under international law, which are governed by that law, are not governed by this Convention, and the activities undertaken by the military forces of a State in the exercise of their official duties, inasmuch as they are governed by other rules of international law, are not governed by this Convention.

Article 19

The State Party where the alleged offender is prosecuted shall, in accordance with its domestic law or applicable procedures, communicate the final outcome of the proceedings to the Secretary-General of the United Nations, who shall transmit the information to the other States Parties.

Article 20

The States Parties shall carry out their obligations under the Convention in a manner consistent with the principles of sovereign equality and territorial integrity of States and that of non-intervention in the domestic affairs of other States.

Article 21

Nothing in this Convention shall affect other rights, obligations and responsibilities of States and individuals under international law, in particular the purpose of the Charter of the United Nations, international humanitarian law and other relevant conventions.

Article 22

Nothing in this Convention entitles a State Party to undertake in the territory of another State Party the exercise of jurisdiction or performance of functions, which are exclusively, reserved for the authorities of that other State by its domestic law.

Article 23

- Any dispute between two or more States Parties, concerning the interpretation or application of this Convention which can not be settled through negotiation within a reasonable time shall, at the request of one of them, be submitted to arbitration. If, within six months from the date of the request for arbitration, the parties are unable to agree on the organisation of the arbitration, any one of those parties may refer the disputes to the International Court of Justice, by application, in conformity with the Statute of the Court.

- Each State may at the time of signature, ratification, acceptance or approval of this Convention or accession thereto declare that it does not consider itself bound by paragraph 1. The other States Parties shall not be bound by paragraph 1 with respect to any State Party which had made such a reservation.
- Any State, which has made a reservation in accordance with paragraph 2, may at any time withdraw that reservation by notification to the Secretary-General of the United Nations.

Article 24

- This Convention is open for signature by all States from .... To. United Nations Headquarters in New York.
- This Convention is subject to ratification, acceptance or approval. The instruments of ratification, acceptance or approval shall be deposited with the Secretary-General of the United Nations.
- This Convention shall be open to accession by any State. The instruments of accession shall be deposited with the Secretary-General of the United Nations.

Article 25

- This Convention shall enter into force thirty days after twenty-two instruments of ratification, acceptance, approval or accession have been deposited with the Secretary-General of the United Nations.
- For each State ratifying, accepting, approving or acceding to the Convention after the deposit of the twenty-second instrument of ratification, acceptance, approval or accession, the Convention shall enter into force on the thirtieth day after the deposit by such State of its instruments of ratification, acceptance, approval or accession.

Article 26

- A State may denounce this Convention by written notification to the Secretary-General of the United Nations.
- Denunciation shall take effect one year following the date on which notification is received by the Secretary-General of the United Nations.

Article 27

The original of this Convention, of which the Arabic, Chinese, English, French, Russian and Spanish texts are equally authentic, shall be deposited with the Secretary-General of the United Nations, who shall send certified copies thereof to all States.

In witness whereof, the undersigned, being duly authorised thereto by their respective Governments, have signed this Convention, opened for signature at United Nations Headquarters in New York on ... 2000.

Annexure I

- Convention on Offences and Certain Acts Committed on Board Aircraft, signed at Tokyo on 14 September, 1963.
- Convention for the Suppression of Unlawful Seizure of Aircraft, signed at The Hague on 16 December 1970.
- Convention for the Suppression of Unlawful Acts against the Safety of Civil Aviation, signed at Montreal on 23 September 1971.
- Convention on the Prevention and Punishment of Crimes against Internationally Protected Person, including Diplomatic Agents, adopted by the General Assembly of the United Nations on 14 December 1973.
- International Convention against the Taking of Hostages, adopted by the General Assembly of the United Nations on 17 December 1979.
- Convention on the Physical Protection of Nuclear Material, signed at Vienna on 03 March 1980.
- Protocol for the Suppression of Unlawful Acts of Violence at Airports Serving International Civil Aviation, supplementary to the Convention for the Suppression of Unlawful Acts against the Safety of Civil Aviation, signed at Montreal on 24 February 1988.
- Convention for the Suppression of Unlawful Acts against the Safety of Maritime Navigation, done at Rome on 10 March 1988.
- Protocol for the Suppression of Unlawful Acts against the Safety of Fixed Platforms Located on the Continental Shelf, done at Rome on 10 March 1988.
- Convention on the Making of Plastic Explosive for the Purpose of Detection, signed at Montreal on 01 March 1991.
- International Convention for the Suppression of Terrorist Bombings, adopted by the General Assembly of the United Nations on 15 December 1997.
- International Convention for the Suppression of the Financing to Terrorism, adopted by the General Assembly of the United Nations on 9 December 1999.

Annexure II
Procedure for Mutual Legal Assistance

- States Parties shall afford one another, pursuant to this Annex, the widest measure of mutual legal assistance in investigations, prosecutions and judicial proceedings in relation to criminal offences established in accordance with Article 3.
- Mutual legal assistance to be afforded in accordance with this Annex may be requested for any of the following purpose:-
    - Taking evidence or statements from persons;
    - Effecting service of judicial documents;
    - Executing searches and seizures;
    - Examining objects and sites;
    - Providing information and evidentially items;
    - Providing originals or certified copies of relevant documents and records, including bank, financial, corporate or business records;
    - Identifying or tracing proceeds, property, instrumentalities or other things for evidentiary purpose.
- States Parties may afford one another any other forms of mutual legal assistance allowed by the domestic law of the requested party.
- Upon request, States Parties shall facilitate or encourage, to the extent consistent with their domestic law and practice, the presence or availability of persons, including persons in custody, who consent to assist in investigations or participate in proceedings.
- A State shall not decline to render mutual legal assistance under this Annex on the ground of bank secrecy.
- The provisions of this Annex shall not affect the obligations under any other treaty bilateral or multilateral, which governs or will govern, in whole or in part, mutual legal assistance in criminal matters.
- The States Parties may apply, at their discretion, paragraphs 8 to 19 of this Annex to requests made pursuant to this Annex if they are not otherwise bound by any treaty of mutual legal assistance. If the States Parties are bound by such a treaty, the corresponding provisions of that treaty shall apply unless the States Parties agree to apply paragraphs 8 to 19 of this Annex in lieu thereof,
- States Parties shall designate an authority or, when necessary, authorities, which shall have the responsibility and power to execute requests for mutual legal assistance or to transmit them to the competent authorities for execution. The authority or the authorities designated for this purpose shall be notified

to the Secretary-General of the United Nations. Transmission of requests for mutual legal assistance and any communication related thereto shall be effected between the authorities designated by the States Parties; this requirement shall be without prejudice to the right of the State to require that such requests and communication be addressed to it through the diplomatic channel and, in urgent circumstances, where the States agree, through channels of the International Criminal Police Organisation –Interpol, if possible.

- Requests shall be made in writing in a language acceptable to the requested State. The language or language acceptable to each State shall be notified to the Secretary-General of the United Nations. In urgent circumstances, and where agreed by the States Parties, requests may be made orally, but shall be confirmed in writing forthwith.
- A request for mutual legal assistance shall contain;
    - The identity of the authority making the request;
    - The subject matter and nature of the investigation, prosecution or proceedings to which the request relates, and the name and the functions of the authority, conducting such investigation, prosecuting or proceeding;
    - A summary of the relevant facts, except in respect of requests for the purpose of service of judicial documents;
    - A description of the assistance sought and details of any particular procedure the
    - Where possible, the identity, location and nationality of any person concerned;
    - The purpose for which the evidence information or action is sought.
- The requested State may request additional information when it appears necessary for the execution of the request in accordance with its domestic law or when it can facilitate such execution.
- A request shall be executed in accordance with the domestic law of the requested State and, to the extent not contrary to the domestic law of the requested State and where possible, in accordance with the procedures specified in the request.
- The requesting State shall not transmit or use information or evidence furnished by the requested State for investigation, prosecutions or proceedings other than those stated in the request without the prior consent of the requested State.
- The requesting State may require that the requested State keep confidential the fact and substance of the request, except

to the extent necessary to execute the request. If the requested State cannot comply with the requirement of confidentiality, it shall promptly inform the requesting State.

- Mutual legal assistance may be refused;
    - If the request is not made in conformity with the provisions of this Annex.
    - If the requested State considers that execution of the request is likely to prejudice its sovereignty, security, public order to other essential interests;
    - If the authorities of the requested State would be prohibited by its domestic law from carrying out the action requested with regard to any similar offence, had it been subject to investigation, prosecution or proceedings under their own jurisdiction.
    - If it would be contrary to the legal system of the requested State relating to mutual legal assistance for the request to be granted.
- Any assistance under this Annex may not be refused on the sole ground that it concerns a political offence or an offence connected with a political offence or an offence inspired by political motives.
- Reasons shall be given for any refusal of mutual legal assistance.
- The requested State may postpone mutual legal assistance on the ground that it interferes with an ongoing investigation prosecution or proceeding. In such a case, the requested State shall consult with the requesting State to determine if the assistance can still be given subject to such terms and conditions as the requested State deems necessary.
- A witness, experts or other person who consents to give evidence in a proceeding or to assist in an investigation, prosecution or judicial proceeding in the territory of the requesting State shall not be prosecuted, detained, punished or subjected to any other restriction of his or her personal liberty in that territory in respect of acts, omissions or convictions prior to his departure from the territory of the requested State. Such safe conduct shall cease when the witness, expert or other person having had, for a period of fifteen consecutive days, or for any period agreed upon by the States Parties from the date on which he or she has been officially informed that his or her presence is no longer required by the judicial authorities, an opportunity of leaving, has nevertheless remained voluntarily in the territory or, having left it, has returned of his or her

own free will.

- The ordinary costs of executing a request shall be borne by the requested State, unless otherwise agreed by the States concerned. If expenses of a substantial or extraordinary nature are or will be required to fulfil the request, the States Parties shall consult to determine the terms and conditions under which the request will be executed as well as the manner in which the costs shall be borne.
- The States Parties shall consider, as may be necessary, the possibility of concluding bilateral or multilateral agreements or arrangements that would serve the purposes of, give practical effect to, or enhance the provisions of this Annexure.

Annexure III
Extradition Procedure

- The offences referred to in Article 2 shall be deemed to be included as extraditable offences in any extradition treaty existing between States Parties. The States Parties undertake to include such offences as extraditable offences in every extradition treaty to be concluded between them.
- The States Parties that do not make extradition conditional on the existence of a treaty shall recognise the offences referred to in Article 2 as extraditable offences between themselves subject to the conditions provided for by the law of the requested State.
- The offences referred to in Article 2 shall be treated, for the purpose of extradition between States Parties , as if they had been committed not only in the place in which they occurred but also in the territories of the requested States Parties.
- The States Parties may at their discretion, apply paragraphs 5 to 18 of this Annex to requests for extradition in respect of offences referred to in Article 2 if they are not bound by a treaty of extradition. If these State are bound by such a treaty, the corresponding provisions of that treaty shall apply unless the States agree to apply paragraphs 5 to 18 of this Annex in lieu thereof.
- States Parties shall designate an authority, or when necessary, authorities, which shall have the responsibility and power to execute requests for extradition or to transmit them to the competent authorities for execution. The authority or a authorities designated for this purpose shall be notified to the

Secretary-General of the United Nations. Transmission of requests for extradition and any communication related thereto shall be effected between the authorities designated by the States Parties, this requirement shall be without prejudice to the right of a State to require that such requests and communications be addressed to it through diplomatic channels and, in urgent circumstance, where the States Parties agree, through channels of the International Criminal Police Organisation – Interpol, if possible.

- Requests shall be made in writing in a language acceptable to the requested State. In urgent circumstance, and where agreed by the States Parties, requests may be made orally, but shall be confirmed in writing forthwith.
- A request for extradition shall contain.:
  - The identity of the authority making the request.
  - As accurate a description as possible of the person sought, together with any other information, which would help to establish the identity, location and nationality of the person concerned.
  - A summary of the facts of the offence for which extradition is requested;

    and
  - The test, if any, of the law defining that offence and prescribing the maximum punishment for that offence.
- If the request relates to a person already convicted and sentenced, it shall also be accompanied by:
  - A certificate of the conviction and sentence; and
  - A statement that the person is not entitled to question the conviction and sentence and showing how much of the sentence has not been carried out.
- If the requested State considers that the evidence produced or information supplied is not sufficient in order to enable a decision to be taken as to the request, additional evidence or information shall be submitted within such time as the requested State may require.
- A request shall be executed in accordance with the domestic law of the requested State and, to the extent not contrary to the domestic law of the requested State and where possible, in accordance with the procedures specified in the request.
- The requesting State shall not transmit or use information or evidence furnished by the requested State for investigations, prosecutions or proceedings other than those stated in the request without the prior consent of the

requested State.

- Any person who is returned to the territory of the requesting State under this Convention shall not be dealt with in the territory of the requesting State for or in respect of any offence committed before he was returned to that territory other than the offence in respect of which he was returned, any lesser offence disclosed by the facts proved for the purpose of securing his return other than an offence in relation to which an order for his return could not lawfully be made, or any other offence in respect of which the requested State may consent to his being dealt with.
- The provisions of paragraph 12 of this Annex shall not apply to offences committed after the return of a person under this Annex or matters arising in relation to such offences, or when the person having had the opportunity to leave the territory of the requesting State has not done so within sixty days of his final discharge, or has returned to that territory after having left it.
- If extradition of the same person, whether for the same offence or for different offences, is requested by two States Parties, or by a State and third State with which the requested State has an extradition arrangement, the requested State shall determine to which State the person shall be extradited.
- When a request for extradition is granted, the requested State shall, upon request and as far as its law allows, hand over to the requesting State articles, which may serve as proof for evidence of the offence. If the articles in question are liable to seizure or confiscation in the territory of the requested State, the latter may, in connection with pending proceedings, temporarily retain them or hand them over on condition that they are returned. This provision shall not prejudice the rights of the requested State or any person other than the person sought. When these rights exist, the articles shall on request be returned to the requested State without charge as soon as possible after the end of the proceedings.
- Reasons shall be given for any refusal of extradition.
- If criminal proceedings against the person sought are instituted in the territory of the requested State, or the person in lawfully detained in consequence of criminal proceedings, the decision whether or not to extradite the person may be postponed until the criminal proceedings have been completed or he or she is

no longer detained.

- The ordinary costs of executing a request shall be borne by the requested State, unless otherwise agreed by the States Parties concerned. If expenses of a substantial or extraordinary nature are or will be required to fulfil the request, the State Parties shall consult to determine the terms and conditions under which the request will be executed as well as the manner in which the costs shall be borne.
- The States Parties shall consider, as may be necessary, the possibility of concluding bilateral or multilateral agreements or arrangements that would serve the purpose of, give practical effect to, or enhance the provisions of this Annexure.

Appendix D

THE SAARC CONVENTION (SUPPRESSION OF TERRORISM) ACT (No. 36 of 1993)

(29 April 1993)

An Act to give effect to the South Asian Association for Regional Cooperation Convention on Suppression of Terrorism and for matters connected therewith or incidental thereto:

Whereas a Convention on the Suppression of Terrorism was signed on behalf of the Government effect thereto and formatters connected therewith or incidental thereto;

Be it enacted by Parliament in the Forty-forth Year of the Republic of India as follows:-

- Short titles, extent and application-
  - This Act may be called the SAARC Convention (Suppression of Terrorism) Act 1993.
  - Definition - In this Act, unless the context otherwise requires:-
    - "Convention" means the South Asian Association for Regional Cooperation Convention on Suppression of Terrorism signed at Kathmandu on 4th day of November, 1987 as set out in the Schedule;
    - "Convention country" means a country in which the Convention is for the time being in force.
  - Application of the Convention – Notwithstanding anything to the contrary contained in any other law, the provisions of Arts. I to VII of the Convention shall have the force to law in India.
  - Hostage taking -
    - Whoever, by force or threat of force or by any other form of intimation, seizes or detains any persons and threatens to kill or injure that person with intent to cause a Convention country to do or abstain from doing any act as the means of avoiding the execution of such threat, commits the offence of hostage-taking.
    - Whoever commits the offence of hostage-taking shall be punished with imprisonment for the term, which may extend to ten year, and shall also be liable to fine.
    - Provisions as to Extradition Act – for the purpose of the Extradition Act, 1962 (34 of 1962) in relation to a Convention country, an offence under sub-section (1) of Sec. 4 or other offence specified in Art. I of the Convention

shall not be considered to be an offence of a political character.

- Offence Committee outside India-
  - When an offence under sub-section (1) of Sec. 4 or offence specified in Art. I of the Convention is committed outside India-
    - By a citizens of India, whether on the high seas or elsewhere;
    - By a person, not being such citizen, on any ship or aircraft, registered in India; or
    - By a person, not being such citizen, in a convention country, he may be dealt with in respect of such offence as if it had been committed at any place within India at which he may be found.
  - Notwithstanding anything contained in sub-section (1), the Central Government may, by general or special order published in the Official Gazette, direct that the offence under sub-section (1) of Sec. 4 or any other offence specified in Art. I of the Convention may be enquired into or tried at any place within India.
  - Previous sanction necessary for prosecution – No prosecution for an offence under this Act shall be instituted except with the previous sanction of the Central Government and the sanction granted under this section shall be deemed to be a sanction granted under Sec. 188 of the Code of Criminal Procedure, 1973, (2 of 1974).
  - Protecting of action taken in good faith – (1) No suit, prosecution or other legal proceeding shall lie against any person for anything which is in good faith done or intended to be down in pursuance of the provisions of this Act.
  - No suit or other legal proceeding shall lie against the Central Government for any damage caused or likely to be caused for anything which is in good faith done or intended to be done in pursuance of the provisions of this Act.

THE SCHEDULE

[See Sec. 2 (a)]

SAARC REGIONAL CONVENTION ON SUPPRESSION OF TERRORISM

The Member States of the South Asian Association for Regional Cooperation (SAARC)

MINDFUL of the principles of cooperation enshrined in the SAARC Charter;

RECALLING that the Dhaka Summit on December – 7-8 m 1985m the Head of State of Government of the member States of the SAARC recognised to seriousness of the problem of terrorism as it affects the security and stability of the region.

ALSO RECALLING the Bangalore Summit Declaration of 17th November 1986, in which the Head of State or Government of SAARC agreed that cooperation among SAARC States was vital if terrorism was to be prevented and eliminated from the region; unequivocally condemned all acts, methods and practices of terrorism as criminal and deplored their impact on life and proparty, socio-economic development, political stability, regional and international peace and cooperation; and recognised the importance of the principles laid down in UN Resolution 262 (XXV) which among other required that each State should refrain from organising, instigating, assisting or participating in acts of civil strife or terrorist acts in another State or acquiescing in organised activities within its territory directed towards the commission of such acts;

AWARE of the danger posed by the spread of terrorism and its harmful effect on peace, cooperation, friendship and good neighbourly relations and which could also jeopardize the sovereignty and territorial integrity of States;

HAVE RESOLVED to take effective measures to ensure that perpetrators to terrorist acts do not escape prosecution and punishment by providing for their extradition or prosecution, and to this end; HAVE AGREED as follows:-

ARTICLE I

Subject to the overall requirements of the law of extradition, conduct constituting any of the following offences according to the law of the Contracting State, shall be regarded as terroristic and for the purpose of extradition shall not be regarded as a political offence or as an offence connected with a political offence or as an offence inspired by political motives-

- An offence within the scope of the Convention for the Suppression of Unlawful Seizure of Aircraft, signed at The Hague, on 16th December 1970;
- An offence within the scope of the Convention for the Suppression of Unlawful Act, against the Safety of Civil Aviation signed at Montreal, on 23rd September 1971;
- An offence within the scope of the Convention on the Prevention and Punishment of Crimes against Internationally Protected

Persons, including Diplomatic Agents, signed at New York on 14th December 1973;

- An offence within the scope of any Convention to which the SAARC member States concerned are parties and which obliges and parties to prosecute or grant extradition.
- Murder, manslaughter, assault causing bodily harm, kidnapping hostage-taking and offences relating to firearms, weapons, explosives and dangerous substance when used as a means to perpetrate indiscriminate violence involving death or serious bodily injury to persons or serious damage to property;
- An attempt or conspiracy to commit an offence described in sub-paragraph (a) to (e), aiding, abetting or counselling the commission of such an offence or participating as an accomplice in the offences so described.

ARTICLE II

For the purpose of extradition between SAARC member States, any two or more Contracting States may, by agreement, decide to include any other serious offence involving violence, which shall not be regarded as a political offence or an offence connected with a political offence or an offence inspired by political motive.

ARTICLE III

- The provisions of all extradition treaties and arrangements applicable between Contracting States are hereby amended as between Contracting States to the extent that they are incompatible with the Convention.
- For the purpose of this Convention and to the extent that any offence referred to in Art. I or agreed to in terms of Art. II is not listed as extraditable offence in any extradition treaty existing between Contracting States, it shall be deemed to be included as such therein.
- Contracting States undertake to include these offences as extraditable offences in any future extradition treaty to be concluded between them.
- If a Contracting State which makes extradition conditional of the existence of the treaty receives a request for extradition from another Contracting State with which it has no extradition treaty, the requested State may, at its option, consider this Convention as the basis for extradition in respect of the offences set forth in Art. I or agreed to in terms of Art. II. Extradition shall be subject to the law of the requested State.

- Contracting States, which do not make extradition conditional on the existence of a treaty, shall recognise the offences set forth in Art. I or agreed to in terms of Art. II as extraditable offences between themselves, subject to the law of the requested State.

ARTICLE IV

A Contracting State in whose territory a person suspected of having committed an offence referred to in Art. I or agreed to in terms of Art. II is found and which has received a request for extradition from another Contracting State, shall, if it does not extradite that person, submit the case without exception and without delay, to its competent authorities, so that prosecution may be considered. These authorities shall take their decisions in the same manner as in the case of any offence of a serious nature under the law of that State.

ARTICLE V

For the purpose of Art. IV, each Contracting State may take such measures as it deems appropriate, consistent with its national laws, subject to reciprocity, to exercise its jurisdiction in the case of an offence under Art. I or agreed to in terms of Art. II.

ARTICLE VI

A Contracting State in whose territory an alleged offender is found, shall, upon receiving a request for extradition from another Contracting State, take appropriate measure, subject to its national laws, so as to ensure his presence for purpose of extradition or prosecution. Such measures shall immediately be notified to the requested States.

ARTICLE VII

Contracting State shall not be obliged to extradite, if it appears to the requested State that by reason of the trivial nature of the case or by reason of the request for the surrender or return of the fugitive offender not being made in good faith or in the interests of justice or for any other reason it is unjust or inexpedient to surrender or return fugitive offender.

ARTICLE VIII

- Contracting States shall, subject to their national laws, afford one another the greatest measure of mutual assistance in connection with proceedings brought in respect of the offences referred to in Art. I or agreed to in terms of the Art. II including the supply of all evidence at their disposal necessary for the proceedings.
- Contracting States shall cooperate among themselves, to the

extent permitted by their national laws, through consultation between appropriate agencies, exchange of information, intelligence and expertise and such other cooperative as may be appropriate, with a view to preventing terrorist activities through precautionary measures.

ARTICLE IX

- The Convention shall be open for signature by the member States of SAARC at the SAARC Secretariat in Kathmandu.
- It shall be subject to ratification. Instruments of Ratification shall be deposited with the Secretary-General of SAARC.

ARTICLE X

This Convention shall enter into force on the fifteenth day following the date of the deposit of the seventh Instrument of Ratification with the Secretary-General of SAARC.

ARTICLE XI

The Secretary-General of SAARC shall be the depository of this Convention and shall notify member States of signatures to this Convention and all deposits and Instruments of Ratification. The Secretary-General , shall transmit certified copies of such Instruments to each Member State. The Secretary-General shall also inform member States of the date on which this Convention will have entered into force in accordance with Art. Z.

IN WITNESS WHEREOF the undersigned, being duly authorised thereto by their respective Government, have signed this Convention.

DONE at Kathmandu on this fourth day of November one thousand nine hundred and eighty-seven, in eight originals, in the English language, all texts being equally authentic.

Appendix E

THE ANTI-HIJACKING ACT

(No. 65 of 1982)

(6 November 1982)

An Act to give effect to the Convention for the Suppression of Unlawful Seizure of Aircraft and for matters connected therewith.

Whereas a Convention for the Suppression of Unlawful Seizure of Aircraft was, on the 16th day of December, 1970, signed at The Hague;

And whereas it is expedient that India should accede to the said Convention and make provisions for giving effect thereto and for matters connected therewith.

CHAPTER 1
Preliminary

- Short title, extent, application and commencement-
    - This Act may be called the Anti-Hijacking Act, 1082.
    - It extends to the whole of India and, save as otherwise provided in this Act, it applies also to any offence there under committed outside India by any person.
    - It shall come into force on such date as the Central Government may, by notification in the Official Gazette, appoint.

CHAPTER II
Hijacking and Connected Offences

- Hijacking-
    - Whoever on board an aircraft in flight, unlawfully, by force or threat of force or by any other form of intimidation, seizes or exercises control of that aircraft commits the offence of hijacking of such aircraft.
    - Whoever attempts to commit any of the acts referred to in sub-section (1) in relation to any aircraft, or abets the commission of any such act, shall also be deemed to have committed the offence of hijacking of such aircraft.
    - For the purposes of this section, an aircraft shall be deemed to be in flight at any time from the moment when all its external doors are closed following embarkation until the moment when any such door is opened for disembarkation, and in the case of a forced landing, the flight shall be deemed to continue until the competent authorities of

the country in which such forced landing takes place take over the responsibility for the aircraft and for persons and property on board.

- Punishment for hijacking–Whoever commits the offence of hijacking shall be punished with imprisonment for life and shall also be liable to fine.

CHAPTER III
Miscellaneous

- Provisions as to extradition -
  - The offences under Sec. 4 and Sec. 5 shall be deemed to have been included as extraditable offences and provided for in all the extraditable treaties and provided for in all the extradition treaties made by India with Convention countries and which extend to, and are binding on India on the date of commencement of this Act.
  - For the purposes of the application of the Extradition Act, 1962 (34 of 1962) to offences under this Act, any aircraft registered in a Convention country shall, at any time while that aircraft is in flight, be deemed to be within the jurisdiction of that country. Whether or not it is for the time being also within the jurisdiction of any other country.

Appendix F

MODEL CIVIL DEFENCE PLAN : CAT 1-'A' CITY NEW DELHI

Delhi has been declared as a Cat-1A Civil Defence Town. This Civil Defence plan has been prepared keeping in mind the aspect of damage by NBC weapons, i.e., Radiation (apart from the Blast and Burn). Radiation can make an area completely inhabitable for long period due to radioactive fall out.

Guidelines for the Civil Defence Plan for Cat-1A Town has been issued by the DG Civil Defence, for handling nuclear attack. Mobile columns for dealing with nuclear attacks on Delhi will be positioned in the nearby towns within the 50-80 miles. The DG Civil Defence has also proposed one mobile column for each police District of Delhi.

Planning. The planning has been done keeping following aspects in mind :-

- There will be comparatively higher damage by Nuclear Weapons as compared to Conventional Weapons attack.
- The assistance required will be from the towns adjoining Delhi.
- Area contamination by the radioactive fall out and downwind wind has to be catered for.

Additional Factors. Radiological Reconnoitre and Decontamination Services will be in addition to the existing recognized services.

Evacuation

- **Policy.** The civil defence policy of the Government is "not to have any sponsored evacuation". Therefore only channelling of sponsored evacuation will be carried out. As and when the Delhi Government feels that the evacuation is essential, in case of imminent nuclear threat, the evacuation will be initiated. Though for a city with a population of 10 million, practical problem of even evacuating 30% of the population will be tremendous.
- **Plan.** In the vulnerable area during the phase of impending threat of nuclear attack, amongst the population, the old, infirm, women and children who are not required in town would be evacuated.

- **Full Evacuation**. The Plan for full evacuation will be launched once the instructions to this effect are received from the Government of Delhi.

Warning System

This existing schemes of the Civil Defence envisages several independently chalked out plans. They are as under :-

- Warning and Communication Plan
  > National Warning System.
  > Local Warning System.
  > Shelter Warning System.
- Radiological monitoring
- Decontamination

Sheltering Plan. Earmarking of the buildings (under ground/basement) Govt. Public and Private buildings, Community centres, warehouses, vital installation DTC depots, industries, etc, for the sheltering in and around Delhi. This will not involve much expenditure. Construction of fall out shelters in the basement of buildings. Regular fall out shelters outside the vulnerable area.

Public Education Plan. To make public aware of nuclear hazards in terms of radiation, large conflagration, shock waves disruption of communications and large scale panic, destruction and rumour mongering.

Radiological Reconnaissance Team. Training and reorganization of radiological reconnaissance team by the permanent staff is mandatory. The DG Civil Defence has projected total 560 reconnaissance teams for Delhi area. These teams are also made responsible for Detection and Decontamination of the assets after the attack and to form Decontamination Service in Delhi. The Decontamination training will form composite part of the Radiological and Monitoring scheme.

- Commandant Home Guard.
- General Office Commanding, Delhi Area
- Indian Air Force (Air Raid warning)

Appendix G

RESPONSE MECHANISM

In the Indian scene, especially in the case of a 'NBC' related terrorist act or incident, a response mechanism also would have to be institutionalized at various levels:

Levels of Response

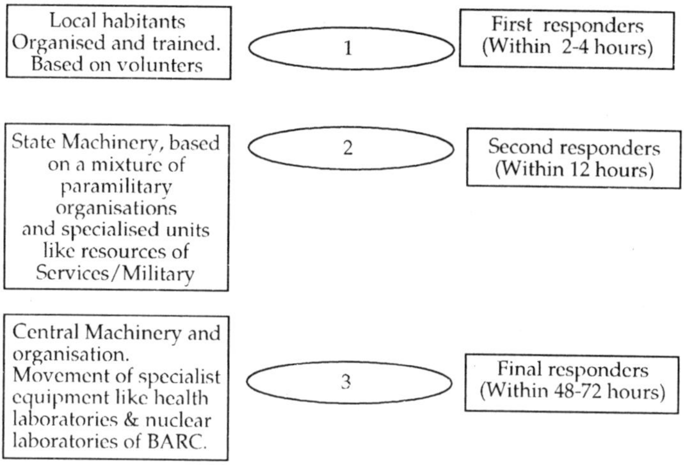

For any specialised unit, a suggested model organisation should include the following technical aspects:

- Identification and Detection team, which carries ACADA, DOSI Meters, BIDS, etc.
- A Security team to isolate and encircle the area, combined with 'capping the source' capability.
- For this one could use 'Foam technology'. Idea is to extinguish the origin of the agent. However, for radio-active material, the methods are slightly different like 'Lead Cages' etc.
- A Quick Reaction Medical Team (QRMT) should also be integrated with such second level as well as third level responders. These could carry emergency kit and medicines which can be applied as antidotes. For example, use of 'Atropine Sulphate' or 'Combopen' injunctions can neutralize, nerve attack. However at the third level, the 'Final Responders' should be able to mobilise medicines at national level through an available 'National Data Base Centre for Disaster

Management'. These medicines could be disposed strategically on a grid system.

- Decontamination teams atleast at second and third levels should be a part of the organisation so as to neutralise and decontaminate persons and equipments before these agents spread further.
- Use of software models for marking and identifying of danger zones and templates be utilized (one such software for various yields of KT in case of a nuclear disaster is already available at Bhaba Atomic Research Center).

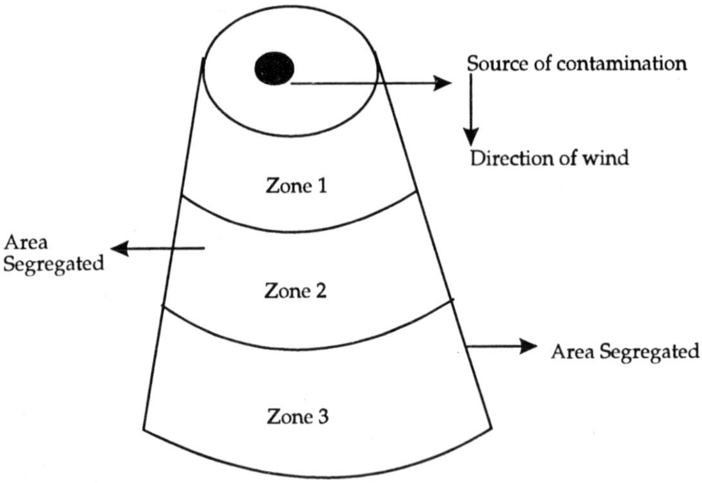

This would enable containment of collateral damage for all the three categories, i.e., N, B or C agents. This has been further amplified in the NBC Technical Manual.

Appendix H

SERVICES PROVIDED BY THE DISASTER RESPONSE BRANCH TO RESPOND TO NATURAL DISASTERS AND ENVIRONMENTAL EMERGENCIES : UNITED NATIONS

In compliance with General Assembly resolution 46/182, the Office for the Co-ordination of Humanitarian Affairs (OCHA), through its Disaster Response Branch (DRB) in Geneva, has established an emergency response system for coordinating actions taken by the international community as a result of natural disasters and environmental emergencies, including technological accidents. The DRB Operations Centre is immediately activated, when necessary, and is specially designed and equipped for the mobilisation and co-ordination of international emergency operations in response to disasters. As the focal point for co-ordinating international response to an emergency, the relevant DRB Regional Desk immediately prepares and disseminates situation reports to emergency relief services of donor governments, the United Nations system, intergovernmental and non-governmental organisations (all together about 600 addresses). In case of a major disaster with substantial involvement of different UN agencies during the immediate relief phase, a United Nations inter-agency mission may be sent to carry out a comprehensive multi-sectoral assessment of the effects of an emergency to ensure coordinated planning and the formulation of an overall UN response.

- When the situation warrants and subject to the availability of funds, OCHA will provide an emergency cash grant to the Government of the disaster-stricken country.
- OCHA is ready to act as an expeditious channel for donor contributions, relying on quick and simple administrative procedures.
- OCHA maintains a permanent (renewable) stock of donated disaster relief items, at the OCHA Warehouse in Pisa, Italy.
- If required, and in consultation with the United Nations Resident Co-ordinater, OCHA can field a United Nations Disaster Assessment and Co-ordination (UNDAC) team to assist in emergency assessment and field co-ordination during the initial relief phase.
- OCHA alerts and co-ordinates Search and Rescue (SAR) teams from different countries when the situation warrants it, e.g. in the case of a major earthquake affecting urban areas.

- OCHA can assist in the establishment of an On-site Operations Co-ordination Centre (OSOCC).
- OCHA can assist in establishing and co-ordinating secure and reliable telecommunications during the emergency response phase.
- OCHA can assist in identifying needs for and accessing technical and logistics resources in support of field co-ordination.
- OCHA can mobilise and co-ordinate the deployment of Military, Civil Protection and Civil Defence Assets from a number of countries and multinational organisations.
- These assets include specialised personnel and equipment required for disaster relief operations (e.g., aircraft, helicopters, ships, nuclear/biological/chemical decontamination facilities, field hospitals, water purification units, etc.).
- A Military and Civil Defence Unit (MCDU) is established within OCHA as a focal point for the use of military and civil defence (civil protection) resources in all types of humanitarian emergencies. Moreover, it can establish an on-site co-ordination centre for multi-agency employment of such assistance. In case of natural disasters and environmental emergencies, including technological accidents, the provision of military and civil defence assets takes place in accordance with agreed upon procedures (Oslo Guidelines, May 1994).
- When requested, OCHA can also assist countries to cope with environmental aspects of emergencies, including industrial accidents, not covered by other existing arrangements.
- OCHA maintains a Central Register of Disaster Management Capacities, which may be available for international assistance.
- OCHA Chernobyl Desk assists in co-ordinating all Chernobyl related activities of UN agencies and major international organisations.

Bibliography

WMD Terrorism

Ajay Darshan Behra, Trans-National Terrorism: Analysing the Political and Social Economic Undercurrents, Asian security seminar held under the aegis of IDSA, New Delhi, 28-30 January 2001.

Ariel Merari, ed, *Robert Kupperman on Terrorism and Combating Terrorism,* (Frederick, Md : University Publications of America, 1985).

Air Commodore Jasjit Singh, AVSM, VrC, VM, *Kargil 1999-Pakistan's Fourth War for Kashmir ,* Knowledge World, New Delhi-110002.

Adam Roberts, *The Strategy of Civilian Defence*, Faber and Faber 24 Russell Square London.

B.H. Liddell Hart, *Strategy,* Army Publishers, Delhi.

Brig. Chandra B Khanduri, *Generals and Strategists from Kautilya to Thimayya*, New Delhi, Patriot, 1992, p. 197.

Bruce Hoffman, "The Contrasting Ethical Foundations of Terrorism I the 1980s' Terrorism and Political Violence, Vol. No. 3 (July 1989) 398.

Brain M. Jenkins, "Understanding the Link between Motives and Methods" in *Terrorism with Chemical and Biological Weapons Calibrating Risks and Expenses,* ed, Brad Roberts.

Bernard Stewart, ed. *'State-Sponsored Terrorism: The Threat and Possible Countermeasures, Terrorism,* 8, No. 3 (1986) 253-313.

Brian Jenkins, ed. *International Conference on Terrorism and Low-Level Conflict* (Santa Monica, California: RAND, 1982).

Brij Mohan and AKL Vats, *Global Armageddon: Emerging Challenges in the New Millennium* (New Delhi Comcare International Publishers).

DV Segre and JH Adler, "The Ecology of Terrorism," *Survival* XV, No. 4 (July/August 1973):178-183.

Gen. Carl Von Clausewitz, *On War,* Routledge & Kegan Paul Ltd. Broadway House, 68-74 Carter Lane, E.C.4 1949 Vol. I.

Gen. Carl Von Clausewitz, *On War,* Routledge and Kegan Paul. Ltd. Broadway House, 68-74 Carter Lane, E.C.4 1949 Vol II.

Gen Carl Von Clausewitz, *On War,* Routledge & Kegan Paul Ltd Broadway House, 68-74 Carter Lane, E.C.4 1949 Vol III.

General d' Armee Beaufre, *Strategy of Action,* Faber and Faber 24

Russell Square London.

General d' Armee Amdre Beaufre, *Deterrence and Strategy*, Faber and Faber 24 Russell Square London.

Ivelaw L. Griffith, "From Cold War Geopolitics to Post-Cold War Geo-Narcotics" *International Journal.*

Jeremiah Denton, "International Terrorism: The Nuclear Dimension", *Terrorism* 9, No. 2 (1987): 113-124.

Jessica Stern, *The Ultimate Terrorist* (USA, First Harwood University Press, 2000).

Jeffrey D. Simon, *Terrorists and the Potential* Use of Biological Weapons, Report R-3771-AFMIC (Santa Monica, California: RAND, December 1989).

Louis Rene Beres, *Terrorism and Global Security: The Nuclear Threat* (Boulder, Colorado: West-View Press, 1987).

Lt. Gen. (Retd) Kamal Matinuddin, *The Taliban Phenomenon: Afghanistan 1994-1997,* Karachi: Oxford University Press, 1999, p. 217.

Major Thomas R. Phillips US Army ed, *Roots of Strategy,* Natraj Publishers, Dehradun.

Magnus Ranstorp, *Hizbullah in Lebanon: The Critics of the Western Hostage Crisis* (London, Macmillan).

Malcolm W. Browne, *The New Face of War,* The Trinity Press Worcester, and London F. 965

Mark Juergensmeyr, "The Logic of Religious Violence", in David C Rapport, ed, *Inside Terrorist Organisations* (London: Frank Cars and Company Limited 1988, p. 183).

Paul Leventhal, Yonah Alexander, eds. *Preventing Nuclear Terrorism: Report of the International Task Force on Prevention of Nuclear Terrorism* (Lexington, Mass: Lexington Books, 1987).

Peter C. Sederbergn, *Terrorist Myths, Illusion, Rhetoric and Reality* (UK, Pretence Hall Englewood Cliffs).

Philip B Heymann, *Terrorism and America: A Common Sense Strategy for a Democratic Society* (Cambridge, MIT Press, 1998), p. 8.

Poonam Mann, "Fighting Terrorism: Indian and Central Asia" *Strategic Analysis,* Vol. XXIV No. 11, February 2001.

Richard A. Falkenrath, Robert D Newman, and Bradley A. Thayer, *America's Achilles Heel: Nuclear, Biological, and Chemical Terrorism.*

Robert Kupperman and Jeff Kamen, *Final Warning: Averting Disaster in the New Age of Terrorism* (New York).

Richard A. Falkenrath, "Confronting Biological Chemical Terrorism"

Survival 40, No. 3 (Autumn 1998) 52.

Samuel Hutington, 'Clash of Civilisation and the Making of the World Order' (New York: Touchstone 1997): See also, Samuel Hutington 'Clash of Civilizations', *Foreign Affairs* summer 1993.

Sreedhar, Taliban's Afghanistan; Looking into Future, Perceptions *Journal of International Affairs*, Vol. V No. 4, December 2000, February 2001.

Walter Laqueur, "Postmodern Terrorism," *Foreign Affairs* 75, No. 6 (September/October 1996).

Water Laqueur, *The New Terrorism: Fanaticism and the Arms of Mass Destruction* (Oxford University Press, 1999) 8-48.

Walter R Lawrence, I.C.S, C.I.E, *Valley of Kashmir,* Kesar Publishers, Residency Road, Srinagar Kashmir, 1967.

Yonah Alexander, Phil Baum and Raphael Danziger, 'Terrorism: Future Threats and Responses" *Terrorism.*

Yossef Bodansky, *Bin Laden -The Man Who Declared War on America,* Published by Prima Publishing, Roseville, California Member of the Crown Publishing Group, a division of Random House, Inc.

Zalmay Khalilzad lan O. Lesser, *Sources of Conflict in the 21st Century,* Natraj Publishers, Dehradun.

Articles

We can, But Don't, Script from Out Look 11 February 2002 opinion by Raja Menon Future Fire "India Today" by Raj Chengappa.

[illegible] (1945–52) [illegible]

[illegible] and the Making of the World Order [illegible] Touchstone 1997). See also, Samuel Huntington [illegible] Foreign Affairs summer 1993.

[illegible] Looking to the Future. Proceedings [illegible] Vol. V No. 4, December 2000.

[illegible] "Postmodern Terrorism" Foreign Affairs, 75, No. 5 [illegible] 1996).

[illegible] and the Future of [illegible] Press, 1999 [illegible]

[illegible] Politics of Kashmir [illegible]

[illegible] and Rajnath Banerjee [illegible]

[illegible] Patterns of Global Terrorism [illegible] California

[illegible] Group, a division of Random [illegible]

[illegible] Sources of Conflict in the 21st [illegible] Publications, [illegible]

[illegible] February 2002 [illegible] Chittagong [illegible]

(b) [illegible]

4. [illegible]

युगपद् [illegible]

5. (a) ज्वरो रोगपतिः [illegible]

क्रोधो......

(b) क्षयस्तमो ज्वरः पाप्मा मृत्यु[illegible]

Index

B

C

D